CW00584904

THE EARTH
CAN HEAL ITSELF-
CAN YOU?

"The Earth Can Heal Itself - Can You?"
© 2010 Anne Shearer
This first edition published in 2011 by Trailblazer Books.
5-7 Station Road, Eddleston Road, Peebles EH45 8QN, Scotland

The Right of Anne Shearer to be identified as the Author of this work
has been asserted by her in accordance with the
Copyright, Designs and Patents Act 1988.

All Rights Reserved. No part of this book may be printed, reproduced or utilized
in any form or by any electronic, mechanical or other means, now known or
hereafter invented, including photocopying and recording, or in any information
storage retrieval system, without permission in writing from the publishers.

A catalogue record for this book is available from the British Library.

ISBN: 978-0-9569977-0-8

Book design and production by
Bernard Chandler, Glastonbury, www.graffik.co.uk
Cover design Bernard Chandler.
Cover painting "Planet Earth" © Moira Russell.

Text set in 11 1/2 pt on 14pt Plantin, with Cochin titling.

Printed and Bound by
CPI Group (UK) Ltd, Croydon, CR0 4YY

THE EARTH
CAN HEAL ITSELF-
CAN YOU?

by

ANNE SHEARER

About the Author

Born in Kent, 'The Garden of England', and reared in a great English Cathedral City, Anne's early life was as a farm and estate secretary, in the beautiful Avon valley of Wiltshire, and the magical countryside in Herefordshire, on the English-Welsh border.

After marriage she moved to the Scottish Borders, where she reared her family, becoming closely involved with the life and organisations of a rural village. This culminated in a 17-year career as a non-political County and Regional Councillor, latterly as Chairman of the Social Work Committee. An interest in the source of stress and addictions led to her training as a psychotherapist. With the assistance of the then Strathclyde Regional Council she set up a Registered Charity, renovating with an army of volunteers a large inner-city school in the centre of Glasgow, where she worked with literally thousands of people suffering from stress from all ages and walks of life in an award-winning voluntary project. Recognising that the common cause behind the multiplicity of symptoms was a restriction in the breathing pattern of clients, she developed the teaching of correct breathing as a major aspect of her work. The initial cause was healed in most cases, and the symptoms disappeared. In other words people learned to heal themselves. The success of this approach has led her in 'semi' retirement to the founding of a new Registered Charity with the aim of universal education in teaching correct breathing.

Also by Anne Shearer:

LOVE, DRUGS...or ANY CITY LIKE GLASGOW
(The source of the Addicted Society)

"In my opinion, the ideas presented in this book represent a change in attitude that, if applied, would revolutionise mankind." Eddie A

Testimonials

*Comments about breathing training
and my relaxation tapes:*

"Your relaxation tape saved my life."
Woman artist

"The inmates said that your relaxation tape
on anger management was the best and most
original they had heard."
Prison social worker

"The surgery would be grateful for information on the
wonderful work you offer."
GP Practice, Glasgow

Some responses by former clients:

"Passed my law exams - B1 - the things you taught
me will last all my life."

"Thank you for showing me the amazing love I have
in my heart."

"Correct breathing has helped my high blood pressure."

"My former low blood pressure is now normalised."

"We will pass on your work to the next generation."

"I think of you as Mother Earth!"

CONTENTS

ILLUSTRATIONS

Dedication

For my children
Colin, Julie & Wendy,
and grandchildren
Claire, Peter, Hannah & Julia.

Acknowledgements & Thanks

Acknowledgements - To all those patient people who put up with my travails as with great anguish in my late seventies I overcame a built-in resistance to learning the complexities of the computer, and simple(?) word processing. Especially Rita, Muriel, John, Hannah, Tommy, Colin. Also the patient teachers on the various courses on the same subject, which I never completed!

Above all to my designer-editor Bernard Chandler in Glastonbury, who has brought the spirit of that special place to his inspired and intuitive understanding of the manuscript. In fact I believe that I had to arrive in Glastonbury by a series of amazing coincidences in order to be led to our meeting and find that special person who was probably the only person who could understand how I have been labouring to bring this book into birth.

Thanks - I owe undying thanks to all those great writers, speakers, and philosophers down the ages whose words have inspired my own need to write a book in which the power of the breath of life deserves to be honoured. In particular Lilla Bek, friend and mentor, who has brought enlightenment over many years to thousands by her inspired wisdom and insights. She told me to retire(?) enjoy my cottage and garden, write a book about breathing, and have fun!

I also owe immeasurable gratitude to those thousands of clients and friends over several decades, who have learned to release their own wonderful gifts, through the correct use of that sadly universally despised force to which we owe our continued existence, the Breath of Life. By their example, I have been given the inspiration to write this book.

Special thanks to Tom.

Foreword

IT IS INDEED CURIOUS that a civilized country which is forever detailing the horrors of illness, disease, social malaise and addictions to the nth degree, seems to remain determinedly disinterested in the appalling misuse and misunderstanding of the way in which the largest portion of our population incorrectly uses the breath of life. The resultant cell damage is, I am convinced, the seed bed from which our collective malaise springs. The precise use of its blueprint, known to a small healthy baby, can regenerate the cell damage imbalance at source and be the missing link to a truly healthy society.

Humility to re-learn is the key, the rebalancing of the creative, intuitive instinct we all possess, in the hidden fight of over-intellectualisation which is stifling our spiritual growth.

Anne Shearer, 26/10/2010

'*There is no habit in life which pays bigger dividends, and pays them more promptly, than proper breathing. It is the source of your health, your cheerful spirits, your energy, your youth and your relaxation. A healthy baby is the perfect instructor.*'

Karin Roon, *The New Way to Relax.*

'*It reckoned that one generation of correct breathers could regenerate the race, and disease would be looked upon as a rarity.*'

Ramacharaka

BREATH IS LIFE

THE FIRST PASSIONATE URGE to write a book is not generally dependent on whether or not it gets published (although obviously that would be the dream fulfilled). The burning need to communicate forces us to put pen to paper (or fingers to computer) in order to create an information channel by which we *need* to share our thoughts with the universe.

Important words, sentences, flow from the brain, which have to be expressed, since to *repress* seems to create a negativity within us, a block harmful to our peace of mind.

Despite this inner urge to 'write it down', the lazy Piscean side of my nature says to me 'I'll remember, but I'll do it tomorrow.' and then I don't. I eventually realise that I shall have to keep a notebook beside my bed, since the best ideas and thoughts come first thing in the morning or during a wakeful period in the night, when an elegant coherence of thought often wings its way into urgent consciousness in the 'absolutely quiet hours'. The source of these thoughts appears to come from a part of my brain, which hasn't even been consciously thinking about these specific ideas, it's as if a power not my own is talking to me. If that sounds pompous, so be it! I have no alternative way to express it.

The clarity of these words seems to come from what I call a spiritual source, even if my interpretation sounds practical and matter-of-fact. The word 'spiritual' will be mentioned quite often in this book, not to be confused with one religion or another, spirituality and religion do not necessarily go hand in hand.

Key experiences and subsequent conclusions of the last twenty years of my life have forced me to set down the following chapters. *Not* to do so would deny the reason and privilege for which I have been given life. I am reminded of a quotation from that inspiring thinker Theodore Roszak who wrote that 'at the end of our lives most people are sick with guilt at having lived beneath their authentic potential.' There is a comforting cliché which says that 'it is never too late', words which I endorse from experience, but I believe there may come a time when it *is* too late to take action and see results anyway in this lifetime.

The last two decades have challenged me as at no other time in my life to justify the purpose of my life. In so doing I, like many others, have been forced to think and act from what to the best of my belief is the core of my being. Reluctantly I have been forced to discard the artificial barriers of non-action created from childhood onwards in order, as I thought, to protect me from criticism. Like many others, as I have shed my own ill-will to myself, largely through the transformative power of correct breathing, the artificial barriers have become unnecessary. Communicating with oneself from the heart allows us to communicate with others from the heart, actually anything less is not good enough.

Proving to myself the loving power of this invisible communication source has given me the privilege of helping others to discover it within themselves. By so doing they have personally healed their own particular life problems be it relationhips (first with themselves) work or home, without further outside help. Their help came from within.

Some of what I write may seem fanciful, mystical or un believable; however, to read on may require you to suspend your disbelief!

A well-known writer once said that afraid as he was of man, he was more afraid of God (or the God of his understanding) if he did not write what he felt from the heart. I find myself in the same predicament, but I do know that out there in the Univese will be people who understand what I am trying to say in this book. Others are beginning to comprehend and, as I once did, need others to lighten the darkness with right words. Perhaps these pages may open a door for those in between these two worlds of materialism and the beginning of enlightenment.

I have been waiting for the date of May 1st to start writing this book. My large desk bought in a Glasgow street market is in my bedroom. Since childhood I have always had a great respect for a desk of my own, preferably a large one! The aim is to have a massive clearance of desk and bedroom, to create optimum conditions for freeing the mind for creativity. That's the idea.

A little unrealistic this, for my mind seems to work better when all around me is self-created chaos for freeing the mind for the planned creativity. The tidy-up envisaged is really a form of procrastination or delaying tactics. Still, I am aware that deep within myself something is stirring which needs to be brought to the surface. We either go forward or back we never stay still, so unless I start to write, my life will go backwards, a state I refuse to contemplate.

One of the books which has been a great inspiration to me for over twenty years was written in the early morning 'quiet hours' between 4am and 6am.

Several times in my life when needs dictated I have been able to move into this early morning timetable, and realised that this was the time slot I needed to take advantage of, if I was to contact the part of me that could think most creatively for writing from the heart. What better time of day in Spring to be alert when Nature is weaving her most magic spell.

Today I failed the 4am time test, tomorrow I'll do better!

So much of what is happening world-wide is creating grief, violence and terrorism. Each person responsible for that misery was once a child-a seemingly innocent child who breathed as correctly as at any time in their lives. What or whose negative energy destroyed that pattern?

The main purpose of this book is to try to explain how the power of our breathing pattern on our thoughts and actions can affect our Earth. When that power is used wrongly it creates earthly mayhem, at its deepest and most precise vibrational level, those who breathe correctly can create heaven on the Planet, for infinite wisdom is so often then revealed to them. Ancient wisdom concerning ourselves, nature, and the Universe.

In my therapeutic work no greater satisfaction is possible than to speak to someone whose life has had more than its share of grief, hatred and violence, who begins to chuckle with the delight of a delightful small child. That chuckle has come naturally from a deep but totally aware meditative state created by correct breathing, a rediscovery of the sheer joy of being alive, when that utter bliss we felt as a child is again re-experienced, leading us to see our personal problems as relatively unimportant. In the words of a modern day philosopher 'don't sweat the small stuff, it's all small stuff.'

This delight in life of the small child is so infectious, you realise the child's joy comes from an internal source not directly connected with the visual world but which is totally real and able to be re-captured by us as adults as we regain a corrected breathing pattern.

The writer Bronson Alcott, father of Louisa Alcott who wrote the world famous book *Little Women*, was a visionary educator whose writings were brought together in a lesser known but to my mind more important book called *How Like an Angel Came I Down*. Bronson Alcott believed

4

that the soul of a child already carries within it the 'imprint of spirit and wisdom'. That imprint is full of laughter and delight at the wonder of life.

At one point Alcott was speaking to children in his Sunday School class. When he asked the children if they had ever seen a miracle, one little boy replied *'yes breathing, the motion of the pulse.'* ('Out of the mouths of babes and little ones' - *Holy Bible.*)

Our breath is a constant miracle, taken for granted, a taken for granted we ignore at our peril. I believe that it contains some of the most minute, finest and invisible trace elements not obtainable elsewhere, which we leach from our physical body when we breathe wrongly, and start to use up these subtle stores deep within our bodies, not discernible to science, which can only be re-introduced into the system by correct breathing. That is what *I* believe, that the air itself contains these trace elements.

No book or scientific article has taught me that. We all possess our own unique jig-saw piece of the great truths of the world, but I am sure that this is so, and we all have the task of bringing that truth into the sum of world knowledge by our actions.

'ALL IS CONTAINED IN THE DIVINE BREATH, LIKE THE DAY IN THE MORNING'S DAWN.'

Old Saying

Chapter 1

THE BEGINNING
AND THE END

LATELY I HAVE BEEN ASKING MYSELF the question 'How shall I know when I have completed this book?' Yesterday intuitively I knew that the time had come. I realise that when you write about something that has come to you through intuition rather than by scientific or intellectual manuals you have to wait for the 'Professional' to catch up with you! This is a wonderfully liberating yet scary thought, probably interpreted by some as pompous. Too bad. Science without intuition is like dough without yeast, and there is too much of this limited kind of science about. For instance I believe that a great deal of the post-hurricane suffering during the Florida tornadoes and subsequent catastrophes could have been relieved if the intuitive response instinct in the appropriate leaders had been at a higher level of awareness. More appropriate assistance would have been available in the vital hours following such disasters.

The world intuitive faculty will have to be developed dramatically to mitigate or even forestall Nature's protests in the form of natural disasters in the years ahead because of our unnatural use of her gifts to us.

In thinking about the kind of people who might possibly read this book, a saying comes to mind: 'To those who understand no explanation is necessary, to those who do not (will not?) understand, no explanation will suffice.' Probably like me you will have bought books over the years which after a brief perusal seemed to appeal, but they have then lain for ages upon your book-shelves until for some unknown reason a book has again come to your hand, and upon opening it you will find as I have that it makes sense, and I mean spiritual sense. We have grown spiritually and are now ready to understand the book, yet the seed of that growth must have been there years before when it was first purchased. No doubt that is what happens when even a single word or sentence had enough meaning, if far-glimpsed, to persuade us to make the original purchase.

It is said that nothing is ever wasted. The true understanding of how such decisions come about become increasingly clear to those who begin to learn 'the language of the breath'.

From time to time during the past twenty-five years I have found (or perhaps they have found me) people, books, articles, research materials, which have mirrored back to me information which had already been shown to me intuitively. Some people call it 'Ancient Wisdom, divinely inspired.' I believe it to be the imperishable wisdom of the ages which can never be destroyed. No one person has the key to all this information, only the Higher Intelligence which created it, but we all possess some unique portion of it, ignore it tho' we may. This information seems to me to be on an electrical vibration, since all energy is electrical, even if we do not yet have the skills to measure the highest fields where this Ancient Wisdom is stored, but it is released through the minds of those who are ready to receive it. It is more frequently released when we are quiet and relaxed, the best receptive atmosphere being through the medium of correct breathing which for many seems to switch them onto a spiritual wavelength. Remember, as I frequently recall, the word breath means *spirit* (ancient Greek).

From my own experience correct breathing leads to a

sense of urgency, leading to correct action. Incorrect breathing may lead to a sense of urgency, but the ensuing action will be incorrect, probably arising from a sense of impatience underpinned by fear, a non-spiritual energy.

At this time of global unease the need to take correct action is critically urgent. The lines of a memorable poem often comes to me, frequently quoted by Sir George Trevelayn.

> The time is now when wrong comes up to meet us everywhere,
> Never to leave us 'til we take the longest stride of soul men ever took,
> Events are now soul-size,
> The journey now is exploration unto God,
> Where are you making for?'
> It takes so many years to wake,
> But will you wake for pity's sake?

When you meet an awakened soul who recognises the correct need for soul-size action to meet the global challenge there is a great feeling of joy and hope. Despite the scale of future action needed there is also a sense of peace and companionship, a belief that the global downward trends are capable of reversal. Such meetings may be brief, you may never meet that person again, but you realise that you are both *tent-pegs*, part of a great army of usually unrecognised enlightened souls whose thoughts and actions are helping to keep the *guy-ropes* of our planet more secure. If the above words don't at present make sense to you, perhaps at some time after you read these pages you will feel drawn to acknowledge your own hitherto unrecognised need to ponder and investigate, and recognise your own special unique information source which for all of us lies at the core of our being. It joins us to the great family of the Earth's spiritual protectors.

I mentioned at the beginning of this chapter that I thought it was time to bring together thought processes and experiences which have beome important signposts in my own personal journey. A number of books and seemingly irrelevant articles in the media have given me a feeling of comfort that there are people 'out there' who are discovering or rediscovering facts about human metabolism which is irrevocably linked to the way in which we are joined to the metabolism of nature and therefore that of the Earth.

A French physiotherapist Pierre Pallardy, like myself, speaks of the area of the lower belly (between the pelvic bone and the navel) as the 'second brain'. It is also the area of the body from which the breath (spirit impulse) arises. The correct breath links the lower (spiritual) brain with the upper intellectual brain and conveys a strong sense of *rightness* which floods the mind when this movement is a constant factor of our natural life-rhythm. It stimulates the auto-immune system, clears toxic blockages, in so doing repairs circulatory limitations, and balances cell oxygenation. It is Nature's preventative against cancerous cell formation; without correct oxygen circulation there is fungal growth, an ideal milieu for cancer.

Pierre Pallardy has discovered intuitively the vital link between the lower and upper brains, the only amendment I could suggest is that his words *deep breathing* might be changed to *correct* breathing as the first so often seems to mean for many people *drawing in* the lower abdomen and thereby *restricting* the expansion of the lower and largest area of the lungs. This then restricts the intake of oxygen and also the communication link between the two brains. *Deep breathing,* as many people understand it, necessitates a *tightening* of the strong muscles of the lower abdomen with a resultant knock-on tightening of all the muscles around the lower lungs, thereby restricting oxygen circulation to the upper brain and limiting its proper function. In other words the life-force is being restricted. Correct thinking must therefore be restricted, leading to inappropriate action.

Correct breath involves a *relaxation* of the lower stomach muscles, thus enabling the great lung expansion that accompanies a maximum supply of life-energy to the system. This expansion is not completed until it reaches the top of the lungs, the lobes just beneath the collar bone, and continues through the respiratory pathway to the upper brain. In exhalation we reverse this process, until the contraction of the lower abdominal muscles at the end of the exhale forces the toxins accumulated during the respiratory process to be excreted. I say *excreted* intentionally since exhalation is an excretory process, and we would do well to remember that. Its limitation or non-completion mirrors the effect of deliberately holding back liquid or solid excretory matter. The excretory function of the out-breath cannot usually be seen, except in cold weather, but its limited expulsion through incorrect breathing results in toxin accumulation throughout the respiratory tract.

The correct contraction of the lower abdominal muscles at the completion of the exhale gives you the feeling that you are (as described by the Barefoot Doctor) 'squeezing a sponge'. I once read in an article that few doctors understand this process fully, with no reflection on their skills, rather the limitation of their training.

Some years ago I discvered an old book in a library which had no author's name or ISBN number. This book was about the writer's discovery that she could use her hands to direct healing energy via her hands to parts of her body which were suffering. This led to her realisation that the nucleus of our physical and emotional centre arises in the pivotal lower centre of the body, behind the sacrum (sacred area?), which is where the breath arises.

She was taught this by French dancers. Naturally dancers have to move from a superb inner core sense of balance. Physical balance leads to mental and emotional balance. I recognise that this area is also the seat of the auto-immune system, and the continual re-commencement of each breath from this area between the pelvic bone and the navel not only strengthens the auto-immune system, but gives a sense of self-identity, empowerment, and emotional balance.

I have taught so many people to breathe correctly from this lower area. We have noticed an almost instant improvement in their health, hardly any colds, greater energy and confidence. The muscular strength of this area becomes noticeable, where before it has been soft, with no sense of strength or 'vitality'.

The author of this old book tells us that the centre I have just described reminds us that its correct use reveals to us our sense of spirituality, and once we are aware of this non-scientific and non-provable fact, we will feel the need to continually stay in touch with it through our breathing *as a basic natural instinct*. The writer suggests that the presence of this centre near the sexual organs creates a confusion about the sexual urge.

I have discovered from teaching correct breathing to hundreds of people whose sexual lives were, to say the least of it, 'in a mess' creates a self-corrective movement cycle being re-established, as a client begins to intuitively sense that a natural feeling of joy in living re-emerges as he or she re-links themselves with this great centre of breath empowerment, without repetitive sexual activity as the only way to stimulate the lower area of the auto-immune system, which of course must be in continual active watch to maintain health. The sexual urge, for some people a sometimes insatiable addiction, recedes into an important, essential but *controllable* drive which can only be fulfilled through a sexual *and* spiritual union.

The book says that our present over-attention to sexuality in all its forms with resultant sexual diseases, promiscuity and perversions arises through a severance of this respiratory and spiritual source of joy. Because this source is so near the reproductive organs the muscular activity involved in 'sexual release' where a person is not in touch with this natural sacral (sacred) centre of respiration and spirituality, results in a very temporary sense of release and joy continually requiring repetition in the same way that an alcoholic or chain-smoker requires another *fix*. The long-term result of any of these addictions including repetitive sex for the wrong reasons, leads eventually to health break-down in some form.

The author of this very wise book referred to in these preceding paragraphs says, 'Children born of true love unions and of bodies who feel this consciousness of being at one with the spiritual body (through correct breathing) will be endowed with perfection.'

Of one thing I am very sure. Any person who we have placed upon the 'Sexual Register' will be out of touch with breathing correctly from this sacral area. The problem with our society is that there are so few people who have the training, understanding and skills to work effectively with those whose damaged spirits lead them to project this damage on little children. Our society is still very immature, the spiritual development of man has still a long journey to travel, we have so much to learn.

From time to time I have noticed historical references to this lower 'sacral' sacred area of the body, the impulse centre from which the fountain area of the breath (spirit) rises. This source of the respiratory impulse between the pelvic bone and the navel appears to have been recognised by early Christian church builders, in the construction and design of the first Christian churches. The nave (navel) and sacristy (sacral), two very important focal points of the building, bear such a close symbolic affinity to the sacred, spiritual centres of the human body. I am sure that the metamorphic stages of the growth of the Christian church which has so often repressed the true spirit of man, has resulted in numerous spiritual teachings of the wisdom of the early Christians to be jetissoned down the ages. Probably because the growth of power within the leaders of the Church depended upon keeping their congregations in a state of submission and fear, so that the correct breathing impulse become repressed down through the ages.

In one ancient culture I read that antagonists fighting to the death would try to kill their opponent by piercing this lower navel area in a fatal thrust, believing that by so doing they would destroy the soul, which could not then return in subsequent incarnations. Yes, they belived in reincarnation even in those days! I believe that the Druids claimed to be able to use the power of divination or soul-assessment by examining the entrails of their victims revealed by exposing this area through sacrifice. Again several examples of ancient knowledge revealed by the customs of the times, the last two not pleasant to imagine, but nevertheless containing an awareness of this soul well-spring of the human body, from which our physical health and auto-immune system can be strengthened.

From what I have discovered about the training of health professionals, this is a 'health education area' sadly unexplored, but could in my opinion produce a quantum-leap in global health understanding and subsequent education.

The extremely practical but also Metaphysical healing of our wounded breath or life source as we eliminate the adverse effects of long-term physical, mental and emotional suppression, brings to mind the saying (was it Jung?) that 'all healing is painful.' This I have found on a personal level, and it has also been reflected in the experiences of those who have asked for breathing correction training. The interesting fact for all of us is that despite this possible temporary period of discomfort, we have all been conscious at some deep level that what we are experiencing is a temporary process, part of what we call 'clearance'. If we have appeared to have lost our true life's path, retracing it is as painful as it must have been for us, usually as a child, to have felt compelled to turn our back on it. It is wonderful to discover that the true path can be re-found, and successfully followed.

The book I mentioned earlier in this chapter, *Your Hands Can Help to Heal You*, refers to the lower belly breath-life-centre as the point of our conception impulse as we began our life-span within the womb, the pulse around which all our growth takes place. Our unique personal spiritual beat (or musical vibrational note) lies within this sacral and sacred part of our body, and to feel separated from it causes us to feel fear, loneliness, and I believe probably accounts for the sense of the 'glass-wall' depressive illnesses suffered by such a large proportion of the world's population.

When the sacral pulse-centre is out of balance, the vibratonal impulses sent to our upper cranial brain from our lower intuitive brain become disturbed and confused like a piece of music which is out of tune, and until our breathing pattern is repaired the confusion will remain. All our upper brain operating function depends on the free flowing vibrationally oxygenated messages sent from the lower sacral brain via blood-cell circulation.

If I frequently refer to the natural breathing process throughout these pages, the intention is deliberate.

The conscious repair of our respiratory movement cannot be done forcefully or too quickly, but only gently and steadily. This repair takes time and patience.

The re-use of this correct breathing movement which may

have been adversely affected since birth, can at first seem difficult, even unnatural, because we are re-using and strengthening muscles which should never have become lazy in the first place, and they are stiff from non-use. Do not expect to notice dramatic results at first, it depends on whether or how much this process has been suppressed, but remember no natural process is *meant* to be suppressed.

Nevertheless you may all of a sudden find that you need to turn the heating down in your home, (an ecological saving of the Earth's energy?) due to better circulation of the heat of the sun throughout the body. It is important to remember that any heat in the body is from the sun's energy, and flows via our blood-stream in the veins to all cells and extremities of the body. Having to turn down the heat in your home is the sign of this success. After about a year you will realise that you have had fewer colds. This is the long-term effect of the elimination of respiratory toxins which will start to take place after you re-commence correct breathing. It will be discussed further under another chapter called 'The Healing Process'.

Throughout the past three decades of my career as a psychotherapist *all* those who have come for assistance have exhibited suppression of the correct respiratory process *whatever their problems or symptoms*. The dawning realisation that when someone re-learns to breathe correctly, naturally led them to reverse and sort out their own life's problems, forced me to revise and extend my therapeutic work to include basic correct breathing as the most important part of that process. This reduced the frequency of sessions, but guaranteed invaluable self-progress by the client between appointments, the taking-on of responsibility for their lives, a pre-requisite to maturation, even while on medically prescribed drugs. The latter does however inevitably lengthen the reovery period, as a client has to go through a period of medical drug withdrawal in co-operation with their doctor.

Obviously many people want to begin to correct their breathing while still on medical drugs, and it is advisable to tell your doctor that you are wishing to do so. Sadly, teaching patients respiratory correction does not seem to be part of GP training, but I have invariably found that when my clients do so, their doctor is usually interested and encouraging. Correct breathing seems to gradually take over the need for most medication. It is a wonderful feeling when a client who has been reliant on chemical medication for many years for various problems, is finally able to become drug free. *It is essential* however that medical drugs are reduced gradually with the co-operation of one's doctor.

It is a great pity that doctors do not have the time to teach correct breathing. I think it would help doctors personally to do so, and perhaps also reduce the high level of suicide and alcoholism in their own profession, and indeed many other professions, particularly dentists.

Perhaps at some future date doctors and all other health professionals will receive personal respiratory re-education as part of their training, although the skills required encompass the physical, mental *and* spiritual. The latter I believe not part of their syllabus. Even so, I fully believe it is the most important factor in regaining full health.

The medical process does not teach spirituality, but the spiritual dimension invariably resurfaces naturally when breath is corrected. Medical articles repeatedly state that respiratory problems form a major part of referrals.

The *professional* who can teach us most about correct breathing is a healthy young baby! I suppose it also takes a certain *humility* to recognise this, but then we have been told to 'become as little children', and 'a little child shall lead us.' (*Holy Bible*). My own personal respiratory corrective period *forced* me to embrace humility in this respect.

I often wonder if it would be beneficial for GPs to be trained to prescribe the concentration and strength of medication according to the breath efficiency of the patient. I would think that medication ingested into a brain-oxygen deficient patient who breathes badly, could provoke an intense reaction not noticeable in a better oxygenated system; in the same way that bleach for example will create a stronger reaction if the same quantity is placed within a sink-full rather than a bath-tub of water. Perhaps this is why two people prescribed a similar drug will experience totally different reactions.

I mentioned earlier that regaining respiratory self-responsibility for health does take longer if someone is on medication, since that person is going through a double de-tox. (a) from medical drugs, and (b) from respiratory toxin clearance. Anyone who has studied the side-effects from prescribed medication will be aware that these side-effects as well as the originating symptoms will have to be eliminated in a toxic form, both physically, mentally and emotionally, a cocktail of all three.

Many years of restricted breathing seem to produce layer upon layer of respiratory toxins which have become embedded in the respiratory system, and these have to be discharged. Originally as they became trappped within the system, they changed from undischarged exhalation, a non-discernible vapour, to watery mucus, and then a wax-like substance which begins to line and block the breathing passages.

The cleansing energy produced by correct breathing appears to dissolve or scour these impure layers of breath-waste which start to *melt*, and are discharged through the head orifices, mainly the nose and throat, but also eyes and ears. Some people experience a limited period of apparent flu-like colds during this *melting* process, but then the excretion of any poison from the system is never pleasant, as the unpleasant originating source of the problem is re-experienced briefly as it leaves the body, in unusually concentrated bodily wastes. Sometimes a period of confused thnking occurs as we learn to trust our own intuition rather than other people's 'shoulds and oughts'. Emotionally we discover we have more courage, and will face situations which before gave us fear. All these are part of the positive symptoms of the excretory process of respiratory de-toxification.

I have consistently found over several decades that clients seem to know intuitively that this period of cleansing is not *re-infection*. 'Clearance' is the term most frequently used. The resulting bonus as better breathing replaces old inefficient habits is that people experience far fewer colds and infections in the following years, due to an upgraded and stronger auto-immune system.

As the health of the physical body begins to improve, so does brain function. Apparently the upper brain, our *operating engine* takes approximately 40% of our oxygen intake for proper function. It only weighs about one and a half to two and a half kilos while the remaining 60% of the oxygen is used by the whole of the rest of the body mass weight.

Brain poison from years of inefficient respiratory clearance takes its own time to become free of toxins. Only a natural and healthy supply and circulation of oxygen to the brain can produce mental health and clarity. This clearance of the upper brain must be matched by a re-connection and re-activation between the upper and lower brains as mentioned earlier in this chapter. The re-stimulation of the latter by correct breathing brings into use the natural expansion of the lower and larger lung area, right through the lung expansion to the lobes of the lungs. This re-connects our emotional and intellectual brains, and the balance of the left and right hemispheres of the upper brain. It beings about a resultant ability to function at maximum potential in our own unique place in the world order.

Thousands of people from all walks of life, age and occupation who have corrected their respiratory function, have reported dramatic improvements in health, reduction in the frequency of colds and 'flu-like symptoms, regularisation of high or low blood pressure, optimum efficient brain function, improvement in circulation resulting in warmer hands and feet in cold weather, and the ability to function easily within a 30% less requirement for artificial heating! The knock-on effect is an increase in calmness, confidence and joy of life.

PERHAPS SUBSTANTIAL REDUCTION IN THE NEED FOR ARTIFICIAL HEATING MIGHT BE TAKEN UP BY THE THOUSANDS OF ORGANISATIONS WHOSE EMPLOYEES REQUIRE TROPICAL-LIKE WORKING CONDITIONS MERELY BECAUSE THEIR CIRCULATION IS INEFFICIENT DUE TO BAD BREATHING. WORKPLACE TRAINING SESSIONS COULD HELP TO CORRECT THIS OVER-USE OF ARTIFICIAL HEATING, DUE TO EMPLOYEES' IMPROVEMENT IN THEIR OWN NATURAL HEATING FUNCTION. THIS SUGGESTION OBVIOUSLY APPLIES TO EMPLOYERS AS WELL!

From my observations of clients over three decades, dramatic reductions have been noted in the need for NHS appointments, in fact one GP 'complained' to me that when she sent clients to my clinic she rarely saw them again! They had in fact put their health back in balance by taking responsibility for breath correction, Nature's self-healing alchemical process, and 'medical' symptoms gradually recovered naturally.

I am certain that all chemical drug medication which 'blocks' symptoms of illness also blocks an area of brain function, which then depresses the lung area connected with that particular brain cell mass. This also acts as a depressant on the lower brain's stimulation of the correct respiratory initiating spark I have met so many people during my work who have been on long-term medication whose physical torso appearance shows a lower stomach distension in varying degrees of obesity, with a sharp contraction of the upper chest area. This 'shelf' represents a blockage in the free flow of healthy emotion and feelings, a tremendous respiratory circulatory inhibition, not only of oxygen to the brain but to the heart. Obviously there will eventually be a health crisis. The use of illegal soft and hard drugs, while creating a temporary flow of inter-brain emotion, is only an artificial stimulant of short term duration, and a temporary lack often releases negative emotions in a destructive way. Possibly responsible for road rage accidents and many forms of social violence, with children frequently the innocent recipient.

As the countries of our global civilisations begin to face up to the growing realisation of the part we have played in the increasing threat from Global Warming, we also have to face up to the quantum leap required in our behavioural patterns arising from our thoughts, which will have to take place in order to avoid climate calamity.

Our cultures and national characteristics arise in the first instance from one individual, who then affects and *infects* the thoughts and behaviour of groups. Never forget that group behaviour originally comes from the mental and physical behaviour of one highly motivated individual of a positive or negative dominating energy. This attracts like-minded individuals, and so the resulting energy produced acts as a magnetic catalyst, creating a mushrooming effect as the group expands. I am convinced that the core individual within the negative energy force will be an incorrect breather, and the core individual within a positive group cell will be a 'correct' breather. If the intellectual juggernauts of our age decide to pour scorn on these sentences, I might lovingly suggest they give themselves an opportunity to experience some corrective breathing sessions, to balance the creative brain hemisphere with their intellectual critical brain dominance.

The extra dimension of awareness gained from corrective respiratory training appears to open up an inner eye of perception full of joy and wonder at the beauty of the world. To me all restricted breathing negativity acts as as a barrier to this sense of joy, love of life and positive creative energy, as it arises like a fountain from the lower-belly well-spring of our body.

I observe with sadness and compassion the limited and incorrect nasal breathing of so many famous people (in the world's terms), who dominate our TV screens, radio and entertainment industry. Much journalistic writing is of a nature one comes to associate with the same disease. I read of the health break-downs of many of these individuals, the addictions, time-out in rehab centres, knowing that at the core of their consciousness must lie unnecessary feelings of limiting self-worth engendered by faulty breathing. You hear in daily programmes on TV and radio the nasal sounds which indicate sinus problems due to long-term incorrect breathing problems. These have prevented efficient excretion of the outbreath leading to mucus-block, and therefore resultant sinus problems. It is said that sinus problems are a symptom of blocked tears. 'Where no tears fall from the eyes, other organs weep.'

I believe that we are 'given' life and we choose to be here to fulfil the purpose of that gift. Its blossoming through our life's journey is a legitimate expression of the joy of being true to ourselves. Only joyful and compassionate people are the true inheritors of the Planet's riches, or can really be true Earth healers. The laws of inhalation and exhalation which decide our health, are also those by which the Earth can regenerate Herself. To regain and re-own this sense of our life's purpose often after great personal tragedy as so many people do, is proof that it exists. It is not a figment of our imagination. Re-own your breath, and you re-own your soul and can pass on the priceless magic of its reality.

Someone once wrote that frightened as they were of the power of man, they were more frightened of the power of God if they did not write as they felt in tune with their own life's purpose. I believe that many more people will have to become aware of this truth and act upon its meaning if we are to heal the Earth. Heal ourselves, stand back and...

LET HER HEAL HERSELF.

Chapter 2

HIGHER POWER OR
YOUR TRUE SELF

THE USE OF THE PHRASES, 'Higher Power', or 'True Self', often quoted these days, may evoke a groan of cynicism or respect, depending on the nature of the speaker and the audience. When I am in the company of like-minded people these phrases usually refer to exploring physical, mental or emotional solutions for our own or a client's problems, knowing that there is a right and wholesome answer to all human problems explored through these beacons of the acceptance of a Higher or True Self.

Sufferers from stress have often been in physical, mental or emotional turmoil for years, perhaps on long-term medication, knowing there must be another solution, and endlessly searching for some other way to relieve their dis-ease. When we begin to use correct breathing we eventually come to a deeper understanding, often when a personal crisis, illness or bereavement seemingly unbearable, suddenly becomes bearable. We have reached out to some hitherto unexplored space in our soul and found a beacon of light. If the cynics scoff at the mention of the word soul, it is not my job to persuade them otherwise. This beacon of light at first faint, is not a search for the unorthodox, but the reawakening of a deep awareness that the solution lies within ourselves. This awareness seems to trigger off a series of coincidences which lead us to a person, place or book which continues to open up this ray of light, and convince us that we have our solution already within us.

Eventually we take some action, often involving great courage, leading to the release of a relationship, addiction or limitation of thought which has, over a long period of time, enclosed us in a prison of our own making.

As our process of corrective breathing develops, we begin to be aware of a long series of non-material 'stepping-stones' along which we are being led. Sometimes we fall off into the earlier chaos, but know that we have to get back on this narrow path of clues which has been presented to us from some unknown source. Our *unsolvable* problems become solvable as beams of enlightenment reveal other more healing ways of using the marvellous energy of loving vibrations in which we are all swimming, and in which we begin to trust.

Finally we see our illness or life-crisis as a blessing, which we are now prepared to release, including everyone else involved, for who we may be grieving, or with whom we are over-emotionally involved. We accept that this was also their and our choice, acknowledging that all traumatic events carry lessons for everyone involved. In retrospect the pain often seems to be about very little, and we comprehend the truth of the saying 'don't sweat the small stuff, it's all small stuff!'

From this growing certainty of a Higher Power, once scoffed at but now rediscovered almost as a Holy Grail, we tap into a Higher Computer Code of understanding the law of cause and effect in human behaviour. Correct breathing releases a newly-discovered energy to transform a negative effect into a positive outcome. There is a divison between those people who can or cannot master man-made computers. A similar kind of division exists between those who begin to master the spiritual computer skills of understanding Higher Power, and those who deny its existence. For many years I was one of the latter. To the latter I can now say 'rubbish, you used these spiritual computer skills to get yourself born, so although you may now deny them, they are still embedded in your deepest consciousness. I have no doubt that at some time in this or another lifetime a sense of utter desperation at the chaos of your life will cause you to have no alternative but to return to their wisdom.' The words 'no alternative' may become dramatically urgent in the forseeable future, as Natures's invincible laws of cause and effect return to mankind the devastation we have created, of her artistry. That is, unless we learn the laws of Higher Power on a global scale. This power includes that of forgiveness.

So what is this Higher Power? The words are suggestive of the use of a greater energy than we normally have available. It might be challenging to question why we don't constantly use this Higher Power, why bother to use a lesser? Unfortunately we are only human. Elsewhere in this book I have written about the electrical energy frequencies that constantly pulsate through the human brain while we are alive. An energy to which the body responds and translates into action or inaction on a higher or lesser level of vibration. I make no apology for the repetition of key information in other chapters of these pages. These core clues wind like a golden cord through the many revelations which have been released both to me and other people in past years.

A repetition which time and again reduces the complexity of inexplicable events down to a formula so simple that it can act as a yardstick to explain cause and effect, and how the meaning of apparently disastrous events are Nature's attempts to restore herself to her healthy vibration of loving Alpha. She has no alternative, and nor do we. Mankind's collective violent vibrational brain energy attracts back to itself violence on an equal scale. This law of cause and effect on an invisible level is only understood by few people at present, but will have to come into universal comprehension before we can reverse the present manic destruction of countless lives, earth spoilation, and 'unnatural' disasters.

More people all over the world are beginning to understand and respect the irreversible laws of Nature. Only when that happens, will the loving energy of such people begin to spread on an unseen but powerful level, and the threat of colossal disasters which we have attracted, begin to recede. There is no other way.

If you can stand fast on your higher light ray energy or Higher power in the time to come, and remain unaffected by fear, help will be given from unseen and unknown sources, attracted to you by your personal vibration of energy. This will be the stronger according to the power you have created from the accurate purity of your breath pattern on your own unique rhythmic vibration.

Every second, minute, hour, day, week, month and year of our lives we have free will to choose which of the following electrical frequencies vibrate through our brain, and are influenced by the way we breathe. These frequencies are:-

BETA. 15-25 vibrations a second.
Constant Beta is contrary to Nature, and creates Stress - there is a dangerous over-production of Beta in Western culture. (Dr. Marsden Wagner of the World Health Organisation said some years ago that Western civilisations have a 60% domination of the left hemisphere of the brain.) A worrying diagnosis of our cultural Beta brain over-drive.

ALPHA. 9-15 vibrations a second.
The same frequency as the Earth's magnetic field.
In Alpha rhythm we feel peaceful and loving. A few minutes of correct breathing will produce this feeling within us, because we are back in synchronicity within Nature's embrace, and feel safe again.

THETA. 5-9 vibrations a second.
The frequency of powerful creativity, healing and meditation.

DELTA. 1-5 vibrations a second. Sleep. Brain virtually at rest.

Small children are said to have a brain frequency of Alpha/Theta. What a terrible shock for them to be confronted by our powerful mass-Beta stressful electrical frequency. The above electrical frequencies constantly flow through our bloodstream like sap through the veins of a leaf. Collectively this man-created energy encircles the earth like a gigantic man-made negative communication system. Its effect is experienced by us personally and by the Earth, it affects us throughout our lives in all our experiences.

When the brain is in Alpha-Theta rhythm, we seem to connect to a higher form of deep, benign, loving communication, which consolidates, is spiritually reassuring, and enhances our power to remain at such slower frequencies, enabling us to heal all aspects of our being. They also release from within us powerful knowledge of a wisdom we did not know we possessed, and allow us to become independent but not rigid in thought, unaffected by other people's negative energy. Reminded of the brain patterns of small children, I recall Wordsworth's prophetic words 'trailing clouds of glory do we come.' How tragic that for so many small children that glory is soon tarnished.

A POWERFUL AND CONSTANT STREAM OF
ALPHA/THETA ENERGY EMANATING COLLECTIVELY
FROM MANKIND TO THE EARTH COULD,
I AM CONVINCED, DO A GREAT DEAL MORE TO
RESTORE HER TO HEALTH THAN ALL THE
NOBLE SPEECHES FROM POLITICIANS.

When the brain slows down to Delta, we drift into sleep. Our present culture seems to be trying to operate on a run-down universal battery as we ignore the need to rest and sleep as a priority. We need to be able to live free from the avoidable stress caused by fatigue-strain from ignoring Nature's 'need to rest' signs. They are there for a reason. Many people suffer from insomnia because they go to bed with the brain at fast Beta, caused by an involvement with over-stimulating energy activities and noisy entertainments of various kinds by which we over-excite the brain. We expect to be able to fall asleep without giving it time to slow down to a calmer rhythm. We are then unable to easily change our brain electrical frequency, and have not been able to become really rested despite having spent 7-8 hours in bed.

I believe we have the right to dwell in Wordsworth's 'clouds of glory' all our lives. Countless recorded cases exist of people who have experienced what is called 'the near-death experience'. Having been pronounced clinically dead from accidents, operations or other trauma, they have returned to life again. All their accounts record a sensation of rising above the body, drifting through a tunnel, and emerging into a beautiful place of wonderful colour where they have been met by loved ones who had already moved on from our present life. Although wishing to remain, they have been told that they have to return to their earthly existence to finish some work, but all repeat that their lives have been profoundly and positively affected by this 'out-of-body' experience. I have met people who have gone through this situation and been deeply affected by their transformation. Their integrity is unquestionable, their renewed joy of living infectious.

Unquestionable too is the information that has been revealed to me from a deep core of awareness which has come unsought, through my own personal experience of using correct breathing. It has changed my life for the better in infinite ways, and the lives of so many people who have been sent to me, with whom I have had the privilege of sharing the simple information on correct breathing. It has transformed our existence. There is no substitute for the reclamation of this rightful knowledge we all possessed as we came into the world trailing our own individual clouds of glory. Our material-worshipping culture stole that sense of glory from the small baby. Far too soon, we closed the prison doors of our own enlightenment as a growing child. We began to lock our own prison doors, our natural ability to maintain the deep spiritual self-healing state of the electrical frequency of Higher Power's creativity, which was our birthright.

When I think of the Earth's continual need to stay in the loving frequency of the Alpha vibration, I am reminded of the words of Jesus that 'a little child shall lead them', or 'except ye become as little children ye shall not enter the Kingdom of Heaven.' This does not mean that we should become childish, but we have the challenge to re-possess in maturity the joy of the young child, which is still within us all. We can rise to this challenge to find again that child, which is longing to be rediscovered, as we reclaim the power of correct breath.

Theta vibration, the highest of all, is in a sense 'out of this world.' In healing work we have to sustain the frequency of Theta rhythm in our own brain in order to bring someone who is stuck fast in the self-destructive vibration of Beta hyperactivity, back into loving Alpha. There is such a lot of work to do, but there is nothing more satisfying than to see someone throw off the dark cloud of constant vibration of Beta materialism by correct breathing, regain the childlike sense of the joy and fun of life, and to trust again in the benign energy of Nature and their own Higher Power.

The compassion which comes to us as we walk the new path, helps us to understand with clearer insight the addictive problems of our times, the chemical, dangerous and unhealthy ways by which masses of people try to regain this Hidden Grail, for that is what they are doing. They are looking for their own lost child by addictive self-destructive methods of drugs and alcohol which rot the brain and physical body, and lead many to a premature death. They have lost the key and our culture has thrown it away. These illusory temporary and damaging glimpses of an artificial Heaven, are addictively clutched, their use is stolen from the natural loving energy of life, to them even an illusion is better than the loss of memory of that other joy, once known but now apparently unobtainable by natural means.

I wonder why the access path to health and joy through correct breathing is so determinedly ignored by our Health Services and public bodies who continue to attach a sneering New-Age tag to those who are advocating more intelligent ways to achieve health. Correct respiratory action triggers off proper circulation, which initiates the discharge of toxins leading to healthy cell life. Only correct breathing can do this, it is an essential, natural, but not a scientific, process. *It is higher than science.* Any left brain egotistically manufactured pharmaceutical chemical recipe will not do your breathing for you.

Increasing numbers of people are rediscovering the power of correct breath, are re-tuning themselves to Nature's power-point of Higher Power, and in so doing are *truly* becoming 'Friends of the Earth'.

I am not sure if the Earth can wait much longer for us to re-nurture her, yet we are all she has.

I suggest you learn to use the air of life correctly if you want to help the Earth and support her loving vibration. You will also rediscover Higher Power as a bonus, re-tune your spiritual motor to Alpha/Theta, and live healthily, probably longer. Above all happier.

THERE REALLY IS NO ALTERNATIVE.

Chapter 3

THE SPIRAL OF
WORLD HEALING

I REMEMBER ATTENDING a dowsing conference some years ago when that gifted Scottish dowser the late Major Bruce MacManaway spoke of the 'spiral of life', meaning that growth exists in all living things in the form of a spiral, observable in a seashell or the rings on a cut tree section. We may not see this growth pattern in a physical way in a human, but when we observe the knots within the cut section of a tree, they represent some trauma which has blocked or upset the smooth evolution of the spiral. These 'knots' also exist within a human being. In therapeutic terms we also refer to them as 'blocks' in a physical, mental or emotional form.

The pattern of our lives is intended to move upward on the spiral as we develop, it is meant to happen naturally as we grow into the next stage of our lives. Our personal blocks represent unresolved trauma yet, unlike the tree, we can remove these blocks. The most efficient way I know is by restoring our respiratory pattern which naturally moves us upwards on our spiral instead of remaining stationary or going even backwards which is not at all pleasant. Correct respiration restores the energy, and repairs spiral damage. Without that inspirational energy of oxygen, food alone is ineffective.

In pondering the chaos in which the world appears to be

enmeshed, I am beginning to wonder if this represents mankind attempting to move upwards in his spiral growth, but in so doing has to bring up to the surface the old energy waste blocks or symbolic 'knots' in the wood of his previous historic past. To those who speak of the 'good old days' where were they? You only have to read the social history of this country to realise how far we have progressed, despite the hideous social black spots which still exist. The rural area in which I live was one of the two areas in Scotland responsible for most witchcraft persecution. I sometimes feel that I can pick up the witch hunt energy still vibrating in the atmosphere.

Irrespective that these pages sometimes refer to highly coloured and inaccurate media programmes and articles, modern media coverage and publicity must eventually ensure that dictators can no longer conceal for ever the sins, extravagances and injustices of their appalling regimes. The washing lines of the world scene are increasingly on view! Just as you cannot hide your light under a bushel, neither can you hide your darkness. Without such media coverage the thought consensus of more enlightened cultures would be unable to express their concerns. Eventually change must happen, the knots in the wood worldwide must be unravelled.

When this occurs we appear to see an apparent escalation in violence and mayhem of all kinds. To be able to stand back and in a concerned but detached way view these disturbances, I have found it helpful to invoke my therapeutic knowledge of Hahnemann's 'law of healing'. Hahnemann was the founder of homeopathic medicine in Europe. In trying to interpret Hahnemann's law on a global stage we need only imagine a human being who has swallowed poison. While it is still in the system the symptoms may appear extreme and violent. If something is given as an antidote or purge to clear the poison, that person may seem to become even sicker as toxicity is excreted. The toxic energy seems to temporarily flood the system on its way out, but they are in fact *recovering*. If we can stand back and look at the horrendous world social 'poisons' and resulting evils which hinder our journey up the spiral of life harmony, in order to excrete these evils they have to appear on the *surface* of society. I hardly dare to suggest that this could be Hahnemann's law in operation but could it, perhaps, be so?

I have seen the same principle in operation within the lives of individuals as they heal. There are no short cuts. Individuals and nations have to go through this same 'eye of the needle'. If healing does not take place in this lifetime thank goodness for reincarnation, but that is in another chapter, and my own opinion.

Corrective breathing appears to follow the same 'Hahnemann' pattern, because it seems to bring up to the surface for self-repair physical, mental, emotional and spiritual disharmony. The spiritual translation of the word breath (spirit) is never far from my mind. I invariably find that spiritual re-adjustment always precedes the physical and mental, even if the individual is not aware of this.

Spiritual poisoning also follows Hahnemann's law. Painful events happen in our lives *often appearing too hurtful to bear, but there is always an harmonious path through the labyrinth.* As we discover this way through, we realise that we are releasing unpleasant aspects of our character concealed beneath our ego. We have to face up to the challenge of loving ourselves before we can love others; our dislike of the child within us has to be redressed.

We finally realise that we are probably releasing generations and layers of man's inhumanity to man, manifested in man's inhumanity to the *child* down the ages. This process of healing the hurt child within us is essential for us to move up the spiral of life, re-integrating right and honest love for ourselves. There is no alternative. I am regularly amazed by the looks of horror which appear on the faces of very intelligent people, who consider it extremely selfish to love oneself. To them self-love seems to mean the accumulation of vast material possessions at the expense of others. Of course that *is* a self-love, which is an addiction born out of a feeling of insecurity, and the exact opposite of loving oneself. Wholesome and necessary self-love comes from a great sense of the wonder and beauty of life in which we include ourselves as part of that great pattern. As the wise woman said: 'God made you and He don't make trash.'

Put it like this. If you say 'how can I love myself, with all my faults, weaknesses and down-right badness?', which part of you is at least acknowledging your weaknesses? It has to be the best bit, the true you, or how could you recognise your limitations? You have to give yourself credit for recognising this, so if there is this good part of you, how can you hate that? So start there, all long journeys start with the first step. It has to be the loving side of you which recognises the un-loving side, or how would you be able to?

Every correct breath amplifies this energy of love. As you feed it to yourself it can be felt by other people, the spread of love which is in global short supply, and can only be spread by loving people. We have to start with ourselves. Correct breathing increases this energy, but also self-starts the respiratory first-aid which is a pre-requisite to sending out this love world-wide, for which Mother Earth is starving. If you think these last few words sound sentimental you are free to change the way that you think. I had to.

Hopefully as you raise your spiral of spiritual growth in this way, you will notice beneficial changes in your physical mental and emotional/spiritual energy. There comes a 'no going back' realisation that you can no longer ignore. You have to make a conscious decision no longer to stay trapped in your own prison of self-rejection. The door to the prison is wide open and really always has been. By making that decision you become a healer of the Earth's magnetic field rather than a liability, your personal contribution to *her* spiral of regeneration through the power of *your* own self-healing.

Healing spirals never stay still, they either go forward or backward; where there is a block of apparent stagnation there will eventually be an explosion of negative health energy within ourselves, and by natural transmission, within the Earth itself.

As man is the Guardian of the Planet, that guardianship will only be healthy if it is benign. There is colossal evidence all around us that this is not the case. We have to learn to give this benevolence to ourselves before the Earth can feel the effect. This book is being typed on an earthly computer which can bring together in a material way all the factual and intellectual knowledge accumulated by our present learning experience. I feel positive that there also exists a *spiritual* 'computer' in the vibrations of space which reveals its wisdom to us through the magnetic frequency of our vibrations according to our individual unique corrective respiratory pattern. We can then 'log in' to a fantastic new special programme only available to those who breathe correctly.

As we learn to give ourselves love and so heal ourselves, I have complete confidence that the Earth will automatically heal herself. The great natural psychologist Jung never treated children. He said 'bring me the parents, the children will heal themselves naturally.' So it will be, as we re-learn to parent our child the Earth. An almost unnoticeable upward spiralling will occur, first in our own spiritual health and auto immune system, followed by the Planet's auto-immune system coming back into balance.

Thank goodness there are more and more people moving up this spiritual spiral; will you join them? The slope is gentle but inevitable.

Re-consider Hanneman's Law of Healing. The process must involve an eventual expulsion of the original poisoning or traumatic energy from the individual or organism, as the healing energy of the remedy begins to take effect. An agitation is seen to take place as the negative energy of the original problem tries to fight off the positive energy of the remedy. If the remedy is the correct one, eventually the originating cause will come up to the surface to be ejected and eliminated. A person may experience this period of ejection as a 'symptom' of the cause; it will temporarily appear as unpleasant or painful. However the *cause* of the problem is actually being *excreted* and is on its way *out* rather than on the way *in*.

If we transfer this *effect* on to the world stage and consider the violence, terror and general mayhem which appears to be engulfing us at the present time, I am beginning to wonder whether this appalling negativity is coming to the surface because of the effect of the groundswell created by the spirit-ual (irrespective of traditional religions) energy now being increasingly generated by many people throughout the world which I believe must be having a 'Hanneman' effect on its negativity. This may not be understood by the majority who through no fault of their own do not yet understand Nature's laws, but is does not mean that *nothing is happening* on this unseen level. I do not know if there is still time, but that is no reason to mistrust its power to change.

The Earth has absorbed our negative energies down the centuries until her need to go on moving upwards, to replen-ish and heal herself, is forcing her to throw off obstacles that block that renewal. *Our* negative energy and its power is the blocking obstacle.

If the increasing numbers of people who understand these invisible laws goes on multiplying, there is a chance that we ourselves may be able to move upwards on our own spiral, so that Nature's increasing protests in the form of 'natural' disasters may become less dramatic.

Loving energy injected into the core of the spiral will still have to work its way upwards forcing anything unlike itself to be ejected. It is said that 'love brings up everything like and unlike itself' (Leonard Orr). The evacuation of poisonous energy which may represent Nature's present turbulence and the cumulative diseases of man, could represent the self-healing process of love.

On the surface of the global spiral we appear to see more and more catastrophes daily revealed to us via TV and press, which *may*, and I repeat *may*, be the collective world violence being *excreted* from the Planet; a negative energy which has been simmering underground for aeons, and is being released because of Nature's irreversible law of Alpha balance.

Only the passing of time will reveal if this law of the spiral is now actually being enacted on the world scene at the human and planetary level, but remember for man and Earth the base of our twin spirals has to be always spinning at the energy of Alpha, a loving energy, the *only* antidote to destruction. Everything you as an individual do with love goes out on to the world stage on an unseen beam of energy *and makes a difference*. It strengthens the loving power of Nature's spiral to eject violence and disease from the planet.

Never think that *your* 'candle-power' of energy is insignificant. If you are beaming out this loving energy that energy will not and cannot be wasted. It must find a home as it is absorbed into the gargantuan body of Universal Higher Energy now being emanated increasingly from enlightened individuals who are involved in healing Mother Earth's loving spiral on which we all depend for our existence.

★ ★ ★

IN SPITE OF ALL OUR WANDERINGS
WE *CAN* RETURN TO THE HIGHEST CIRCLE
OF OUR SPIRAL.

Chapter 4

ENLIGHTENMENT

IN MY DICTIONARY, the interpretation of the word *'enlightenment'*, as a verb, means to *'enlighten'*, to free someone from a false belief. As a *noun* the state of enlightenment is referred to as being marked by spiritual insight, freedom from false illusions.

In my own experience, my personal enlightenment has come about from the near miraculous ways in which respiratory correction and relaxation training has brought me an extra dimension of joy of life beyond my wildest dreams. Even so the retraining period has not been painless, as I shed my protective illusions, and probably experienced what Jung referred to as 'the dark night of the soul.' This latter is probably a prerequisite if you are going to be working at a deep empathetic level with people who may have been traumatised in childhood, and as adults project that hurt on themselves, society, and in various ways often unnoticed, under a veneer of respectability.

I have often thought that teaching correct breathing and such activities as yoga in schools, universities, prisons, etc, would be of great benefit not only to the students and staff, but also to the *enlightenment* of the general atmosphere.

Therefore it was with concern that I read some time ago of a prison experiment in teaching yoga, which of course always involves better breathing. I think it was in Norway or Sweden, but certainly a Scandinavian country. The experiment had been discontinued as some prisoners had apparently become violent. I have no idea what form of yoga was being taught, it did not surprise me if there was occasionally some form of apparently disturbing reaction, but what concerned me was the fact that those responsible for this provision were possibly not aware of, or provided appropriate therapeutic explanation to the prisoners for the *abreaction* as to what was apparently happening.

A sudden release of tension can sometimes be followed by a period of disturbance as negative energy is released. This is a temporary situation, its possible symptoms must be explained to any participant *before* embarking upon such healing activity, and appropriate allowance made in the form of professional psychotherapy or similar help.

The problem is that pioneering methods in prisons are often short-term and done on the cheap. Apart from the apparent lack of therapeutic professional understanding, the excellent reputation of yoga, as in this case, is given a negative connotation. Now I may be incorrect in these thoughts, but I felt regret that a healthy source of desirable enlightenment had gone so wrong. In my experience teaching yoga, which includes breathing training, represents a wonderful way for someone to release themselves from fear and violence, but that *release*, which is a release from these perhaps long-term repressed traumas, may on the surface seem to be a disturbance when it is in fact a natural and transitory excretory process!

There are two other points worth mentioning. I have met some inadequately trained yoga teachers who did not breathe correctly themselves, and therefore could not teach others the process. Anyone who wishes to be taught correct breathing, relaxation or yoga must do so *voluntarily,* because they *wish* to do so, and no degree of coercion or persuasion must be involved. I do not know if the latter situation was part of the prison yoga and relaxation experiment, if not I am not surprised that it went awry. Any form of pressure in this kind of activity will invite an unconscious resistance often resulting in over-reactive behaviour.

A prerequisite and willing participation in such enlightened work means that we are now ready to face up to our unconscious terrors and repression, and with appropriate help release them in an enlightened way. This also means that we are willing to move on spiritually, however intense our released pain may temporarily feel, in which case we are prepared and able to neutralise it in a non-harmful way to ourselves or others. We realise that the repressed fear and pain has been responsible for the problems we have created in our lives. The resulting spiritual growth and sense of natural love for ourselves and others, teaches us that love is greater than fear, and gives us courage to continue with the process. (The onion-skin effect.)

When deep-seated fears come to the surface without this necessary *pre-lining* of spiritual awareness which implies an acceptance to grow and mature, the energy of the released fear and negativity can make us panic, feel threatened, and project on to others this amplified energy created by the release of apparently overwhelming panic, rather like the fizz when the stopper is pulled out of an over-aerated bottle of liquid.

From my own experience of working with people who have been in prison for various crimes, their childhood years have been destructive and rejecting, and so it did not surprise me that the prison experiment proved a disaster. It has now probably gone on record in the pioneering country as an unsuitable method of rehabilitation. Unfortunately such records can prevent a very positive, wholesome, natural and healthy experiment from becoming a recognised part of *prevention* of future violence and re-offence.

Yoga is not the only process that results in better breathing, but better breathing as an essential natural habit always leads to enlightenment. In fact I believe that the process can only be a partial one if breath is not the core catalyst. Teaching yoga and breathing in a prison situation needs to be carried out by someone who also has a training in psychotherapy, including spiritual enlightenment. The probable release of deep tensions requires a continuing therapeutic supportive environment in which staff understand the process, and an ongoing explanatory dialogue is made possible with the participants.

We cannot reach any form of enlightenment without getting rid of all the physical, mental and emotional negative baggage we have been carrying. It is a form of poison often invisible but keenly felt by those around us. The air can be laden with what I can only describe as a negative electrical charge which has to be dispersed or it can affect other people without them understanding why they feel so negative. Until there is enlightenment, there cannot be present the power of a positive electrical charge strong enough to dissipate the negative discharge of *baggage clearance*.

In this chapter you may feel that I have spent too much time on the prison experience, but is has enabled me to raise a voice in protest at unenlightened attempts to provide a beneficial service, which deserves a rather more enlightened approach.

You know when you are becoming enlightened, because you feel loving. Even in negative circumstances, you feel a new unshakeable certainty that you have discovered *why* you have been given life, and what you are meant to do. You notice beauty everywhere, you respect and nurture yourself and others, through Nature's lens of joy.

In particular you have a loving, greater understanding of childhood, a sense of wonder that creates an enchantment to each day. I have noticed that every time I feel I have gained a greater sense of enlightenment, I see children as even more beautiful. The question then begs itself 'do people who haven't yet started to walk on the golden carpet of enlightenment really like children?' Some people who profess to love children do so from questionable motives, a need to control, to *use* the child in some undesirable way. There are plenty of them about. I give thanks for my slowly increasing sense of enlightenment as it helps me to communicate with children in a special way, no words need be spoken, but an *unspoken dialogue* indicates that the child *trusts* you, feels safe with you, and that is a great privilege. Only now do I understand the hidden message behind the words that 'a little child shall lead them,' and 'except ye become as little children.' You realise that the child is teaching *you*, it is the language of love. This empathetic harmony is also felt in the animal kingdom.

To return to the story about yoga and the prisoners. I believe that the violence mentioned was letting off steam which had been simmering under the surface which would have been responsible for the original offence, and also perhaps a reaction to the prison regime. If it is not properly understood in the way I have suggested, it will probably erupt again and involve further offending with a return to a custodial sentence.

Many people from all walks of life receive homeopathic treatment; it is understood and accepted that this process often makes you feel worse before you feel better, with an apparent recurrence of the original symptoms, which is a *positive* reaction.

It goes without saying, that enlightenment means a release of everything within us which is dark rather then light, and depending on the level of our spiritual blocks the dark can be very dark indeed. The release of apparent aggression can vary tremendously in its intensity, almost minimal to acute, but does signify a cleansing, necessary for growth to occur.

In a properly understood and supportive environment, the steam can be released in a gentle way, the effect of which is fully understood by an individual whether prisoner or 'ordinary' man or woman in the street, if there is such an individual.

I believe there are few individuals who would not feel very much better and healthier for a gently supervised opportunity to improve their respiratory action and be able to let off the steam of their stored-up stress in a safe environment, which, with permanently improved breathing, will not re-occur. So many people are prisoners in their own self-imposed cells, in which they have been incarcerated since childhood. It is the imprisoned children I am most concerned about.

The ills of addiction, and the disturbed childhood symptoms we see on our streets, merely represent the extreme symptoms of imprisoned children who cannot be released from their cells because their jailers, i.e. most of the community, are themselves imprisoned within their own rigid confinement, even if the Highest Power has never closed, and never will close, the door.

In quoting the prison example of probably *unenlightened* enlightenment teaching I have over the years encountered a number of yoga teachers who seem to have missed out on some aspect of their training in that they still do not appear (as least to me) to be breathing correctly, and you cannot teach what you cannot do yourself. Without correct breathing I would not have had the courage at one point in my career of undertaking breathing and relaxation work, on two separate occasions, with prisoners on parole who had been convicted of murder, one an axe murderer. This in a big empty former school with no other staff on site, on a Saturday morning. Such a situation is probably not conceivable in these enlightened days! The appointments had been made at the request of a social worker who knew of my work. I do not know of the long-term outcome, but one did contact me several years later for a further copy of my relaxation tape! I hope such a statement does not sound conceited but when you breathe correctly, a contact is made between your own core reality and that of another person, which creates an atmosphere of trust and good communication without tension and fear.

That wise old psychologist Jung declared that 'you can only heal to the level that you have suffered yourself.' Perhaps my apparent 'death' at birth helped me to understand the parole clients at a very deep level, but I can understand the meaning of Jung's words.

The people who have most influenced me in my quest for wholeness have been people whose wisdom carries the truths spoken of by Jung. Considering the sufferers of this world of whom I was once one, we need so many people who have 'walked the walk' of reversing suffering into joy. Anyone who has faced up to an *apparently* agonising life situation, and learned how to turn disaster into creativity, fun and fulfilment has had to learn about, and embrace, Higher Power. In addition, for me and many others, the clearest and *cleanest* route is from breath correction, for the secret formula is already within the air we breathe, and is distilled into the brain through correct oxygen use. A process more finely tuned than the most sophisticated scientific or mechanical device so far invented, or *could* be invented by man, the *key* to health.

In addition, I am convinced that the air we breathe if used properly, keeps us 'topped up' with very fine trace elements contained in no other substance. The more stressful we allow ourselves to be, the more we deplete these trace elements upon which we depend, and they cannot be replenished except through the correct breath. In the same way that a great machine invariably relies upon a very tiny cog or minute piece of mechanism for its proper operation, and breaks down when that minute cog fails, I believe that the human machine relies on trace elements not discernible to scientific research for full function from the core cog of our being.

We can never change the past for all our *intelligence*, but the effects of so-called disasters can be diluted and rendered powerless by using the healing power which flows into the brain by the right use of air and correct breathing.

An intricate mathematical figure can be reduced to the power of nothing. Since mathematical function comes from the left (analytical) side of the brain, I am persuaded that we can reduce past suffering to the power of nothing through the power of the right creative, intuitive side of the brain.

In my personal journey I have come to see reincarnation as a sensible and logical process, which includes the thought (however it may seem to others) that we choose how and when we depart this present existence. That is my personal belief, and is discussed in another chapter. You have the right to your thoughts on these matters, and I have mine. These have been reinforced by living examples of people I have met over several decades and from all walks of life who have come to the same conclusion from their own personal life experiences.

What else is enlightenment about? Enlightenment in its purest sense is perfect love, which directs an invisible vibrating beam to heal our pain. Healing cannot tolerate pain.

There is no greater joy than to be able to share this self-healing formula with someone who requests help, but it cannot be assimilated unless a person has reached the stage of understanding that only *they* can heal their own pain. I cannot heal or enlighten anyone. As Enid Smithett, (a wise old dowser) put it in a talk to The British Society of Dowsers 'we are equipped by Nature to find our own way.' The fact that you yourself have discovered the way, qualifies your role as a silent trusting supporter, enabling someone else going through the temporary pain of healing to stay with their own individual process and not give up.

The path to enlightenment is the same for us all. That path can encompass each individual without encroachment on another. If we personify Lower Power as the direct opposite of Higher Power, it stands to reason that the Higher is meant to cancel out the lower. You can't have your cake and eat it! Thinking of Higher Power as a relentless force for good can also help to cancel out the chewing-gum fixative properties of Lower Power. The latter has had a nice, cosy bed and breakfast stay in our psyche for so many years. Its removal resembles the struggles of a toddler at the tantrum stage, who we are attempting to remove from a dangerous situation, but who doesn't see the danger and resists removal with all its physical and vocal strength. Such descriptive metaphors can often be helpful as we go through healing change, while removing the recalcitrant child from danger you still have to love him or her, even if you don't like them very much at the time!

Whatever the level of enlightenment we reach in our lifetime, we make many mistakes on the way, but if we are *trying* to stay in that safe place, it is as if we are protected from the negative effects of our fall from grace. You have probably heard the wise saying: 'It is better to seek for perfection and miss, than to seek for mediocrity and find it.'

When we have committed spiritual errors, which have not been cancelled out before we pass on, then I believe we have to return again and again until we get it right, after all time is timeless. Jesus said: 'In my Father's house are many mansions.' I suppose we go to whichever of these rooms we are spiritually ready to enter after an earthly 'death,' enjoy a recovery period, a spiritual wash and brush up if you like, and see a re-run of our previous existence, a personal heavenly video of our recent life. Probably after consultation with our own Guardian Angel we then decide to 'have a go' at another earthly existence to try and learn more spiritual lessons. I do not think we re-enter the earthly plane at a higher spiritual level than we left it; this planet is the Training School of Spiritual Learning. That's my opinion.

To would be-suicides I have suggested that you can do it any day, and even if you do, you will have to come back to earth at the same spiritual level you left it, so there's really no copping out This situation hasn't happened often, but no one I have worked with in therapy has ever taken the ultimate decision to end their lives.

You may find I am using rather hum-drum language, even slang to talk of intense human experiences, but sometimes a pithy metaphor can do more good than heavy-weight therapeutic jargon. Many of my clients have been superb spiritual heavy-weights, but with very limited skills acquired, from our present over-intellectualised educational system. I was overjoyed to hear today that schools in England and Wales are to have five hours of creative and cultural activity each week, which one cynical educationalist says is impossible. I could wish the ratio was for five hours intellectual activity a week, with the remainder of the time devoted to cultural and creative activity! Can you hear me Rudolf Steiner? Up There?

My present level of enlightenment helps me to love virtually everyone these days. This doesn't mean that I have to like their actions, we are told to love the sinner, we don't have to like the sin. We have to forgive, otherwise someone is still controlling our thoughts and actions. The most effective way to diminish the power of your opponent is to forgive him or her.

It is a great joy and relief to share relationships with people who know these laws. We get a lot more fun out of life, to be with those who are more or less on the same path of enlightenment means you get more achieved with less hassle. Such relationships are never boring, pompous, ego-centred, superior to others; they are always fascinating, full of coincidences, humorous and downright delightful. My deepest and happiest relationships have only been able to come about after I set foot on this narrow but totally safe path.

It was probably Leonard Orr who stated that 'enlightenment is certain knowledge of absolute truth.' My admittedly amateur study of scientific 'truths' gives me the impression that its goal-posts are constantly shifting. It gives you a feeling of total security to have discovered the 'absolute truths' revealed by correct breathing.

The invisible power of respiratory directed thought infused with love is, I believe, the most powerful energy in existence, exceeding all man made concoctions of military might, the huff and puff of the present state of our 'enlightenment', but that must change, I am sure it *will* change, perhaps from the extremity of our despair when we *have* to find another way. Maybe when we *really* understand how each nuclear 'test' affected and still affects the sensitive balance of the Earth's magnetic field.

This delicate all-powerful energy is invisible, but can pierce the densest matter and initiate change, so much so that the recipient of this laser beam of energy cannot withstand its benign influence. Once accepted and comprehended, the recipient then has no option but to use this energy in all their activities. Situations *then* can change for the better in *the twinkle of an eye*. The only condition is that that the initiating laser ray of energy must be utterly benign.

I have no doubt that at some time in the not too distant future we shall be forced globally to make an illuminative quantum leap of enlightenment in order to avoid massive global and human disaster. The shallowness and lack of insight of mankind's collective thoughts and actions contained within our unspiritual cocktail of accepted over-intellectualised 'intelligence' may have already spawned an inevitable downslide of chaos as we ignore the laws of Nature which are always spiritual.

Unless the growing spiritual energy of enlightenment being steadily switched on in the minds of thousands globally, of all races and religions, can create a spiritual anchor strong enough to deflect this enormous destructive energy we are producing, which is attracting back an energy of greater destructiveness, we could be facing total chaos.

Those who are walking the path of enlightened breath must use its all-powerful healing energy and love, in complete faith that it is a truly *unstoppable* force which implies 'thus far and no further' to the forces of disharmony obvious to all who view life from a spiritual dimension.

Many of our children are more enlightened than ourselves. If we refrain from using our own similar power it will make it virtually impossible for them to keep our great global vessel on a collision free course. Fortunately I am an optimist.

As a child I remember we had painting books with clean pages, which when painted with clear water, emerged as many coloured pictures. I often think that the effect of correct breathing has a similar effect upon the spirit of a formerly unenlightened soul. What emerges like the brush of water on a plain page is the rainbow-like beauty of a newly enlightened spirit.

Yesterday I was wondering if my remarks abut the danger to our Mother Earth were too strong. Today I was reading a speech given by Prince Charles to the European Parliament. He spoke of the 'Doomsday clock of climate change ticking even faster to midnight. If we are not courageous and peacefully revolutionary in our lives, the result will be catastrophe for all of us. In this sense it is surely comparable to war. If we fail, none of us will be forgiven by our children and grandchildren.'

Perhaps my remarks about the danger to Mother Earth were not too strong after all.

ENLIGHTENMENT CAN ONLY BEGIN WITH
YOU AND ME, ME AND YOU.

ENLIGHTENMENT IS CERTAIN KNOWLEDGE
OF ABSOLUTE TRUTH...

Chapter 5

THE CORRECT BREATH

WE EITHER BREATHE *correctly or incorrectly*, Nature has invented the process. At some stage if you go on reading this or other books on the subject of breath, it may be possible for you to comprehend as I was forced to, that breath is also Spirit, God if you prefer, whatever seems right for you.

Since breath is also life, when we cease breathing we can no longer remain alive. We must accept that to breathe incorrectly means to limit the life energy, resulting eventually in some malfunction throughout the three areas of our human function, physical, mental and spiritual.

There are several chapters in this book about various aspects of the invisible energy of oxygen which keeps us alive, and the way in which we maximise its potential through correct breath. It is also a spiritual energy, largely unacknowledged, apparently despised by virtue of that lack of recognition.

A visible substance to which we think we owe our survival, i.e. food, is presented to us ad nauseum via advertising and the media, yet we can survive for a number of days without food, and only a few minutes without oxygen. A major outbreak of a throat condition which prevented whole communities from swallowing food would be considered catastrophic, with gigantic world-wide attempts to solve the problem, yet we ignore the shutting-down by millions and millions of people worldwide, of lung areas which are vital for a disease-free existence. The financial cost in uneconomic health-care cannot be evaluated, because we are not using that part of the brain which would allow us to understand the invisible causes of our death-oriented society.

Please try and be patient with yourself (and me!) if some of what you read in these chapters at first seems a little puzzling. That is because you may not have been asked to use your brain in quite this way before.

You may think I pay too much attention to air and the way we use it, but then it is the only thing which keeps us alive. Like myself, as I later describe, you may put a book such as this on a shelf for a while, and then take it down again when, hopefully, chapters which once appeared meaningless, suddenly become meaningful.

I can only share what others as well as myself have discovered, so I am not talking out of the top of my head! The words that come from a deeper understanding of the power of correct breath seem to create a new language which takes time to comprehend. As the saying goes 'suspend your disbelief!'

As I said in an earlier paragraph, we often buy a book because something about a title or paragraph read while in the bookshop appeals to us, but when we get it home we find it difficult to concentrate on, and consign it to the bookcase. It may be years before we take it up again for no known reason, but find by an apparently miraculous coincidence that we cannot put the book down again. What we are reading mirrors something important that is happening in our lives. The book we have neglected sometimes for years, becomes one of the most important in our collection.

Remember the phrase 'coincidence is God's way of remaining anonymous.' Such coincidences often remind us of the sense of wonder we experienced as a child, when our lives seemed full of this exciting and heady feeling.

This sensation of sharing a wonderful new truth, however

stumblingly even painfully discovered, is now mirrored by the words from a book, which has lain dormant on our shelves for years. It gives us a powerful link with the author, often sharing some great truth with that writer, a truth that we were not told at school or University. It's like a personal discovery of the wheel, only much better. Usually we may never meet the author but the knowledge that they exist or have existed creates a relationship, becoming more important than many other relationships in real life which are now less important to us.

We are growing in maturity, and friendships based on a lesser maturity are no longer relevant. We do not have to feel guilty, for we have opened another door in our lives which we have to go through. We cannot take all our friends with us, they will enter when they are ready, so there is no way in which we must have expectations, criticise or condemn. *We must however go through that door,* when we see it open, or we will go backwards spiritually, which is not required of us.

We are progressively starting to think much more independently for ourselves and trusting our new thinking. Some higher invisible intelligence is telling you to trust yourself, and like me you may experience a great sensation of relief. A trust in your own judgment, after years thinking that other people were right, knew more than you did.

A great feeling of relief and confidence in ourselves may also bring up a sense of freedom, also sadness that our religious, health, business and political hierarchies seem to be operating in ignorance of these great truths. Surfacing within as a result of correct breathing, they are also bringing our loving joyful wise child to the surface, who we will no longer deny.

The information being released to us from our centre, by correct breathing, is continually confirmed by the illuminations from wise books by great masters which seem to be so *sensible.* A widespread knowledge of their truths could revolutionise and enrich our institutions, not least the now crumbling financial golden pyramid to which we have in the past paid homage.

This steady accumulation of new priceless knowledge is never more dramatic than in the process of rediscovering correct breath, until that is the only way in which we can fully integrate each new intake of this wonderful substance, which becomes so magical when we use it in the correct way.

The description of breath as a priceless substance implies that it has a solid structure, and indeed in one way it has. We see the exhale on icy mornings, when we notice a cloudy vapour being excreted from the mouths of those who exhale through the mouth. You will have read of their breath freezing on the mouths of arctic explorers. I wonder if this phenomenon is as noticeable when the exhale is processed through the nose. This vapour contains the substance of the waste product of the breath. *We hardly appear to notice this phenomenon when a person exhales correctly through the nose.* This seems to me to give credence to my thoughts that we have, built into the back of the throat the human equivalent of the catalytic converter which is built into the exhaust-pipe structure of a motor-vehicle. It purifies the pollution. In a human it purifies the exhale.

I have yet to hear any scientist confirm this, but it does not affect my own belief that when we breathe out through the nose we are discharging *less polluted CO_2 into the atmosphere,* a perfect way to lessen our personal carbon footprint.

Seventy per cent of the waste material of the body is excreted from our exhale, that seventy per cent is either filtered out in a purified or toxic form, depending on the way we breathe.

So what is correct breathing? Obviously there must be a *correct* process, because Nature is a professional, and her rules are exact, more exact than the most sophisticated and exact scientific experiment we can devise. Any infringement of Nature's laws will produce disharmony and disease.

In his wonderful book *The Science of Breath*, Ramacharaka states that 'the percentage of civilised men who breathe correctly is quite small, and that eminent authorities have gone on record to state that one generation of correct breathers would regenerate the race, and disease would be looked upon as a curiosity.'

As my knowledge and use of this exact science of the breath increased, so did my certainty of the truth of the above words, and the enormity of the task of teaching correct breathing in all our training institutions. Also *to the whole world,* for to do so would reduce disease, violence criminality, sexual perversion, child cruelty, and other social ills.

We seem to be lacking in a necessary sense of natural urgency to take such action, because of our over-intellectualised educational culture, which assumes it is better equipped to act on a crisis if it can be seen, heard, or touched physically. The crisis we are facing is very subtle and can only be seen by those who see with the eyes of nature and spirit, yet not to act is, I believe, to attract a human health disaster created by the breaking down of the human collective immune system.

You cannot get a degree on the subject of correct breathing. No professors exist as far as I know, who can speak authoritatively on this subject, the complexities of which, together with accumulated information down the ages, could fill a library. Not however in the Universities of the nations, even although it is the sole contributor to human life on the planet. The subject falls between the three options of health, education and spirit. The Health and Religious institutions do not seem to be competent to take up the challenge.

The ancient translation of the word spirit as breath just cannot be disregarded. It is the wonderful and irreversible result of obeying the basic law of the way we use the energy of Nature. It is not something which can be controlled by man. but it is the *yeast* of life which rises automatically from the correct use of the life force. It raises our activities from the bestial.

You will never find a hospital patient, or chronically sick individual who breathes properly. I believe this lack of respiratory health training places a strain on the medical profession which must know, at some level, that people have an innate knowledge of self-healing but do not connect this link with correct breathing. This serious shortfall in medical training leads, I believe, to a high level of alcoholism and suicide in that profession. It implies a lack of the knowledge of the great strengths which correct breath gives to the individual. Dentistry carries the same problems.

Their training is not good enough to meet the challenging expectations of their professions.

The GP who at a conference said 'take away my knife, take away my tablets, take away my drugs and I have nothing', spoke a bitter and intuitive truth.

When your level of breath awareness is developed, many of the available entertainments on TV or radio become puerile, our daily encounters with other people give ample evidence of their lack of tone and joy of just being alive, so sadly obvious in many young people. Ample evidence of a cancerous if unintentional disrespect for the laws of nature.

We are so fixated on Global Warming and degeneration in the animal and bird world that we do not note the degeneration in homo sapiens who is disobeying the exact laws of Nature every time he breathes incorrectly, which some say is most of the time.

The effect on young children of adults who breathe wrongly is a matter of great personal grief to me, as I note the look of sadness in the eyes of so many children, and the 'acting-out' behaviour which we criticise and condemn, yet it is *their* reaction to *our* stress. A trained breathing teacher would have a powerfully beneficial effect on the child, without a word being spoken. At a deep level the child is full of relief at being able to relax in the company of such a person because they do not pose a threat in the way that is presented by a tense, incorrectly breathing adult.

The child is straight off Nature's production line, and has been taught by that great teacher before birth how to use life by the way it breathes. The knock-on effect of parents, teachers and other key adults in the child's life whose respiratory pattern is distorted, damages the child physically, mentally and emotionally without even touching it, or uttering a word. A badly-breathing child can turn into a sick adult, physically or intellectually, an addict, a damaged genius, a pervert; there are quite a wide variety of occupations open to it, once the door of wholesome life-use is barred.

These things I write may seem harsh, you may condemn me for being outspoken, but again I quote the saying that I am more fearful of the wrath of God than man if I do not speak out.

As a therapist one is initially enthusiastic to share one's knowledge and skills to be able to help someone who is going through problems. You soon learn however that particularly with breath correction it is only possible to help when some-one is aware that they are breathing incorrectly. Otherwise they are not yet ready to accept training, even if by so doing they will be able to change their lives for the better in every way. *My* mind was barred to this work for many years, there is always the 'right time' when a person is ready for change. Our minds become so closed, that we cannot conceive that we have the power within us to change and help ourselves.

When I first started my work as a psychotherapist an old lady came to visit me, but not for help. She reminded me of an elderly Mary Poppins, and had come (I am sure she was sent) to bring me a tattered copy of a book called *The New Way to Relax*. The author's name was Karin Roon.

The old lady said that she was part of a little group who met regularly to study the book, and she had found it so helpful that she wanted me to have her copy. In saying good-bye she said that she did not think that we would meet again, and we never did, but she left me a wonderful sane and invaluable book, which I later bought in quantity and sold to clients, in order for them to have a great aid in the various stages of their recovery.

This book has been a constant source of comfort and help to many people over the years. In no way could it be called *New Age* or *Complementary*, nevertheless the comments and chapter on breathing are some of the best I have ever read. I can think of no more important sentence than the one which says, 'There is no habit in life which pays bigger dividends and pays them more promptly than complete breathing. It is the source of your health, your cheerful spirits, your energy your youth and your relaxation. A healthy baby is the perfect instructor in breathing and relaxation.'

This wonderful book reminds us that 'at the beginning of your relaxation practice you will observe that the expanding movement of the breath starts above the stomach.

'The better you learn to relax, the lower the starting point of your breathing will be. Complete breathing when you achieve it will give you the sensation that your abdomen is lifted from a point between the pelvic bone and the navel. When the breath rises above the navel it is an indication that your breathing pattern has not yet *regained* its proper function.'

The Correct Breath which is the Power of Life is to be cherished, as we would a little baby, it is our birthright, it is so gentle and tender.

IT LOVES YOU.

Chapter 6

GOD

WHEN I LOOKED UP THE WORD '*GOD*' in my dictionary, the definition was 'a prime mover, an infinite force.'
Funnily enough, there is no mention of this God as a benevolent force. Of course a man-made God such as a statue or
idol, which is still worshipped in many parts of the world is
seen by the worshippers as a prime mover and an infinite
force. So I have no intention of trying to persuade you that
God is other than just that. The God of *your* understanding.

What I have found however is that many people start to
become deeply interested in defining God to themselves,
once they begin to correct their breathing pattern. Without
any words from me they eventually reach a point of inner
consciousness, where they become aware of an infinite
force of great benevolence, with which they seem to be in
touch, and can never afterwards reject. A journey has begun, a
search which will not go away. It is not in any way connected
to established religions but does not make them hostile to
established religions.

They do however gravitate to those religions based on
love, not everlasting damnation!

I think we over-emphasise sporting prowess as something
to be *worshipped*, we create man-made idols and turn them
into Gods. They usually topple off their thrones eventually!

Let us consider what *does* happen when say a footballer
against all odds scores a winning goal. Contacting a centre
of such powerful inner consciousness that timing, precision

and perfectly directed energy, allows the player to do the seemingly miraculous.

Only a few sports personalities can constantly contact this vortex of power.

Perhaps we could also consider the fact that this finely directed energy power can be used in many other areas, once we remove our fascinated gaze from what is called gross motor activity. Ways which can also give seemingly miraculous returns. We used this precision of focused energy when we brought ourselves into life. Sometimes against all odds, no one gave us a medal! We did, however receive the crown of life, the sporting highlight of our lives. Everyone can be a spiritual sporting hero, without needing the applause of the crowd. The Earth needs breathing sporting heroes, and heroines!

I was reading *The Tao of Physics* by Fritjof Capra yesterday. He often mentions Einstein in his writings. Admirer of Einstein that I am, we share the same birth date, I always look for quotes by this eccentric genius particularly with reference to energy. Einstein strongly believed in *Nature's inherent harmony*, which all too few scientists seem to me to respect. He also said that the most challenging issue for mankind are the words 'is the Earth friendly?'. Too much scientific work would appear to disregard this inherent harmony, and if you think of the sports person and birthing baby, one is forced to concede the existence of a natural electrical frequency precisely focused at our birth, and always available to us, but used by too few of us later in life.

Sri Aurobindo talks of 'a new vast and deep way of experiencing, seeing, knowing, contacting things.' I am sure that a birthing baby is in contact with this process, during and after birth. A sports person achieving unbelievable new records, for a fraction of time, only briefly maintained.

A healer bringing in a strong pure energy to relieve a stress sufferer is, I believe, using a similar force from worlds unrecognised by our cynical culture. The precise centred focus reinforced by spiritual sporting breath.

Do *you* feel a little cynical when you hear of someone visiting a healer? Have you ever visited someone who uses healing energy? Obviously with anyone who advertises themselves as a healer, you have to use your intuition and discretion as to who you contact, but have you wondered why some people do seem to have what are called 'healing hands?' The healers of great integrity who I have had the privilege of meeting seem able to use this all-powerful focused energy, in order to help a sufferer to absorb a healing electrical frequency to reverse the negative energy which has caused their particular problem. This use of a power we can trust to do miraculous things is no mere accident, the energy is all around us. ''Tis ye, 'tis your estrangèd faces, that miss the many-splendoured thing.' (*In no Strange Land* by Francis Thompson.)

I have been fortunate to work with many people, who in the process of correcting their breathing action have discovered this energy within, and have changed their vibrational potential, to heal themselves naturally, which is what correct breathing accomplishes.

Once having been found we know that we must hold on to it, as a secure rock to trust which allows us to chart our true path. Even if we stray, as we are bound to do at first, we know that we must keep in touch with it in order to be safe.

In re-finding this miraculous world that exists within us, which has not been taught to us by any accepted educational process, we rediscover a joy and spice to life which is accompanied by almost miraculous coincidences. It reassures us that we have an invisible friend or colleague, certainly not of this Earth, name it what we will. God? Well it certainly seems to be a prime mover and infinite force, using coincidence as God's way of remaining anonymous. Refer to Chapter 22,

The Power of Thought, in particular Section Two.

In trusting a Loving Universal energy, we begin to realise that the old excuses as to why we stay in the same old negative rut will no longer hold water. We want to change, and it becomes an urgent need. We have to take these first faltering steps by ourselves, bringing into reality the energy change behind the words, 'Am I ready to let go of who I am, in order to be who I have not yet become?' The unnoticed, unrecorded acts of great personal courage needed by us to be all we can be, are ones I have encountered time and again; working with those who are using the restorative healthy vibration of correct breath to re-build their lives. Yet this is what we all did at birth, we 'let go of who we were, in order to be who we had not yet become.' We did not know if we would make it, but we did it all the same. Into the unknown.

If the ancient translation for the word breath is spirit, and the Christian religion talks of Father, Son, and Holy Spirit, did the early Christians understand that the correct use of breath must lead to an inner spiritual recognition of a force as yet unable to be analysed *nor ever will be* by scientists? Spiritus = spirit. I have read that some scientists, particularly some physicists, have recorded this possibility. It must take some humility, given their training, and I congratulate them. Good old Einstein was probably the first.

I believe that anyone who has taken this step of contacting the inner Higher Power, or God (prime mover or infinite force), are the ones the Earth can trust to help her heal herself. They are spiritual light points on the Earth's surface.

All violence, wars, lethal weapons, over-materialistic production for greed, hunger for power, competitiveness are fuelled by Beta-energy, the result of incorrect breathing, or incorrect use of spirit.

The Earth is empowered by loving Alpha energy, and the Earth is alive.

By the law of magnetic attraction all energy frequencies attract an identical energy back.

Therefore the Earth has to attract Alpha in order to maintain her balance, health, and ability to support the existence of mankind, the dominant species.

At this present time in our earthly tenancy, we are sending out so much Beta (stress), as the discharge from our dominantly Beta energy production. It is attracting Beta energy back, which is interfering with the ability of the Earth to attract back the Alpha electrical frequency she needs as she discharges her own waste Alpha energy. In the conflicting interface between the two opposing energies which the Earth must win in order to stay on balance in the planetary system, a growing disharmony is being created by man which in reality is man acting in opposition to the Earth. What an impertinence!

I do not know for how long the Earth can put up with mankind's behaviour. When I was a child I was told that man had to conquer Nature. In my childish way I imagined him hacking his way through endless jungles! Nature was presented to me as a force for evil.

Now I know and thank goodness so many others know too, that the Earth can exist quite nicely without mankind, thank you! Can mankind exist without nature? I don't need an answer to this question.

I do not know how much time we have left to put *ourselves* right, because that is the only way in which the Earth can heal herself of her man-made wounds; remember it is not enough to talk the talk, we have to walk the walk.

The only road to the exact information we need, is to get ourselves back into a state of love, as *little* children, for our treatment and lack of understanding of the child in our midst, reflects the way we have damaged the Earth, you cannot separate the two.

When we collectively breathe correctly as the child, who is the prime mover and infinite force in our midst, the magical blueprint we have been given will fall into place. Breath can unite the nations, for the right use of breath brings love into blossom. Jesus said 'Except ye become as little children, ye shall not inherit the kingdom of heaven.' This I interpret as the Kingdom of Heaven *on Earth*.

I don't need to talk any more about God, an infinite force is just that, *infinite*, there are no adequate words. Call it enlightenment, a white light, or the heart that in breaking open upon the Cross contained the whole Universe?

In virtually all religions there was an original emergence of a Divine Figure, an Anointed One whatever name is given to that figure by its followers. No matter how the followers of all religions seem to have interpreted the true meaning of the original message, so we must eventually come back to a force of love, which can only be experienced by the opening of the heart. Our correct spirit breath leads us to that place within. What more beautiful words to complete this chapter than:

'THE GREATEST MYSTERY OF ALL TIME
LIES IN THE WAY THAT CHRIST
LIVES IN THE HEART.'

The Aquarian Gospel - Levi Dowling

Chapter 7

THE BRAIN

I WAS ABOUT SEVEN YEARS OLD when my brother was born. It must have been some months later that I remember being sent to the local butcher after I came home from school. I sometimes had to do this at lunch-time, often to buy sausages, but on this occasion *brains*. I think sheep's brains as my baby brother was being weaned onto more solid food.

The brains looked horrible on the butcher's block, white, shiny and slimy! Horrible. The smell as they cooked was pretty awful too. I thought that they were also meant to make my brother brainy. Obviously they didn't give me sheep's brains when *I* was a baby!

Getting back to the subject of this chapter, I realise that some, even quite a lot of what I write, will be referred to in other parts of this book. This is inevitable, as so many of the processes connected with correct breath are interlocking. In explaining one of these processes, it will be necessary to mention another, which cannot be ignored, but all do bear constant repetition. To learn correct breath, for some time the process must be uppermost in your mind, like learning an essential important new skill.

As I start writing these particular pages, I invite you to think of a figure eight, and to put a vertical line down through the centre of the number. The top part of the eight was to represent the two halves of the upper brain, and the lower part was to represent the lungs. The left intellectual upper half of the brain is connected to the right lower lung, and the right creative upper half of the brain is connected to the left lower lung. You might find it helpful to make a little diagram to help illustrate this information.

ONLY CORRECT BREATHING SUPPLIES THE BRAIN WITH CORRECT OXYGEN

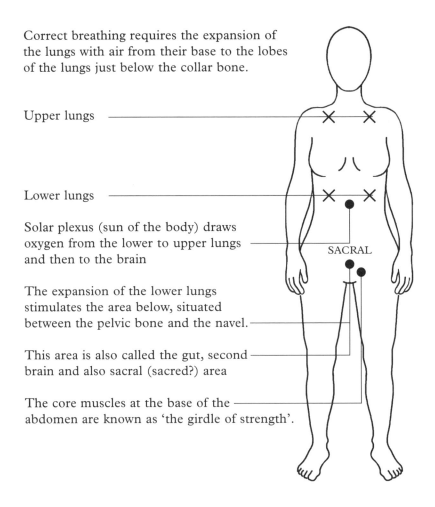

Correct breathing requires the expansion of the lungs with air from their base to the lobes of the lungs just below the collar bone.

Upper lungs

Lower lungs

Solar plexus (sun of the body) draws oxygen from the lower to upper lungs and then to the brain

The expansion of the lower lungs stimulates the area below, situated between the pelvic bone and the navel.

This area is also called the gut, second brain and also sacral (sacred?) area

The core muscles at the base of the abdomen are known as 'the girdle of strength'.

SACRAL

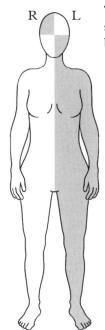

R   L

The left side of the brain controls the right side of the body, and the right side of the brain controls the left side of the body.

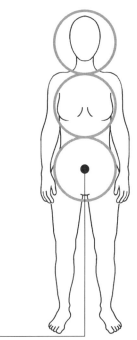

I believe this area to be the site of the auto-immune centre strengthened and inspired by breath. ——

Although the above words are correct, I cannot talk about the upper brain, without referring to the second or lower brain, situated between the pelvic bone and the navel. It is only brought into correct use when the breath rises correctly from the lowest and largest area of the lungs, whch I understand is also just above the invisible centre of the auto-immune system. I am told this lowest area is linked to the invisible higher world of consciousness *not* invented by man. There you go, three for the price of one. Someone not connected to this centre through incomplete breathing, doesn't know what they are missing! For me it would mean only living half a life, and feeling lost and alone.

Going back to the strange way in which one half of the upper brain controls the opposite lung and side of the body. Nature has planned it that way, but keeps her secret as to why.

This brain/opposite lung of the body can be recognised if you know of someone who has suffered a shock or heart attack. When you learn which side of the brain has been affected, you will notice that the person is physically affected in the opposite side of the body. A person who has been critical and rather materialistic, will seem to become quite soft-hearted, while a quiet, timid person may become talkative and aggressive.

I find this left/right interaction fascinating, in observing my own and other people's reactions. For instance it helps to make boring TV programmes more interesting, when in an interview, someone is asked a question, and you see their eyes move to the right, you can be sure that they are watering down the truth, or trying to find an answer that they think you want to hear. Not necessarily the truth. If their eyes look to the left, you can be pretty sure that they are honest and searching for the right answer possibly a spiritual answer. A good tip this if you are interviewing a witness in court or a job interview.

I recall an article about Ghandi the Indian spiritual leader who deplored the fact that with the demise of the use of the spinning-wheel, India, had lost *its left lung.* Of course spinning, a creative skill, uses the right side of the brain, stimulated by the activity of the left lung. It was a universal household activity, superseded by factory processes, so that the creative home spinning became redundant. Quite a dramatic example of Ghandi's unusual intuitive awareness.

I often think that children would find this kind of information very interesting as part of the school curriculum. On the other hand it might provoke a school strike if they understood that the government was trying to educate them out of their right brain, by the lack of creative subjects such as art in the timetable. I wonder if this constitutes abuse, as we rear children who are starved of creative subjects, rendering them easy fodder for the first drug pusher lurking at the school gates, offering a little tablet that sends them on a colourful psychedelic journey to regions of the brain long locked away in tears of stolen childhood.

If my own childhood, so long ago, had contained more creative subjects, I am sure schooldays would not have seemed so boring. Children learn by osmosis; they are natural workers. I certainly did not learn to read at school but from a little book brought home by my father, from which I read several paragraphs with him when he came home each lunchtime. The book was called *The Land of Nod*. After that my reading took off.

From then onwards the school reading books were so easy and boring, that reading lessons were a waste of time. My brain marked time during much of my primary school years, but with forty children in the class, progress had to proceed at the level of the slowest in class. Nowadays I believe that particular policy has improved.

I believe most sleeplessness arises from an over-stimulation of the left hemisphere of the brain by our present culture. I may have mentioned elsewhere in this book, that if you are lying down with your eyes closed, try to roll your eyes round under the closed lids to the left-hand side. Immediately you are bringing the right brain back into focus, which helps to slow down the over-active left (doing) brain and helps to bring the right natural brain function into focus, including the relaxation ability. Nature then usually does the rest of the work.

The policy of TV programmes to run violent murder films late at night is, I believe, a sign of a total misunderstanding of the needs of TV viewers in the later evening hours. It is quite shocking to read how channel after channel screens these late-night horrors, implying yet another example of irresponsibility for the mental health of viewers.

Watching such violence suggests a deliberate violation of sensitivities of the public, actors, producers, and all involved in such productions. All these people wrapping their minds around such horrors, hour after hour. Standards have slipped so steadily that we do not notice this rape of our natural good taste. Our brains and senses slip into grooves which get even more hardened, so that we become indifferent to the real horrors stories from all over the world, where the violence of war erupts into untold suffering to which our brains have become hardened.

The dominant world culture, which prioritises power, speed, materialism and competitiveness can only do so by the over-domination of the left side of the brain by putting nature on the back-burner, but she will not for much longer be so abused.

There is an urgent need for us to reunite the information link of the upper head brain with the lower auto-immune lower belly brain. It starts to come about in a natural way as we correct our breathing and relax tense muscles which suppress the carrier breath.

Here is a little experiment. Next time you forget something very important, and have spent ages 'wracking your brain' to find the answer or word you are looking for, stop trying. Instead speak to your lower belly brain and ask him/her to give you the answer. Then ignore the problem and get on with other things.

Sooner or later, often sooner, the answer will come to you, apparently unbidden and effortlessly. As you use this process more frequently, you will realise that you are bringing a hitherto ignored part of *yourself* into use. Yes, *yourself*. You may ask where has this important part of you been all these years. It was there when you were young, but began to be ignored as you absorbed the culture of our times It was a very important part of you and now is the time to reclaim your whole wonderful self.

You see, no matter what the problem, it is said that some level of the brain always knows the answer. This lower and also spiritual brain was written about by the Hopi Indians, and some Yogi teachers. So if you give this area of the body an instruction, which lies between the pelvic bone and the navel, let it do the work. It seems to be our link with Higher Power, which will always work for your greater good, if you give it a chance. It will not work if your thoughts are negative, and not for the betterment of man.

Some of the most wonderful discoveries are the *rediscoveries* of the marvels nature has stored *within* you, to me they resemble the sense of wonder Columbus must have felt when he discovered America. In this case we don't have to travel so far!

If you have read the paragraph which speaks of the necessity to use *full lung function to obtain full brain function,* you must also take into consideration the fact that there exists this second unseen brain (that is unseen by scientists in its meaning) in the lower belly. So perhaps we need to see the shape as an 8 with a further 0 at the bottom, i.e. 8 plus a lower 0. This makes a symbol representing the lungs in the centre, with the upper and lower brain beneath and above the lungs, the emotions in the lower 0 and the intellect in the upper 0. To be understood and expressed, emotions have to be communicated to the upper brain. Intellectual knowledge has to be communicated via the emotions, if it is not to come over as cold, hard, and boring. When the breath is correct, the brain is also balanced, and communication is processed through the heart in a natural and loving way.

From the massive number of people in all walks of life and

from all professions, whose two brain plus heart synchronicity is out of balance, the sheer scale of resultant physical, mental and emotional ill-health in global society represents a cry of misery of such magnitude that an all-encompassing solution needs to be embraced. To do that we have to go back to nature, to reflect on the real meaning of Einstein's words when he spoke of 'Nature's Inherent Harmony', or Fritjof Capra who stated in his book *The Turning Point* that 'Our present Society does not reflect the harmonious interrelatedness we observe in Nature.'

Britain can never be a world power again in the empirical sense, nor even a financial one, if we read between the lines of the present economic crisis. The people who have brought about such a crisis will certainly not be breathing correctly, or they could never have acted in such morally corrupt ways. Think about that, I do not have to meet them to make such an observation. It is said that the only thing which could create such a crisis is that 'good men do nothing.' Or have done nothing, so that we are all implicated.

Media and Government regularly expound profound solutions to our present national malaise, but suggest totally blinkered solutions as to how we can arise as a nation from the present morass. Economic solutions unaccompanied by spiritual growth still leaves a hollow vacuum. There is no other way than a spiritual understanding which rises supreme over any economic solutions, in fact spiritual growth means that our material needs *will be met*. The colossal power then available to us through such understanding will always override any narrow political solutions, whatever the external implications.

The wasted unused lung and therefore brain space from cradle to grave in our population is also an indication of the ignored pollution that is slowly and surely weakening the vitality of our country. Blocked circulation blocks not only blood flow but the vital information we need to pull ourselves out of the abyss. I believe we could in one generation reverse our current national deterioration, but there is only so much time left.

I repeat, the only process which goes on in the brain is either negative or positive thought. Inadequate oxygenation of the brain increases the negative bias from which those thoughts and subsequent actions spring. Negative thought leads to nothing or less than nothing. All the social ills of our culture arc the collective diseased weeds of negative thought and action which pollutes all strands of society.

Such a force of negativity, which is always preceded by breath limitation, one of Nature's unrecognised laws, leads to the inevitable over-production and excretion of human CO_2, which occurs from unnatural breathing.

The CO_2 pollution from 20 people who breathe badly, locked within a closed room for 20 minutes will be quite measurably greater than from the same 20 people breathing correctly under identical conditions. In the former case the unpleasant atmosphere and odour in the room will be greater than that from the latter which will be noticeably sweeter, and create less pollution. I know this has been scientifically proved, but the implications seem to have been taken no further.

Think of this in all the homes, offices, factories, shops and buildings including schools, colleges and universities throughout the country, often poorly ventilated, which are used by millions of people. Add to that the electrical vibrations produced by millions of computers. We seem to completely ignore the effect on children of such toxic emissions. Don't forget the toxic emissions in space with which we are all so concerned, will hardly have been produced by people who breathe correctly, are spiritually positive, have brain balance and whose personal toxic emissions do not damage the planet.

All incorrect breathing produces negative thought, and subsequent negative action, which must by default go against the wholesome vibrations of nature, and will add to the toxic emissions in the atmosphere. Think of this on a Global level.

The science of Kirlian photography illustrates quite graphically the energy balance in the brain expressed through a photographic image of the fingertips which projects brain energy. A big disparity in the pattern of the left and right hand reflects a similar imbalance in left/right brain use. This is just one of a number of ways in which we can visually see unnatural harmonies at a personal level.

When I was ten, I took what we called at the time the *Intelligence Test*. I marked up a hundred and twenty-eight out of a possible hundred and thirty, and my brother achieved one hundred and thirty plus. This test made no reference to a child's emotional IQ, which I believe to be the most vital part of any assessment.

Of course emotional IQ has to be undertaken by those who are emotionally balanced, how can we bring that concept into today's assessment of the child? On that basis, looking back I am not sure that the emotional harmony of either my brother or myself would have rated the same high level as our intellectual IQ. Probably by that time we were struggling with the left brain demands of an educational system already deciding where our 'intelligence' could be best used on the State's economic treadmill.

Hyperactivity in a child does not have to be 'corrected' by drug medication. Teach the child to breathe correctly, and before long it will once more tune itself into the Alpha activity of the Earth, which in a child means that its own brain activity will be restored to natural Alpha. The hyperactivity will resolve itself. If you disagree, find me a child diagnosed with hyperactivity who can breathe correctly;

you will find that their lower belly immune response and oxygen intake is completely out of synch, as will their natural brain harmony.

DON'T BE BRAINY, BE IN BALANCE
WITH THE EARTH.

Chapter 8

JOY

WHEN I BEGAN TO WRITE THIS BOOK BY HAND, I had no idea that I would create fifty plus chapters. I gave them all a number and title, and have been selecting them one by one as I type them, very proudly using my newly acquired word-processing skills. So now I come to this title of Joy, which it gives me great joy to write.

What a short word, yet so many people would look at you in cynical amusement at the thought of its single syllable ever passing their lips, or being included in their vocabulary. For a man it would sound embarrassing, and to many women a state so seldom experienced that both sexes frequently avoid it.

Yet we are all looking for joy.

The dictionary calls it 'a condition or deep feeling of pleasure or delight'. Perhaps to many it represents such an unattainable state, that it is better to avoid using the word at all.

A most challenging and precise clarification of its meaning came to me vividly via a young woman, who told me she had given up a very steady and lucrative job in banking, sold her flat, and left an unsatisfactory relationship. She moved to a small town, bought a shop selling crystals and alternative books, and ran courses with complementary therapists.

She spoke some words which have remained with me ever since, indelibly imprinted on my memory. In changing her life around she told me, '*I decided not to do anything or be with anyone who did not give me joy.*' I think that's a yardstick which we could all do well to emulate, remembering also that we can *choose* to create joy from any former mundane tasks. Also that we can choose to be joyful in any situation, but the latter is more easily attained when we have repaired our breathing, and regained enjoyment in simple pleasures. We then seem to begin to trust and understand Nature's Universal Laws.

The words of my young friend may seem like a selfish statement, but it is necessary to think more deeply about the meaning of joy. *Joy is not a shallow emotion.*

Most of us, although sadly not all, can still remember from early childhood the sheer bliss and pleasure of just being alive. This joy we can see on the face of a small child, or children at play. Yet all too often as an adult, it remains as a memory, seen from the present as impossible to achieve.

During the years when my great changes were taking place, I began to realise that I had to acknowledge the presence of a Higher Power, which was an always available energy source, greatly heightened by correct breathing. It gave me joy, a new fresh joy, accessible when I was on my own. Lilla Bek, the writer and expert on the Laws of Higher Power, once said to me: 'It is only when we are on our own that our guides, our helpers, are always available, so that even the silence is pregnant with possibility.' How right she was. I am never lonely now.

Even so in those early days my joy was too often determined by outside events and by other people's moods.

In our development we never stay still, as soon as we contact our inner core, we either move on or go back. If we decide we are not prepared to move on from that deepest centre we regress spiritually, and by so doing eventually become unwell. As we finally accept that our thoughts create our environment, we reach an important milestone in our spiritual progress which is that we can no longer tune into the addictive mind-set of being sorry for ourselves. This is the dead-end option which prevents us from exploring the undiscovered territory of learning that we can *choose* to pick joy out of the air.

This leads to discovering a new horizon of being able to convert apparent loss into gain, solely by the power of a thought. This may at first feel rather wobbly, rather like learning to walk again. Then we begin to realise that we have chosen a new 24/7 existence, totally opposite to the ways we have absorbed from our upbringing and environment as to what constitutes worldly success. We are no longer interested in worldly success, unless it brings us joy.

Our pioneering thought choice of plucking joy out of the ether yields rich returns, for we then have to let go of expecting our dearly-laid earthly ego-plans to work out. As we trust our new ego-less thoughts, what happens is a subtle influx of unexpected happenings which we know, but cannot prove, has arisen from this new life-mode. The words 'should', 'never' and 'can't' are excluded from our vocabulary. They are all parental words, unlikely to give us joy, rather to attract negative energy. They have to be mentally shot down with labelled thought arrows which say, if you forgive the slang, 'sez you!'

The refusal to be sorry for ourselves, and avoiding negative words, is a process which takes its own time during which we may occasionally rant and rave, and distrust. Then at some point we say to this apparently mischievous Higher Power, 'OK, what are you trying to tell me? What do I have to learn?' The answer is all about stopping talking, and starting to *listen*. Increasingly the answer will come from within, the still small voice, with great clarity like an internal laser beam.

Before long you will be glad that the 'shoulds' and 'oughts' never materialised. A super alternative and better way will have come to you. It is usually simple but so totally *right* that you can only feel joy at the result.

You begin to realise that this kind of joy has not and never has been withheld from you, and that joy is indeed in the ether. Heaven is there in every grain of sand. Your days become full of wonder, you have discovered the alchemy of life, well worth the earlier angst. The correction of your breath will strengthen the process.

A new, better and more joyful way of life has been awakened within you.

Another aspect of this *no other option* way of being alive is a much more accident-free existence. Increased mental awareness leads to fewer accidents, living in the *now* creates an economical efficiency, which highlights priorities. If we obey the priorities, I have found that other activities fall into their appropriate places. I don't really like the word efficiency, but this is a kind I can live with very happily.

The word 'efficiency' has in the past been equated in my mind with the word 'boredom'.

I referred to the accident-free existence as being one of the perks of this new life-style. I have come to the conclusion that there is no such thing as an accident, rather it is the magnetic attraction of negative energies. Violent disagreement may be your reaction, but I am sure that if research was carried out into the accident rate between those who breathe correctly as opposed to those who do not, the former will have a dramatically reduced accident ratio.

I'm all for reducing accidents and pain in the world. I read once that our upright stance of feet being earthed and heads being drawn up into space, allows us to draw information from that higher space, call it Heaven if you will. All our thoughts are drawn from the energy of the air or oxygen we breathe. Since energy never disappears, we might suppose that the air or space around us is filled with the energy of the thought processes of everyone who has ever existed. This space-filled energy is known as the Akashic Records, and becomes available to us through our unique vibration.

I believe that our higher energy, or spiritual breath, enables us to absorb higher spiritual thoughts into our own energy-space. By the same token we can also absorb lower level energy and make it our own as we often do. Higher energy space is infinite, as is our capacity to attract it to us, while we are still earth-bound.

There are many people alive who have recorded their certainty that there is a heavenly place beyond, which they have discovered after going through what is called the 'near-death experience'. That is, having sustained a physical experience of such severity that they have been pronounced dead by the medical authorities, and yet have returned to consciousness. During that interim time-lapse they all report the identical sense of travelling through a dark tunnel towards a great and beautiful light, where loved ones may appear. They want to stay but are told that they have to return to life. I have met several such people. The resultant feeling common to all of them on their 'return' is the experience of *joy*, a transfiguring sensation which has stayed with them. Perhaps to tell *us* that *it is now safe* to allow ourselves to feel joy.

If we do not know how to rediscover joy, we shall sell ourselves, our children and Mother Earth short, by the boring emotion of negativity *or joy starvation*.

WHICH WILL YOU CHOOSE?

Chapter 9

HEALING

THE WORD 'HEALING' can be used in many ways, most of us carry an impression perhaps from schoolday lessons on the Bible when the word applied most frequently to the work of Jesus, who healed in diverse ways. My childish recollection comes from the Biblical words describing the actions of Jesus. 'And he laid his hands upon them, and they were healed.' At that point the sufferer's problems disappeared.

In the past couple of decades I have heard a number of eager beavers declare that they were healers and my cynical side, which I try to repress, says 'Oh, yeah?' At one time such people appeared at 'New Age' seminars often as males with ponytails, ear-rings and a glazed look. The female of the species often wore cotton paisley skirts and much chunky jewellery. Also the glazed look. Perhaps they were, perhaps they weren't (healers), but I have since given a great deal of thought to healing; who has the power, and as far as I am concerned I still fight shy of those who say that they are healers. I can go along with those who say that they are able to use the healing energy, but they say this with humility, and claim only to be a user, never the inventor. They don't have glazed eyes.

I believe you should avoid those who can't wait to put their hands upon you without request or permission, and tell you that you are in need of healing. At any one time, most of us are to some degree or other. To say such words implies to me that the healer needs a little bit of their own medicine first! Remember the words of Jung, repeated elsewhere, that 'you can only heal to the level that you have suffered yourself.' There is a feeling that you can trust someone who has healed their own pain at whatever level was necessary.

The most doubtful healers are the newly-qualified ones who have recently attended training, buzzing about only a step lower than the Angels, looking for the needy on whom to practice their new-found skills. Yes, I've been there, worn the tee-shirt only for a short time thank goodness, but that was before I had been forced to 'walk the walk'. Don't worry if that last statement is not yet quite clear to you.

As I have mentioned, I always feel wary of those who call themselves healers. The fact that they say they are brings in the ego, a false sense of importance, which immediately limits their healing power. Even so they must take credit for at least conceding that there is a force called healing, but when they look soulful and pronounce themselves as healers, I always want to giggle. Some people who know they are out of harmony and know they need to be healed, may consent to be a recipient, as a way of pleasing the would-be healer, but from what I have seen this is a sure-fire way to becoming a failed healer, working on a reluctant healee. It won't work, the healer often reports feeling re-energised, but the healee feels de-energised, because the healer has in fact *stolen* energy from the patient, a nasty form of vampirism.

When I first became aware of the power of using the healing energy, I approached a Church of Scotland healing organisation, wishing to share my joy and wonder that we all had the power, even if we didn't know how to use it yet. It appeared that the word healing was very hush-hush, only the ordained Minister could be allowed to use it, it was not for the common man (or woman like me) to use such powers. I came away with my tail between my legs, even although the words of Jesus came to me in my slightly flattened state. 'Go and do ye likewise.' 'What I have done ye shall do more of.'

Not having investigated that particular section of the established Church since, I am not sure what is the Church's attitude these days to the man in the street being able to heal. I don't feel I have to ask priestly permission in order to use healing energy, to help another human being. Jesus gave us permission 2,000 years ago.

We not only have to recognise that we need help, but have to find the courage to ask for it. Often a person will go for years trying to hide the fact that they are in distress. It is extraordinary how long we will suffer in silence, even enduring physical or mental breakdown, before help *has* to be sought. Sadly medical treatment may require surgery, a nervous breakdown takes many months or years for recovery, and intensive drug medication can sometimes produce a zombie-like personality change. Symptoms are treated, but the cause is only too frequently suppressed. I believe this is what they call 'medical healing'.

Yet I do believe that we are all born with our own do-it-yourself healing kit, since we are part of nature and have a built-in survival knowledge. It seems to have been weakened by modern technology and the parental attitudes of Big Brother government organisations, from education to health. Despite their influence, more and more these days, we are waking up to Nature within ourselves and its power to heal.

Pangs of hunger are a warning sign that we need to eat, thirst that we need to drink. We have to be able to recognise the early signs that we are in stress and need help or healing. Obviously situations which are causing us stress may resolve themselves, but all too often our unconscious actions and attitudes attract problems which we cannot solve, and subsequently produce similar situations throughout our lives.

So what is healing? It is an energy applied from within or without which restores wholesomeness. I have always liked that word, either from a physical, mental or emotional perspective, although I have never met anyone supposedly suffering in one of these areas who was not also affected in the other two.

Whatever the *symptoms* presented, I will recognise without a shadow of doubt that there will be a restriction in the breath and blood circulation, which needs to be restored to Nature's rhythm. Where the circulation is restricted there will always be a suppression of one half of the brain; it may be the left analytical, or right creative, but if one side is suppressed the other will be over-active, and full brain potential will be limited. The brain will go into negativity, and the emotions into fear. This sounds a simple explanation, but from a scientific viewpoint is approximately what happens when someone in under stress. The situation becomes serious if the brain is not able to return to balanced function. Then the individual is stuck in an internally chaotic block.

The severity of the symptoms can sometimes be deceptive, in that their severity may be masked by the inability of one person to communicate, while another person may exhibit strong disturbance, yet not be suffering as acutely.

It is essential to understand that if only the symptoms are relieved in any form of healing, then the unaffected *cause* will go on gradually sending even stronger symptoms up to the surface. Many apparent healings only relieve surface symptoms, which give temporary maybe even dramatic relief, but that is all they are, temporary.

Some of the people I have met over the years go regularly for 'The Healing'. One pair of ladies I knew always followed up their regular Saturday afternoon healing sessions at the local Spiritualist Church with a fish supper! As long as they had this weekly prop they could cope with the rest of the week, but I do not think this is what healing should be about.

Am I wrong to think it can often be a prop, over-reliance on someone else, without spiritually moving on to take more self-responsibility for our problems? The Saturday afternoon healing sessions followed by a fish tea has its humorous side, and for some seems to be a part of Glasgow life, and probably similar rituals exist in many cities all over the country.

I believe everything that happens teaches us something, but where would we be if we are in a situation where we only have ourselves available? No spiritualists or fish and chips! It is so important to recognise that improved breathing brings healing information into our thoughts which we learn to trust, and restores our self-confidence. It teaches us that there is an infinite energy already within us which is there to contact, a spiritual healing energy of the highest order.

Many people are terrified that the cause of their terror may be suddenly revealed and overwhelm them, but unless the cause is repaired at its causal level, dis-ease in some form will eventually surface, just as poor material in the foundations of an apparently strong building will eventually cause the weakening and possible collapse of the whole structure.

There is no set-in-stone time scale by which healing can be guaranteed. It may be suddenly if we are ready, but is often best resolved by shedding regular layers of long internalised toxic energy, understanding that we have to fill the vacuum left with creative energy supplied by correct breathing. There is a quotation that 'Nature abhors a vacuum.' Trauma released too quickly requires that we must fill that empty space with positive energy. A shoring up of right thought, until that hollow space once filled by the negativity of restrictive breathing is firmly inhabited by the sure knowledge of our own power that comes with the constant habit of correct breathing.

The origin of the former negativity and fear usually lies

deep in the unconscious mind and while the reason is not able to be recalled, it still casts its shadow on the present, rather like a deep-seated phobia of some common object or situation. It has a paralysing effect on a person trying to live a normal existence.

Whatever the trauma, corrective breathing perhaps for a time with appropriate guidance by a therapist who also breathes correctly will, usually over a period, help to release the effects of this original cause; until the core of its negativity loses the power to cause distress.

Obviously there are as many degrees of repressed stress as there are skins of an onion, and each healing situation effects a different time-scale of improvement, but the main purpose of healing is to restore full responsibility to the individual for life-harmony. Any so-called healing which maintains lengthy reliance on the healer is to be suspect.

There is another aspect of healing work which I feel should be mentioned, and that is the word *'thankyou'*. It is amazing how many people fail to give thanks for this form of help, much of which is given without payment. The question of whether payment requires to be made is one which I am not at present addressing, but the graciousness of saying thankyou is evidence that healing is taking place. I did not invent the saying that 'praise and gratitude is love in action.' (probably another of Leonard Orr's one-liners). I became increasingly aware of its moral strength as it became an important necessity in my own life. Now, giving thanks frequently throughout the day has become a moral necessity for all sorts of encounters and happenings by which I am being blessed by Higher Power. Before, I would have been insensitive to the need for the grace of gratitude.

I wonder why we have become so conditioned by the parent-figures of our bureaucratic institutions who seem reluctant to believe that we lack the power to heal ourselves unless by their explicit permission. We have come to believe that too.

We need to understand that at some point we actually *give ourselves permission* to make ourselves ill or out of harmony with Nature, even to the extent of accidents of all kinds. I mention this latter for you to think about. This fall from perfection is recorded in our brain-diary, but we can reverse what we have done, it is never too late. For this information to be retrieved, the brain must contact the data, and the brain works best with an adequate supply of oxygen.

The process was known to us at birth through the direct link between the auto-immune spiritual system, the breath and the brain.

A small child has a powerful self-healing, in-built knowledge of this natural function, which so often becomes severely damaged as the child is exposed to the unnatural culture of our times, so that the link is broken down. It can however be retrieved by the use of corrective breathing over whatever period of time is necessary. Once the process has been re-started, it is rather like reversing the momentum of a wheel to its opposite direction.

After a while the new movement picks up another rhythm, which increases the energy supply instead of depleting it. This has a catalysing effect, which restores correct circulation, cell regeneration, and effective brain function. The left and right brains function in synchronicity, establishing a balance of harmony, and ability to take right action

There will always be negativity when one brain hemisphere consistently dominates the other, which means that the smooth mechanism of the mind/body/spirit trilogy is out of harmony, and our sense of self becomes distorted, the *grating of non-oiled areas* of the great machine which is you or me.

Spiritual truths of the healing process are our birthright, destined to protect us, otherwise we go through life feeling like a musical instrument which we know is wonderful, but is forever out of tune.

If we can find someone who is in tune with correct breathing we can re-tune ourselves. It is a process of alchemy, bringing mind/body and spirit into one great melodious vibration when we *know* that we are healing ourselves. Fears drop away, sense of self is restored, and we become aware of our importance as a person and *our right work* on the world stage.

We have been given back our own-self healing pack, never to be mislaid again. Re-rooted in the real world of nature, not that of man-made artificial priorities. The indestructible tapes of the laws of global wisdom are uncovered within our psyche, and we find ourselves constantly referring to them throughout the day, no matter what other people give us as *their* version of right or wrong. You can imagine that we each have our own spiritual laptop on which is recorded the true path of our potential. How can we attain it, and remove obstacles as if we were correcting a programme we had typed, which contained errors? There are many ways in which we can use creative imagination to reach the goal of our potential, each correction we make is through the power of changed thought. Thought is an energy. When it is combined with the love impulse continually strengthened by the healing energy of correct breathing, it is as powerful as a laser beam which takes all before it.

The loving energy of our own unique vibration has already recorded our original living, loving soundtrack, the path we have agreed to try and follow, which no one else can copy. All other life-paths are different to our own. The only reason for us to think that we can attain our goal by straying off that path, is fear that we cannot risk staying on it. A mistake. Such straying from our own self-chosen pathway can never bring fulfilment, will usually bring despair, even though we may try to disguise it from others. Why else do people commit suicide?

The wonderful thing is that the path, however overgrown from non-use can always be rediscovered, and the debris of incorrect decisions and action cleared away by the power of our individual right action. This propels us forward and that momentum will continue as long as we listen to our own 'laptop' programme. I can tell you that this does work, but only your core voice knows *your* route. As my favourite poem goes:

> Just list to that voice and all tumult is gone,
> Your life is the life of the infinite one,
> In the hurrying race we are conscious of pause
> With love for the purpose and love for he cause.

My Law - attributed to a Maori

This healing poem which I have quoted in full at the beginning of this book, has been a blueprint for me for the last twenty years, the nobility of the words always having the power to soothe and inspire.

No one can tread our own healing pathway, although they may *lead* us to our own vibration of Higher Power or energy. Neither can we walk another's healing pathway, all we can do is to show them how to access their route through the magic of correct breath. *If they ask us.* And if we have the knowledge.

This walk along our own pathway has been likened to a dance and I like to think of it in that delightful way, because you know it really does resemble a dance. The dance of a joyful child. When the dance seems to stop is a sign that you have stepped off your path.

Our correct breath rhythm is our only guide. I received an email from Canada today, with a poem about the word guidance.

G = God, U = you, I = I, the rest of the word spells *dance!*

However cynical you may be, however embarrassed you may feel as you say the words 'Higher Power' inside your head at first, or are able to think of its energy as a joyful dance, we have to acknowledge that the effect of human energy change *can* be scientifically recorded. Even although the individual using the power of correct breath to dance their own dance, is using no man-made scientific energy or equipment to bring about what we personally see and *feel* are amazing changes in our lives.

Organised science will only admit the truth of anything it declares to be fact after it has proved it to be so after lengthy trials and the placebo effect used as a back-up support. Any other manifestation of healing energy processes used by society since time immemorial, even in order to survive, are still classified as non-scientific.

This denial by Science of the use of another energy which produces results gives credence to the saying that some scientists are 'rather like people in wheelchairs, they operate better on flat ground!'

More and more we are looking back to the people of primitive times, in an attempt to understand the way they used the power of nature to survive, realising more and more frequently that they understood instinctively much of the information that science is only now rediscovering. I do not think it is correct or safe for our present society to rely zombie-like upon what scientists have *so far* discovered. We have to use our own individual intrinsic deep links with nature as our true scientific guide in order to survive the global climate changes with which I am positive we will be presented in coming decades.

I find increasingly as I notice the way people speak, see and particularly, breathe, I can only really trust those whose words and actions are dictated by their close link with Nature.

If those critical signs are not present I realise that they are unknowingly taking their point of reference from an unreliable source, even if they think that this source supplies their livelihood, and allow that to dictate their lives, conceding no other alternative.

If we rely on any source which cannot be proved to be linked to the true vibration of Nature, it will ultimately fail us. This truth is already set in invisible stone.

The ancients understood the laws of electricity in a way that its power affected human behaviour. Sadly nowadays, scientists, as far as I can see, do not study the way *they themselves* use energy in a personal way, before they pontificate on what they maintain are scientific truths. If physically, mentally and emotionally they are not personally using the energy of Nature correctly, which is correct scientific breath, I ponder on the thought processes behind much scientific research.

The brain only *thinks* correctly when we *breathe* correctly, that it the only scientific truth I find acceptable. It is a rarity to find any scientist who will acknowledge this truth, because I have yet to meet a scientist who does breathe correctly!

One notable exception is the physicist Fritjof Capra who, in his book *The Turning Point*, states that 'various methods of stress management and relaxation are likely to play an important part in all future therapies. Correct breathing is one of the most important aspects of relaxation and thus one of the most important elements in all stress-reduction techniques. When the organism is fully relaxed, one can make contact with one's unconscious to obtain important information about one's problems' This book was written in 1982, and defines, to my mind, exactly what self-healing is all about.

At one time when I was going through great changes in my own life and in particular trying to prove to myself if it was possible to measure the energy of the human brain in order to satisfy myself that my life and work with sufferers from stress was based on sure foundations, I discovered the process of Bio-feedback. The Master of this work was the late Maxwell Cade, who wrote an important book, *The Awakened Mind*. I was privileged to attend workshop training with Maxwell, whose biological measuring inventions, which included the 'Mind Mirror', trained a student to learn relaxation, and study the effect of that process on their brain electrical frequency. Maxwell Cade's training helped his patients and students to achieve the ability to re-train the brain to stay in Alpha and Theta rhythms. These are the *anti-stress* vibrations, and their constant use helps a person to regain health, optimum brain function, and subsequent reduction of negative situations in their lives.

Maxwell's pioneering work as a well-known brilliant inventor, engineer and pioneer in this important field, allowed him to recover from a near-fatal motor-cycle accident. Without this work it is highly unlikely that he would have recovered in such a remarkable way, to carry out some of the most important research work for humanity in his lifetime.

Before I encountered the work of Maxwell Cade, I was building up my own intuitive information bank on the use of energy in healing. As someone who hated science as it was taught in my school, I was nevertheless committed to learning about human energy and its vibrational effect as an important factor in the use of our self-healing abilities.

I travelled to London thinking in my naivety at that time that I could see Maxwell without a prior appointment! In his absence I was fortunate and privileged to meet his wife and assistant, the writer Nona Coxhead. She showed me the 'Mind Mirror', a piece of equipment resembling a flat box, the surface being divided into two, intersected by lines along which small flashing lights showed the electrical energy going on in the two hemispheres of the brain.

It showed how relaxation revealed that these lights demonstrated an equal symmetrical brain alignment, denoting brain balance. Otherwise there was an uneven light-up shown by the light display of the box, indicating an unbalanced use of the brain. One hemisphere was in domination over the other, leading to negative thinking and resultant action.

After some conversation, in one of those spontaneous 'happenings' which have lit up my life during the past twenty-five years, Nona suggested that we should each be attached to a separate Mind Mirror, which was done by putting a band round the head to which were fixed electrodes which picked up the electrical energy frequency in the left and right brain hemispheres of the box.

At the same time I worked on her feet in an interesting form of foot stimulation not to be confused with reflexology or massage, but which works only on the spinal reflex of the feet. It is called The Metamorphic Technique and based on pre-natal development. Its effect can be felt sometimes throughout the body as a tingling sensation which produces a sense of release, and seems to work through the neural pathways.

Metamorphic treatment is carried out in a very relaxed and detached way, without emphasis on results, so that the force of the intelligence of life within the client begins to make correction from a deep level without regarding symptoms, which seem to disappear naturally. The process takes about an hour, and also includes working on the hands and head. While I was working with Nona I was unaware of what was happening to the lights on the Mind Mirrors to which we were attached.

Nona seemed quite excited when the metamorphic session was completed. It appeared that while I was working on her feet, she had experienced quite profound tingling sensations, which moved up through her body, which I was able to interpret as an opening up in her circulation. Her excitement was because she had observed what is termed the *'dowsing'* signal on my own Mind Mirror, synchronised with the very calming sensations she was experiencing. In other words, while I was working intuitively with my hands on the spinal reflex of her feet, my brain was operating as I knew from past experience in a rhythm of alpha/theta. Nona was picking this up. This was confirmed by the flashing of the lights within the box measuring electrical energy levels. My work in the metamorphic technique was inducing a profound relaxation response which had been scientifically measured. Such an experience defined an experience in which healing took place. In this case it was completely intuitive, and the metamorphic technique could have been any therapy of integrity.

All I was doing was working at a non-scientific vibration which was instinctive. Some of us call it dowsing.

This was a most interesting experience for me, as I was already using the skill of dowsing, but the vibration had never been demonstrated to me in this way. I also know and have experienced how the use of this Alpha/Theta brain vibration, entirely harmonious with Nature, can bring healing to a stressful situation, without words or touching involved. It could be called the use of loving thought, or as my copy of *The Aquarian Gospel* by Levi Dowling says *'Love reinforced by thought is God's great sovereign balm.'*

This greatest power or charge of love, projected and reinforced by the power of correct breathing, carries no tensions or negativity to block the beam of its energy. It needs no physical contact to wing its way to someone who has asked for help. The process known as the metamorphic technique is one of the few therapies which carries with it no intent or attempt to relieve symptoms, its detached approach frees the client to maximise the intelligence of their own life force to effect change.

This use of our life force intelligence is never more dramatic than when we use it to bring ourselves into the world, the most difficult and dangerous event of our lives. We used a deep intuitive knowledge to find our way, and in self-healing we use the same process trusting our deepest intuition and investing all our energy on the vibration of nature within us. *It worked,* assuming that you are alive while you read these words. You've already been successful in the most difficult challenge of your life!

It will always work, when we trust this process. All forms of healing lead us to this threshhold. In the end we all have to take responsibility for own healing. Whoever may inspire us, they cannot carry us, or we will always be dependent on someone else. As Enid Smithett, a grand old dowsing friend, said in a remark I have always remembered. '*We are equipped by nature to find our own way.*'

The saddest thing is that so many of us have mislaid this only true way link with nature. I am so glad that I re-found it in time. I'm not saying it has been easy, but otherwise I would have missed my life's purpose. The power of self-healing was vividly recounted to me some time ago by a remarkable elderly doctor, Dr. Arthur Rowbotham, then in his late eighties. *'Robbie',* as he was affectionately called by the many who loved him, held numerous imposing degrees and qualifications, but was a man of great simplicity. He had studied at the Vienna School with Freud and Jung, was a Yoga expert, and a great advocate of the healing power of breathing.

In his late seventies he had been involved in a near-fatal road accident, and broken most of the bones in his body. He was not expected to live, and told with great humour how he had been taken to the hospital mortuary twice, but each time a flicker of life was noticed and he had been taken back to the ward. He attributed his recovery to his knowledge of healing through breathing, and using this power effected a full recovery. His knowledge of visualising the oxygen repairing the damaged areas and cells of his body was all he used. A wonderful loving man.

I strongly believe that we all have this power to self-heal; whether or not we have the faith and trust to use it is another matter, but I am convinced that the mind brain charged correctly by breathing from the lower brain low in the abdomen can work miracles. Using this energy we then draw to ourselves, the all-wise power and energy of the universe. That is how my good friend healed himself.

Even with accidents, I believe that the brain, that miraculous computer which operates as fast, or faster (?) than the speed of light, instantly records on its neural pathway any deviation or change of vibration caused by accident or dis-ease, because it is in opposition to the vibration of nature which controls the universe.

Healing applies to an energy which restores us to our intrinsic need to *lock-in* again with nature, in order to vibrate in harmony with her unalterable laws. The most important and direct way to achieve this is by the repair of the respiratory system. (Remember again the real meaning of the word breath, which is spirit.) Once our brain rhythm is functioning naturally on the frequency of Alpha/Theta or between 5-15 vibrations a second, we naturally heal or bring our cells back into synchronicity with the Earth's vibrational field.

In mentioning the rhythm of Theta which is most frequently displayed by a loving small child or when we are in deep meditation, it stands to reason that the slower we can reduce our vibration the easier it will be for the body's energy to restore healing. Just as the first space ship or any great mechanical device requires to be capable of generating a degree of higher energy than is actually required in order to touch base or achieve fusion, so the brain can accelerate healing by operating in Theta 5-9 vibrations per second, which is on a higher level than Earth frequency. The nearest we can get to God?

Remember the words of Fritjof Capra who stated in his book *The Turning Point*. 'It is only when we are fully relaxed that one can make contact with one's unconscious to obtain important information about one's problems or illness. The communication with the unconscious takes place through a highly personal, visual and symbolic language similar to that of dreams.'

I believe that real healers, whose brains function naturally in Alpha/Theta heal by their very presence in any group. There is a desperate need for such people. They are the only ones who can help to re-stabilise Mother Earth. Indeed what we are all required to do, in gratitude for having been given life, and to use our unique gifts on that frequency. This seems perfectly normal to a healthy small child. Until we impose the 'shades of the prison house'.

It is the only alternative to the violent Beta-based energy ever predominant in our present culture.

The Earth can heal herself, and so can mankind. The energies and frequencies I have mentioned need to be fully understood, publicised and practised by everyone, *including* our medical authorities, leaders of all our national organisations, institutions and educational bodies. This is truly a case of *'to hear is to forget, to see is to remember, to DO is to know.'*

We either go forward or back, heal or destroy, there is *NO* middle ground.

They say that in the presence of a real healer, you do not know who is the healer. Anyone who has self-healed emanates healing energy naturally, and in that presence you feel purified. I believe the possible catastrophic escalation of killer diseases predicted by some, could far out-strip the ability of man-made medical science to cope, because it has closed the door on the knowledge inherent in us all of our God-given ability to self-heal.

We have to re-claim it.

THE ONLY CERTAIN THING IN LIFE IS CHANGE.
IS THERE STILL TIME FOR US TO REMEMBER
HOW TO HEAL OURSELVES?

Chapter 10

RELIGION

IN MY *Reader's Digest Universal Dictionary* the word 'religion' is given three separate descriptive phrases; the one that appeals to me is number three. *'The spiritual or emotional attitude of one who recognises the existence of a superhuman power or powers.'*

The other thing that struck me was how few words there are in the Dictionary beginning with the letter 'r'. Has this to do with man's evolutionary lack of verbal skill in clearly pronouncing that distinctive letter?

The dictionary's description of the word 'religion' more or less corresponded to my hitherto unwritten thoughts about its meaning.

We are all aware of the multitude of ways in which tribes, races and nations have over the centuries created their own ideologies, creeds and different religions. Each have expressed core beliefs, according to their own unique interpretation, of what that superhuman power thinks, how it directs their lives, and how they should live as a result. Whatever their belief, it is always a power greater than themselves, for good or not so good. Love or fear, all too often fear.

In referring to the words of the dictionary which talk about religion as an *emotional* attitude, like others I have come to the conclusion that there are only these two emotions, love or fear. All our other *feelings* are really sub-divisions of these two. Rather like a family tree. When you think of all the range of positive or negative states of mind, you will realise that they can be categorised as being motivated by either the love or fear impulse. From my present age (elderly), I don't think you can have it both ways; a religion based on love cannot contain fear, or one based on fear contain pure love.

When I was a child I attended what was then called a Church of England school, called St. Mark's, which came under the umbrella of the Church of the same name. The church was called 'high'. It included incense swinging, and a great deal of ceremony. The vicar seemed a being apart from a small child's perspective, and a curate who appeared as a lesser version of the superior and distant vicar. One thing of which I was certain, they were both perfect and sinless beings, a state to which I could never attain.

At night I would hop into bed, determined that starting the next day I would be *absolutely perfect*. Unfortunately the inevitable lapse of grace would occur in a frighteningly short time the following morning for some childish misdemeanour. I was confirmed in St. Mark's church, my memories of that event consisting of a series of pre-confirmation talks by the curate at which my attendance was only 50%, followed by a confirmation ceremony conducted by the Bishop, when my best friend and I just managed to contain our giggles. The suspender holding up my stocking slipped, so after the confirmation ceremony I had to walk back through the congregation clutching tightly to the suspender through my skirt in order to prevent my stocking from collapsing. Not a very dignified or holy start for a new communicant.

My early religious training did leave me with one conviction that there definitely was a hell to which I had reasonable certainty of being committed, and that there was a Judgement Day which marked the end of the world, when all the graves gave up their dead!

Funnily enough, after I married and my son was born, I remembered a picture I had seen in the curate's house where the long ago confirmation talks had taken place. The picture was that of Jesus, to me a most beautiful face, full of wisdom and compassion. It was entitled *'And the Lord turned and looked at Peter, and Peter remembered.'* If my communion preparation only yielded the lasting impression of that picture perhaps there was hope for me. I was able to obtain a copy of it after contacting the curate (who without doubt had no cause to remember me with fondness), and it hung on the wall in my son's bedroom. I hoped as he grew up he might think that was an inspiring reflection of the possible face of Jesus. I was still not familiar with the word spiritual, but now I realise that to me that painting represented a truly spiritual being.

My emerging thoughts about the world's religions and their origins is that I respect and empathise with any which reflect the Higher Power of love as their basis, and find it impossible to accept any which include the reverse. Of course within those which talk of everlasting love, are many followers whose philosophy and history demonstrate the reverse.

Very few human movements can encompass the purity of thought of the founder, when they are separated by centuries. It took the book *The Aquarian Gospel of Jesus the Christ* by Levi Dowling, in which Jesus speaks frequently of the *'Holy Breath'* to come into my possession virtually at the same time as Ramacharaka's *Science of Breath* (Science you note!) to recognise how they both emphasised the power of breath. My subsequent random exploration of other religions always leads me to search their books for references to breath (spirit) for me to embrace an affinity with the writings.

I have realised that all institutions, events, religions, wars, and political structures have at their epicentre the thoughts of one individual who attracts to themselves others who see an opportunity to latch-on to some of the power. Unfortunately the self-growth seen by some followers involves self-interest, and so the movement begins to lose the true meaning of the inspirational founder.

As I developed (I hope) in spiritual understanding, I began to realise that as far as my earlier religious training was concerned, the ritual, pomp and ceremony seemed to come between me and the Higher Power I felt comfortable with. I continually wanted to 'place a little child in the midst of them' and relate to the spirit of the child who breathes true to spirit, in order for the child to show us the right path.

Bronson Alcott, in his book *How Like an Angel Came I Down*, believed that the soul of a new-born child 'already carries within it the imprint of spirit and wisdom.' I have come to apply this yardstick to all the religions and sects which embrace a particular guru or prophet. The word 'God', which is nice and short, sums up the source-inspiration of most, but some Gods are loving and forgiving, others harsh and punitive. One generating love, the other fear. Some of the most wonderful, creative and inspiring expressions of faith and courage have generated from the former, appalling cruelties and suffering from the latter.

The fundamental meaning of the most complex and important issues for mankind can be encapsulated in the fewest words. Perhaps our tendency to preach, analyse, and write ad-nauseam about the subject can distil the essence of its true meaning to nothingness; yet whether we realise it or not, the urgency and importance of that true meaning under-lies all our thoughts and actions. The urgency of a global commitment to spiritual consensus, the greatest challenge facing us all. We are under threat from the collective non-love magnetic energy from our own and past generations.

At the lowest point in my life when I was terrified of risking a decision in order to move forward, the turning point was when I had to make a stand for what I believed and trusted in. I knew I had to trust myself in order to grow spiritually. I had to act from an awareness of what was good and right, for not to act was to allow and condone harmful energy to dominate. I realised as I took the decision to *trust*, that the tide began to turn in favour of what was good and right, but I had to take action *without knowing that I would succeed.* What did happen however was that almost immediately circumstances began to act in my favour as if I was being protected. The harmful energy disappeared like water down a drain, and positive events occurred to solve the situation. All this because I found the courage to trust in right action, without being sure of success.

Looking back I know without a doubt, that the agony of mind I experienced at this time was also the turning point of a belief in God. I became aware, as far as I was able in my limited way, to have some idea of the sufferings of Jesus. I was not physically threatened, but I was in danger of losing everything of value (non-material) I had built up.

I began a daily meditation involving as guides, mentors and protectors, a number of important spiritual men and women down the ages who had inspired me. I do not know how I would have got through this nightmare period without this spiritual connection with the God of my understanding, the love of Jesus and my guides. I still maintain my daily meditation, having added several other spiritual friends, not now in this world, who have never let me down. I do not believe that death prevents the 'cross-pollination' of thought energy.

The situation to which I refer was a confrontation between good and evil, when the latter seemed to be on the winning side. Later I invented an original saying 'the power of evil is as great as the power of good, but the power of good is greater.' It is only in facing up to evil and holding fast to love, that evil cannot prevail. It was the certain knowledge that this power of good was a loving, living energy that could be trusted, which became my religion. In learning to act on this truth, its energy and strength was available to me, a power greater than my own. Available yet non-provable on many subsequent occasions, but spiritually verified non-material truths for me to pass on to others having to face the same choice of trust, when every nerve and sinew cries out to give up. To use this protective energy you can always defend, but never attack.

As a therapist you have to know, and have proved the truth of such spiritual laws, for people come to you with apparently unsolvable problems in their lives. While you cannot tell anyone what they *should* do, the fact that you know what works, allows a delicate web of verbal interchange to take place, to help give your client the trust to take right action.

Jung calls this process 'the dark night of the soul', which in retrospect is also the catalyst for the switching on of the light.

You cannot talk about religion or God to a client, unless they raise the subject first. I have however noticed time and again that the correction of the respiratory pattern almost always seems to arouse a desire to speak of deeper issues such as God and spirituality, as if the breath had watered these issues within a person without me saying anything. It was evident that it was of supreme importance that I could talk with some personal confidence and certainty on such subjects naturally, without trying to *impose my own opinions.*

It has been obvious that many people have felt immense relief at being able to discuss spirituality, as distinct from a named religion, without detracting from their own religious faith, but the teachings of their faith seemed to have left a vacuum and unanswered questions or resources. There is a saying that 'Nature abhors a vacuum.' The non-spiritual vacuum of fear within them had been their weakness when faced with a powerful stress problem for which they had sought help. If I had been able to face my own 'dark night' and found a light and faith not dreamed of, I knew that was possible for all, even when there were no external indicators that their problem had a solution. I knew there was *always* a solution, and to quote a platitude (what's wrong with platitudes?): 'There are no problems, only solutions.'

Having become convinced that love is stronger than fear which I think is a pre-requisite for a therapist, I know that loving faith, sustained and undiluted by fear and negativity is a very strong unseen energy. All energy vibrates and resonates, attracting back to itself the same power on a higher frequency. This is because Higher Power, unlike your Bank, pays dividends of greater value than mere cash. It is an invisible alchemy which works for good in all situations of spiritual trust in love energy.

Everything I have written in this chapter, or in fact this whole book, is about *my* personal experiences. I remember how many books I have bought over the years, sometimes many years before I actually read them, and yet I must have bought them for a reason of which at the time I was not aware. Even so, without knowing why, I turned to each particular book maybe years later when I unknowingly *needed* a special book and there it was on my bookshelf. I was now ready for it. Sometimes I did not have to read the whole book, and yet there were sections which were vital for my spiritual growth, important parts of the jigsaw of my life. Although I have never met them, the authors have become my spiritual friends, often closer than the friends with whom I exchange regular social interaction. I was ready to experience what these writers had to say, because their words matched and confirmed my present life experiences and questions. Previously their words would have washed over me, a perfect example that 'to hear is to forget, to see is to remember, to do is to know.'

Perhaps this book will be one you buy before you are quite ready, but I hope that some of the words will have the same resonance for you, as others have for me.

When I started writing these pages, the TV and the media were full of the London tube bombings. Here in Scotland and my own rural hideaway the horror affected us all, although it is the Londoners who bore the brunt. Its immediacy broke through as I learned that my son, who works in London, could well have been on the fatal Kings Cross tube at that time, but his planned journey was changed to the following day.

I had to ask myself if all that I have said above would have sustained me if he had been involved? I cannot tell you, except that my reaction and ability to deal with personal trauma would have been entirely different if I had not been able to deal spiritually with my former crisis. *Then* I learned that there is a spiritual reason for all human dilemmas and apparent tragedy. Also that the only way to disarm an enemy is to forgive them, otherwise they have control over you. Don't let them have that control.

Acts of terrorism and cruelty, based on the supposed words of any religious preference will always be based on a fear source, a weaker energy, and the perpetrators will not be using the correct breath, or they could not morally commit such actions. The only higher vibration available to us, that of love, must prevail simply because it is more powerful. It may seem simplistic to write these words, but as I have said elsewhere a global quantum leap will be necessary, yet of such simplicity that our over-used intellectual brain does not yet have the emotional intelligence to embrace such a creative leap. At least it has the capacity, but possibly will not use it unless there is no other way to turn, but when we do, I am convinced that Higher unseen Power will then be able to come to our aid. 'The mighty powers of worlds unseen do not send forth their aid 'til man has done his best, they only help when man can do no more.' *The Aquarian Gospel* by Levi Dowling.

While empathising with our successful bid for the 2012 Olympic Games, shall we ever see an equivalent jubilation generated by the enthusiasm for some great spiritual break-through which was non-competitive? We shall have to set our spiritual aims many notches higher in order to gain the Olympic gold for winning the race to outrun religious terrorism.

In all the spiritual wanderings and educational messages for personal growth which I have been sent, the most important ones have been *sent* in a way which involved no living person, media or postal information, although all these are channels for spiritual tips. Enormous insights have also changed my life from some very small books, many alas out of print so I cannot buy them for friends. They have brought great comfort and reassurance, their brevity and succinct phraseology encompassing immortal truths that can never date or change. 'If something isn't spiritual, it isn't.' 'If religion isn't love, it isn't.' Short and pithy, eternal truths, safe to build one's life upon. Simplicity is their keynote, as all religion should be, brevity is not weakness.

It is difficult to extricate loving truths in religions hemmed about with so much dogma, ritual, enormous buildings, pomp and ceremony, when as far as I can discover Jesus lived in complete simplicity and built no buildings. Many religions with their ceremonies seem to create a barrier to the spirituality which is what religion is supposed to be about.

Would it be so wrong to imagine that the future of spirituality could involve the dissolving of religious boundaries to be replaced by a great groundswell of global comprehension of unalterable universal truths, the power of self-healing made possible by common understanding of the Holy Breath of non-fear? The everlasting continuity of this great power being lived within the family, small groups, communities, knowing they are still universally linked within the great family of Spirit. All will be equal leaders in the automatic healing of Mother Earth that will follow.

Several years ago my continuing search for sifting the wheat from the chaff in diverse religious practices led me to a preoccupation with a comparison between Jesus and the Buddha. I had a number of friends who embraced the Buddhist faith. For many years I have been a student and admirer of the life and work of Rudolf Steiner. His book *From Buddha to the Christ* gave me the answer. 'Buddha came to open the mind, and Jesus came to open the heart.' The perfect explanation to me of those two great streams of consciousness.

I understand that the heart chakra is the last to be opened, the heart chakra is the love centre, the point when we dare to really allow ourselves to love ourselves. Its opening means the release of love, believing that the little child is our teacher, leaves me little choice as to where I can look for my spiritual inspiration. Always the loving little child in our midst, who is trying *despite us* to breathe correctly. A new religion? Is love spirituality or religion? Why complicate things? The universal religion shown to us by the child definitely must be love as it is the highest power. If we can all agree with that, no problem, but until we do there will be religious conflict.

Chapter 11

ONE GENERATION OF
CORRECT BREATHERS

'ONE GENERATION OF CORRECT BREATHERS would regenerate the race, and disease would be looked upon as a rarity.' These words were written by a wonderful yoga teacher Ramacharaka earlier in the last century, in his book *The Hindu-Yogi Science of Breath*. As I developed my own understanding of the power of correct breathing, I understood and totally agreed with his visionary words.

I realise that virtually all the chapters in this book encompass the truth of this statement, which many might consider extraordinary, and find difficult to comprehend, as at one time I would also. From my vast store of untraceable quotes, most of them snippets perhaps going back over half a century (do not call them platitudes!) the following words are so true. 'To hear is to forget, to see is to remember, to do is to know.'

One of my hopes is that after reading or even dipping into this book, you may feel drawn to find a teacher to at least start you on this exciting path of regaining your correct breathing rhythm, and in so doing, releasing the wonderful gifts and talents you have been storing away. You cannot plan this personal sunrise, it comes as you are ready, when an adequate supply of life-enriching oxygen/breath has stimulated your potential.

Once rediscovered, you have to follow your own path, often realising that the path you have been on for many years had only been a side-road. Don't worry, nothing is ever wasted, all our experiences are here to be used, often when we least expect it.

The biggest life-shift in our better breathing habits is in health improvement, not only physical. You have more energy, reverse ill-health patterns, sleep better, and feel warmer on cold days as a result of better circulation, to name but a few. You find that you have greater powers of concentration, clarity of thought, and creativity. Gradually you realise that old fears which have prevented you from being all you were meant to be, can be confronted and over-come, bringing with their release a wonderful sensation of relief and achievement. The final and unexpected awareness is that of spirituality.

As you develop your own personal corrective breathing rhythm, the more you want to share your experience with others. The problem seems to be that they often do not seem to be interested, your enthusiastic words slide off them, and you may feel disappointed. Here is an important lesson, *you can't change anyone else.* I believe everyone who breathes badly knows that they are doing so, but because the reason for this lies among the unspoken fears of childhood, they are not yet ready for this change. It would be wrong for us to give them the impression that they 'should', or they will see us as bossy parents which may affect our friendship. In this work, you have to be 'as wise as the serpent and as gentle as the dove.'

One the other hand it is ok to sow seeds, very often they later germinate, and your friends will start to ask you questions about correct breathing which will tell you that they are more interested than at first appeared.

Obviously it is very satisfying when a person goes on to take a training in correct respiration, and you will find that your friendship blossoms because there is so much more to share about the beauty of life as they release their own understanding.

I have mentioned my own thoughts elsewhere about the possible origins of yoga. The word means *to join up*, which to me has always implied our breath. Like every other subject yoga teaching can be excellent or less than excellent. I have worked with many people who have studied yoga for years, and still do not breathe correctly. Re-learning to breathe correctly involves, I have discovered, an inner form of yoga. The continual action of proper lung expansion seems to massage and stretch tense inner muscles, surrounding the vital interior organs including the lungs, and resembles a deep form of yoga.

As I like to boast, my own ability to place my palms flat on the ground without bending my knees at eighty is due to a supple spine created by my own breath correction, and not due to formal yoga training. Again do not suddenly attempt this exercise, a little at a time is the best stretch activity for the back, or any other form of exercise.

Let us go back to Ramacharaka's statement about one generation of complete breathers regenerating the race. On a personal level it has certainly worked for me. During the quite long period of several years when I was going through my own breathing renewal, I was aware that each level of improvement persuaded me to face some fear or other, and overcome it. Subsequently it seemed an easy thing to overcome, but while I still held that particular fear within me, it represented a restriction of my breath. Once released life appeared to be more beautiful.

I believe that when you have conceived a beautiful idea it becomes a reachable goal, and can then materialise. Each time you decide to make time to breathe better, you have sent this thought out to the atmosphere which holds all man's creative thought, and its magnetic energy will try to help.

That is because it also benefits the planet to which we owe our existence. Our breathing has, I believe, an effect on the Earth's magnetic field.

Higher Thought tells us that the earth was given to man to protect, nurture, cherish and enjoy. If he learns to do that, he will reap untold blessings. From what we see all around us at the way man has abused his inheritance, we could be poised on the edge of appalling natural repercussions, symptoms of which are already apparent. From the vantage point of enlightened breath/spirit such a rebound is all too easy to comprehend, as our violent, mechanistic and anti-natural scientific activities, negate the reverence due to Mother Earth.

She has been created on a Heavenly principle of love (Alpha Vibration), and any man-made creation in opposition to that frequency damages the Earth's magnetic field, which also supplies man with the oxygen he needs for his survival. I cannot prove this, intuitively I don't think I need to. If our predominant collective energy is Beta, and it has been scientifically proved that the Earth's energy vibration is at Alpha, to keep her place in the planetary system she may eventually have no alternative but to brush man off her surface as an annoying parasite.

How we breathe decides our vibration, and its effect on ourselves, our surroundings and the Earth Herself. Incorrect Universal breathing, the abuse of our *only life support mechanism*, could eventually destroy us by its magnetic reverse energy attraction, and the earth will be our unwilling destroyer, in order to save Herself.

Of course we do have an option, we always have free will to breathe correctly. As we begin to understand the speed by which correct breathing revolutionises our lives, restoring ourselves and our surroundings to health and harmony, so we restore our individual relationship with Nature, and the Earth can heave a sigh of relief as one more human soul comes to Her aid.

It is a very awesome thought, but maybe it is time we did some awesome thinking; thank goodness I believe we are still capable of such thought. The Earth will protect us if we learn to protect and heal ourselves. I am positive that it helps Her to re-balance also.

Consider how we can regenerate the race. Simply by breathing correctly, which relaxes muscles, including those which are squeezing the lungs, preventing them from inhaling life-giving oxygen. When that pressure is removed, the lungs absorb ample life-force, and the circulation of oxygen in the blood-stream can be taken to every cell for regeneration. That is all we are composed of, *cells, cells, cells.* Obviously each cell has a specific function. By the same token the Earth is also composed of cells. All cells need healthy stimulation in order to regenerate. As long as the cells are able to regenerate through the correct use of oxygen/life, health will be assured. Correct breathing also ensures that the waste products of the body of which 70% are excreted through the breath, are discharged in a way that the atmosphere around us can absorb and dissolve it without polluting the environment.

Adults who breathe correctly ensure that their children will also breathe correctly, for the children will have no reason to be afraid of their parents. The blood stream, the only available force of life to us, will flow healthily through the veins of their children, regenerating their cells. Their thoughts and spirits will be joyful, they will be healthy. Disease will become a rarity, all that is needed is for man to *know himself,* and the purpose for the gift of life given to him will be understood.

A generation of adults who breathe correctly, will produce children who breathe correctly, the race *could* be regenerated in one generation. *I believe that is the only option left to us.*

You may not believe it, but you have free will. What are we handing on to our children and grand-children if we do not face up to the fact that a large proportion of the Earth's population is suffering from self-imposed oxygen starvation, a degenerative disease?

'EMINENT AUTHORITIES HAVE STATED THAT ONE GENERATION OF COMPLETE BREATHERS WOULD REGENERATE THE RACE, AND DISEASE WOULD BE LOOKED UPON AS A RARITY.'

Ramacharaka.

Chapter 12

INSIDE OUT - OUTSIDE IN

FOR MANY YEARS, when I have spoken about repairing the respiratory process I have deliberately avoided the words 'breathing techniques' or 'deep breathing'. To those who come new to this training the word *technique* seems to stimulate the intellectual side of the brain as if breathing was an unnatural activity, only repaired by a man-created scientific process. If you ask someone who needs help in this natural instinct to breathe *deeply* they will usually pull *in* the lower abdomen, thus constricting the expansion of the larger lower lung area, and therefore *deprive* themselves of air.

These days I only talk about *correct* breathing, which instantly cuts out a lot of the wishy-washy thinking about this wonderful gift of life, and enables re-teaching to become simpler and more easily focused. I say all this because I have very often needed to help people to *cure techniques* and *deep-breathing,* taught, I suspect, by an enthusiast who obviously does not understand *correct breathing*! Amongst the all too rare books I possess about the breath, I find I have greater empathy with the even rarer writers who talk about *correct breathing* as distinct from the other two methods I mention above.

The words 'deep breathing' often trigger off a physical constriction of the lower lungs, the largest lung areas, and in the way many people interpret the movement also results in the expansion of the upper chest and an elaborate raising of the shoulders. If this movement is continued for long, it could produce hyper-ventilation, as the oxygen/carbon dioxide ratio becomes out of balance. A high proportion of the population hyperventilate.

One of the other techniques in current vogue is alternate nostril breathing. I believe that the understanding of the functions of each nostril is very important, but few teachers mention that each nostril is related to the opposite side of the brain; ie. left nostril right creative brain and right nostril left analytical brain. More detailed facts about the left/right brain function is given in another chapter. If I occasionally find difficulty in sleeping, I usually find that my left nostril seems a little blocked, which means my intellectual brain is over-stimulated by some pre-sleep activity, and I need to cover the right nostril for a little to activate the right creative brain, from which arises the sleep impulse.

I do not think that anyone who teaches correct breathing can disregard its spiritual implications, which are revealed little by little, as each layer of our impaired breathing is repaired. This process is inevitable, neither therapist nor client wills it to happen, it comes into consciousness because it has always been there from birth, has been hidden by fear, and contains within its activation the great moral truths of life which we bring in at birth. They can of course be obeyed or ignored, the latter brings disharmony to our lives, the former harmony and joy. We always have free will. To obey these moral laws takes courage, but as we re-build them into our lives we wonder why we had been afraid.

Most of my present understanding of correct breathing has come about through my personal intuitive re-awakening of this magical process. I find that referring to breath correction as a *technique* or *deep breathing* does in my estimation devalue the deeper implications of this work and demeans it. It can never be a purely physical process, the *mind* decides the quality of each breath, and the spirit moves the mind.

This is an unalterable fact, a law of nature.

As I write, I am sure that my thoughts on correct breathing may provoke analytical scepticism from some quarters, but as I mention elsewhere, I am reminded once again of the words of a past philosopher who said that he was more afraid of God's disapproval than that of man, if he did not write what he felt to be true. This feeling applied to my thoughts as I wrote many chapters of this book!

Becoming aware of the need to obey the spiritual truths revealed by the breath, one of my clients once declared that 'it is not for the faint-hearted', but I am convinced that there was never a time when our civilisation was in more need of the strong-hearted.

I am personally certain that correct respiration is in fact a matter of choosing longer life or earlier death, the length of our life-span, whether we end our lives from some unnecessary disease, sudden organ failure before our natural time, or alternatively finish our days in the twilight zones of Alzheimer's disease or senile dementia, requiring appalling quantities of other people's energies to keep us alive in an existence virtually devoid of quality of life.

I believe that the efficiency of our long-life respiratory health is the determining factor. As far as I can discover, this critical information seems to be virtually disregarded and goes unnoticed in a health service influenced to an ominous degree by the commercial interests of the pharmaceutical industry. The reported high levels of suicide and alcoholism in the medical profession, our core health provider, proves to me the lack of understanding of man's capacity to heal himself by the correct application of the vibrational frequency of natural breathing, Nature's great healing alchemical medication.

Surely if doctors breathed correctly themselves, their acquired vision would debar them from such a step.

Here are two quotes for you by deep-thinking people of unknown origin.

'If you do not develop that which is within you, what you do not develop will kill you.'

'If you do not follow your heart and your emotions, sooner or later you will fall ill.'

Prophetic words describing a heartless culture which so often imposes an over-intellectualised education which stifles the spiritual gold within the growing child.

The only reason we do not follow our hearts or develop our talents is through fear and lack of confidence, both symptoms of which are relieved through breath reclamation. Un-relieved, this fear creates a knock-on effect over the years, of holding in the breath, tensing the muscles, resultant restriction of circulation of blood to the cells; cell malfunction and whatever form of disease and health breakdown is thus created by the deterioration of the energy life-force of the individual. The ultimate symptom is of course death. When faulty 'upside-down or outside-in' breathing leads to this ultimate state of degeneration, we become like any other man-made machine, worn out and unable to be repaired.

Except that, *EXCEPT THAT* we are *not* a man-made machine, we are a *nature-made* machine, and if we catch ourselves in time, the re-introduction of the vibrational frequency of correct breathing can reverse the present collective world life-destructive process, allowing nature's great healing rhythm to repair from the inside out. I have seen this miracle happen so often that it appears entirely natural and find it surprising that the process is understood by so few. Even those who call themselves 'green', and fanatically support any activity which is supposed to heal Mother Earth, but not man himself.

Curiously many scientific and intellectual people find it difficult to comprehend the concept that correct respiration leads to the relaxation of muscles, better circulation, therefore cleansing of toxins and regeneration of cells, the mind and emotional spirit being totally involved in the whole process. The end result is *re-connection* instead of *separation* from the central core or hub of nature, from the inner to the outer self.

The complete reversal of ill-health as opposed to extended sickness survival can, I maintain, only happen through the above continuous pattern of breath which brings into mind that statement by a great Yogi teacher that 'one generation of correct breathers would regenerate the race, and disease would be looked upon as a rarity.' (Ramacharaka, *The Hindu-Yogi Science of Breath*.)

I feel so privileged to completely understand what Ramacharaka meant by the above words, believing it a tragedy that his wonderful little book seems to be out of print, as are a number of such 'special' books on the subject. It's almost as if there was a highly charged negative unseen energy at work trying to sabotage vital information which could release man's ability to heal himself. Who makes the decision not to re-publish such gems? I can only think of someone who is totally out of touch with the only valid natural process which keeps us alive.

A very profound and definite muscular action is meant to take place in order to relocate and centre the respiratory activity just below the base of the lungs from the area between the pelvic bone and the navel. As Karen Roon (the wise author of a pivotal book titled *The New Way to Relax*) says: 'When the lift of the breath starts above this point it is an indication that our breathing has not yet *regained* its proper function.'

Regaining full respiratory function necessitates the regaining of this action, the site which I have come to believe also houses the initiating source of the auto-immune system.

The full lift of air requires lung expansion to rise from

127

this point to the lobes of the lungs just below the shoulder blades. Obviously not every inhalation occurs to the fullest extent, there is a wide variety of movement according to the relevant activity, but where the suppleness of this process is restricted by long-term fixed muscular tension there will always be physical mental and emotional symptoms of dis-ease, perhaps not yet diagnosed by the 'specialists', but observable to a correct breathing therapist, and certainly born out by short or long-term evidence in the life-history of that individual.

To some extent the physical exercise of correct breathing resembles an inner form of yoga, as the expanding lungs give a form of massage to the vital organs, relaxing the surrounding muscles and enhancing the life-giving blood circulation of oxygen. I do not believe that any form of massage externally applied by an orthodox masseur can equal or reach these deep inner tissues; there is no substitute for such self-generated healing.

The regaining of a vital function which comes naturally to a young child can only be re-taught to us by our own inner teacher. The movement is embedded deep in our unconscious mind, and starts to communicate itself to our conscious mind and spirit via correct breath, so that *as human organisms we really understand how we are constructed and meant to function.*

IF MAN HAS DISCOVERED HOW TO GET TO THE MOON, WHY IS UNIVERSAL IGNORANCE OF OUR BASIC LAWS OF HUMAN CORRECT FUNCTION SO COMMON?

The above lines represent for me the need to regain the pearl of greatest price, the true self, a pearl I would not exchange for the money owned by the wealthiest millionaire, a pearl we all possess at birth but agonisingly lose as we *conform* to the 'civilised' pressures of our culture.

The internal yoga I mention above is not taught as far as I know by any yoga teacher I have yet met, but it needs be to be reincorporated into our natural life pattern for full health to be restored at all levels. This power of self-repair or do-it-yourself healing does require self-discipline, (a phrase which I don't like very much being a Piscean!) but self-discipline of this kind can be very joyful, and bring to the surface of the mind and emotions a sense of our own *uniqueness*. The process is never violent, always gentle, but does require to be practiced several times for a few minutes each day, if possible. It is really all you have to do.

To get the most benefit from the exercise, also read the chapter on the correct use of the nose and if you can, when you practice, lie down comfortably, flat on your bed or better still, on the floor. I have been amazed by how comfortable the apparently hard floor seems if you are breathing correctly, it's as if you create your own invisible respiratory mattress. In fact I can sleep quite comfortably on a hard wood floor if I am really tired, something which at one time I would not have believed possible.

Natural respiration restores to us the information stored in our right creative brain. I look upon it as an art form by which the beauty of our own unique gifts are eventually restored to us, revealing potential beyond our wildest dreams, potential of which we are the sole owner and nurturer. This vital corrective movement of the breath arises from the epicentre or core of the body. This 'bulls-eye' between the pelvic bone and the navel, sends up its energy through the lungs to the brain, dispelling layers of toxic physical, mental and emotional tension and misuse. A clarion call on a subliminal level which releases our power, our sense of purpose and destiny, a call that cannot lightly be disregarded. If we do, we have a continuing sensation of being homeless within ourselves.

During this time of re-connection we may go through a temporary period of confusion, as Leonard Orr puts it: 'Confusion is two opposite thoughts of equal worth.' It is a time when our old outworn self of negativity wants to hang in there. We have given it bed and breakfast for so many years, and it won't go down without a fight. The rigid confines of our upbringing and education, whatever is incompatible with our true spiritual nature must be released to the garbage heap of our untrue self. We can no longer dismiss the homing cry of our true identity, no longer pollute it with other untrue man-made doctrines. We are once more on the spiral of our own blueprint from the inner, overcoming the negativity of the outer.

As we progress on the centrifugal force of our re-spiriting breath, we can no longer ignore often quite dramatic improvements to our physical health, mental clarity and emotional joy. We will never again give this priceless gift away lightly. Even as we become increasingly aware of the non-spiritual pressures surrounding us, we have to defend it. In this re-growth mode we have to release relationships which are no longer meaningful, work, often homes. Somehow we are protected as we realise that the spiritual source of our security is a non-material Higher Power which sends to us *at the right time* right relationships, work, and a home base whenever needed.

In this inside-out repair process from the core of our being, the healing vibrational transformational energy breaks through the outer crust of the suppressive intellectual restrictions of our time, and we know beyond a shadow of doubt that we are becoming who we were *meant to be*, our own non-tangible book of inner wisdom is opened up to us. It can never now be mislaid, as we continue to tread the path of nature's breath. In this transformational process, no one has ever really given us therapy or healing but ourselves, no one has given us medicine, massage or manipulation. A teacher/encourager may be required for the first few sessions, who will remain detached, quiet, but observant, and able to share questions and discussion.

Much of the dis-ease work of our present health providers appears to me to be totally lacking in this most profound, inexpensive and reliable process of return to health. I read recently that if something is not spiritual it *isn't*, in other words, it's worthless and so it seems to me is so much of present-day medical practice. I say these words from a professional practice where I have introduced thousands of clients to restored respiratory action, and I have heard about their symptoms *appearing to dissolve*, having been previously treated for many years by pharmaceutical prescription, without the cause ever being located. I have seen dramatic long-term reversal of symptoms by the return to natural breath, the improvement corroborated by relatives and friends. I have never tried to help the physical problems of these people, but realised time after time that their symptoms were being cured from the inside-out.

The reliance on what I call 'alternative' medicine, drugs, etc., may certainly leave us feeling relieved for a period, but so often again there is a build-up of the same symptoms and usual side-effects often feeling worse than the original problem. We seem to take it for granted that those not actively being treated for health problems are in fact healthy, but those we read about being treated by the NHS are the tip of the iceberg, with most of the remainder of the 'ice-mass population' existing in a permanent acceptance by whole societies of sub-surface physical, mental and emotional/ spiritual respiratory ill-health.

Finally we have to remind ourselves that (as we are constantly being told by those who do not have the necessary tools to show us,) *we* must take responsibility for our health, but do not tell us that to do so we must rediscover via our breathing that the maintenance of our auto-immune system is within our own control. How can they teach what they do not understand themselves? Babies have a strong immune system particularly in the first six months, they have this internal heating and healing ability. Babies are straight off the production line and their breath impulse is from the inside-out, they are in touch with their spirit, as Bronson Alcott (father of Louise Alcott) believed. He maintained that the 'child's spirit at birth brings with it the imprint of spirit and wisdom' in his book *How Like an Angel Came I Down*. This knowledge is given back to us on the breath, our joyful, loving child, how could we let that child down again?

No one can make us healthy, we already know what to do; the Earth also knows how to regain her health, and I believe the people who use her air/spirit correctly are the ones who can help her, because these people support her, and do not *take* from her. They can be of greatest help to her, so that she too can repair herself from the inside out.

It is said that the most courageous thing a man or woman can do is to be true to themselves. This has been my own experience too, and in this journey back to our true selves we may become afraid and turn our back on the process of self growth integrated by correct respiration. Of course we always have free will, but I have found that although this does sometimes happen and you may see a person's forward progress seem to 'stall' perhaps for years, our lives can never actually stand still, we either move forwards or backwards. I have repeatedly noticed that when someone has experienced the light of the Higher Power or true self at the end of the tunnel, it is always there encouraging us to move forward, and sooner or later you observe this growth movement once again in a person's life. The truth will never go away, and its quiet internal whisper cannot forever be ignored.

Then we find the courage to move on from damaging relationships, free ourselves from work that never makes use of our true creativity, find a new place to stay, a home which may be much less affluent than our former dwelling, but one in which we truly feel *at* home. All this has been waiting for us, new relationships, work, home, but it cannot come to us while we are still trapped in our previous false security.

More and more we trust the guiding spirit of our breath which will never let us down.

A great deal of therapeutic time works on the external symptoms which seem to be causing distress, and often a dependency situation can be created by too frequent appointments and the reliance on someone else's energy, a stimulant of voice, hand, or calming balm to heal us, but what if we are isolated with none of these available? To be able to go inwards on the wings of our breath and find all that we need, is the only permanent healer known to me.

This true core at the epicentre of our own and Nature's force field keeps our vibrational field in harmony with the Earth, its implosion throughout the layers of consciousness forces out the negative rhythms which cause physical, mental and emotional/spiritual disharmony so that the dis-ease impulse cancels itself out as the auto-immune system is regenerated.

I long for the day when the Universal health fraternity understands this process of the breath. It will create a more mature approach to those suffering 'ill-health', the patient will lose a child-like and unhealthy dependency upon health professionals whose training will include a much wider and practical training in the medicine of the spirit of the breath. This will allow them to drop an unhealthy aura of paternalism and elitism which is becoming increasingly out of date with the needs of our times and universal awareness...*Inside-out health, rather than outside-in symptom treatment.*

Chapter 13

PRIORITISING

WHEN I BEGAN TO PRACTICE and study the art of breathing and relaxation, an unexpected but very important benefit became apparent to me. I realise now that it happened because the end-product of natural breathing is a calmer brain, and when the brain is calm our thought patterns change. This is brought about because of the drop in the brain's electrical frequency from Beta 15-25 vibrations a second, to Alpha 9-15 vibrations a second (approx).

I suspect that I, like many people, at the beginning of the day create, if not via pen and paper, at least a mental list of what we wish to accomplish. We usually prioritise the things which appear most important, hoping that we can also fit in those which do not seem so urgent.

As the day progresses, after breathing and relaxing, I have discovered I usually have to change the order of priority in my planned list, for it seems to have reorganised *itself.* What I had earlier considered important lost its urgency, while what I had considered to be the least urgent activity had jumped to the top of the list. What's more I realised that the second list was really the better, resulted in greater satisfaction and a more harmonious day in every way. I think that this has been one of the most important lessons of life I have ever learned. Whenever I make lists nowadays, I make allowances, and am prepared for total subsequent flexibility, and change of plan. It has brought about a certain feeling of humility and relief that there exists a greater power than my own(!)

which knows what is best for me.

It is really comforting to realise that I am being looked after in this way, and I have developed a far greater patience in handing over the path of my life to this Higher power. It gives credence to the old saying 'man supposes, God disposes' (never in a destructive way). I have also found it easier to admit if I have been wrong or made a mistake, knowing that it is not a personal failure. The work of the breath has taught me that it's ok to make mistakes, and we don't have to be perfect.

Sometimes the beneficial result of my revised daily list is not apparent for days, weeks or even months, but I have gained a strong faith in its accuracy. It has proved time and time again how inaccurate my original list of priorities had been. What is even more significant is that while to an outsider and also to myself, the first plan seemed perfectly logical, the changed order put spiritual, what appeared to be mundane activity, first, which I later realised had had a spiritual basis. The changes gave a much greater sense of harmony to my days.

The more experienced I became as a psychotherapist, the more I realised the truth of a remark by Leonard Orr which has become part of my life. 'I am never upset for the reason I think.' The temporary irritation at accepting a changed timetable taught me to let go of being annoyed, or I would miss the important truths being shown to me as a result. What I had once thought of as being of urgency was urgent no longer. Instead what had once seemed of little importance became the new urgency.

The important issue here is that often when we are feeling upset and then have the self-discipline to allow ourselves to breathe and relax, our tensions and anger seem to reduce or disappear after we have used time in this way. The issue now is that if all our thoughts and subsequent actions are as a result of these two contrasting states of mind, which is the most valid?

I may have to persuade you reluctantly, as *I* was once reluctant, that we have to *spiritually* admit that our thoughts and actions *after* relaxation are the ones most likely to *reveal* the reason for our earlier anger. If we transpose this prioritising solving behaviour on to the world scene, we may understand how much of man's inhumanity to man could be averted and eliminated by a more relaxed approach.

There is one other important result from this more *merciful use* of life energy, which is the growing realisation that as we change our thoughts to loving, we seem to attract a corresponding invisible energy. It pours a benign healing solvent into situations, suddenly creating long term solutions. The blocking force which prevents this world-wide solution to all our ills is our *universal ego*, which has its origin in suppressed fear.

The symptoms of our anger are never the real cause for our heightened reactions. I have already quoted elsewhere 'I am never upset for the reason I think.' As we find the strength of mind to relax, we discover the real cause, which is usually related to our own personal problems. This remedy also applies to world leaders. Television programmes reveal more than they realise of their personalities. If we persist in unresolved anger, we become fatigued by the energy we are using to hold it in, and the fatigue causes us to the see the problem through 'emotional magnifying glasses', as one writer succinctly put it. It is important to know that we are allowed to *own* our anger, or tell someone that we are angry, but to give vent to our anger puts us at a spiritual disadvantage.

Eventually we metaphorically throw our daily lists over our shoulders as we send a thought out to this Higher Energy about what we would like to accomplish for that particular day. Then we listen to our intuition, stay relaxed, and discover the wonderful way in which our day is re-processed by an energy not apparently our own, and yet it is our own!

The whole day then seems to flow like magic with amazing inexplicable coincidences occurring to lighten it, often in an amusing way. Don't forget Higher Energy has a great sense of humour! Intuitive prioritisation teaches us to listen to what the heart is saying. Not the sentimental way we often think of the use of the heart but the deep all-knowing way we all have of acknowledging the loving song of the heart's true beat.

The use of the intuitive song of the heart may appear totally mundane to an onlooker, may only involve us in deciding to change the library books before going to the supermarket on a particular day, but if we listen with the heart to what we are to do next, boredom becomes a thing of the past. Minor events turn into an adventure, so we go to the supermarket before the library, and something happens. We might meet a special person we had been longing to meet, which would not have happened if we had used the head only and chosen the other option. We had usually lost the address or phone number of this person, but the meeting may change the whole course of our lives. All because we had trusted the heart. Coincidence? God's way of remaining anonymous.

The new prioritising game becomes a fascinating aspect of our lives, replacing the need for constant exterior stimulation such as TV chit chat, newspapers, computer games or lottery tickets! Natural unplanned magic appears round every corner, a constant diversion, more exciting than computer games or gambling.

On a more serious note there is a wisdom in the words that *what works with the microcosm, also works for the macrocosm.* Taking the heart-thought process to the political, economic and scientific scene, we have been given a sure-fire alchemic formula which, if adopted, could revolutionise and spiritualise the daily decisions which affect us all. Being spiritual, they will always be for every-one else's advantage as well as our own.

I remember reading of one important international humanitarian committee which always preceded its meetings with a short meditation session, and the resulting discussions were acknowledged to be more harmonious, took less time, and achieved more beneficial results. What a quantum leap of humility and dropping away of the destructive force of ego would result in a Universal adoption of this idea! At all Government metings? Could it reduce the barriers of religious bigotry? Probably.

Regular corrective breathing and relaxation always improves our ability to prioritise, and this ability can never be of more use than when we have to respond to an emergency or crisis, a fire, accident or other disaster. The fine line between losing or saving lives. Some time ago I was able to register the breathing patterns of several firemen, and found with concern that they responded to *their* idea of correct breathing by *holding in* the breath. If someone in that occupation needed to go into a burning building, surely a full lungful of breath would enable them to survive longer before being overcome by smoke. The difference between life and death, the saving of a life?

Many people at the end of their lives must echo the thought: 'If only I had known, if only I had done this or that differently, and now it is too late.' I do not think that these will be our final thoughts, if we learn to breathe correctly, relax and prioritise. It is then hardly ever too late. Our lives become the fulfilment of our gifts and talents.

As we heal our breathing and learn to give priority to thoughts and resultant actions that our Higher Power releases, we begin to be faced with the negative things that happen to us when we ignore this unseen prompting.

These negative results are continual reminders which

become increasingly urgent in their message, and we are reminded that we disobey them at our peril. We have discovered a new way to live, and the painful result of disobeying the breath message becomes a way of teaching us new rules for our lives. I am reminded of that wonderful Bible *The Aquarian Gospel of Jesus the Christ* by Levi Dowling, which states 'a little sin in him who walks in Holy Breath, is greater far than sin in him who never knew the way.' It makes sense doesn't it? Breath teaches intuition which teaches right prioritisation. We disregard it at our cost.

In healing our injured breathing, we become *entrusted* with the responsibility to obey our inner voice of *right action*. If we continually ignore this voice, we also learn that as soon as we acknowledge our omission, the law of forgiveness and reversal of negative results begins to operate, but only when we are honest or humble enough to mentally apologise to our Higher Power for our neglect! Often we make spiritual mistakes unintentionally, and we become quite upset thinking we are being punished, but our *apparent* suffering is really a sign of our progress. We are developing an increasingly heightened conscience which helps us to avoid similar future spiritual errors of judgement.

As we learn to walk this spiritual path of prioritisation, we can be of greater assistance to others who may ask us for help. We cannot *walk* the path for them, but we can help them to open the door to their own greater ability to walk their own right path.

In personally increasing our skills in the fascinating game of right prioritising, we recognise the truth of Leonard Orr's words: 'There is no good or bad, but there are consequences.' The consequences of right prioritisation are always positive.

I have noticed that small children have a much stronger sense of their own priorities than we parents who *care* for them, and their passionate and often, to us, annoyingly vociferous protests, are the only way they can express their legitimate priorities, often before they have the gift of speech. The respiratory and intuitive restrictions we have placed upon ourselves prevent us from proper communication and intuitive understanding of their needs. So the prison doors as Wordsworth puts it, 'Close around the growing child.'

Don't let it happen to your child, or the child within you. If we close our own prison doors, we close them on our children.

What continues to console and delight me is the way in which everything in our lives falls back into balance and grace once we obey the law of breath prioritisation. I give thanks to have continually experienced this sense of astonishment and delight. Time after time in the past two decades of my life I have had the privilege of being used to help other people to learn these unseen magnetic and immovable laws of corrective breath and spiritual prioritising. This may not bring great material wealth, but our needs seem always to be answered, and that is enough.

A child always knows what are its own priorities. If we do not listen to the child, it will start to put itself and its true needs on the *back burner*, and begin to neglect what is right action for its true spirit. As an adult it may take some time to regain the listening ear to our own true priorities, but only then will we feel our lives are fulfilled. We will also see that fulfilment in the lives of our children, who are linked to us by lifelong unseen bonds.

WHAT ELSE DO WE NEED?

Chapter 14

COURAGE

In sudden fear we all catch our breath for the
moment,
Some children have a lifetime of catching their
breath, and holding it,
The sign of a well-reared child, is its ability to
breathe correctly,
It shows that it is not afraid of life.

Extract from *Diary of a Friendship* - a letter from
Wilhelm Reich to A. S. Neil (Founder of Summerhill School)

THE ORIGIN OF THE WORDS 'Dutch Courage' probably
arose from the story of the little Dutch boy who blocked the
hole in the wall of the dyke by stuffing his fist in it, thereby
preventing the sea from crashing through, and flooding the
town. I believe other help arrived in time.

I don't remember often using the phrase myself, but surely
it means to summon the energy and courage from some
unseen source irrespective of personal safely, to retrieve an
apparently impossible situation. To take action in extreme
circumstances when the odds seem loaded against you.

Last night on television I saw a mass of protestors facing
and attacking the police on an issue which may be justified
public protest, but not the kind of abusive violence caused
by a collective artificial courage sustained by the aggression

of those around you, which is really a form of mass hysteria. An example of the defiance which comes from a repressed childhood. Those participating in this and other ugly mass scenes of a perverted sense of courage, need others' energy to back their own, because they are really cowards at heart. Such actions give us an apparently legitimate opportunity to use otherwise unacceptable aggression, in an artificial courage situation.

This is not to say that all crowd protests are unjustified, but I have seen too many of the self-indulgent 'showing-off' versions from those who are only looking for a chance to make mischief, like a little child who has had too little love, and needs a tough bully-boy to hide behind. This is not courage, however loud the noise.

My virtually inexhaustible supply of pithy statements evoke some really basic truths about courage, the one I believe to be of greatest importance says. 'The most courageous thing a man (or woman) can do is to be true to themselves.'

So many of us received severe psychological bruises and blows in our emerging childhood, from a culture to which our poor parents gave blind acquiescence at our expense. In many cases their decisions to pay lip-service to avoid disagreeing with the powers-that-be, or what the neighbours would say, left us vulnerable and alone, since *we* were the ones most in touch with nature from whom *we* took *our orders*. I remember in my own childhood that we were told that man had to conquer Nature. Sadly, eighty years on in my lifespan, it is becoming only too obvious that Man has no chance whatever of *conquering* Nature, and his attempts to do so could lead to his own self-destruction.

I am probably one among many who, I expect, were brought up with the words *'what will the neighbours say?'* It was heard frequently in the background. Not surprising that to be true to ourselves, the joyful, loving child within needs to reject as an adult many of the artificial standards by which our society is stuck together. As an adult, rejecting these artificial standards often means overcoming the considerable fears we have carried within us since childhood. Believe me that takes real courage.

The person who first said 'Give me a child until the age of eight, and I will have him for life,' knew the truth of what he was saying. I know how hard the cement of our early upbringing can set to form an almost impenetrable rock-face of adult beliefs. A cement of negative thought through which the green shoots of natural joy find it almost impossible to penetrate.

When we eventually come face to face with a great crisis in our lives which can eventually prove to be a wonderful turning point, even if tragically painful at the time, we finally recognise how many of the unquestioned norms and beliefs of our childhood have led us to this crisis. We have no known solution, and at first turn to others for an answer, but somehow we have to find a chink of light to guide us in our dreadful internalised darkness. For many years without question we have accepted the externalised darkness of an artificial and trivialised *culture,* which we have mindlessly accepted as our own, assuming that *they* knew best.

This life crisis so common today, described frequently as *mental ill-health* in varying degrees of severity, and invariably treated with drugs, has arisen because we have ignored the irreversible laws of Nature, the most inexorable of which, is that if we do not breathe correctly, *sooner or later we shall become ill.*

A small child naturally lives by the laws of nature, until as Wordsworth says 'shades of the prison house close around the growing child.' Emerging from this prison after many years, even although the door has always been open, since Nature has never closed it, is one of the most courageous journeys we can take.

The onion skin layers of fear which affected our positive loving development, began to form early in childhood, and caused blocks in our maturity. In order to remove them, we have to re-awaken our childish fears of we know not what, including unjust punishments metered out to us for misdemeanours we could not comprehend. Often before we were even two years old. Punishments given for even minor infringements of what our parents considered *good* behaviour, which was what *their* parents considered good behaviour. Back down the ages those customs can be traced so that even now, however socially sophisticated we consider ourselves, we are still affected by the lingering echoes of previous decades; when most people were enslaved by the power of the great landowners, and the giants of the early ages of the industrial revolution. To oppose their rule meant deportation, imprisonment, even death, grinding poverty, separation of families. Enslaving conditions on farms, in factories and grand houses, sometimes from the age of four or five.

It was not so long ago, and the echoes of inherited unnamed fears still undermine our imagined freedom of thought and action today.

One of my earlier fear challenges came about when I decided to stand for a local county council vacancy in my rural village. It was in an area where I was told that the retired colonels, lairds and landowners ran the council. Here was I, an ordinary housewife at the time, but I had done my stint in a number of local voluntary organisations such as secretary of the village hall. My *maiden* speech led to the first nursery class being set up in our rural county. Also an occasion where a discussion about grants to help support local playgroups produced a speech in opposition by an elderly local Baillie declaring that such organisations were to give the young mothers an opportunity to drink coffee and gossip!

I became very aware in those years of how difficult it was to make a dent in the village power-sharing forum of the local laird, retired colonel, the minister, and the head teacher. An inherited situation when such a group were, not so long ago, the only people in a rural village in Scotland who might have the necessary qualifications to understand County Council minutes.

As a young wife and mother, confidence and courage were certainly required, at a time when I had not yet discovered the enormous power still to be found from correcting my breathing, and gaining access to a Higher Energy, which would have eased my path.

I remember vividly the words of a wise old lady, who said: 'You don't have to live your life by other people's megalomania, and you don't have to ask permission.' I have never acted outside the law, but these words allowed me to dispose of the many levels of formerly unrecognised fear and self-limiting behaviour, which then enabled surprisingly exciting adventures to be undertaken!

As I began to throw off my own years of negative conditioning, her words have constantly been an inspiration, as I began to push the boundaries of my aspirations. I realised that the number one priority in life was to be true to oneself, and you cannot then hurt anyone. So much of our thinking is limited by feeling guilty for carrying out such a concept, but it really means that if you are not true to yourself, you are not true to others, and as a result you are really *harming* other people. The sin of omission.

Another aspect of our behaviour which has to be faced as a result of being true to ourselves, is that we have to learn to say *no*, where formerly we would have said *yes* in order to please other people. This latter results in other people controlling *you*.

I did find to my relief that finding the courage to quietly

say *no*, produced unexpected benefits; each time I said the no word it became easier to say. I lost the fear and aggression I expected from others at my use of that word, and found that I seemed to gain more respect. You can decline, even using quite pleasant phraseology that nevertheless can be contained within firm intent and with no chance of a change of mind. In other words the answer is still an irrevocable '*no*.'

There is a considerable skill in being able to be 'as wise as the serpent, but as gentle as the dove.' A skill well-worth cultivating.

Obviously we have to make sure that saying the no word passes spiritual scrutiny. When you do this, you will almost universally find that the other person accepts your decision, and you will both grow spiritually.

You begin to realise that if you had said 'yes' to the other person, you would have taken action which would have undermined your spiritual integrity, with a resultant action which would have led to negative results for both parties.

So often in a therapeutic situation I have been able to support a client on the first rung of this ladder of self-realisation, who then began to remove themselves from a controlling and egotistical influence of a domineering other person. The first time we say '*no*' is the worst, it is sometimes amazing to see a change in the atmosphere and feel a surge of confidence as we realise, by results, that we have the right to decline domination by anyone else.

Again the instinct to hold back and seek permission from another person for a quite simple decision or action we wish to take, undermines our natural courage to take a necessary step forward in growth. As we begin to regularly trust our own ability to act according to our own true instincts in every decision we make, on the information coming from our true self, we realise that if we act from this core authentic self we *cannot* hurt anyone else. People who have dominated us may take *the huff,* but that is because our standing straight is forcing them to do the same. That must be when *they* are ready, but is *not our responsibility.* We have no obligation to *try to make* someone grow in spiritual stature. We can of course share information about the way we have been able to free ourselves from domination by another, but only if our advice is requested. This journey must allow each to develop their own courage in their own time, or we will halt our own spiritual growth.

This spiritual journey is the same yet different for everyone, as we are all separate individuals with our own life agenda. We must go through our own spiritual door, and can take no one else with us. If our former friends are not ready when we are, it is the wrong time for them, and we must never try and influence the timing of their journey. We are not leaving them behind, our friendship was appropriate during the time of that relationship. Others are now waiting to meet us on the other side of that door of courage. These we are meant to meet because we have some joint work to do. Our spiritual vibrations are similar. For a special period of time they become our *family of the spirit.*

As I gradually grew in courage on my own path, I discovered that even although I realised I had to leave some long- term friends behind, which at the time seemed sad, there was no real loss. Those friends, although still loved, did not really know the latest *me*, we were living in different worlds of understanding. A relationship of any value has to be on a fairly similar vibration, otherwise it is just an illusory friendship based on habit.

If we do not develop the potential that is within us, we are unlikely to make real relationships of the spirit, which are based on each person relating from the core of themselves. In this situation, one plus one is always the sum of more than two, whereas *habit* friendships are equal to one plus one being *less* than two in spiritual strength.

We cannot develop that which is within us if we are constricted by fear, when what we need is courage. Fear results in repressed breathing, which leads to lack of brain and cell oxygen. Eventually like any machine requiring energy, the system closes down and finally shuts off before the work is done, for under such conditions there is no purpose in keeping it going.

I have always loved the following words: 'Be outrageous, those who achieve greatness are always outrageous.' Anyone who has forged ahead to move the boundaries of man's understanding has always been considered outrageous and even been persecuted, until the inevitable truth of their words and actions make such sense that they cannot be ignored.

Every time you extend the boundaries of your own world as a result of correct breathing you will feel a little outrageous, because you are becoming a pioneer, extending your life into unknown boundaries, and pioneers have no maps. Don't worry, trust your breath and your intuition, what seemed outrageous yesterday, will by tomorrow become accepted and normal.

When we are able to release ourselves from our own and other people's fears and doubts, we rediscover the beauty of spontaneous right action unspoilt by negativity. We release the ability of being totally true to ourselves, making time work for us, instead of being dominated by other people's time restrictions. Time has, after all, been given to us as a priceless gift, and we must live by our own time rules.

We may never become great in the world's terms, but since we are all unique, becoming outrageous enough to be true to that unique joyful child within us, releases our personal spiritual greatness which no one can destroy, and gives joy, importance, and purpose to our lives.

Next time you doubt yourself or become afraid, think about this... You have *already* succeeded in the most difficult and dangerous project you will undertake - what is that? The act of your birth. What did you do? You left the safe place, to which you could never return, you came along a time of confusion to go somewhere you had never been before, and didn't know if you would make it.

You had to put all your eggs in one basket, make a supreme effort and then a bit more. Did you make it? *Yes*. For here you are, you have already leaped the highest fence you will ever jump, so don't sell yourself short, you had and have the courage, don't waste it.

To fulfil your potential, you have to be prepared to take the same journey that you did in order to give yourself life, and you succeeded. You have already jumped the highest hurdle, everything else you face is a lesser challenge.

GO FOR IT!

Chapter 15

METAPHYSICS

THE WORD *Metaphysics* is one I sometimes find difficult to define. I know the meaning in my spirit, but my intellect can find it harder to put into words. So I consulted my large and heavy Reader's Digest Universal Dictionary which helped quite a bit. It stated: *'The branch of philosophy that systematically investigates the nature of first principles and problems, ultimate reality... The study of being, and often the study of the universe. Excessively subtle, abstract or speculative meaning.'*

I hope this leaves you a little wiser! When the word Metaphysics came so strongly into my mind, it was the only one which seemed effectively to describe a philosophy into which some years ago I was being increasingly drawn.

I left school at the ripe old age of sixteen years and four months. I had just obtained what was then called London University Matriculation Exemption, gaining three distinctions and five credits, quite a reasonable result. In fact a better result than either of my two brothers, both of whom went to University. I sometime ask myself if I was jealous. I had been told by my mother that my father had said that I had to leave school at sixteen, even if I went into a shop!

At that time all I wanted to be was a PE teacher, but there were no bursaries in this particular career for girls. I had two brothers, and my father's dream was that his sons should go to university. A girl's place was with her mother, with some kind of a job which earned her keep until she got married! This was a difficult period just after World War Two, and I am sure that my father, an insurance superintendent, would have had limited resources. My elder brother by eighteen months had been awarded a University place at the same time I took my Oxford School Certificate at sixteen. My chances of further education weren't even discussed!

In some ways I can understand my father's attitude, natural at the time for a man who was intelligent but had had a hard upbringing in the early 1900s. To send his sons to University was a considerable achievement at that time. This was also at the end of World War Two.

Looking back, I don't remember ever being bitter about my father's attitude. I had enormous energy, and did not feel I could have tolerated the constrictions of University life. I did however love reading, psychology, poetry and philosophy. The local library had been my second home since the age of seven. Nine was the official joining age, and I think that my mother must have fibbed to the librarian about my age. As we stood at the high reception desk and my mother told me I could choose a book, I started to say with childlike honesty 'but I'm only seven,' when she gave me a little kick on my foot, and I was in!

The sound of words, their nuances, their unknown Metaphysical meaning has probably been a factor underlying my awareness all my life. I think most beautiful poetry is about some aspect of nature, so perhaps the opportunity which came my way at sixteen to become a farm secretary, led me to spend the next ten years of my life very closely in touch with nature. Mostly in the beautiful Wylye valley in Wiltshire, and latterly in the equally beautiful and mystical borderland of Herefordshire near the Welsh Border where, I felt strongly, I must have lived in a former existence.

My typing and shorthand skills were what I would call adequate but as my employer, a gentleman farmer, dictated at about twenty words a minute despite being a Cambridge graduate I got by. One of my nightmares which re-occurred long after I was married, was that he would suddenly start dictating shorthand at sixty words a minute, when twenty was his norm. On the other hand, the glory and exuberance of the farming and country year seeped into my blood never to leave it, giving me a strength and stamina which used my endless energies. It is still an inheritance of my later years.

This joy in life despite its ups and downs, has left me with a strong sensation of a power beyond anything materially observed, which has great wisdom beyond that normally considered adequate for life by our inadequate culture. It alone really guides our lives.

This wisdom contains unalterable truths about any conceivable human situation, into which we can tap to explain the inexplicable in our lives, and to give us help, hope and comfort. At that time however, I did not have the key to unlock this information.

Marriage and the raising of three wonderful children then took over, and it was not until I began training as a psychotherapist that the word *Metaphysics* entered my vocabulary in a profound way, bringing with it an immediate and strong sense of recognition. A meaning that, unrecognised, had been underlying all the decisions of my life until then. So many of the wise and true sayings of people long gone who must have been in touch with hidden and higher truths, had influenced my life decisions. Particularly now when, becoming a psychotherapist, I was placing myself in a position of trying to assist others in finding a way out of their problems.

From the 1950s and even before, a growing number of books had begun to come on to the market, firstly those which could be classed as self-help, followed by the birth of the complementary and alternative health era. At the beginning, many of these books were kept under the counter in the local library, (together with books of a sexual nature, pretty mild stuff at that time). Nowadays there are thousands to choose from on the open shelves. Many of the self-help variety helped me enormously, as I came through a painful time of change in my life. Very often a book that I *needed* to read would come my way, almost miraculously, by the law of coincidence to which I refer in another chapter. One or two seemed to fall off the shelf in different book shops.

Looking back, it seems laughable that the under-counter category in which many of these books were placed, and now on general display, reveals the great changes that were beginning to affect the way in which we viewed health. In particular the way in which mind, body and spirit are inextricably linked. What we recognise as spirit (as distinct from religion) which, when out of balance, is probably the core-generator of disease.

All these changes are coming about despite earlier hostility. Nowadays grudging but increasing acceptance is sometimes voiced from church and medicine that there may be scientific and spiritual truths not yet known or recognised by them but already known to some non-scientists and spiritual people. Such people are not often part of organised religion, but they seem to be able to assist in a way which can help an individual to heal themselves. This is by making contact with, and obeying, the irreversible laws of something known as Metaphysics, not taught by either of the powerful hierarchies of medicine and church.

At a time when I was going through painful life changes, I came upon the work of a lady called by the singular name of Florence Scovel Shinn who taught Metaphysics in New York, and changed many people's lives for the better as a consequence. Her sense of humour, optimism, spirituality and clear perception taught through her work and books on Metaphysics, conveyed everlasting truths in the minimum number of words. They have enthralled not only myself, but also many of the people who came to me for help with problems of stress over the past twenty-five years.

Many of the books which have helped me in my life-growth have been short, as were those of Florence Scovel Schinn. I recall only four, written by her, including such titles as *The Game of Life and How to Play it, Your Word is Your Wand, The Secret Door to Success, The Power of the Spoken Word.* One of her sentences is fixed in my brain, and has probably been of more help to numerous sufferers than many weighty books of helpful advice. 'The door to my greater good is open wide, and it is nailed back!'

I do not know when Florence died, but thousands including myself, owe her a great debt of gratitude.

I realise nowadays that the circumstances of the first half of my life led me to make many wrong choices. That it to say decisions which took me on paths not in harmony with my true nature. Such decisions cannot be made unless one is free from fear, and looking back I realise that despite all I have talked about in this book about my early years, which gave me joy, the potential of which I was capable was restricted by nameless fears. At that time I was not aware that I often held my breath.

Looking back at the lives of my parents, I recall that my mother lost her own mother at the age of nine after being aware in her childish way that her mother must have suffered several miscarriages during my own mother's formative years. Expressed as she put it by seeing *something* carried down the stairs on a tray, covered in a blood-stained cloth.

Her father remarried after three years, someone who appeared to have been the typical hard and hated stepmother. The first war broke out when she was thirteen, with air-raids over London where she was living, and I realise now that she must have suffered some kind of breakdown in her late teens, being sent to the home of family friends in Kent to recuperate.

There she met and married the son of the house, my father, whose half-Italian mother treated the men of the house like minor royalty, to whom all the females were an inferior breed!

This assumption that the men were on a higher plateau than the females was probably unwittingly maintained by my mother who, although no doormat, was also full of nameless fears, caused I now realise by the events of her early years.

In her eyes the worst was always likely to happen, which became the usual self-fulfilling prophecy, and I am sure she passed it on to me. I never questioned my father's attitude to women until I was in my teens, but he was not a demonstrative man. I don't remember him giving me a spontaneous hug as an adolescent. In retrospect I was always aware and afraid of some deep brooding anger beneath the surface of his outward presence, which might erupt in violence if sufficiently provoked.

I give thanks when I see the natural affection between my son and his two daughters, where an affectionate hug is a natural part of their relationship when they are together. This might explain my own unexplained fears, which had to be lanced before I could begin my life's work, and this clearance took quite a few years. 'No growth without pain.' (Jung)

I think we can survive many limitations in our childhood, if there are also some special adults, maybe teachers, who fill in the gap. Usually unconsciously, which helps us to maintain a strong feeling of our identity and sense of vocation. Without such mentors we can feel bereft and lonely for many years.

We need recognition by these special adults in our formative years. If our own parents were too troubled themselves to give us as children this elixir of life, we can be vulnerable to the problems of the psychologically walking wounded. The latter eventually have to heal themselves spiritually, despite the needle, knife and tablet approach of a medical profession, who find it hard to acknowledge the spiritual because it cannot be seen visually or proved scientifically.

I thank God that I have always enjoyed excellent physical health. Something must have been right!

Our culture and national priorities leave much to be desired in the nurturing of the young child's spiritual potential. Apart from supplying material needs, that to me is the only quality that needs to be nurtured. All else falls into place, because all else is subservient to the spiritual, and will come into being in a natural way by the law of vibrational attraction. The child knows how to grow itself.

Returning again to the laws of Metaphysics, rooted in the work of the ancient philosophers such as Socrates and Plato. They are nowadays reflected in a new breed of philosophers such as Louise Hay, Eckhart Tolle, Depak Chopra and many others. All alive at this present time, their words are applying a break to the materialism of our age, and attempt to halt the downward spiritual slope of our global culture.

I mentioned at the beginning of this chapter, the fact that my earlier education did not include its extension to College or University. As I developed my work on breathing, and began to realise how its deeper meaning had begun to change my fear levels, I realised that I either held on to my fears and restricted my development, or had to move into the creative space formerly occupied by my fears. That space needed to be filled by right thought and action.

Correct breathing was leading me to become filled with thoughts and actions which reflected the *true me* rather than the negative me. These I knew were acting as a wall behind which I was hiding, rather than risk exposing that true self to the world for anticipated rejection.

I knew that the courage required to overcome my fears was being supplied by correct breathing. What I can only call a parallel spiritual development assisted by the study of Metaphysics was giving me greater wisdom and confidence.

Over the years it was as if I was being shown another University of great truth and information, totally different to the information I might have been given if I had attended Higher education in my earlier years. I began to feel so glad that this University of Spiritual Truths was the one I was proud to be attending, even although it was invisible!

It was around this time that I began to realise the power and support available to me in this interim period of moving from fear into courage. The value of the work of such masters of Metaphysical truths as those taught by Florence Scovel Shinn were of infinite help not only to myself, but hundreds to whom I had the privilege of introducing these ideas.

Many of these people were going through crises of growth in their lives, when nothing they had learned through upbringing or education had enough integrity of certainty to act as a spiritual hand-hold. A certainty of truth to help them to move onwards and upwards to develop the courage to rely on their own latent gifts, skills and power. The courage to return to their own true path, from which the false materialistic priorities of their earlier lives had distanced them, was brought into being by the healing energy created by correct breathing, consolidated by the laws of Metaphysics.

If the learned facts drilled into us in childhood have no spiritual basis, they will be powerless to help to solve the inevitable life problems which confront us on our path to maturation.

Metaphysics presents spiritual truths in a way that is acceptable, piquant, often witty and even humorous. Eventually, as we begin to see these rays of truth, creating comfort and reliability, we integrate them into our lives. We even invent our own Metaphysical truths to overcome our personal life difficulties. Finally we understand that there is no problem for which there can never be a good and positive resolution.

A neat and brief sentence containing a world of Metaphysical truth has been circulating recently. '*There are no problems, only solutions.*' Just a few succinct words that can have the power to re-direct the mind away from the hopelessness of the counter thoughts of the internal voice of 'it's too late,' or 'things can never be the same again.'

Eventually we begin to have a great deal of enjoyment, even fun, studying the material of this new and illuminating way of living our lives, and realise that its value is priceless. We produce our own invisible degree courses. Somehow this work needs to be available to future generations. Taught in schools.

Metaphysics cuts to the bare bones of the truth in a wise and acceptable way. It is supported by the hindsight and wisdom of past ages; re-invented and re-interpreted through understandable words in the culture of the day.

Such truths will never alter in the future, they are based on *spiritual* truths which are irreversible. Any structure, plan or project not based on such truths can never succeed, and will eventually collapse.

At the time I started this chapter, I was on holiday in rural Portugal in the heat of the summer. The truths of Metaphysics applies to whichever part of the world in which you may be living, whatever you may be doing.

Few people go through life without at some time encountering a crisis which they seem to have no resources to solve. Various degrees of fear, desperation, anguish, horror and desperation are encountered, as they appear to be descending into an apparently bottomless pit. There are two alternatives. One which many take is to take the easy way out and accept second, third or fourth best. Any hand held out is grabbed at, even if the ensuing relationships are controlling, jobs taken providing no real satisfaction, dead ends in terms of creativity.

Often the deep sense of lack of fulfilment leads to health breakdown in the second half of life, brought about by the fact that that their lives have been based on negative choices.

The alternative is to *face the fear*. Out of the recesses of my mind comes someone else's words. 'Fear knocked on the door, faith opened it, and there was no one there.' Unless the fear is faced, however tremblingly, help cannot be freed from unseen sources, *which are already waiting in the wings*. Such help will emerge never fear, in the form of unimagined helpful coincidences, people, information, and resultant insights which help us on the next stage of our recovery.

This is where the emergence at this time of hundreds of books on right thinking and philosophy written by people who have themselves faced the abyss, found the way through, and can support others to find their own path, is so inspiring.

In the forefront of such information, are books on Metaphysics, and I place the work of Florence Scovel Schinn in that forefront, because it has an immediate, humorous and wholesome approach presented in a non-intellectual way. Books to carry in a bag or briefcase, to be referred to so many times during the day, as we often feel compelled to do in the early days of recovery from stress.

We take our first haltering steps to self-healing, but like a small child learning to walk, require the equivalent of a helping hand to maintain progress. A therapeutic appointment several weeks away is just not good enough. In so many cases, help needs to be on the spot, and on the spot is where such books are nowadays always to hand.

In my own work on myself at a critical time, and with others who have asked for help, breath correction provides the re-rooting of the spirit, and Metaphysics provides a very unique supporting scaffolding structure. When that spirit becomes vigorous enough to stand alone, as the true personality grows strongly re-rooted, its master plan can be fertilised in those new but at first tender roots, by the trust-worthy words of Metaphysics.

If the roots are those of a daffodil, we must grow as a daffodil, and not try to be a tulip as we may have done before. We may have mistakenly thought that the daffodil was not good enough. It is useless trying to be any other self than our own blueprint, which is already perfect. Thinking we have to be someone different is in effect what so many people are trying to do, and wondering why their lives are full of frustration and disaster.

In emerging from the shadows of despair, at first the light of hope may seem flickering almost appear to go out just when we thought it was re-lighting our path. Having left the bottom of the pit, we have to climb out ourselves, sometimes the next foothold only presents itself at the last minute. We dread falling back but are not sure of the next rung.

One of the most important support systems is that pro-vided by the Universal Truths of breath and Metaphysics. These truths become our own truths as we slowly progress. Eventually we realise that even if we are still climbing out of our own particular abyss, with much yet to learn, we can never fall back again.

One of the amazing facts which emerges from this spiri-tual climb, every bit as difficult as the ascent of Everest on an unseen level, is that as each truth comes to our aid from an inspiring Metaphysical source, we begin to realise we knew all this when we were a small child!

I have spoken elsewhere of the writings of Bronson Alcott (father of Louise Alcott) encapsulated in the book *How Like an Angel Came I Down*, who believed that the soul of a young child came into this world already full of spirit and wisdom.

Deep within us then we already have the plan for our lives, Metaphysics acts as a star to steer by. To recognise our individual *angelic* origin.

I have a very thought-provoking article (author unknown) on the subject of relationships, which emphasises the need to be true to ourselves, or our relationships will have no true meaning. The article suggests that at the end of our lives so many people are *'sick with guilt at having lived below their authentic potential.' Do you agree?*

I am sure that we knew this potential at the beginning of our lives, we may have mislaid the way, but its voice can still be heard when we pause to listen to its quiet but insistent echo. The quality of this present culture of immaturity in which we are immersed is rarely sufficient to be able to prescribe the required alchemy for healing.

It is often other souls who may have lived thousands of years ago who had the pioneering courage to discover these perfect truths. They wrote them down for us to rediscover so many lifetimes later. They speak to us in a way that cuts through our cynical, cold, analytical and often patronising medical science to illuminate the path of our spiritual homecoming.

Eventually we can look back, *be glad* and give thanks for our suffering, because the wisdom that we have now gained to pass on to others has become a pearl of greatest price. This pearl makes the materialistic ambitions of so many million-aires impoverished and laughable.

We give continued thanks that we have been given back the means to heal ourselves, integrating a joyful wisdom of so much greater depth than any psychological degree based on the left brained educational training wastelands of our universities and colleges. Much degree-based trainings can quench rather than nurture the thirst of so many students who enter these courses full of the searching and dynamic enthusiasm which often springs just once in a lifetime.

Sometimes it is *despite rather than because* of such intellec-tually based degrees that we find our true path in this field of such great need. To be a catalyst, so that our pithy knowledge of Metaphysics may enable others to re-grow from their roots. Help them to prune out the parasitical untruths which we have been told to prioritise, and rediscover the right truths of Higher Power as criteria to live by, and pass on to our children.

Metaphysics is about simplicity. When we are trying to find a way out of the stress of being on our wrong path, our need is not to be presented with lengthy and wordy so-called solutions. It is for the sentence and words, brief yet succinct, which stirs into life the equivalent truth within our psyche, that acts as our *tube-strap hold* until the next lifeline of wisdom is revealed to us. Revealed it will be, once we start to listen, and act on that wisdom.

The words of Florence Scovel Shinn have been for me and thousands, the strap-hangers designed to inspire just at the right time. I have quoted the titles of her books earlier in this chapter.

I have known many people whose lives were falling apart, bring themselves back from mental collapse by a combination of correct breathing, and a sudden awareness of the power of right words discovered through Metaphysics in the work of such wise souls as Florence Scovel Shinn.

The power to self-heal discovered through this combination of breath and right thought, has been repeated in my experience time and again during several decades of close involvement with the true energy of healing. Breath and Metaphysics are the duo which puts us back in touch with Nature in our nature.

When I was running a stress centre in the heart of Glasgow we had a little box of Metaphysical sayings on a side table in the kitchen waiting-room.

This box was rarely mentioned, but it was interesting and heart-warming to discover how clients and visitors while waiting for an appointment would make a bee-line for the little box and select a page at random, which was then put quietly back without comment. Later discussion often revealed that the page selected contained a really appropriate message for that person on that day. It has also happened to me on many occasions. It is said that the saying we pick *is the one we need*.

It seemed to bring an instant lifting of the spirit, a dive into the deep end of some of the world's truths contained within just a few totally appropriate words.

These little Metaphysical sentences always seemed to reflect the present need which suited that particular individual. A statement of everlasting, I should say divine truth.

We are deluded by the *untruths* of much of our cultural training in which we are expected to swim without the real truths which help us to move confidently through the waves of life. A support which has never before been presented to us, we have been left to drown by our *civilisation*.

If we give perpetual lip-service to these half-truths of our present culture, we shall surely become just another number in the frighteningly high total of those whose lives are distorted by physical and mental illness, of wrong thinking, wrong decisions, wrong relationships, wrong work. *This does not have to be.*

That one relationship which needs to be right, that of ourselves with ourselves, which has been out of harmony with nature and our own true nature since childhood, can be healed, can be triumphant.

CORRECT BREATHING BACKED UP
BY METAPHYSICS CAN BE AN
INVINCIBLE PARTNERSHIP.

Chapter 16

COINCIDENCE

IT IS ONLY IN RECENT YEARS that the phenomenon of coincidence has assumed a greater significance in my mind other than something perhaps to remark upon and then forget. Nowadays I see it as a sign that a Higher, wiser power than mine is trying to tell me something, even if it is to remind me that such a Power exists. To me it is a very comforting happening, and enlivens my days, wondering when and where coincidence will occur again in my life, so that I can have the fun of interpreting its meaning.

I expect most people recognise coincidence when they meet someone on the street who has recently been in their thoughts, particularly when that person has not been in their mind perhaps for years. Usually we leave it at that, but nowadays I look for a deeper meaning, because there may be an underlying reason as to why I have to meet this person again. It happened to me this week, when someone I had been thinking about a few days before, who had left the area some months ago, suddenly said 'hello' to me in a little country town five miles from my home.

The reason for her return was because of a house sale, but she said that she had been thinking about me, and intended to ring. As we parted I knew that before long we shall probably be working together in some way. The house sale may be a way of bringing her back to the area. Coincidence can only work in an apparently matter of fact way.

The energy which brings about coincidence is, I believe,

a meeting of vibrations on an unseen level which creates a magnetic attraction, causing a coming together on a visual plane. We are electrical beings whose magnetic frequency is amplified when we breathe correctly which, in my experience, seems to increase the frequency of coincidental happenings. This has been demonstrated by such processes as *Kirlian Photography* which reflects the electrical energy emanating from an organism.

Elsewhere in this book I have referred to the wise statement that 'coincidence is God's way of remaining anonymous.' Now what could be more illuminating than that?

This wonderful phrase explains the coincidences which often happen quite frequently when we begin consciously to move along the path which we realise is the right one for our soul's journey. Often, finding that path and staying on it requires a special kind of courage. We usually have to make great changes in our lives, sometimes misunderstood and even disapproved of by those we love, so that we may feel quite lonely for a time.

It is at such a critical and sometimes lonely time of our lives that coincidences appears to happen more often, as if we were being reassured that we had made the right decision. They may seem so remarkable that we somehow know that they could only have happened because we *have* made the right choice. They appeared to mirror our thoughts.

When I was a child, I used to try so hard to see God. I would lie on the grass on a Summer day, trying to pierce beyond the infinite blue of the sky, sure that if I concentrated enough I would see Him. I was so sure that Heaven located beyond the sky.

All too soon I began to accept that what I saw was all there is, and God moved away from me, or so I thought then.

Years later I remember a speaker at a conference on spirituality saying that we all have a Guardian Angel, and the atmosphere is infused with energy that we can attract to work on our behalf. That is not to say that all we have to do is sit back and do nothing; cultivating the right attitude to allow this energy to manifest requires a discipline of thought and behaviour to try and exist in an atmosphere of love. Everyone knows how difficult that can be. However we are all imperfect, and make mistakes all the time. I believe, as I have said before, that we get Brownie points for trying, and so often are met more than half-way.

This is when I now believe that coincidence speaks to us.

Recently I was chatting to a friend, who told me that some time ago she was in a small village in Scotland, called Carnock, and for no known reason a very strong feeling of love flowed through her. It was such a significant experience, that it stayed in her mind, as it did not seem to be associated with any person she was thinking about at the time.

The name Carnock rang a bell with me, and when I returned home I checked with several small books I possess about the life of St. Kentigern of Glasgow in whom I have an interest. The brief references were in connection with the Saint visiting an old man, Fergus, in Carnock, who was dying. Fergus asked Kentigern to place his body on a cart drawn by two oxen, and travelling by *the straight road that has no track*, burying him where the oxen stopped. This turned out to be The Necropolis in Glasgow, consecrated as a burial ground by St. Ninian in the fourth century. Did my friend *pick up* Kentigern's love from his time in Carnock?

None of the books I possessed gave more than a passing reference to Carnock. The following day I had to go to Glasgow, and intended looking for a stationery shop in the city centre where I understood the prices were quite cheap. I had some difficulty finding the shop but, when I did, was surprised to find it sold mostly cheap knick knacks, and little stationery. I was disappointed at its tawdriness.

On one wall were some shelves of the usual cheap paper-back novels that people read once, and return for second-hand sale. There was quite a big empty space on the bottom shelf, and lying in the middle of that space was a book entitled *The Life of Kentigern*. I lifted it up almost unbelievingly, wondering how such a book could be in such an unlikely place. In purchasing it (naturally!) I looked for a reference to Carnock as the name was in my mind. There were about *six* pages telling of Saint Kentigern's time there, staying apparently for several years, *which I had never known nor read before*, and where, according to the book, he was first ordained a Bishop. Coincidence? You tell me.

Of course this chapter is not about my favourite saint, but I tell of the incident at length, because to me it was quite an extraordinary coincidence, given my interest in Saint Kentigern, and the experience of my friend. It gave me a great sensation that *someone up there* was communicating with me.

I am positive that the Highest energy is always trying to communicate with us; it lies just below the surface of our consciousness. When I am in harmony with it everything in my life has become and remains more vivid and pleasurable. Colours, the spoken word, art, music, nature, one wonders at the masses of people who feel bored with life. Our over-intellectualised culture has created an over-analytical and criticising mind-set, so much so that we can miss the mess-age spiritually meant for us alone. The coincidences which came my way seemed to occur more and more frequently as I was improving my breathing, which helped to sharpen my awareness, and see below the surface of life.

> The Angels keep their ancient places,
> Turn but a stone and start a wing
> 'Tis ye, 'tis your estranged faces,

Which miss the many-splendoured thing.
But when so sad, thou canst not sadder
Cry, and upon thy so-sore loss,
Shall shine the traffic of Jacob's ladder,
Fixed betwixt Heaven and Charing Cross.

Frances Thompson - *The Kingdom of God.*

The coincidences which have happened to me have certainly seemed to represent a Jacob's ladder. Such experiences can illuminate all our days, once we begin to live our lives by *breath awareness and intuition.* These words are for me some of the most important words in the language. I have experienced wonderful coincidences arising from this life-choice which I now trust implicitly. I understand that you may doubt my words if you have not yet had a chance to try this magic formula for yourself. For me it came about through correct breathing, meditation and a calmer outlook. This takes time, you have to walk the walk. I found out for myself that it does not work only by talking the talk.

Through the *walking* route we gradually prune the negativity from our lives, we raise our electrical frequency, and thereby our energy, thus creating favourable situations in our lives, often when we least expect it, frequently by amazing coincidences. Their regular occurrence can make our days a dance of fun. A treasure chest always overflowing, but only available to us when we use the mystic key. The wonderful thing is, we realise that we had the key once as a child, the circumstances of our lives may have stolen it from us, but once we have rediscovered it, we will never let it go again.

This reliable power works in such simple ways that we often forget that all bigger ideas and projects work by a similar process, often after a combination of numerous smaller actions. Recently I received a delivery of eighteen ten foot railway sleepers at the front of my house, for the purpose of constructing two raised beds for vegetables. They had to be transferred via a neighbour's side drive to my own back garden. I could not think how I could find someone to help transport the heavy sleepers up the path to my garden, a good fifty yards. When I ordered the sleepers I had no idea how I could get them moved to my rear garden. On the same day I had for a long time been wanting to see a local councillor concerning a matter of importance to a number of people.

Everything I now do has to come from a sense of right timing, particularly intuitive right timing. Even the time we leave home when there is no other pressure except to decide just that.

So I had two important problems to solve. First of all I had to travel to the nearest little town five miles away for some messages. I chose the time to leave by intuition.

On my way out of the village, I saw a young man in a garden cutting grass, and recalled that a neighbour had suggested that he and his brother sometimes helped out with garden jobs. I suddenly remembered my railway sleepers. Within three minutes he had agreed to come with his brother and help. Date and time arranged on the spot (Scottish weather permitting). Within ten minutes I was in the Post Office, and who should be beside me, but the local Councillor I needed to see. If I hadn't left home at my *intuitive* time I would probably have missed seeing both these two people, who coincided with my needs. The intuitive faculty heightened by the power of the breath.

As with small issues, the same process would also apply to world issues, that is when world leaders understand the language of correct breath.

The Law of Coincidence, or playing the Game of Life as I think it should be played, is developed most inspiringly in four small books on Metaphysics, the invisible laws of right living, or as the dictionary says, 'investigating the problems of ultimate reality.'

These books, by Florence Scovel Schinn, I mentioned in the previous chapter on Metaphysics, describe most vividly the way in which we attract our greater good to us. They have helped so many people, myself included.

Ultimately of course it is learning to use the power of the mind possessed by all of us in a creative and positive way.

I have found that so many small inexpensive books contain information beyond price.

Young children seem have a natural knowledge of the law of coincidence, seeing it as a natural happening which they can use. I remember as a child wondering why my parents and others used other beliefs based on negative pessimism which seemed to attract problems which I thought could have been avoided. Of course I have no way of proving this but I know what I knew then, *and knew that I was right*! How can you tell your parents they are wrong when you are five years old?

Using the laws of intuition and resultant coincidence, we can walk in our own energy all our lives, and correct breathing will keep us on course. As a result we seem to be able to avoid being dominated by other people's energy, the sure way to an unhappy life. Living dominated by another person's negative energy is the perfect way to attract disaster and ill-health into our lives.

We can never hurt others by acting from the guidance of our own breath, regulated by intuitive thought energy, constantly referring back to what our heart dictates. Whatever mistakes we have made in the past can be healed, particularly when we fully comprehend the laws of karma and reincarnation, although these illuminations can only come to us when we are ready. I do not expect everyone to share the thoughts expressed in this last sentence.

Our children will benefit when we return to our right path, the invisible cords which bind us seem to vibrate back to them the positive happenings which are coming into our lives from the rules of coincidence. Often without verbal communication taking place. We may have become separated by disharmony arising from our own disharmonies as young adults, when we did not know the Game of Life and the laws of coincidence.

I have seen miraculous reunification of disunited families through the above Universal Laws, after years of discord. Of course Nature's laws are constant and irreversible.

It is never too late, these unseen laws are more powerful than those which have been written by man down through the ages.

Unplanned and unforseen coincidences are, I believe, a delicious way in which Higher Power lets us know that we don't know all the tricks!

Chapter 17

CHILDREN

Your children are not your children
They are the sons and daughters of life's
longing for itself.

Khalil Gibran - *The Prophet*

MOST PEOPLE have heard or read the above words, the opening lines of a beautiful poem called *Your Children* by Khalil Gilbran, in his book *The Prophet*. Really deep-thinking spiritual poetry about children is all too rare. Gibran's words have been quoted so often that it is easy to forget their deep meaning.

Before I married and had children myself, I found small children a bit of a nuisance. They needed to be controlled, seen but not much heard. I wasn't an advocate of corporal punishment, but accepted that possibly they needed to be occasionally lightly chastised.

Nowadays when I hear people talk about children in such a dismissive way it breaks my heart. Much has happened to change my thoughts to respect and humility, concerning the small beings who have come to remind us about what love is.

I certainly was not a punishing parent, but then one's own children are always more special than anyone else's, aren't they?

As my children began to develop, two very important thoughts came into my mind.

175

(a) Despite being born into the same family, each of my children had a vastly different individual personality. Same parents, same house, same environment, yet there must be other inexplicable factors which decided their individual natures. That fact in itself gives scope for a sense of wonder of factors beyond a lifetime's ability to solve.

(b) I realised almost without exception that when my children *played up*, became cranky, or behaved badly in the world's terms, it was invariably when they were tired or hungry. Not enough attention had been given to their limited ability to function as mature beings, in a world totally geared to adult needs. In other words children, like adults, have limitations. When we need to rest or eat, we should not ignore that need. I once read in an unidentified article, that when we are tired or hungry we see the world through emotional magnifying glasses. We feel irritable, hostile to other people, become quick tempered. Why should we expect children to behave differently? Yet we often treat tired and hungry children as *naughty*, when they appear to become unmanageable as a result of *our* limitations.

Often when we criticise a child for being cranky, we forget that a small child does not have the verbal equivalent of saying they are at the end of their tether in adult terminology. All it can do when we have over-taxed a child's nervous system is to make loud sounds of protest. As we learn to respect our own personal limitations, so we need to respect those of children, and arrange their timetables accordingly.

I note that small children from five onwards just starting school, often leave home at about 8am. Many are taken when school finishes to after-school activities until they are collected by working parents sometimes not until 6pm. A ten-hour working day, with no facilities to lie down and rest. We interpret their subsequent over-excitability as having too much energy or being naughty, when in effect their hyper-activity should be seen as over exhaustion, they are out of control, and we have made them so.

You have only to be walking in a city-centre, often in over-heated and over-crowded basement stores to see protesting children being dragged around, shaken when they cry, expected to 'behave', when it is in fact our own behaviour with regard to a child's endurance capability, which is out of control. Our prime parental skill is to be able to identify and avoid whenever possible those situations which over-tax a child's nervous system.

We are all inheritors of the positive and negative aspects of our own upbringing; becoming a parent requires us to un-learn the negative aspects, and convert them into the natural parental wisdom with which we are all intuitively born, rather than the so-called norms of our inherited attitudes to children.

We note the often publicised inadequacies, faults and injustices within our present culture, believing that the adults are the victims, and yet it is the children who are the first sufferers from man's inhumanity to man. Whatever the limitations of my own upbringing, I can never remember a time when I came home from school at lunch-time without my mother having ready a main meal and a dessert, despite the fact that six of those years were during wartime short-ages. I was an adolescent then and always hungry. That is a memory I increasingly cherish. Many children weren't so lucky.

Conversely I remember times before I started school, when a memory surfaces of a piece of chocolate withheld for some days, because I had not eaten the dinner that was on my plate. It is amazing how at 80 I can still remember my thoughts about what appeared to be the problem. I can vividly remember not being *able* to eat everything that was placed on my plate, just because I was not hungry enough to eat it all. A normal human reaction. In an adult this was acceptable, but apparently not if you are a four-year old.

I was never smacked for not finishing my dinner, but the pressure to eat what is put on your plate is really forced feeding, an unacceptable factor if you are an adult. I wonder how much of these early-feeding patterns affects our subsequent disposition to bulimia or anorexia. Luckily neither of these has ever affected me!

The need to finish what is on one's plate, as seen from my present age, is probably a relic of the days when food was so scarce it was a sin not to finish our food, because you never knew when the next meal was coming from. This was even more true in the war years.

I am sure that all children being nearer to nature than the adult, know exactly how much they need to eat or drink, but when I was a new parent, I still thought as my mother had taught, about the need to finish what was on the plate. I do not think that lasted very long, somehow my own common sense came to the rescue, but I do remember that my youngest daughter always wanted to eat raw vegetables, and the conflict in my mind then was that all vegetables needed to be cooked. She was right and I was wrong. Nowadays eating raw vegetables is considered a plus health factor, and an important part of my present vegetarian diet. Just as I knew my food needs as a child, so did my daughter. I think I have apologised to her! The lessons we inherit from our parents die hard.

Looking back on my earlier years, I remember possessing a great sense of injustice, to myself and others, an enormous energy of passionate feeling and refusal to be dominated. I probably over reacted in certain situations.

In later years I came to understand the possible source of my intensity of feeling concerning the needs of children. I heard from my mother, about the way in which I was raised in the earlier months of my life. At the time of my birth the baby-rearing fashion of the day embraced the methods and opinions of a New Zealand doctor called Truby King. As a victim of his methods I wish I could confront him face to face now.

I have a fellow feeling for the famous novelist Doris Lessing, another recipient of his monstrous regime which became popular in the 1920s. It must have been a form of near-torture for the new-born baby, who was only lifted and fed every four hours, despite the needs of the baby, whose only protest was to cry. The crying had to be ignored as the infant was *broken in* physically, mentally and emotionally to the fact that its needs did not matter. A good grounding for producing an adult with a feeling of worthlessness. What a great way to break a baby's spirit. Oh yes, it can be broken at such an early age. I also speak of this regime in another chapter.

Truby King invited parents-to-be to have a nurse in their home for several months after the birth, to break the baby in to his methods, which they were assured would make later child-rearing much easier (a non-protesting zombie?). My parents fell for the hype, perhaps it gave them a sense of importance to have a resident nurse. My mother only briefly discussed her Truby King experience with me, when I was a parent myself, certainly she was very concerned when my first baby was born if I did not respond immediately to his crying. I have a feeling that after the departure of the nurse, she listened to her natural instincts and fed me on demand, but I am sure that the earlier experience of Truby King's unnatural methods were responsible for some of the insecurities I was, fortunately, later able to heal as I corrected my breathing.

I think some of his training was still in the air when my son was born in a small-town nursing home, for I have strong memories of the Matron warning us not to lift the baby every time it cried, and to try and keep to four-hourly feeding. When I returned home, I was confused and distressed as I tried to be a good mother, trying to cope with conflicting instinct and guilt. I don't know if shades of Truby King training still trail their rigidity in the maternity wards, but I hope not.

It was with a sense of affinity that I read an extract from Doris Lessing's autobiography, and to read of her own sense of outrage from having been subjected to the Truby King method of cruelty to babies. It gave me a sense that I was not the only one. I wonder how many more casualties there are who are still alive?

You may think I make too much emphasis on the early routines imposed upon young babies, but these imposed patterns start to shape the child's character. Children try to communicate to us, as small babies, their only means of communicating unhappiness being the sound of crying (weeping?). We have to learn to listen. Our only means of responding to their attempts to communicate is by finding the source of their grief, since they cannot get up and make their own food, change their own nappies, etc. For those who say that they are only looking for attention, well why not? The younger they are, the more they will need our attention, which will either be loving or less than loving. If it is frequently the latter, they will form their rooting opinion of life as a negative condition. They will begin to be afraid of life, and to restrict the correct breathing pattern with which they were born.

I have a most unusual book, a series of Sunday School sessions written between 1835 and 1837, entitled *How Like an Angel Came I Down*. It consists of conversations between children and their Sunday School teacher, who in this instance was A. Bronson Alcott, the father of Louise Alcott, who wrote the timeless classic book *Little Women*.

Because of the period when these sessions were recorded, the names of some of the children obviously belonged to another era, Nathan, Lemuel, Josiah. On page 303, the class were talking about miracles, and Mr. Bronson asked if anyone had seen a miracle. To which George answers '*Yes.*' Mr. Bronson: '*When?*' George: '*Why breathing, the miracle of the pulse.*' The wisdom of the child should *not* be disregarded.

Are we a lost generation who cannot understand the miracle of the breath? We never seem to talk about it, only the miracles of science. Is breath a science? Which could we do without, breath or science?

Bronson Alcott believed that the psyche of a child already carries with it the imprint of spirit and wisdom. Where has our generation lost these precious gifts?

It was only as I was made to take my own journey of self-discovery that I was forced to take a much deeper look at childhood, obviously my own, and also that of my clients.

While I am certain that we must not live in the past, I believe that whether we wish to or not, we have to face the limitations we have imposed on our potential by our perceived childhood loss of that *imprint of spirit and wisdom.* How it has led to sorrow and problems in our lives, our nameless fears, negative thoughts, and wrong decisions.

In our lack of wisdom we can drink, smoke and take drugs, hurt other people. Or re-learn to breathe correctly. In that case we shall not need to drink too much, smoke, take drugs, or hurt other people We shall regain our own imprint of spirit and wisdom, live longer, be healthier, get more fun and joy from our lives, like a really happy child, of which there are all too few.

The miracle of the pulse of the breath has allowed me to heal so many of the negative aspects of my childhood. Even now I can occasionally become tense and anxious, but the moment I return my breath to correct mode, they vanish. Most of our fears have to do with a feeling of inadequacy, of other people having control of our lives, yet the moment we restore correct breathing they all begin to disappear, because correct breathing balances the brain pattern, and relaxes the muscles. It is usually not the circumstances themselves which cause the stress, but the value we place upon the circumstances. Back to the saying: 'Don't sweat the small stuff, it's all small stuff.'

I am positive that the value we place upon any situation arises from the conditioning circumstances which happened in our earliest months and years, when the people who created the circumstances were almost invariably our parents.

With the best will in the world few parents are perfect, so at some stage in our lives we have to let go of our unhappy child who feels so sorry for itself, and find some way to heal that child. We are the only people who can undertake this self-healing process, and we are the only people good enough to do so, combined with the spirit of the correct breath. Obviously we have to forgive our parents, which is a must if we expect our own children to forgive us.

At the time I left school some sixty plus years ago, a friend began a teacher-training college course. I remember her telling me that the motto of the College was: *If a child wants to, let it.* Quite advanced advice at that time. I wonder if that motto is still observed.

As a slightly more than amateur gardener I know only too well how vital are the early nurturing conditions for the young seedling. Despite the greed of our culture, its impatience, its ego-dominated power base, it ignores the essential growing conditions of the plants it wishes to raise for pleasure or profit, at its peril. No observance of Nature's laws, no pleasure or profit. Yet we do not raise the human plants for profit, so we ignore many of Nature's laws upon which healthy growth depends. The only way to raise the human child is to respect its natural needs and demands which are as integral to healthy growth as that of the plant. Does the *no profit* return create blinkers in our attitude to children?

The only way to know children is to watch and observe, to give them the same attention as a naturalist studying the habits of a rare species.

The more I advance in the knowledge and ability to breathe correctly and live in calmness, the greater my sense of wonder at the miracle of childhood. A child breathes most correctly in those early years because it is near to nature, and without realising that cause, we feel a great joy in observing the joy of life of the young child. We find a great sense of empathy and closeness to the child, who will respond instinctively to that love, particularly if we are breathing correctly, thereby creating a calm secure atmosphere.

A child grows itself from a cell to a baby in those nine months within the womb, no one advises, teaches, or shows it how to grow itself. The baby is in touch with a deep creative wisdom from which it receives its instructions. That source of knowledge is still essential, and is available to the child particularly in the first eight years of its life. Nevertheless that child is also expected to have to try and adapt itself often to the false values upon which so much of our culture is based. In effect to sell itself short from its authentic links to nature. It needs to survive in this world, but what a world, as distinct from the world of natural wisdom from which it has grown itself. The child tries to make sense of this *adult* world into which it is expected to fit, the word of noise, addictions and artificiality.

One of my greatest joys these days is to study a small child, to share without words its interest in what surrounds it, its delight in a miniscule object as it learns about its shape, what it can do with it, how it watches other children, animals, the deep thoughtfulness behind all its actions. To catch the eye of a child and share its sense of wonder at life, is the nearest I believe that one can get to heaven on earth.

To be trusted by a child is such a great privilege. 'Sentimental' you say?

The Great psychologist Jung would say when asked to see a child. 'Don't bring me the child, bring me the parents.' It is we as adults who have lost our way.

'Tis ye, 'tis your estranged faces,
Which miss the many-splendoured thing.

From *O World Invisible we View Thee* -
Frances Thompson.

So many of us as adults are sad, worried, frightened, anxious, lonely, depressed, violent. All these aspects of our nature belong to the sad, worried, frightened, hurt and lonely child still within us. Correct breathing can heal all these negative aspects of non-joy, and evolve us into a mature adult, so desperately needed by that child. The necessary changes at cellular and hormonal level are brought about via the vibration of correct respiration.

In her wonderful book *The Secret of Childhood*, Maria Montessori wrote the following words...

Society up to now has never claimed that the family should prepare itself in any way to receive and fittingly care for the children that might come to form part of it. The State so rigorous in demanding official documents and meticulous preparations, and which so loves to regulate everything which bears the remotest trace of social responsibility does not trouble to ascertain the capacity of future parents to give adequate protection to their children, or to guard their development. It has provided no place instruction or preparation for parents.

These powerful and moving words were written in 1966; has very much changed in the past half-century?

Again, moving words by Michael Quoist, in his poem, *I like Youngsters*:

> But above all, I like youngsters because of
> the look in their eyes,
> In their eyes I can read their age,
> In my Heaven there will only be five-year old eyes,
> For I know of nothing more beautiful than
> the pure eyes of a child.

I cannot complete this chapter on Children without reminding anyone who reads these words, that less than 10% of children in our schools can breathe correctly. For me it is the equivalent of a perpetual horror story, of what we are doing to the next generation of soon to be adults, who are supposed to help save our planet.

What better words to remind us of the great responsibility we bear towards our children than those of Karin Roon from her book *The New Way to Relax*:

> There is no habit in life which pays bigger dividends and pays them more quickly than complete breathing. It is the source of your health, your cheerful spirits, your energy, your youth, and your relaxation.
>
> A healthy baby is the perfect instructor in breathing and relaxation.

Jesus said: 'A little child shall lead them.'

IT COULD, BUT WHEN SHALL WE
BE READY TO FOLLOW?

Chapter 18

CIRCULATION

THE SIMPLEST WAY TO DEFINE CIRCULATION is of something going round and round. Blocks in circulation, whether it be traffic jams, information, drinks and refreshments at a party, good communication, petrol in your car, water in a stream or river, mean that the energy of movement is halted. In either a human social activity, or block in a natural process, that which is expected to happen does not happen.

The result of any block can result in chaos, irritation leading to negative actions, sometimes catastrophe. In water such as a stream which is blocked up, the result can be stagnation. Changes in structure, toxicity, often a disease source. Cancer?

I have often thought that most of us know more about the problems resulting from a petrol block in a car caused by *dirty* petrol, which can result in an accident if the car suddenly slows down without warning on a motorway, than we do about our own vital circulatory process of the blood stream. That great scarlet river without which healthy life cannot be maintained.

For many years my work on breathing and relaxation took place in an old Victorian school in the centre of a large city. The heating system was not very efficient since its original installation in the first half of the twentieth century. The main rooms we used for therapy had to be supplemented with portable heaters, because the work could not be carried out in cold conditions. In any case, I would take it for granted that most of the clients would feel the cold anyway. Like most stress sufferers they had poor circulation, cold hands and feet. Their circulatory problems in many cases would have been probably classified as a medical condition. Invariably they would be receiving drug medication. An additional and, just as important, frequently undiagnosed problem would be that they suffered from fear and anxiety. An un-diagnosed large part of the problem was resultant restricted breathing.

By the time they had completed several correct breathing sessions, the shivers had gone, and I was being asked to turn the heating down!

In other parts of the building where we could only afford basic background heating, new volunteers who arrived to help, would sometimes disappear quickly, unable to cope with the low temperatures, but those who stayed usually gained a basic knowledge of breath correction, and would often say 'when I first came here I really felt the cold, but now I don't even notice it.'

A suggestion for a national energy-saving drive. Natural too.

What had happened to all these people? What had happened was that improved breathing had resulted in relax-ation of muscles. This reduced pressure or block on the blood-carrying veins, which then allowed the blood to flow more *efficiently* to the brain, spine, and round the body to the extremities of the fingers and toes, and *warm* them. Few people realise that the warmth of the blood in our veins is directly related to how we use the warmth of the sun, the earth's sole central heating system on which we all rely.

I was often amazed in the bitter Scottish winter how people would arrive for help, who complained of the cold. They often wore short-sleeved shirts T-shirts or blouses, with no pullover. They had got so used to the (to me) over-heated rarefied warmth of business, government, or educational establishments, that they assumed this was a universal norm. Many homes reflect this domestic over-heating with individuals seeming to ignore that the most important and sensible way to protect oneself in colder weather is to purchase and wear warmer clothing to deal with a drop in temperature. *Before* turning on the heating. It is as if they were ignoring self-responsibility, and assuming that something or *somebody else has the responsibility to heat them.*

I have observed that everyone who corrects their breathing saves at least 20% in heating requirements. From a national viewpoint this would be an enormous saving in artificial energy, and an equally enormous increase in health from better circulation (to which I'll refer later in this chapter). Plus a knock-on reduction in demands on the health services. In addition a great national and personal financial saving in energy costs.

You can think of our blood as the sun within us, as I suggested, our own personal central heating system. When we internalise and maintain tension, the extremities of the body, are the first to feel discomfort. Because of the invisible link between the mind and the body, cold hands to me always indicate mental tension, and poor circulation. When a system is under threat it will draw energy from its furthest distribution points in order to maintain the supply to the centre. Obviously, continuing reduction in the supply eventually leads to the breakdown of the whole system, which is how I view heart attacks, strokes, probably all other diseases.

I become really frustrated when I hear of all the advice given to elderly people about keeping warm in winter, and the highly commendable literature on energy conservation. However the one factor which would help the elderly to keep warmer naturally, and reduce national artificial energy demands, corrective breathing, is totally disregarded. The more we block our circulation, and only *we* can *unblock* it by natural means (surely the most important ecological lesson we can learn) the less artificial energy we need. Without seeming to boast, at eighty years old I have felt perfectly comfortable this past winter with an evening temperature of 55°F (plus a knee-rug! Sometimes a hot-water bottle at my back), hands and feet comfortably warm. The sole reason for this is correct breathing.

I am not suggesting that this is right for everyone, except that improved breathing leads to less reliance on artificial heating. Even 5% reduction in heating demands would create a fantastic national saving in artificial energy.

I could afford to increase the temperature, and would do so if I felt it necessary, but why bother if I am comfortable at 55°F? When I hear of sad cases of hypothermia, I know that limited breathing will have been an important contributory factor, which no caring agency would have picked up. I would suggest that the main causal factor represented a life-long self-suppression of the body's basic breathing heating system. Good circulation, preceded by good breathing, leading to the strengthening of the auto-immune system. These problems will not go away in one generation, but we can remind ourselves, as Ramacharaka predicted in *The Science of Breath,* that 'one generation of correct breathers *could regenerate* the race, and disease would be looked upon as a rarity.'

The more the circulation is self-blocked, the more artificial heating energy we have to purchase. We are constantly reminded that we are headed for a global energy crisis. I attended a University lecture some months ago on this crisis, given by an eminent energy adviser to the Government, whose doom and gloom warning was of a 5-10 year deadline for termination of North Sea gas supplies. We were left in no doubt as to the urgency of the situation, and the need to find other energy sources. Just as my clients and colleagues reported an improvement in circulation from correct breathing, many have, like myself, reduced the use of artificial heat by at least 20%. Surely a practical national educational programme on corrective respiration would result in a sizeable reduction in heating demands, assisted by publicity and media co-operation. A vast information drive would be needed, but the benefits would be far-reaching in many areas.

We might question why we were not made aware of this vital information while at school. Perhaps we need to home in on Mother Earth's laws rather than looking for life on other planets. It appears as if we do not know how to make use of life on our home planet. Has science missed the point?

I wonder what would be the attitude of the National energy companies if there was a drop in human energy demands, and therefore lower consumption and profits. Would vested interests try and inhibit the circulation of vital life-saving information? It has happened before.

You will probably have read of the rapid spread of the flames when windows and doors are opened during a house-fire. The effect of the stimulus of air on heat to spread the fire. So the intake of air through correct breath spreads the heat of the sun through the body, the sun's circulatory effect within human tissues.

Correct breathing ensures that this circulation is efficient; many people who over-breathe take *too much* air in, or the opposite, *too little*. There is a *correct* way, which restores the circulatory warmth of the sun throughout the body in a natural way.

Obviously we cannot go from seriously limited respiration to correct breathing in one easy step, it takes time and practice like any other skill or craft. The bonus is that we do already have this skill recorded in our body/mind/emotional make-up from birth. It is a matter of retrieval.

Whenever I hear of the installation of a new wind-farm I

give an internal cheer. I view them as works of art, things of beauty. I am sure we shall require an enormous expansion of this harnessing of the natural energy available to us, circulating the gifts of nature in a non-polluting way.

Twenty years or more ago I met a New Zealand ex-Air Force pilot called Bruce Cathie, a writer and brilliant mathematician. For some years Bruce had been carrying out research into the harnessing of the oceans' power to create electricity, by erecting rig-type installations on points of the earth's grid system. Bruce was positive that ample electricity to supply world demands could be obtained in this way, again circulating the energy gifts of nature in a non-polluting way. Bruce told me that his books had been confiscated by the Government and taken out of circulation.

Elsewhere in this book I may have quoted the lovely phrase 'coincidence is God's way of remaining anonymous.' Many who may read these words know exactly what I mean, if not I hope you may, perhaps sooner rather than later. Let me give you an example.

As I was writing the above words about harnessing wind power, a newspaper item the following day carried information about a Scottish-built invention to harness *wave* power, consisting of a large tube-like structure which floats on the top of the sea creating a process which generates electricity in a way that my non-scientific mind can comprehend and accept, but not *understand* if you see what I mean!

The country which has purchased the ingenious invention for generating wave-power electricity is Portugal, a country I always associate with inventive imagination. Perhaps they have been the first country to see its potential. The coincidence between me writing about Bruce Cathie's thoughts, and the simultaneous item about the wave-power electrical energy invention, both within a few hours, was for me *God's way of remaining anonymous*. Higher Power's e-mail system.

Attempting to write intuitively means writing in the dark. Coincidences such as the above are to me Higher Power's way of saying '*Yes.*' A very comforting thought.

I believe that Nature's immovable laws have already provided the answer to man's ability to extract harmlessly from the atmosphere all the energy he requires. The only restrictions are those which he imposes upon himself. Or imposed upon us by mega-power companies committed to huge profits. As Francis Thompson said in his poem *No Strange Land*:

> 'Tis ye, 'tis your estranged faces,
> Which miss the many-splendoured thing.

Nature's ability to provide all our needs is limitless. *We* have to discover them. When we are ready to let go of our egotism, and release the humility to understand and absorb it, we shall truly become partners and caretakers with Nature in understanding Earth's breathtaking mysteries. How to keep her healthy, despite taking from her all the energy we need. I refuse to call this science, which to me often appears cold, clinical and heartless. Such are not the real laws of Nature.

When we have discovered how to tap into the colossal energy renewal potential available to man himself by harnessing the power of correct breath, I believe we will be able to understand how to direct human electrical energy to reduce and reverse by correct thought and action, natural catastrophic disasters such as Global Warming. Man has been given power over the earth which he has abused, and is now facing the backlash, as Nature tries to keep her circulatory balance, to stay healthy. It is her *right*.

The power of loving thought, as distinct from thought *not* reinforced by love is the greatest power of all. From thought, all man's activities both positive and negative have resulted, and given birth to our present civilisation. Only thoughts of egotism, power, greed and materialism have produced the circulation of the harmful energies we interpret as Global Warming. Is it inconceivable that catastrophic natural disasters could fall away once we individually and collectively comprehend the miracle of Nature's healing energy. To project it through the loving thought of perfect breath, the greatest power there is? Not only to heal ourselves but the earth at the same time. I believe it is possible, can you? We have to retrieve this impeccable power of Nature from the toxic knowledge blocks within us. Trusting the circulating power opens the door to the miraculous support of unbelievably wonderful coincidental solutions to our problems.

Nevertheless we have to heal our breath first to draw on this power. It takes its own time even when we have become enlightened and determined. The respiratory muscles which either constrict or relax must become supple. We must never breathe too quickly or violently, thinking we can speed up the process. Naturally and steady is the answer, as the alchemy of the breath unlocks the information already stored in brain cells which, until now, has been locked in the vaults of the mind. This information has to be decoded and externalised into right spiritual action, which can be circulated on an unseen level, and picked up by others ready to absorb its truths.

A great groundswell of unstoppable energy would then be circulated, an energy which could heal mankind of violence and negative thought forms in an unbelievably short space of time. This decoded understanding through the power of right breath has to be externalised into right action, spiritual action, which in its circulation would completely override the present global destructive malaise.

Have you heard the story about the monkeys on a tropical island who discovered a new and better way to crack certain nuts, hitherto not known to them? No other monkeys until then had discovered the ingenious way to do this. However within an inconceivably short space of time the monkeys on an adjacent island who had no contact with them also began to use exactly the same method to open the nuts! The circulation of information by the power of animal instinctive energy. We have the same power, and we are supposed to be a higher species!

That, I am certain is how loving spiritual energy can be circulated globally. There are those who forecast doom and gloom for the future. The circulation of the power of spiritual energy has the power to dissolve without violence the violence in all its forms which causes so many to despair of any solution to mankind's misery.

We are all influenced by each other, that is inevitable. We are in constant contact with others, or they contact us. There is however, an additional factor which has often re-occurred in my life, and in this I am not alone.

One of my first and continuing experiences in the circulatory nature of unseen energy is the fact that we then become open to extraordinary coincidences. We may go into a bookshop for instance, and as I mentioned in another chapter, discover a certain book for which we have been searching, or need to read, which quite literally (!) falls off a shelf in front of us. We are delighted but often ask ourselves how could this be? The answer is of course, and I am prepared to be challenged, that there exists an inexplicable law, inexplicable by the laws by which we were raised and educated. It is nevertheless an alternative powerful law which we would be wise not to ignore. It always makes me feel, *cosy*. Safe and befriended by a loving energy which has a *sense of humour*.

The book has been important, as if it was waiting for me. I may not read it for years, but I *know I have to buy it*. More often I know I am meant to have it now because it answers questions for which I have been searching, also because it is comforting to read of others who have been travelling a similar but not identical path to myself. Our coincidental life experiences makes me more confident of the path I have chosen, and the circulation of the information within the book is intended for many others besides myself.

Other books, people or events have appeared in amazing diverse ways, often when something has not gone according to plan, and yet the altered course of the day has led to an unplanned meeting which has resulted in being given vital spiritual information.

A vital book, person or happening has come my way. It is an occurrence which has led me to alter negative thoughts when a planned activity appears to go awry. Nowadays I am inclined to ask the Universe what pleasant surprise it has in store for me instead. *Man supposes, God disposes.* This has led me to the truth of another statement, often quoted to reduce the tension in apparent disaster. '*Don't sweat the small stuff, it's all small stuff.*'

I remember being aware of much of the information I have shared in this chapter when I was a young child, not in an intellectual way, but knowing for certain that there was a great power which could solve problems, and being frustrated that my parents did not apparently use it. They seemed to prefer, to use the negative approach that difficulties were insurmountable. I knew that I had the answer to the solution but could not convince them.

I did not then as a small child and do not now think, that any difficulty is insurmountable, if we bring the right energy to it. Sadly my earlier certainties became overlaid by childhood conditioning, and I had to go through many apparent problems in my middle years before I was able to retrieve them with gratitude through correct breath training. The energy had merely remained dormant in my mind, because I had been too frightened to go on trusting it. I had blocked it off, but now regained the courage to trust it again.

Through the magic of breath.

I do not know how much time is allowed to us before the spiritual evolution necessary to save our planet will demand our urgent and undivided attention. If a quantum leap takes place, it could happen with amazing speed. We may not be able to avert considerable disaster until we are literally on our knees. '*To those who understand no explanation is necessary, to those who will not understand no explanation will suffice.*' I am sure that whoever wrote these words will not mind me quoting them.

At this present time enlightenment and its circulation are really our only ammunition, For the first time in history offensive or defensive weapons cannot be an answer. There is a saying '*Give a plant a chink of light and it will grow to it.*' Thank goodness there are many chinks of light in existence towards which it is safe to grow. For me the priority is the understanding of the correct breath. The light never goes out, even if we shut our eyes to it. When our own light does begin to grow, it positively helps to generate the light of others, the millions of all our counter parts become dazzling, and the earth begins to heal as we heal.

All our thoughts and actions circulate out into the great stream of human energy consciousness, and represent a rippling effect of energy which attaches itself to a similar energy like itself. It affects and hangs around in the atmosphere as a benign or negative influence, and attracts back to itself the quality of its nature, for good or ill.

We need to take responsibility for that vibrational personal energy we circulate. Saving our material rubbish is nowhere near enough, our negative words and thoughts become recorded in the atmosphere either as a benign or toxic energy. We cannot see this energy, but we can *feel* it. I am sure that my negative thoughts and actions damage the earth, I do not want them to circulate in this way. Being mindful of my breath keeps me safe, in touch with Nature and is by far the most powerful way to offer my carbon footprint to the reversal of Global Warming.

JUST CIRCULATE LOVE.

Chapter 19

THE SUFFERING
THERAPIST

THE TITLE OF THIS CHAPTER may cause you to raise your eyebrows; surely therapists are meant to be past the suffering stage of their lives, or how could they present themselves as being able to show others how to heal their own particular suffering?

I have met numerous therapists from many disciplines during the past twenty-five years. The ones who have impressed me most for the depth of their wisdon and compassion (two essential qualities in this work) have been those who have at some point in their lives experienced considerable stress, pain or tragedy. Not necessarily all three, but in coming through their own personal trials and discovering a philosophy which has enabled them to solve their crisis, they have discovered a way of transcending life's even more acute problems.

In contemplating these personal tribulations most of these people will admit that they had indeed attracted their own unhappiness. Discovering a way to overcome and rise above it had given them a visionary understanding of an approach for healing which they could pass on to others, knowing that the intense suffering and despair being experienced by a client is also a great catalyst for beneficial life changes.

Now I am not saying that you have got to go out and find ways of suffering in order to be a therapist, but from my own personal experience, and as Jung once said. 'You can only heal (or be of help to a fellow sufferer) to the level that you have suffered yourself.' Too many of the therapeutic practices approach balancing mental stress from an *intellectual* level. No one I have met who suffered from stress problems moved forward in their lives until their *hearts* began to heal, and this change only began to come about when the intellectual brain took a back seat. Some therapists become disillusioned when their clients *refuse* to heal after weeks and weeks of mental battling, and numerous expensive appointments. Doctors of course usually have another tablet to prescribe, find that a certain medicine may not suit their patient, so the prescription is changed. Many mind-orientated counsellors have only one arrow to their bow. It probably has a fancy name, but when it fails to do the trick, it is all too easy to blame the client rather than the process.

Of course some people seek help believing that therapy is like taking medicine which is supposed to do the trick with no help from the patient, and many people believe that is how therapeutic change happens, with no effort from the client. In that case, however well-trained the therapist, failure is bound to be experienced.

The former alcoholics or drug addicts who have turned their lives around are often to be found at the centre of some project to help others free themselves from these addictions. Unfortunately, from such centres I have visited in the past, the tobacco habit has still been very obvious. My experience as a therapist has convinced me that freeing oneself from the nicotine addiction is more difficult than giving up heroin. The link between the oral satisfaction of a cigarette between the lips and frustrated breast or bottle feeding has always been so obvious to me, but is seldom mentioned in addiction literature.

The problem of immaturity is invariably behind all addictions or stress, a news item this week suggests that 70% of the population have some fear or phobic problem. So many questions present themseves when hearing such figures; for instance, can immature parents produce mature children?

When my first child was born, one of my deepest thoughts was how little any part of my education had prepared me for the experience of giving birth, the great gap in understanding how to be able to manage this life/death experience, to which there must be total commitment, and no going back. You can't change your mind in the middle of labour; in fact giving in to the demands of nature which had to be listened to, created the sensation that I was disobeying the rules and training of my early years. So far had my conditioning taken me from my deepest links.

The damage which had been done to my true instincts by the culture of the times had produced deep grooves of disassociation from nature's unalterable laws, together with the ability to flow with them, so intense in childhood.

I have never heard others express these sensations in so many words, but the same experience must happen to the majority of young mothers struggling to come to terms with the demands of parenthood. As my awareness of this gulf strengthened, it occurred to me that elephants look after their young babies and mothers in a more sensitive way than the human race. Although I did not give birth to my second child under a tree as I had intended, like some native mothers, the second time I was in charge in my own home, and the visiting midwife said that it was the happiest birth she had ever attended!

This separation of self from nature is, I am sure, at the root of virtually all our problems. We are beginning to pay for our worship of the material dimension, and the enormous increase in anxiety and nervous problems in a high proportion of the community is the irrefutable symptom of our pain.

The life-styles which are our substitute for life, create addictions in many forms such as substances, sadness, depression, fear, phobias, anxiety, bad health.

For all the above, we have to go back to the root of living by the laws of nature if we are to heal. The fundamental law of nature is to take in life through our breath, both inhalation and exhalation completed to a *correct formula*, and those who do this correctly will begin to heal themselves. The therapist who understands the rules of breath will have a head start above all other alternative processes, whether their training has a medical or complementary basis.

I have never known a therapist to suffer from the frustration of being *stuck* with a client where the latter wants to heal their lives, who has completed a process of breathing correction. It is amazing, almost miraculous, to observe the reduction in what the therapeutic world calls *presenting symptoms* after two or three sessions of corrective respiration. The disappearance of endless tears, meaningless chatter about countless symptoms, blaming circumstances, blaming others. A couple of breathing training sessions and you become aware that the person is beginning to catch a glimpse of a real identity beneath their despair. Their own inner guide.

Within the space of a few weeks the sufferer's relationship problems seem to drift away or become solved, they have decided to change their job, pursue a course of study, their overall health has improved. If you mention their former problems, they seem puzzled as if all that happened to a different person. The miracle is that all this has occurred without any counselling, hardly any conversation, and certainly no analysing.

The growing addiction to using the power of correct breath begins to provide a sure and safe source of retrieving the feel-good factor once provided by the other addictive excuses for living, with no side-effects except for confidence, hope, eventually joy, improved health. The ability to take right action, and regain self-respect, and respect for others.

This work on addictive breathing cuts across all boundaries of class, culture, race and religion. I believe it is the missing link in our confusion and despair, as we look for world healing in all the wrong places.

I believe that we need hundreds of thousands of breathing therapists to introduce the art of correct breathing to all the walking wounded stressful people who crowd the waiting rooms in health centres, or occupy hospital beds. We are told that 90% of those who seek medical help are really suffering from stress.

Everything that lives has a frequency; that frequency fluctuates in a human being according to our health and vitality. As we raise this power through respiratory efficiency we find that we seem to be able to sail through what were former difficulties. People who breathe correctly will also not be slaves, they cannot be bullied.

To all women who are in abusive relationships the art of breath management will enable you to free yourself from your abuser, because the higher frequency must always override the lower. Anyone who abuses will have a low fequency, and if you trust your breath, circumstances will change in your favour in a seemingly miraculous way. I have seen this happen time and time again.

There is so much wisdom available to a therapist who has undertaken the discipline of repairing their breathing pattern; this wisdom supercedes intellectual training, which seems to overlook the fact that everyone possesses their own innate ability to self-heal. Once *breath* is the therapist, a unique and wonderful self-counselling relationship commences of *self with self.*

The addiction to correct breathing, which instantly draws us into the natural cycle of the earth's vibrational field, is always waiting for us like a patient child stuck with an impatient and irritable parent. Its side-effects of confidence, assertiveness and right action cuts across national boundaries, its unseen waveforms are faster than the speed of light. It can create a boundary which cannot be violated by violence, for violence is an immature energy which must be subservient to higher energy. To save the Earth we are going to be forced to generate this higher energy, by re-finding a great power we all possess but have mislaid, and which is the only energy powerful enough to dissolve the cancerous energy of violence spreading its diseased tentacles worldwide. It is a degenerative vibration causing chaos to us all and the Earth herself, for the Earth pulsates on a vibration of love, Alpha energy, and is harmed by any vibration lower than love.

Therapists are thought of as people trained in some sort of therapeutic discipline which is made available to help those who suffer. I find it difficult to empathise with any so-called healing practice which does not include the enlightenment that correct breathing brings to anyone who offers their servces to reduce the pain of others. The help we offer must be compatible with the laws of nature whatever the therapeutic approach. Results may not be seen instantly, depending on how long the client has been abusing these laws. If the therapist is grounded in right breathing they will not be affected by thoughts of personal failure by the length of time it may take for the *penny to drop.*

Considering the suffering to which mankind has subjected the planet, she is needing many thousands of Earth therapists who are vibrating on her same wave-length, in order for the gigantic turn-around that she must make in order for her to re-stabilise. It is understandable that as our Earth-Mother she may no longer be able to support or tolerate those who are using her energies in a parasitic way. Those who think of her as inanimate or able to remain forever tolerant of our abuse will have to re-think their actions.

We have to accept the fact that our relentless development of the God of science detached from the heart impulse has brought us to the edge of a global collapse. We might wonder if there is a vital area of life-regenerative energy that our science-worship has ignored and suppressed. *There is.* This regenerative energy is the only one now available to us. It can be regained by re-surfacing the required information from within, through the alchemy of correct breath, which infuses the information through the blood stream to the brain. It is then translated by that pure flow of unpolluted information into re-nurturing nature within us, resulting in earth healing corrective action. The process is the same as that which heals the individual, its retrieval gives us the information as to the Earth's true needs. As far as I can see, without it, the existing public information on avoiding climate change seems anaemic.

Knowledge of the earth's true nature is encapsulated within the customs and intuitive information possessed by some of the so-called *primitive* tribes of the world that we have *civilised.* Jung said most aptly, 'Let us forgive our European selves for what we have done to the African within us.'

A true therapist, I am convinced, has retrieved their intuitive information from within, and it acts as a firm basis for working with people who have lost themselves. Unless you have this foundation you can be badly affected by the negative energy of your clients and become a suffering stress victim yourself.

I have been approached by many *qualified* therapists in the past two decades whose self-confidence has been badly shaken by trying to treat people suffering from many forms of stress. They have been overwhelmed by the formidable negative energy of their patient, and have decided to give up their practice, because they have become so badly affected by the dark places within the psyche of the client.

The therapist may have possessed a string of paper qualifications, have impressive notepaper, but the intellectual bias
of their training did not ensure the rugged spiritual strengths
given by a training in corrective breathing, which I believe
must be the initial grounding for all who offer themselves as
therapists. This grounding, which brings a sense of humour,
practicality and wholesomeness, essential to a therapeutic
session, will assist by creating a positive invisible atmospheric
energy wthin a room, which will be picked up and absorbed
by the person who is suffering, even if no words have yet
been spoken.

In order to be of any use to a stress sufferer, a therapist
must have rediscovered the joy of living themselves, find
delight in small things, the ability to see 'Heaven in a grain
of sand.' Such attributes can only be gained from an inner
certainty of having discovered the truth of what life is meant
to be about. Without this confidence we will affect our client
with our negative carbon footprint.

A therapist with such qualities will never become
de-energised by the other person's negativity. Their strengths,
based on a sure foundation, will always be able to be quickly
replenished. Such people will be like gold dust among the
many thousands who have lost the way. They are capable of
soaring above the cold psycho-analytical approach behind
much therapeutic training, which is so often the best that
seems to be on offer.

Graduates of such methods through no fault of their own,
are thrown out at the deep end on the world scene of chaotic
human behaviour. In the arena of psychiatry, so many graduates with impressive paper qualifications, but still infants
in personal maturity, will dispense mind-altering drugs, or
pass the client on to yet another specialist. Such specialists
themselves may be sadly lacking in the rock hard sureness of
spiritual certainties which I see as essential for anyone who

has the temerity to offer themselves as a help for those in the turmoil of acute stress. Spirituality does not of course mean organised religion.

The above words do not in any way lessen my respect for those in the field of psychiatry whose humility of approach has earned my profound admiration; I wish there were more like them.

I have met many students hoping to offer themselves on the therapeutic market as counsellors, whose main subject was psychology, but whose immaturity renders them totally unable to encompass the coal-face of human stress drama. Them themselves become personally stressed when the going gets tough, and the client does not respond positively to therapy. Failure on the client's part to make progress will be seen as the fault of the client, rather than inaequacies in the therapist's training, which has been totally lacking in anything other than an intellectual approach.

There are many phrases in which a few words embrace an enormous wealth of truth. One is embodied in that seldom quoted piece of wisdom, 'The eyes of suffering see the furthest.' The therapist who sees the furthest has probably gone through his or her own personal suffering, been strengthend by the experience, and seen in retrospect how much of that pain had been self-made. It finally appeared as a helpful rather then a negative period of learning the unchangeable truths of right living. Another common but so true saying then becomes applicable, 'don't sweat the small stuff, it's all small stuff.'

A therapist who has been thus self-healed will be able to empathise rather than be swamped by the pain of others, will be much more likely to help the client to come to terms with their problems, see them in a more illuminative way, and be able to take the journey forward to self-healing. A therapist who sees their own problems as problems has not yet learned the other succinct phrase, 'there are no problems, only solutions.'

In reading of the lives of many famous men and women who have laid the foundation stones of present psychological training on which numerous therapies are based, we read time after time that their childhood had been beset with tragedy and problems. In later life understanding and reversing the effect of such trauma has led them to their life-work of helping others.

I admire their courage in developing their own particular line of psychological reasoning, but believe that much of their work with patients entailed months and years of frequent appointments which could have been reduced if they had also included work on corrective breathing. For example I ask myself if Freud would have died of cancer of the throat if he had breathed correctly. Jung smoked a pipe constantly, and ended his days as a rather angry old man. If he had healed his respiratory pattern, his passing might have been more peaceful.

Even so, Jung's remarks when confronted with *problem* children were 'never mind the child, bring me the parents.' They have remained with me frequently when I have been asked to work with a disturbed child. All disturbed children will also have a disturbed breathing pattern, and I have always tried to involve parents very closely in the process of repairing their own respiratory limitations irrespective of the child's problems.

When parents have done so, there is an immediate improvement in the child's disturbances within a very short period. Of course not all parents are willing to face up to the fact that perhaps their own behaviour patterns had set off the upset within the child, and it needs a great deal of tact, I might say *guile*, on the part of the therapist to bring about understanding and co-operation by the parents.

I recall many occasions when parents and child took on as part of their homework the responsibility of correcting each other's breathing in an enlightened atmosphere full of fun and affection. It worked wonderfully well, acompanied by love and humour.

Jung would possibly not have made his pungent remarks on seeing the parent rather than the child if he had not been able to recall his own less than happy childhood, with a mother who suffered regular periods of mental illness.

The knowledge of humanity and breadth of compassion which must lie behind the work and words of the skilled therapist, what to say and what not to say, are skills unobtainable by intellectual training of the mind. These gifts, together with intuition (a therapist's most valuable tool), must come from the heart, and use of the right creative brain. The right use of the heart does not imply sentimentality as so many may think. Such skills are worth their weight in gold.

In a therapeutic session they are invaluable and essential to a therapist, and never more so when he or she has *walked the walk* of healing.their own personal suffering. Not to have done so, and merely *talked the talk* will lead to the suffering of the failed therapist.

As Jung said,

'YOU CAN ONLY HEAL TO THE LEVEL
YOU HAVE SUFFERED YOURSELF.'

Chapter 20

BREATHING AND
THERAPISTS

NO DOUBT, LIKE THOUSANDS OF OTHERS, I find among the pages of the daily newspaper articles I wish to retain, because of an inexplicable coincidence or interest. For me the concerns match issues I have just raised or wish to raise in a chapter of this book. Often however, the content level is such that I despair at the lack of general in-depth understanding about solutions to issues which any intelligent 10-year old could solve. Other articles may give key information to questions I have been asking myself for years, forgotten about, and there is the answer.

That day I feel too tired or can't find the scissors, put it off until the next day, when another paper arrives, which puts yesterday's on the back burner. It then gets mislaid among the other piles of 'important' information to be perused when time allows. Usually time does not immediately allow. Days later, because the subject has been often on my mind, I search frantically for the paper or magazine, only to remember that it has been put out with the refuse collection. Does this sound familiar?

I live in Scotland. The main item of today's news quoted Glasgow's crime and violence figures soaring to a record high yet again. I wonder if anyone has carried out research into the religious affinity, if any, of those who commit the violence. I've never noticed this figure within a news report.

Even today when fatal stabbings in London have reached such a disturbing level.

Years ago I read that the possible source of the violence in Ireland could be traced to the period in childhood we call the 'terrible twos' or the tantrum stage. This is the time when the personality and character of the child has to develop and needs to find expression, but has not the requisite maturity to verbalise very strong feelings. Resultant frustration is vented in screaming, biting, rolling on the floor and other symptoms of intense anger, so familiar to parents trying to contain the behaviour in a positive and yet loving way. Transfer this scenario to the Ireland of several centuries ago, a nation controlled by a rigid and authoritarian mix of patriarchal religion, politics and great estates of wealthy landowners. The latter required an enormous army of impoverished and dependent slaves in the form of the local population who depended upon such despotic control for all their needs. Carrying out demeaning work for their barest livelihood and Heavenly approval.

Not to toe the line would invite excommunication from God and the loss of one's home and livelihood.

The article I read on the Irish violence suggested that it was the direct result of small children at the tantrum age being severely punished and repressed at what was probably then seen, and may still be, as evidence of the Devil arising within the child. Added to which I would suspect that female workers with small children at this age of important development would have to keep the child suppressed and respectful, not to annoy their priests, lords and masters (or mistresses). The obvious way was probably punitive, unjustified chastisement of the child, or risk loss of basic needs.

Such habits of child rearing are hard to change, and although the article I read did not suggest, as I have, the historical probability for the present problem of much of the violence in Ireland, it does makes sense to me. It can result in an adult outwardly too keen to please other people, while holding hate in the heart. An intuitive observer can recognise the underlying conflict which conceals a deep and dangerous anger.

I have no intention to cause offence to anyone from the much-loved and beautiful country of Ireland, a land which, probably unrecognised, is responsible for influencing our own rather staid national characteristics to be infused with a sense that magic and mystery can still have its rightful place in the human psyche.

The scenario of early repressed strong anger incorrectly managed by parents as mentioned above is, I am positive, the main source of many social problems, not only recently in Ireland, but worldwide, probably from the same causal core.

Such symptoms do not of course apply to any one nation, but can also be frequently encountered in a therapeutic setting, where an over-pleasing manner by a client can almost overnight turn into an antagonism of equal energy, which can challenge the self-confidence of a 'highly-trained' therapist. In fact I know of some psychotherapists who will only offer three appointments to a client, having previously been badly affected by a growing animosity from a client in the therapeutic situation, by which they feel too threatened to allow continuation of that therapy. Suppressed client anger has come to the surface, which a trained therapist is meant to deal with in order to *diffuse* and understand such strong emotion. This anger can seem very frightening if it appears to be projected towards the therapist. It is actually part of the necessary release of deep suppression, which has to happen and be dealt with correctly for personal growth to take place.

At one time I too would have felt inadequate if confronted by the force of suppressed anger as it broke surface, but for many years I have been in possession of a therapeutic 'secret weapon' which has enabled me not to be afraid of the anger. Through correct breathing a client will affinitise with its source; the frustrated small child within will be able to re-associate with this angry child, and heal it and themselves through the insights revealed through the lens of right breath. In fact I usually mention such a possibility at the commencement of therapy, so that the client receives forward warning of the 'anger syndrome intensity', and understands that this will be a symptom for a limited period only. As it comes to the surface, the breath will itself reveal the source of the anger. Self-understanding reduces the sense that you are controlled by forces beyond your control.

I have discovered that all requests for therapeutic help and advice mask symptoms of anger suppression. The child comes into being with a great sense of love. It grows and needs to express itself, long *before* it has the words to verbalise. Because its love is so powerful, its anger is equally powerful. If that anger is treated without understanding, and the child is punished and made to feel bad, the anger can become 'swallowed', but is still present, registered both within the mind and body as a suppression.

The child then becomes afraid, because its love and anger has not been understood. To the child its anger is part of its *legitimate* love for itself, in fact *is itself*, love. Having been denied self-expression all it has left is fear. In good therapy that fear has to be lifted, which then releases the anger which has suppressed the love. I see this process as resembling a three-ingredient sandwich. Take one layer off, it reveals the next, take this layer off, the last and best; love can then be revealed. There is a saying in the breathing work, again by Leonard Orr, that 'love brings up everything like and unlike itself.' In other words the love cannot re-surface until fear and anger is resolved and dissolved, for to be effective and long-lasting love must dominate.

The power and intensity of repressed childhood anger boiling over in an adult can be terrifying, unless you can understand and know how to neutralise and deflect it. In our culture today of violence and terror-motivated crime, addictions and sexual perversion, such understanding can save lives in a threatening situation.

Society finds it difficult to see all these as arising from badly managed childhoods, but I believe it is the truth. From what one reads and hears via the Press and TV, prison seems to have little effect, and unless and until our Society gives sufficient time, attention and finance to prevention of the abuse of the child, the adult violence will continue. By abuse I do not only mean the physical and sexual abuse publicly reported, but the colossal abuse of lack of understanding of the care and nurturing required in childhood, in order that these tender plants are brought into full bloom in the same way that devoted gardeners care for their plants. *The most important time for that attention is in the earliest stages to ensure good rooting and growth. This is also true with the tender young human plant.*

What is suppressed in a young child will not go away. It remains, festers and smoulders, until the explosive energy of adolescence through the misuse of the child by parents and society, creates a man-made sub-community of fearful individuals, bullies and martyrs by which the bottled-up anger is released, and expressed in a violent manner. Aggressive eruptions appear to be occurring with greater frequency in communities country-wide, more dramatically recorded in our cities, but increasingly in smaller towns and communities. It is surprising that so many parents do not seem aware that their teenage youngsters have been responsible for appalling acts of violence, saying that these young people were quiet and no problem at home. Is it because many of them were still constricted by childhood fears of such parents, but felt able to break free and wreck their aggression on Society, within the apparent safety of the gang culture?

Rural areas contain their own horror stories, where the benefits of living nearer to Nature have been darkened by the effect on young lives of unnatural and unloving parenting. Human volcanoes exist everywhere, nowhere is safe from man's inhumanity to man, the direct repercussion from man's inhumanity to the child.

I refer back to the possible explanation offered as the basis for the decades of violent turbulence in Northern Ireland. The suppression of the child's powerful attempts to express itself at the formative tantrum period due to religious and civil oppression of the masses of the poor. This perhaps later attached itself to an aggressive political party to express in a 'legitimate' way the pent-up hatreds of childhood. The saying 'the sins of the Fathers contaminating the third and fourth generation' might clearly be recognised in such a scenario.

The peasants, the bulk of the population, were dependent on the landowner for every crust of bread or hope of employment. If keeping small, noisy children severely suppressed, quiet, and apparently non-existent in order to have food and employment, small wonder that the child had to be trained in fear and subservience.

It is a law of Nature that everything suppressed must eventually be expressed. Let us give thanks that the Irish nightmare seems to have been replaced by the delightful emergence of the Irish gift of creativity, humour and sense of mysticism without which, as Einstein tells us, 'we may as well be dead.'

You may ask what has the foregoing and subsequent sections in this chapter to do with Breathing for the Therapist? Well I'm coming to that - eventually. Have patience! A therapist has to be able to empathise, possibly back several generations, in order to help a client free themselves from the binding chains of fear. The word empathy is a very important one; it does not mean sympathy, which I regard as condescension, relegating the sympathiser to a higher level than the individual who is being sympathised with. *Empathy* is an intuitive way of *associating* oneself with another person's problems. By introducing the power of correct breathing into any situation, it is possible to radically reduce the frequency of appointments. Discussion is then between adult and adult. Such empathy is not lightly attained, it helps if you have been there and worn the t-shirt. You have to have 'suffered' yourself, but discovered how to transform that experience into joy. In other words redeemed your own fear and anger.

A recent news report tells us that maternity provision in Britain is the worst in Europe, with the exception of Poland and Czechoslovakia. Now how could this be in such a *civilised* country as ours? I recall deciding after experiencing the birth of my first child in a small town maternity unit, that I would have my next child squatting under a tree, a recognised practice in countries such as India. The caring aspect had been non-existent.

I eventually realised that the chief reason for this decision was my growing certainty that all women in labour have the right to their own special environment in which to give birth. Before this illuminating vision, I was still under the impression that everyone knew better than me about how birth should be handled. Now I realise that the emotional surroundings are as important as the intellectual knowledge provided by the birth attendants. To ignore the former, as was my first experience, can make the work of the mother and, by implication, that of the baby so much more difficult. Cerebral dominance by doctors or nurses creates a tension around the mother, which at a deep level of need to protect means subconsciously having to *defend* herself from the *carers* around her, instead of being able to devote all her energy to the overwhelming demands of the birth process.

Looking back, it was this lack of *emotional* support at such a critical time, which I now realise resulted in a year of post-birth shock trauma, which spoiled that first year of being a new parent, and able to enjoy my lovely baby.

In hindsight it was the sheer *clinical inhumanity* which pervaded that first birth experience, trying to control severe labour pains, and not to cry out while having to lie there in the main ward on visitors' afternoon, with a number of visiting fathers sitting around. Being refused permission to go into a side-ward, to be alone, a natural instinct, and finally being sick and waters breaking occurring simultaneously while trying to make polite conversation with my husband, and trying not to cry out. *Only then did they bring the screens.* No one had told me *anything* about what to expect in the progress of labour.

I only realise now the *legitimacy* of my subsequent anger as I have finally lost the need to conform without a sensible reason to do so. The lack of kindness, empathy, encouraging words at that critical time still has the power to evoke a deep sense of outrage, as one continually hears of this lack of compassion by attending professionals supposed to be helping the mother in labour. Labour pains are reckoned to be equivalent to first-degree torture, because such pain in varying degree of severity inevitably accompanies the act of giving birth. There is no excuse for those who are paid to assist the process to exhibit such frequent examples of man's inhumanity to man, or women in this case.

In retrospect I remember the legitimate despair I later felt, but did not think it valid to allow to surface as I assumed 'they' knew better. The only time in that seven days after the birth, except for one-off bath training of the baby that I was allowed access to my new healthy baby, was at feeding-time. Strictly every four hours, and not between 10pm and 6am. No chance to hold my baby as I needed, to deepen bonding, to learn from intuition so many little signs of recognition to which every mother has a right. The natural development of the nurturing instinct which can only come from contact.

All we mothers had to do was lie there while the babies were in a downstairs nursery. You had the feeling that the babies belonged to the nursing staff, and the mothers were there on sufferance! Nowadays (not possible in my 80th year!) I would have stormed downstairs and taken my baby in my arms, and dared them to interfere. The reason given was that the mothers needed the rest. I am sure that particular regime ensured that being denied the closeness of proper bonding made me feel exhausted, helpless and depressed in that first year, as we had both been deprived of an important post-birth close relationship. After all the baby is inside one for nine months, there must still be a deep need for direct close bodily contact after birth. This can only happen in a restful, nurturing environment.

Our first experience of life must never happen in a factory production-line approach.

These days, of course, mothers are ejected from hospital so soon after birth that they never get time for what I think is a very necessary rest. Having spent eight formative years in an agricultural setting I still retain strong memories of the farm stockman insisting that prospective animal mothers-to-be were always given appropriate time to adjust to a new environment before birth, and never moved into a new one immediately after the event.

Pigs in particular will eat their young if their peace is disrupted after farrowing. The human species needs just as much understanding! I read once that the pig is the animal whose metabolism most closely resembles that of humans.

My next two babies were born at home. *I* was in charge, and gave myself and my babies time to get to know each other. The visiting midwife said that one was the happiest birth she had ever attended. Confirmation that listening to my true feelings produced right results. It was still some years before listening to myself became my first rather than second priority. My conditioning was still too often persuading me that 'they', that is, other people, knew better than myself what was good for me.

Obviously I do not include any existing excellent and caring midwives and doctors in my remarks about the birth environment. I only tell of my own experience, but I do know from many young mothers and midwives themselves that the caring provision is all too often absent even now. Fifty years on from when I first gave birth. It was only later that I read about the wonderful work of two French obstetricians, Drs. Leboyer and Odent. *Then* I realised what should by right be the ideal birthing environment for every woman. Sadly I know of no other British counterparts. There is no substitute for intuitive caring birthing professionals.

A patriarchal, over-cerebral macho-minded mentality springing from an unconscious Calvanistic mind-set still poisons the atmosphere in many maternity units. It is death to the environment necessary for a satisfying birth experience for mother and baby, and probably contributes very often to a difficult birth which otherwise might have gone smoothly. Women and progressive *loving* midwives must have a much greater say in the design, function and atmosphere of birthing units.

As long as we have a male-dominated majority making critical decisions over an experience which, with due respect, they can never experience personally, proper progress will be slow. Never having personally experienced this primal peak experience themselves, how can they empathise with the irrevocable loss to the vital natural needs of mother and baby by ignoring the importance of what I can only describe as a necessary beautiful birth ambience? Of all the priorities and energy we expend on other aspects of what we call civilised existence, many are reduced into insignificance beside the one event which if not managed with sensitivity and enlightened loving competence, can affect negatively the future lives of mother and child.

The mother has quite enough work to do in responding to the inner movements of her child, to have to feel as if she is being threatened by a beta (stress) environment created by those meant to be assisting her.

It does not surprise me to learn that our maternity provision is rated so low in the European league tables, or our pregnancy deaths the highest.

I write at length concerning this issue, because as a therapist re-teaching correct breathing, its beneficial effect on easier births has to be understood and empathised with, before many stressful individuals can be assisted by sensitive therapy to make progress in all aspects of their lives. Including childbirth, if one is a female. I believe poor breathing to be a main factor in conception problems. Correct breathing has a long-term influence on physical mental, emotional balance, and the circulation of the blood. The birth experience if mishandled can create a block of malfunctioning cells which continually send their damaged vibration to the outer surface of the human structure, restricting maturation.

As I paused for a coffee break and to have a quick look at the daily paper, the first page two headline that caught my eye read 'Busy NHS leaves no time for caring.'

A further article revealed that Scotland has almost twice the birth fatality rate of any other Western nation.

The various news items quoted which have so concerned me since I started this article, represent our direct inheritance from the ice-cold mind set directed towards children of an un-loving and un-spiritual culture, whatever its religious face. It has badly damaged our children down the ages. The future parents. A heartless scientific ideology has stunted the correct natural growth of countless children reared under its poisonous influence. I believe that the long shadow of man's inhumanity to the child has become a virus more deadly than the physical ones which fill our hospital wards.

You may think the preceding pre-amble rather lengthy if you refer to the title of this chapter 'Breathing and Therapists'. I make no apologies because anyone who calls themselves a therapist, (a much scoffed-at word) will frequently be faced by a lethal cocktail of negative attitudes towards life which will confront them in their therapeutic practice. In my experience no amount of *talking* therapy is going to change the negative thinking or fear of life which became embedded in the psyche of their clients often from birth onwards during the most formative periods of their lives. *The cement has set hard.*

In our daily lives, we are often confronted by different household breakages which require a certain solvent and glue in order to effect a repair. Usually only that particular substance will solve the problem.

In the human condition I give everlasting thanks that there *is* a solvent which acts as a permanent glue to effect repair to a person who has been damaged in some way. That *glue* is correct breathing. Whatever the presenting problem, the source of the mind-set that has attracted that problem will always be found in childhood, and the child's breathing will have become affected by fear. The intransigence of its severity can present a problem for which there may seem no solution. It takes a brave therapeutic heart to confront an extremely deeply-seated fear which can present itself as intense hostility or over-desire to please, each symptom an iron-clad defence mechanism, which seems to imply, 'I want to change my life, but I'm not going to change myself.' Almost like a smoker asking to be cured of the smoking habit, as long as they can still smoke.

Often the 'three appointment only' therapist will be able to claim success, since they have applied their cerebrally taught training methods by the recommended recipe, and the client goes away to think it all through, before long ending up in another therapeutic consulting room. The original therapist is never put into the position of admitting anything other than another success story. 'I prescribed the therapy, if it didn't work, the client will not have taken it in, it's no longer my responsibility. *Anyway I don't have any other resource skills to offer.'*

It is obviously ethical for a therapist to tell a client that it is not possible for them to assist that person with their problem, and can suggest someone else who may be able to help. I wonder how often that happens. I still believe that without breath knowledge the problem will never be fully healed, but the client of course has the right to refuse to explore the correction of their respiration. *I* did not have the right prescription until I had discovered correct breathing, and how it has worked for me, and for so many others over three decades of experience. It showed me how to solve my own problems, and that this solution was already within me, no doubt revealed by the opening of additional brain cells which had become dormant due to lack of cellular oxygen. I have certainly never applied the three-appointment only principle in my therapeutic practice. In understanding the process of corrective breathing, (sadly as yet too few therapists are trained in this work), I realise I have been given a golden key to help others to open the door to their pain and let the light in. This miraculous panacea has now helped thousands of people to take responsibility to help and heal themselves. Other therapists, trained in breathwork will I am sure endorse my words.

The light of illumination is always there. It can beam into the darkest stagnant corners of the mind and spirit to change, erase and convert all past pain to healing. Remember Jung said 'you can only heal to the level you have suffered yourself.' I would add the rider that you have then converted your own suffering into wisdom and insight. Thereby healing your own pain.

The problems of our society today, highlighted graphically in the daily news, is revealing a degree of stress intensity whose intransigence remains unmoved by mainstream stress management therapies. The complexity of the addictive scene, the pill poppers of all classes and all ages, is ensuring a dangerously high percentage of mental illness, burnout, breakdown and sheer unhappiness in every community. Much of it goes on behind closed doors, only revealed when a fatality, random act of violence, or horrific family break-down is revealed.

Sheer unrelieved unhappiness in our society is running like a tainted stream below the surface of apparent harmony. Its presence is producing an army of 'walking wounded', who are looking for a way to make sense of their lives.

It has also produced another army of counsellors, thera-pists, New Age, (isn't every new day a New Age?) of alternative disciplines and techniques, healers, psychics etc. All part of a national and international First-Aid 'patch-up' process to help the millions who are struggling to find themselves. Any integrity of the therapist will ensure that 'nothing good is ever wasted'.

I have found that those who are most successful in any of these fields, are those who have experienced personal stress in its many forms, and have found the way through the eye of the needle by which all must pass to find this 'true self'.

They must be detached from personal involvement in the client's problems. Without being directive, enable the client to make personal growth in order to be able to solve what appeared to be unsolvable problems, which had been causing them intolerable stress for many years.

The countless casualties of our historical inheritance from rigid non-religious religions, unimaginitive educational regimes, heartless industrialisation; the imposed class barriers of those who held the power of social standards from inherited wealth going back to feudal times, have collectively laid a thick layer of insensitivity on our culture, which is then imposed upon thousands and thousands of our children; constricting them as they grow up in a mental prison of unrecognised fear, where the key for release seems permanently lost.

I think it is eventually essential for those who in any way have been trained to assist suffering clients from any therapeutic discipline, also to be trained in breathing correction in order to be aware from 'the gut' of all these restrictive forces and attitudes which make up their client's pain. You cannot breathe wrongly and still be fully sensitive.

Using the word *client* for those who seek help, sounds better to me than the word *patient* which denotes to me a paternalistic attitude. I have never met a client in a therapeutic situation who did not teach or educate *me* in some vital aspect of important knowledge of the human state.

Reference to the gut in the above paragraph leads me to the symptom which is universal, and whose reversal is the essential factor in taking self-responsibility. To breathe correctly is to breathe from the lower stomach or gut, and if your counselling or therapy training does not achieve the elimination of gut-avoidance breathing, then the cure will never be permanent. The client will be back again, or seek help elsewhere from the army of other stress-help counsellors waiting in the wings. Unfortunately few of these will breathe correctly themselves, and their own stress level therefore will once again do no more than paper over the cracks.

If the gut area is not re-awakened*, because its revival triggers off the expansion of the correct breath, the client's life-span will be shortened, due to whatever illness develops at a later stage in life, through lack of oxygen to the brain and cells, and resulting lack of strength of the auto-immune system. [*see diagrams on pages 72-73]

Having been around now in the therapeutic world for some decades, I have known a number of therapists who have also become ill due to that same reason. Repressed and inadequate breathing. How can you help others if you are not healthy yourself? To be a healthy therapist, you must be able to breathe correctly, ensuring good cell and brain-oxygenation. As a result, you and your clients will develop true wisdom, be loving, have a great sense of humour, sensitivity, be calm, patient, detached, free of personal tension. These are the by-products from breath re-training. Above all intuition. This last, together with lovingness, are vitally important. Without them, you may be wiser to consider another career. I try to use these virtues, but please don't assume that I claim perfection, rather that these virtues are attainable through the breath.

In my personal experience the mental and spiritual strength to decide to be free of tension at its deepest level means to be in perfect control of correct breath yourself. The result is to be able to hold on to your own quiet core of calmness and certainty, to be able to translate and master the backwash from a temporary concentrated and potent atmosphere of hostility and negativity from a client. Particularly one who loathes themselves and therefore you! This can be unleashed suddenly, unknowingly and unintentionally, from your client, but contains a recipe of violence scarcely contained. Hatred, anger, and any other of the turbulent, dangerous and destructive emotions they had erected as a smokescreen when deprived of love, and given its opposite from a very early age.

Believe me if you are in this work as any kind of therapist, either conventional or complementary, *it is not for the faint-hearted.* Only someone who has healed their own core is able to enable a damaged soul to rediscover that same core within the essential inner centre of love from which all self-healing flows. Even if you think you have healed yourself, never feel a failure if despite working from integrity, a client does not respond to your skills. Very often something you have said intuitively to help understanding, will be understood by your client, perhaps many months, even years later. Thankfully no good is ever wasted. I believe in the saying that it is 'ok to make mistakes', and 'you don't have to be perfect.' If we were I do not think we would have needed to return to this existence.

I have discovered that if you trust the perfection of your own centre, when you do make a mistake, it is as if you are being helped by the higher energy in existence and your mistakes seem to be cancelled out. When you have done the best you can the words which come true from *The Aquarian Gospel* make sense. 'The mighty powers of worlds unseen do not send forth their help 'til man has done his best, they only help when man can do no more.' When a deep attitude of evil seems to be projected at you from a profoundly hurt human being, it is good to know and prove that there is a higher power at your elbow!

An apparently terrifying energy can pour from your client, and be a veritable 'sword of Damocles', whether you are involved in the health profession in any way from the NHS, or are a complementary or alternative therapist. I have often wondered what *alternative* the traditionalists can produce to oxygen, breath or spirit. The violence reported in the news media in our hospitals mostly comes from those under the influence of alcohol or unable to get a drug fix, and therefore in a state of withdrawal. Such violence can only erupt from a deeply damaged child within the adult, however frightening it may appear in an adult form.

I feel so strongly that a comprehensive training in breath understanding would be a great asset for all involved in health care in any way. My true self would like to *insist* that this is *essential* training, and an automatic and necessary part of health care education, taught preferably at the very beginning of any course. Just as an animal is more likely to attack if you are afraid, the same applies to the human animal. If as a member of the NHS or a therapist you have cured your own fear, your clients and patients will feel secure with you.

I have never been afraid of physical attack, even in some pretty 'hoary' therapeutic situations, but I am aware that my breath-induced calmness kept the situation under control. Without that protection I would not have been competent to handle it without fear and possible unfortunate results.

I believe this gap in therapeutic training is behind the problems of the numerous therapists who have come to me as clients, who are suffering from stress, despite having performed very competently in their training and exam results. Letters after names give no protection against the vacuum in essential awareness which I believe can only be filled by a proper educational training in respiratory knowledge.

Without this training, any course, however apparently intellectually adequate will, I believe, usually fall far short of that essential ingredient of breath-awareness. The therapists who I have seen professionally have virtually all exhibited restricted breathing patterns. The knock-on result being stress and fear, which spoke of an important reason for their stress. They had been doubly affected by the negativity of their clients, which had swamped them emotionally, drained their confidence, and either led them to seek stress help, or caused them to give up their therapeutic practice. What has happened is that the lack of teaching in correct breathing and omission of attention to the importance of this non-intellectual aspect of any of their training courses, has sent them on to the battlefield of human stress without adequate protection.

At one time I would have been in a similar position if I had not had the good fortune to discover or been led to the increase in personal power and energy which was the result of using breath correctly. It was quite a long process as muscles around my lungs began to relax, and I noticed this increase in energy, and decrease in negativity. Some wonderfully enlightening books and articles began to drop 'into my lap', usually after I had mastered another level of understanding from within myself. The writings and thoughts of another person perhaps long since departed this life spoke to me loudly and clearly. These corroborated the new information I had recently been given, which had come from *within* me.

I realised how few good books there were in existence on the subject. Some of the gems of knowledge came from as far back as Plato, and other writers down the centuries to the present day. It represents to me something like the passing on of a Holy Grail of precious knowledge that must never be lost. I feel sad that so many of these books, which contain priceless information about breathing and its spiritual meaning, have been deemed as worthless by 'up-to-date' publishers. It is as if some malign non-spiritual influence was trying to suppress truths that need to be rediscovered. Are publishers so out of touch with true realities?

We are now discovering how we have been polluting the very air we need for survival, the presence of that magical layer of life-giving ether, which in the endless space around us resembles only the thickness of a layer of varnish on the surface of the trunk of a giant oak tree.

As newly-qualified therapists from all disciplines (and there are an increasing number of both), proudly hang their certificates of authority to practice on their walls in the sanctuary of their freshly decorated and furnished therapy rooms, complete with a framed copy of *Desiderata* and the odd herbal incense stick; (I never did the incense), I speculate as to how woefully inadequately prepared they may be to face the deepest human problems. The fear, hurt, and suppressed violence from past generations that awaits them in the jungle of psychic pain which requires to be healed within our communities.

Yesterday I read that about 70% of the population eventually die in hospital from malevolent diseases, which to me represents the backwash of the symptoms of a 70% unlanced mental and physical abcess and the terminal inheritance of our earliest environmental influences, from birth onwards which created infant terror. Resulting in the self-rejection of air, the essential essence for staying alive healthily. Who was it said 'give me a child until the age of seven, and I will have him for life'? At least one dictator I do not wish to remember.

This statement can however be applied universally. Frequent graphic accounts of the enormous increase in mental illness, which taken with the addiction upsurge, violence on our streets, etc., confirm the fact that an enormously powerful anti-life and anti-Nature force has been and still is rotting away at the roots of our Society. This hand-me-down from past negative attitudes to the gift of life is still contaminating our children, most of whom breathe in a distorted way by the age of eight, although nobody notices it, least of all HM Inspector of Schools, or the leaning tower of the NHS.

So we prepare the crop for another generation of inadequately prepared therapists to harvest, themselves bound down by the intellectually narrow boundaries of their training; in which the medical profession fares no better. I remember that the old school where we ran a stress centre was near a nursing training college. You could drive past, and see many of the students smoking outside and in doorways during coffee breaks. Piles of cigarette stubs. One nurse who came to see us out of interest could not tell me where the upper lung ended.

Walking wounded crowd our streets, we need a breathing revolution of understanding to turn the tide, but turn the tide we must. The origins of the word breath, respire, or re-spirit has its roots deep in ancient history. I am certain that before long, therapists of any discipline will have to be breath-trained.

In the future with possible great global changes, nothing less than spiritual gladiators will be required, who are breath-trained, mentally 100% positive, strong and healthy as a result. Such training must be far in advance of any courses at present being offered by Universities and Colleges, which seem to be restricted by the vagaries of Government legislation and profit hungry commercial organisations.

Whatever our therapeutic or health-related discipline, and while there is yet time, I believe that a thorough and practical training in correct breathwork is a must, in order to qualify for any field of therapeutic or caring work. Otherwise unresolved stress within the professional will create an unnecessary tension within the therapeutic appointment situation. This will be conveyed to the client, who will obviously be tense anyway. It will block communication, create more appointments than necessary, particularly important in a fee-paying arrangement. The basic problem is unlikely to be resolved. The lack of correct breath teaching will also deprive the client of an essential self-help tool which would have positive life-long health benefits for mind, body and emotions.

PHYSICIAN, HEAL THYSELF.

Chapter 21

RELATIONSHIPS WITH CHILDREN

I REMEMBER on a number of occasions meeting that wise old Scottish psychologist Winifred Rushforth, who sadly died shortly before achieving her ambition to reach her century. Winifred founded The Davidson Clinic in Edinburgh, before psychology and psychiatry became available on the NHS. The Davidson Clinic was homely and artistic. People paid according to their means. Winifred was joined by a number of well-qualified psychologists, and much of the therapy encompassed the philosophy of Carl Jung, who Winifred had known personally. I have referred several times to Jung's remark when asked to see a child. 'Never mind the child, bring me the parents.'

The last time I saw Winifred was at a meeting in the Salisbury Centre in Edinburgh, when she arrived with Laurens van der Post; the latter attended her funeral not long before his own wonderful life came to an end.

I always remember Winifred's story at a conference, that some ladies were very incensed by her words that 'children have to learn to forgive their parents.' They were sure that she had got it the wrong way round, and that parents have to forgive their children. 'No,' said Winifred, 'I meant what I said.'

The word *forgiveness* must come into the minds of many parents as we try to struggle with the apparent hostility and

233

acting-out of our children, almost until they leave the home nest, and even many years after. At the same time we often forget that we ourselves may be trying to sort out the forgiveness problem with our own parents as they become older. Unresolved relationship difficulties still remain to block the loving communication that should be there. Sadly very often it isn't. Instinctively we don't want them to die with bad feelings still remaining between us.

Often when we become grandparents and seem to have another chance with childhood, our relationships with our grandchildren are, thank goodness, so often loving, and can even give us the feeling that perhaps we weren't such bad parents after all!

Sometimes our new recognition of the sheer beauty of childhood makes us wish we could start all over again with our own children. We see the babies from our own babies with eyes of greater maturity, and often wished we had handled many things differently.

Going back to Winifred's words and our own parents, we realise that we do indeed have to forgive them if we wish to be forgiven by our own children. We may recall our often unintentional sins of omission with cringing sorrow at our own lack of understanding.

Increasing spiritual wisdom that comes with age teaches us that there may come a time when it will be too late to reach our parents in this life, if we have not at least made an attempt to heal old grudges.

The Biblical words of the 'sins of the fathers being visited upon the children until the third and fourth generation' has frequently come into mind when as a therapist I have been confronted with family hurts and grief being truly handed down through the generations. Negative thought forms and prejudices many attribute to severe conditioning, narrow religions, harsh industrial conditions, and oppressive educational systems. All having their influence on the in-human way that children have been treated. Our children pick up the symptoms of our collective disregard of our own natural and acceptable needs. Negative thought forms, seeds of unresolved fear, which bring sorrow and chaos to the younger descendents of each family tree.

Teaching these last-born casualties of such a diseased inheritance to breathe correctly, for they will always have a restricted respiratory pattern, a symptom of the inherited fear, has the effect of applying a brake on an out-of-control vehicle inevitably racing downhill. I have so often observed three and even four generations of a family all displaying identical breathing patterns, with similar physical and emotional problems.

I find it hard to subscribe to the easily spoken words, 'it's all in the genes.' As if there was nothing which could be done.

Time after time, as a consequence of working in correct breathing with a young teenager or adult who exhibits the stress of such an inheritance; I have seen the release of this dis-ease. Breath correction seems to re-teach the mind/body/ spirit's ability to understand the negative influence of the inherited mind-set. All in the genes? I'm not so sure.

There follows recognition that the freed spirit can then understand that the permanent effects of inherited stress are *not set in stone,* and can be permanently healed in one generation. The power of correct breath balances the human system and restores harmony. I have seen this releasing energy of love and forgiveness directed back down the existing generations by a subtle alchemy well known to those who understand the process.

During the period of my life when so many important truths have been revealed to me, my understanding of these truths have been able to help overturn the stagnant and self-deceptive peace in which many families exist, until the silent poison erupts in a tragic crisis of a physical or mental breakdown. It has been very satisfying to help to avert such breakdowns by the re-teaching of the basic natural way to use the life-force.

Some of these important truths are:

Children have no *duty* to parents: Relationships which flourish in later life can only do so because of love, respect, friendship and forgiveness.

Too many children grow up having to act as surrogate parents to their own parents, which blocks their own development and maturity. This creates the likelihood of such children making marriages themselves based on a parent/child dependence, an unhealthy alliance.

It is never too late to say 'I love you.' These are often the only words needed to start the healing process.

People often wonder how one child in a family can seem to be a *success* in the world's terms, while another can appear to be a complete *failure*. You hear it all the time, often it may be the middle child who seems to have an identity crisis, apparently taking longer to find their place in the world. Yet the middle child often has a great talent for acting as a family healer.

A little thought can help us to realise that each child is born during a different period of their parents' ages and relationship. Financial and social pressures can vary enormously within a marriage. A change of home or work by a parent can create a severe strain on the family unit, etc., etc. Without taking into account broken marriages. All these situations have different effects on children of different ages, who react accordingly.

These may have a powerful effect in terms of stress levels on parents too. I wish I could look back and think that I had been the perfect parent, the best that most of us can say is that we did the best that we could at the time.

I possess a wonderful little book, with great pictures, and little script. What there is, is very potent. It is about a family of mice, and is called *Noisy Nora,* by Rosemary Wells. Nora is the middle child. Each page depicts what Mother does with the youngest baby, and what Father does with the eldest son. Somehow Nora unintentionally gets left out, and as you can imagine gets into mischief, usually of a noisy kind, which disrupts the family. It is only when Nora disappears that they realise how much she is missed, and their concern reflects their real love for her which has of course always been there. It did take a lot of noise however for Nora to get herself heard!

Noisy Nora was first published in 1973, and may probably be out of print, but I would love to see it in every public and school library in the country, as well as on the book shelves of anyone engaged in any form of counselling and therapy. There is more wisdom conveyed in its thirty-six pages than many mighty tomes on the human condition.

Perhaps Nora's problems struck a cord with me, because I too am a middle child! Are you? On the other hand an eldest child will complain that they were always expected to be more grown-up than they felt they should be, and the youngest hates feeling that they are always treated as the 'wee wean' as we say in Scotland. Often getting away with more misbehaviour than the rest of the siblings just because they will always be seen as the baby, and nothing is expected of them. The eldest is often expected to parent the others, which if both parents work, may place too heavy a load on an eldest child who is still very young.

Nora is restored to the bosom of her family, once more feeling wanted and loved.

I suppose most of us will have experienced something of the family stereotypes mentioned above. *Noisy Nora* is one of the cheapest, shortest, non-intellectual yet graphic portrayals of the family saga I have read.

Unless the Noisy Nora aspect of our own childhood is resolved, we will grow into adults either estranged from our parents, or forever trying to please them. I have said elsewhere that so many are endlessly replaying the scenario of our received parental message, 'however hard you try to please me you never will, but keep on trying.' If we accede to this blackmail, our marriage, children and other relationships may be sacrificed to an insatiable mental vampirism which may go on for generations.

Parents and children are bonded to each other by cords of Nature stronger than those of an imposed civilisation. When an adult from a traumatised family unit *grows* through a period of corrective breathing and self-heals their personal family wounds, they understand the irreversible truths which help to make forgiveness possible.

There is one truth which can be of comfort. We *do* have to love everyone but we do not have to *like* them or what they do. We can hate the sin but love the sinner.

As an individual goes through the corrective breathing process, a very subtle change of energy seems to happen. Waves or cords of energy appear to be sent, obviously in an unseen form, to help heal discordant links which bind us unhealthily to our parents, siblings or social relationships.

We accept that we cannot personally change anyone, especially our parents. We do eventually release our hurt childhoods and childish need to be loved, having discovered through correct breath that there is a Universal natural energy which always totally supports us lovingly. It goes deeper than the relationship between parents and children, and once re-integrated into our psyche can never be lost again. Being loved by the Highest Power there is, we no longer *need* love and approval from anyone. Of course it is wonderful to be loved and approved of by others, but if we *need* that, the need comes from our un-healed child and not from our mature adult. In other words we still have work to do on ourselves.

Such an impregnable force of love permanently at home within ourselves, allows us to forgive our parents and anyone else in our lives requiring to be released. If we refuse to forgive anyone, we are giving them control over us, and we must never submit to this control from an unloving energy.

We have a living example of such a philosophy in the form of Nelson Mandela and his relationship to his captors over very many years, in which he speaks so positively of retaining one's sense of self-respect and dignity.

Many families are breaking up, the marriage having been formed by immature men and women, coming to the marriage ceremony carrying unresolved emotional scars which are still stunting their existence. Then the first child arrives, presumably untarnished, who before long begins to produce the symptoms of their damaged parents, many of which are described throughout this book.

In my philosophy there is a truism that 'there's nothing either good or bad, but thinking makes it so.' If we constantly label the inevitable break-up of such marriages as wrong, we ignore the essential underlying state in all of us of our search for personal truth, otherwise we continue to affect each generation in the same way that diseased plants produce poor seeds. This search for truth continues all our lives, even if we are unaware of it. To be untrue to ourselves is to be untrue to our children.

After many years of working with clients searching for their own personal truths I have come to the conclusion that in general one loving parent is better than two warring ones, whose constant state of conflict must inevitably damage the emotional growth of their children.

Many adults whose battling parents had stayed together

for the sake of their children, have expressed to me the opinion that they wished their fighting parents *had* separated, so that the children were relieved of the burden of carrying the terrible often unspoken tension that must exist in such an unstable emotional environment.

At the end of the day, despite anything negative that has happened between us, we find that eventually we *can* tell our parents that we love them, without in any way feeling vulnerable or two-faced. We can hug even if no love or hugs were given to us as children, feeling totally sincere but totally within our own control.

I have faith that the spirit can never die, that we do indeed return to this earthly existence time and again, until we have learned, digested and reversed by correct action, some activity which has been harmful to others in a previous life-time. I believe that when we die, our spirit is returned to a universal sea of loving Higher energy, where we review our most recent existence and eventually decide to try again. This sounds very simplistic, but why not? We re-enter this world, almost invariably having no recent memory of a past life, coming back certainly as a beautiful innocent child, but carrying within our as yet immature spirit the mark or karma of past harm we have committed. Just as an apparently healthy young plant which as first appeared healthy develops in its growth, a fungus or blemish not observable when the plant was very small, despite ideal growing conditions, so our personal human frailties become apparent as we age.

My beliefs do not come about from studying Eastern or Western philosophy but from an utter certainty arising from my therapeutic encounters with an enormous number of people from all walks of life, including my own, whose personal stories and experiences, sorrows and joys indicate a knowledge beyond the material world. The inner teachings revealed by correct breathing have revealed to me and others, truths and wisdom not taught by our education system. We reject these truths at our cost.

I do not ask you to share my beliefs, but one idea has occurred to me, which is that such a shared belief on a deep level could be a unifying force to unite all people. You cannot unify people from any temporary material treaty based on economic dependency, however attractive such a cosmetic arrangement may seem. I do think that you can unify people by 'breathing with one breath', as President Obama said in an election speech. He may not have understood his words in the way I use them now. (How I wish he did.) If that breath is correct according to nature, the positive effect would be far-reaching.

The highest spiritual resources of both East and West will require to be stretched to the uttermost at some point, possibly in the not too distant future. We shall have to come to terms with disasters, both man-made and natural, embodying fear and violence, where in order to sustain global sanity, we shall have to delve much deeper than the shallow mind-set which at present allows us a superficial sense of national security.

Many people who have come to embrace a natural and strong belief in a life beyond this present existence have subsequently found it makes such obvious sense. A mingling of Eastern and Western philosophical thinking could create a stronger common bond in understanding events still to happen, when only a strong belief in an eternal wisdom may allow us to survive the shock of possible catastrophic earth changes. When those who are left may not consider for a time that life worth living, and cease to consider survival as a desirable option. An East/West brotherhood will be an essential factor in harnessing spiritual resources for global regeneration. If we watch small children of differing nations playing and communicating happily together, that is the example for us all. We need to look no further to learn global co-operation.

The words above represent the inner teachings revealed to me as a consequence of my personal experience of correct breathing, not taught consciously, but unable to stifle. I know there is a growing body of like-minded people world-wide. All changes at a deep level begin with a few people recognising non-visible or provable truths, from which roots a great groundswell erupts as an irresistible force of positive energy.

From my own inner teachings I believe that when we die, our spirit returns to some universal place of loving higher consciousness where we possibly receive a spiritual 'wash and brush up'. We consider our past life, its spiritual credits and debts, sins, (also of omission) and virtues, then agree to return to earth life again through human birth. Purified by that soon forgotten experience of recent heavenly sojourn. What the world sees is a beautiful innocent baby, but on the child's soul is registered its karma, representing the total non-loving energy activities of our previous life, which are revealed in the emerging character of the child.

As the child grows, it is obvious that its behaviour begins to reveal these inexplicable traits and problems, difficult to understand in an initial study of its birth family, for how could such traits arise when other siblings of the same family do not show such problems?

Each existence gives us a fresh opportunity for self-study, and to cancel out the stains on our soul by loving action. This is not punishment and we always have free will. If we do not start to pay-off this karmic debt which is not punishment, the negativity we carry attracts by its negative magnetic energy continuing disasters into our lives. Our wrong use and abuse of others in past lives has to be paid off in the same way as a financial debt, but this is a non-material spiritual transaction.

In order to realise the truths of the above sentences, I

believe that we cannot always see the working out of this principle in one lifetime. There exists the challenge of learning to trust the truths contained within the spiritual laws we cannot see, but which do exist as inexorably as the laws we create in the material world.

You may strongly disagree with my words, and have every right to do so, but I am glad I know what I know. I have expressed them in order to set the stage upon which I believe we all step as we come through human birth.

It has been said that we choose our parents and they choose us because of their and our karmic debt, and remember different children's place in the family may represent *different* aspects of their own and their parent's debt, not just to each other, but to the universal community.

It may be very difficult to comprehend the demands made by parenthood, until we have personally become parents, which tests our own ability to give and hold the love impulse to the utmost, often in almost impossible situations, where if the child concerned was not our own, our anger might be aggressively directed without the saving power of love.

Even in the glow of new parenthood, the challenge of love can be virtually exhausted by nights of broken sleep, and our inability to satisfy or understand interminable hours of lusty crying from such a small bundle. The baby cannot communicate verbally, the source may be unable to be discovered, yet having dealt with all the possibilities, still it continues. Our own conditioning and upbringing has distanced us from the intuitive path to the source of the baby's distress. Indeed as new parents, we may feel that our own *civilised* way of life is the right one, and any disturbance being vocalised so strongly by the small child is the unnatural one. *A recipe for disaster.* Our allegiance to the trendy life-style may make us feel guilty as we try to cover up the child's sorrow. It may render us apologetic to others in taking adequate time to attend to the child's needs, so that the earthy and earthly requirements of the infant are brushed aside as *unnatural*.

So here we have the spiritual needs of both parent and child dishonoured, in our present culture of artificiality. The schism continues throughout childhood and explodes again at adolescence, both sides in total conflict, often resulting in a violent and unhappy parting of the ways.

Both warring partners are left resentful, guilty and unforgiving, a recipe for long years of estrangement, sometimes never healed. The death of a parent before the rift is healed, then makes physical reconciliation impossible in this lifetime. A growing unvoiced grief can then poison the happiness of those who remain.

We may never like our parents for what they did, but in order to regain love and respect for ourselves and be able to live with our conscience, *we have to forgive*. Their negative and often unintentional neglect of our needs now no longer controls us. Our own children will then eventually forgive *us*. Despite the apparent barrier of death I have known many cases of parent/child estrangement healed by some inexplicable trust in a communication of loving thought that seems to cross the barrier between the two worlds.

We have to be able to say 'I love you.' That does not mean to say we have to like what they have done. We all have a spark of divine spirit within us, and we have to love that spirit. Loving energy does not belong to us, it is a gift from a higher power, and is never withdrawn from us even if we withdraw from it. It heals us, as well as anyone to whom we pass on its light, irrespective of whether another person accepts or rejects it. That is not our problem. Love is pure and impartial and never attempts to control or impose on someone else's personal space. As parents, we have to accept this discipline of free detachment in our relationship with our children.

Giving love in no way weakens us, it only strengthens us. We are not spiritually allowed to withhold love from anyone, even if as I say we do not have to *like* their actions. I remember some years ago being alone on a Saturday morning in a big building in a therapeutic appointment with an axe murderer on parole. He told me how his mother had abused him on many occasions as a small boy. On this particular one she was holding him by his neck against the wall with his toes almost off the ground. He told me that all he could remember thinking were the words '*I love you Mum.*'

I believe that everyone, however evil their actions, has a spiritual essence however dormant and unused it may be. It must at least be acknowledged for we all come from the same sea of human consciousness.

Looking back in my life on those few people who I know have wished me harm, it is from these painful experiences that I have learned the most valuable spiritual lessons. I think of those occasions now with gratitude.

At one point in my life when I had to confront and resolve unfinished painful questions from my childhood, I came upon that wonderful little book *Heal Thyself* by Dr. Edward Bach, who produced the beautiful Bach Flower Remedies. This small book has been for me and so many others a source of welcome comfort in its wholesome explanations and advice to many who had carried unresolved issues of guilt and grief down the years. The sense of relief in being able to come to a loving release of any controlling influences in our lives, has brought closure and a healthy ability for thousands to look back on their childhood years as a positive time.

This fine little book also reminds us that we have a responsibility to remove ourselves from any controlling influence in our lives. It gives advice on how this can be achieved, and assures us that our sole duty is to develop our own gifts and talents without allowing *the least interference.*

Otherwise we shall eventually be overtaken by mental and/or physical illness.

This whole process can be achieved with love. From several sources I recall the words. 'If you do not develop that which is within you, what you do not develop will kill you.' Another reminds us that, 'if you do not follow your heart and your emotions, sooner or later you will fall ill.' In thirty years of experience as a therapist, both these remarks are completely accurate. Now at eighty thank goodness, I have tried to personally follow this advice, certainly in the last thirty years, and proved its accuracy!

If there is a gift or talent within us which we do not develop, it will invariably be fear that will be holding us back. The amazing thing about correct breathing is that it removes fear and reminds us that we have the right to develop the real magic of who we really are, in other words being true to ourselves. This can only arise from a sense of correct love for ourselves. That comes from *pure* love. Pure love cannot hurt anyone, it allows anyone who has been leaning on us in a wrong way to stand up straight too. How good that we have been able to teach them that lesson!

REMEMBER THAT GREAT SPIRITS ARE
OFTEN BORN OF LESSER SPIRITS.
IF WE DO NOT FORGIVE OUR PARENTS,
OUR CHILDREN WILL NOT FORGIVE US.

Chapter 22

THE POWER OF THOUGHT

A gift to Therapists and the Reader

BEFORE I TEACH ANYONE more advanced work in re-training themselves to breath correctly, which we all knew how to do from day one of our lives (before long sadly becoming distorted), I have found it essential to share with them a session about the Power of Thought.

The reason for this is that as soon as we begin to improve our breathing, we improve the oxygen supply to the brain resulting, I believe, in brain cells releasing information to us about right decisions to make for our lives, which has until now not been consciously available to us.

You may have seen a diagram of a cross-section of the brain, it looks rather like a half walnut, or a brussels sprout. If you have a garden and grow brussels sprouts, you will have observed how the baby sprout grows quite large before being ready to pick. Think about a half section of a small sprout compared with a half section of a fully grown one. I always liken the small section to our human brain, before breath correction, and the larger to the better oxygenated brain. Quite an expansion! The bigger sprout section represents development of our potential. I have a diagram of a cross section of the human brain, which bears a striking resemblance to the walnut or sprout.

There is an urgency about this new information, we cannot disregard it. I speak about brain cells which we think of as residing within the head, but once we improve breath another set of cells appear to become active from what has been called the second brain.

This feeds the upper brain with oxygen from the lower belly gut area, which becomes re-activated by the regeneration of the lower largest lung area.

The work of Pierre Pallardy (famous French physical therapist) mentions this second brain. His book *The Gut Instinct* is well worth reading.

The second brain exists in the area between the pelvic bone and the navel, and in repairing respiration we activate oxygen from the lowest and largest area of the lungs, bringing a whole new unused area of consciousness into the upper brain, as the link between the two brain areas is improved due to a better oxygen supply. This lower stomach area, which Pierre Pallardy refers to as 'The Second Brain', triggers our emotions. The biggest bonus from this self-repair activity is that we become much more aware of the importance of intuition, listening to our feelings, and realise how vital it is that we listen to this silent yet audible inner voice.

It takes quite a while for this reconnection to take place, so that for some time we are living in a world where we are often directed by our earlier thought habits, while a new set of thinking is gradually making itself felt within us, as we breathe better, and become conscious of a deepening of awareness. It can seem like a time of confusion as the old struggles against the new, while sensing that the new thoughts are the ones to be obeyed.

Even if at first we disobey them! Old habits are hard to break.

Such changes of thought must almost certainly involve other changes in our lives, usually involving shifts in relationships, work and home. We begin to realise that we are no longer happy with second-rate relationships, work that does not fulfil us, although often when a better career option is available, we have to move our home. Another change requiring courage.

All decisions which present a challenge, can bring up fear. Improved breathing improves confidence, and allows us to have the courage to make what may seem a risky leap, yet if we are to fulfil ourselves we have to say 'yes' to a question which goes like this '*am I ready to let go of who I am, in order to be who I have not yet become?*' (I think this remark was first made by Leonard Orr.)

This chapter describing a session on the *Power of Thought*, is to remind ourselves that we have already been successful in the most difficult and dangerous task we shall ever have to undertake. In other words we have already succeeded at the greatest challenge we shall have to face. *Our birth.* We had two choices, to live or die. We chose life, so why are we faltering over any other challenge in our lives, when we have already jumped the highest fence? Challenges such as giving ourselves permission to make changes in our lives, releasing relationships where others are dominating us, or we are dominating others, the typical parent/child conflict in adult relationships in which so many are wasting precious time which cannot come again.

In this transitional stage, spiritual awakenings seem to arise, often in someone who would have scoffed at such thoughts until now. In the course of this chapter I have tried to introduce a concept which allows the non-believer to accept that there exists an un-alterable loving energy which cannot be destroyed, and *upon which we can totally rely*. It is also a scientific fact, although I don't think that scientists have yet realised its implications. Otherwise they themselves would personally have to operate from this concept of correct breath, about which many non-scientific people are already aware. They would have to submit science to Nature's laws, and might not be prepared to do so.

The session I am going to describe has fallen naturally into three sections.

1. *Thought - the sole and only activity of the Brain.*
2. *The Proof of a Higher Power.*
3. *You can have your heart's desires.*
   Inherit the Treasure of your birth.

There are quite a lot of books and personal experiences these days about what is called 'channelling'. I prefer to call it *heightened intuition*, an absorption of the collective wisdom of the ages, which I believe we attract in a form of osmosis through correction of the breath.

Energy can never disappear, it goes out into the atmosphere. Each life has its own unique vibration and although we may no longer be alive our energy vibration will still exist on the ether, and can be picked up. The information in this chapter came to me during an intensive self-educational time of my life as an individual when what I learned was not contained within any book I then had in my possession. In my training as a therapist, I was trained to *talk the talk*. The knowledge which I drew in from the co-operation between my breath and the unseen world led me to talk the talk of my soul.

This information returns to us the conviction that we have *the power to heal ourselves*.

The combination of correct breath and the power of love is a laser-like energy which can re-arrange the tissue of our cells. This is the message which I am sure is on Einstein's *Fourth Dimension*, not provable by science.

At an unconscious level many people are afraid to let themselves feel good, or that it is safe to trust that it can be so. An unloved and difficult childhood, possibly with abuse, often turns a loving, optimistic trusting child into a pessimistic, negative immature aggressive, even dangerous adult. An adult who is unable to make contact with their deepest needs, substituting distorted relationships, materialism and plastic pleasures as an apparently outward feel-good factor. Within is a cold oasis of despair, cooking up all kinds of physical and mental health problems waiting to explode in later life.

It takes a forceful change of thought and action to reverse the thinking of such a powerfully disfunctional person and make an axis-shift of thought and action to reverse such a negative energy.

In a physically damaged building, the foundations and framework have to be strengthened and reinforced, before the permanent re-build takes place or a weakened structure will cause the building to collapse again. A plan has to be prepared in order for the re-build to be successful.

The same process can be applied at a personal level in the re-building of someone's life. Someone who has been damaged, and then damages themselves and others. *Their thoughts have to change.*

As I healed my own breathing I became aware of the power of breath correction as *the* thought repair material for human foundations. Foundations, framework and rebuild. I found that before this took place it was essential to create a thought-plan so that the changes which begin to happen particularly in thought-activity could be understood. This plan, like any architectural plan, needs to be drawn up *before* the reconstruction work begins, in which the clients themselves becomes the architect, builder and all trades.

It depends on the free will of a client how often they want to take time for a correct breathing session, people vary enormously. After every session information seems to come up from the unconscious mind, which acts as material to be transformed into action before the next appointment. The process cannot be hastened by frequent sessions, people can only move at their own pace of re-structure.

While someone is in correct-breathing mode I do not talk or counsel except for gentle encouragement, and explanation, if asked for. A client can continue with the process and still ask questions about what is happening, without interrupting the flow of the breath or the session.

Someone may talk quite a lot when commencing the first breathing session. This is a sign that the left verbal, analytical brain hemisphere is still in charge, but before long the creative voice of the right hemisphere will be speaking to them from the intuitive sense, and the talking will slow down. The creative voice has no verbal sound, but is very clear and concise, and gradually the outward talking gives way to internal listening. I try to encourage a client to stay with the breathing, and after a while they become relaxed enough to become more interested in the world within them, which I am always pleased to observe, for that interior world is their real teacher.

A client may choose to wait days, weeks or months before they make another appointment, a period I always liken to the yeast rising in bread-making! The whole re-build may take several years, but is in my opinion an infinitely more reliable re-structuring than any other therapeutic work I know. I am in agreement with the well-known popular writer and philosopher Eckhart Tolle in believing work on healing our breath to be much more cost-effective than any other therapeutic alternative. A large part of the repair process is carried out by the person themselves, which is of course cost-free, as Eckhart Tolle says. Through the improvement of brain-oxygen supply ideas begin to flow into the mind, which have to be understood and converted into action before the next breathing adventure begins.

I mentioned earlier in this chapter the damage that has

been done to so many children, and the resultant distortion of their adult person, but obviously everyone can benefit from this work, for few of us emerge un-damaged from our childhood years.

The ideas in this chapter may appear challenging, but this work will only be meaningful if it *is* challenging from to time. The interaction between the client and breathing teacher is in the form of question and answer.

In the context of this book, will you be prepared to be my client? *Challenge and disagree as much as you like, but try and persevere. Give it a chance.*

When I was challenged to accept the idea that my first breathing session was intended to help me accept that I could have my heart's desires and even deserved them, I was somewhat sceptical. Subsequently as I walked along I began to visualise the possibility of its reality, with a sudden lift of exhilaration in my heart which has never left me in twenty-five years.

First of all get comfortable, really comfortable. I love the saying 'never stand when you can sit, never sit when you can lie!' I'm all for saving energy (I once knew an architect who always locked his office door and stretched out under his desk at lunchtime.)

Have a large pad, and a pen, perhaps a coloured one as well for under-lining.

PART ONE: NOW WE START TO THINK!

Q: 'Is there anything at all that you have done today
     which was not preceded by a thought?'
You may say 'No, I did this that or the other, i.e. cleaned
     teeth, drove car, etc., etc.'
'Yes I know we believe we do these things automatically,
we don't have to keep *learning* how to do them. However to

do them at all requires an action, movement of some part of the body, directed by the nervous system via the spine from the brain. All that goes on in the brain is thought, nothing else.

What else can you think of goes on in the brain? Remember, to decide to do nothing requires a thought first!'

I hope I shall be able to persuade you that you have done nothing at all today without a prior thought. Obviously this has to be acknowledged eventually, despite gnashing of teeth. It's like getting blood out of a stone with some people! Once we have agreed on this you will have to accept that you did nothing last week, last month, last year, or all the years of your life without a thought first. Take your time to think this through.

When you have been able to acknowledge this fact, it follows naturally that our lives have been created by our thoughts.

Apparently we have about 80,000 thoughts a day, give or take a few either way.

Q: 'How many kinds or qualities of thoughts are there?'
A: (eventually!) 'Positive and negative.'

'In which case we must accept that we are all going round with our own proportion of positive/negative thoughts. There must be 80,000 x 80,000 variations within this possibility. I wonder what is *your* ratio of positive/negative thought?

Has it a life-enhancing or a life-destructive bias? How shall we find out?'

Q: 'Can you get a positive return from a negative thought?'
(Most people will agree a 'no' to this question.)

On the other hand an interesting aspect of this question is the idea that if you realise that you have sent out a negative thought, which you then realise transgresses moral law, you *can* quickly send out a mental positive thought to erase the negative one! I am sure this works, but you have to have reached a point in spiritual development to realise the truth that an unremitting negative thought sent out does attract an equivalent negative energy back to you through the law of magnetic attraction. You may call this bad luck.

Q: 'Can you get a negative return from a positive thought?'

A frequent reply is 'Yes, I've sent out a positive or loving thought to someone, and got a negative return.' Unfortunately the thinking here needs to be revised because a truly positive or loving thought *is* just that, truly loving, it is unconditional, and real love does not expect a return. Otherwise it is *conditional*, an *un-loving* energy which is saying 'if I send you love, I *expect* you to send me love back.' Do not despair however, for if you send out a truly loving or unconditional thought, the first person it benefits is yourself for you have sent out pure energy which protects you and enhances the Universe.

Even if you don't immediately see the result, at some time in your life, at the right time, the Universe will return your loving unconditional energetic thought sent out on the air-ways. Maybe days, weeks, months, even years before your unconditional love will be returned to you in surprising and wonderful ways.

A really positive thought you might ponder, is just that. Who needs a return from thinking you need a reward for thinking something which enhances your own energy and sparkle, and protects you?

Now we come to another question.

Q: 'Can you see a thought?' Someone might reply 'Yes.' However the answer is 'no, you cannot see a thought. A thought is not a material object, it cannot be touched. You may think that you know what someone is thinking, but that is not the same as visually seeing and touching that thought. Therefore we cannot *see* a thought.'

Q: 'Can you accept that thought is energy?'

A: 'Yes.'

Q: 'Can you see energy?' The answer is generally in the affirmative, but is incorrect. In querying how energy can be seen, the reply will usually be to quote for example a horse racing, a car moving, a person swimming, etc., to which the contra-reply must be that "of course you can see all these things moving, but you cannot *see* the energy of life which moves them." After some consideration your client will have to agree.

Q: 'Can you see life?' The answer given will be similar to that above, but in the form of humans, plants, animals. Back we come to the fact that we can see the *result* of what has been created by the energy of life, but we cannot *see* that energy. It is invisible.

Q: 'Can you accept that all our thoughts are about life?' Eventually the answer will have to be in the affirmative.

Referring back to all our thoughts, you may have heard the two lines of verse which go like this (Author unknown):

'Two men looked out through prison bars
One saw the mud, the other the stars.' (Positive or negative)

Now, here's the crucial question:

Q: 'If all our thoughts are about life, when would you suppose you had your very first thought about life?' A variety of answers meet this question, from a range of ages usually

256

from about five to eight years old. These are what a person will think is their first _memory_, but that was not the question. The question was first *thought*.

It takes a little while to realise that a small baby can have thoughts! How could they not? If an infant can cry and be hungry, we must recognise that a thought is required for the baby to know this.

Eventually we have to agree that the moment of our birth was the first time we had a thought about life. Some people come up with the suggestion that we probably had thoughts *before* birth. I cannot disagree with this, but perhaps our first active thoughts about life occurred at the point when we emerged from our mother's body into this life.

We then have to think about the energy and activity present at our birth, including the atmosphere and material surroundings. Think about any of these which may have applied to your first entry into the world. I will mention the possibilities:

Your mother may or may not have wanted you, when she realised she had conceived. Some mothers are dismayed at an unwelcome pregnancy. This negativity towards an unwanted child may last some months, but I believe that by the end of the pregnancy most mothers welcome their child.

At most births there will be about three other people present, say a doctor and two nurses. Apart from dentists, I understand the medical profession has the highest level of alcoholism and suicide of all the professions. It is likely that one of your birth attendants may have been quite stressful, i.e., their energy will be at high *beta* frequency. The first person who held you may have had this frequency, yet I understand that of the baby will be Alpha/Theta (loving). A conflict there. A new baby is highly sensitive to that person's energy. A high Beta energy person holding a new baby will give it a shock of tension.

The birthing room may be too hot, too cold, too bright, too noisy, the new baby's first encounter with what appears to be life.

The birth may be by Caesarian section, premature, forceps, breech, (dragged out) epidural delivery, premature or late. Of course it may be perfectly natural.

The umbilical cord may be cut too quickly. If that happens, the baby's oxygen supply will be severed, while it still needs oxygen via the umbilical cord, and before its little lungs are ready to take full responsibility for breath. A good slap on the buttocks is the recipe, a short sharp shock to force those tender little lungs into action before they are quite ready. A severe shock it really is.

Don't forget that it is Nature which has orchestrated the exact timetable required for birth, and time spans forced out of the correct rhythm can have a shock effect on a delicate mechanism. It occurs to me that delicate scientific procedures are handled with much more sensitive understanding than the exact science of the birth process.

R. D. Laing, the famous Scottish psychiatrist, suggested that 'breathing and the rhythm of the heart can be damaged, perhaps for life by cutting or throttling the umbilical cord *while it and the placenta are still fully functionally us.*' I believe that too. I have been with many clients who were in a correct breathing session, who suddenly jerked as if experiencing a shock. Although they carried on with their breathing session, I have come to the conclusion that this experience represented the shock of the cutting of the umbilical cord, when it was cut too soon, the negative internalised energy coming up into consciousness for healing.

Again others have reported severe pain around the head which could have been the grip of forceps, in many cases these people knew that theirs had been a forceps delivery.

So here we are, you have been born. You have just emerged

from the most difficult and dangerous experience that you will ever undergo, for you only have one chance, and you can't go back.

Remember all those present at your birth *did their best,* even if the predominant energy they created was high beta, *STRESS,* while yours was Alpha/Theta, *LOVE.* It's no fun projecting love, while you, such a wee person, meet such fast Beta stress at the most important time in your life, when you had your very first thought about life.

So, given all the options I have suggested in this chapter so far, let us wonder what was *your* very first thought about life, what were the impressions *you* received? It's understandable if you thought they were trying to *stop* you when you were trying almost against all odds to succeed in the most difficult and dangerous job you will ever undertake, to bring yourself into life. It could be understood if your first thought about life was a negative one, because you may have thought that life was dangerous, difficult, *against you.*

However here is where you may have made a great mistake in your summing-up, that life was against you, in fact was a hostile energy. A frightening feeling, particularly when from somewhere within you would have realised that you had your whole life in front of you. Here is a point to remember, that before we have a feeling, that something is frightening, *we have to have a prior thought that it is so,* because thoughts come before feelings.

A little further on in this chapter you may be able to sort out what was *your* first thought about life upon which all your other thoughts have been based, i.e. your foundation thought. Negative? Very likely for many babies. So from this powerful first thought on what we *thought* life was about, all our subsequent thoughts have been based, except that this was <u>*an erroneous thought about life*</u>. *However it may have affected your thinking all your life.*

259

As we have already proved, life is a loving energy. Just because the energy at our birth may have been less than loving, that was just the energy created by all those present at our birth, but not necessarily the correct energy of life. We shall have to go back and revise that faulty foundation stone of the life-plan to which we may have been referring all our lives. It has to be *re-set*, and can be reversed *whatever your age*.

We will call our first thought our *Personal Law*. It was either positive or negative. As we have proved, there are only two kinds of thought.

On the other hand remember what you accomplished at your birth. You left the safe place within the womb to travel down the birth canal, to go somewhere you had never been before, and did not know if you would make it. You had to put all your eggs in one basket and then a little more. You did not try to please anyone, or ask anyone's permission. Did you make it? Yes you did, congratulations, *so you have already succeeded in the most difficult and dangerous work you will ever attempt. Nothing can ever be more difficult or dangerous.*

In order to re-structure your life, you will have to use the same kind of energy you used at your birth, giving total dedication to your right path, putting all your energies into it, not trying to look over your shoulder or placate anyone. *Just go for it.*

If, however, you have been treating life as if it was dangerous, you will find it almost impossible to achieve your potential, because the *fear* residue of your first birth thought will be with you still, holding you back, through restricted breathing, and negative thinking about life. What a pity! How can you undo this block to your potential? It can be done.

★　★　★

STAY WITH ME FOR
PART TWO: THE POWER OF THOUGHT

If you find this at all difficult, remember you will almost certainly have conquered the complexities of the computer world, don't expect this will be any easier because you, like me, will have to open up new brain thinking in order to do so. The end result will be to improve your physical, mental and emotional harmony, as it has done for many, allowing us to see life as a benevolent energy rather than a destructive one.

I have consistently found that one of the problems which seems to prevent someone moving forward in therapeutic work is that they are afraid to trust themselves feeling happy in case everything goes wrong again, so that it is better to feel bad about life, you cannot then be disappointed!

How are we going to convince someone that it is safe to feel happy about life?

I have to find out if they have a faith, not necessarily a religion, so am usually quite straight forward and ask if they believe in God. They don't have to say yes to please me.

You may consider this to be a simplistic or confrontational question. Nevertheless quite a high percentage of clients will either say 'yes' or 'no'. Some will say that they have a belief in a Higher Power, even if they have fairly hazy ideas as to the nature of that power.

Anyway, to the non-believers among my clients or readers, I would ask for patience. To the believers in God or a Higher Power I ask if they consider this to be a totally loving power. The answer is usually 'yes', but sometimes 'no', so I point out that a perfectly loving power would never send them any-thing bad or it would not then be perfectly loving! This statement is often accompanied by a hesitation as if, despite a belief in a loving power, the client still wishes to maintain a little doubt over anything existing which is perfectly loving.

i.e. totally to be trusted.

To the non-believers and believers further questioning is needed.

Q: 'Has man the power to create a Universe such as the one on which we live?' The usual answer is 'no' although some people might disagree, illustrating this with all the discoveries of man and the cultures he has created. A little further discussion reveals that man's intelligence has not yet resulted in him creating a Universe i.e. planet Earth for instance, or he would have done so already.

It must then be supposed therefore that there exists a Higher Intelligence or energy than that of man.

Q: 'Is the Earth alive?' Some say 'yes', some say 'no'. Ask the 'no's to hold on for a moment or two while you ask a question of the 'yes"s. 'How do you know that it is alive?' Well, living things grow on it; this could not happen if the Earth was dead. The 'no"s usually then have to concede this point, the Earth is not a *dead* organism.

Q: 'Can you accept that everything which is alive has the life-force flowing through it, an energy, in fact an electrical frequency?'

A: 'Yes.'(virtually without exception.)

Q: 'Is that energy measurable?'

A: 'Well if it is an electrical frequency, yes.'

'Correct. Well if that is so, which frequency is it?' I explain here that electrical frequencies run in four gears or bands. Beta 15-24 vps (vibrations per second.) Alpha 9-15 vps. Theta 5-9 vps, Delta 5-0 vps. (All approx., and depending on which scientific data you refer to.) Frequent high Beta produces stress, hyper-activity. In Alpha you feel peaceful, creative and loving. In Theta you will be in a form of meditation or healing, spiritual mode. Delta is sleep.

It is now that we have to consider which is the electrical frequency used by the Earth, which as we have already agreed is of course alive. The answers will vary between all four, usually Beta or Delta. I don't know why anyone considers the Earth to be asleep.

Anyway it is a scientific fact that the electrical frequency of the Earth's magnetic field is at Alpha. A loving rhythm or energy. These are called Schumann waves.

I suppose if that changed, the Earth could go out of orbit, which would upset all the other planets, since they are all in some mathematical synchronicity inexplicable to me. It has to be maintained to avoid planetary mayhem.

A few years ago a nuclear physicist called Robert Beck went round the world measuring the brain rhythms of healers or spiritual people. He found that they were in the Alpha rhythm. People who were of perceived spiritual power, i.e. loving, like the Planet.

As we improve our breathing, and learn to relax and be calm, the electrical frequency of our brain will revert to Alpha, and we will feel loving and peaceful, like the Earth. We will also have re-connected ourselves to Nature. Ecological in the best sense.

If the electrical frequency of the Earth's energy is in a constant state of love, then the intelligence which created our universe must be a loving one, which never changes, and can be relied upon. Whether you wish to call it God or not, I don't suppose He would mind very much, as long as we can agree that surrounding us is a loving unchanging energy. People and nations can and do use that energy in the wrong way but it is always here, and a constant support when we trust it, as do babies and little children whose brain rhythms fluctuate between Alpha and Theta, love and highest spirituality. At least until they are about eight years old, and have had time to be contaminated with our cultural high Beta virus.

The Rhythm of Alpha is also the rhythm of Nature. When I was growing up I remember hearing a lot about man having to *conquer* Nature, as if She was evil! What rubbish! We have not got much time left to resonate with the force of Nature and help the Earth to heal Herself as we *get off her back*. *We* have to be conquered *by* Nature - Alpha the loving rhythm.

Q: 'Do you believe in God?'
A: 'WELL I NOW HAVE TO ACCEPT THAT THERE IS A CONSTANT LOVING ENERGY ALL ROUND ME, EVEN IF I DO NOT ALWAYS CHOOSE TO USE IT.'

I think that statement deserves CAPITAL LETTERS!

If, by the questions answers and discussions above, a client feels they can truthfully accept that there is a reliable loving energy all round us that will never let us down, *then I will have made it!*

I have found that I *have* to share these discussions with a client before they start on advanced work on breathing, because before long their breath will have taken them into a natural brain space where God or a similar power exists. It helps to have proved beforehand that this is a concept which they can trust, and upon that trust can rebuild often shattered lives.

This is during the period where they have left their negative thoughts about life behind, but have not yet completely firmed the cement of trust in a Higher Power.

This however is not the end of the story. Let me explain. If you are going to re-decorate your house, or even build a house, make a garden or do any creative project, the one thing you cannot avoid is preparation, and in some cases this requires almost as much time as creating the finished product.

In general we give little thought to breathing, since it is always there, the long slide from perfect correct breathing takes just that, a long time, so by the time it is recognised how badly we are malfunctioning in that respect our 'contempt' for our breath is so abysmal, that we have the nerve to think that we can repair it in one easy lesson. Not so, and because whether we recognise it or not, long-held fear is the major factor behind our damaged respiratory process, it is necessary to create in advance some sort of scaffolding or breathing plan to support us.

When our breathing changes and improves, our thoughts and emotions change. Not as in black versus white, but a subtle receding of the old as it becomes gradually overlaid with a new enlightenment.

Just as black goes through many forms of grey before it becomes white, our personal environment changes because of our improved breathing. Sometimes this change may appear confusing, even a little frightening. As Jung once said 'all growth is pain.'

People vary very much in the way they move through this process. It may take several years, with great surges of joy and true awareness but there can also seem to be emotional pain, and it takes a while to realise that it is the long-held suppressed pain from long ago which is *leaving* us, not entering us. The hurt child. We do not have our parents to support us as we may have done as a child, possibly they did not support us anyway. We are now in process of re-creating ourselves.

This process of breath repair is a period when we have to *re-parent* ourselves.

In his wonderful book *The Voice of the Earth* Theodore Roszak comments

'There is no mental health in our cities until we reawaken our psychic links with nature, observing that our very earliest subconscious awareness is about such ties, which are *deeper even than our much-explored relationship with our mothers.*'

I have found this to be a wonderfully liberating and helpful idea in the therapeutic situation, where so many people come to us who have had disastrous parental deprivation, and believe that nothing can change that earliest absence of love. Yet as a person moves through the re-build of their psyche in the breath-repair training a wonderful thing happens.

I have discovered that they have re-linked with their deepest loving ties with nature, which can override their former despair, that because of the damaged parental relationship, the resultant mistrust of love is permanent. It does not have to be.

The profound relaxation which is a by-product of correct breathing reminds me of another wonderful book *The Turning Point* by Fritjof Capra, a well-known physicist who wrote these profound words, which helped to reassure me about my own convictions:

Correct breathing is one of the most important aspects of relaxation, and one of the most vital elements in all stress-reduction techniques... When the organism is fully relaxed, one can make contact with one's unconscious to obtain important information about one's problems. The communication with the unconscious takes place through a highly personal, visual and symbolic language similar to that of dreams. Embracing various methods of relaxation, they are likely to play an *important part in all future therapies.*

(*Note: You cannot relax correctly unless you are breathing correctly.*)

★ ★ ★

266

STAGE THREE

*Now let us have some fun, for in this section
I shall be your fairy Godmother!*

Q: 'If I could grant you three wishes, what would you
wish for?'
A: (Generally) 'Money, happiness, success, love.' (the
love wished for here is usually romantic love.)
I have to reply that 'if you had your three wishes you
would have these things automatically, i.e. they will be a
by-product of your efficient wishes. Let's go back to base
and perhaps think about the love you mentioned.'
Q: 'What are we in when we have love?'
A: 'Well,' (often after a lengthy pause) 'A relationship.'
'Right, well what's wrong with having that for your
first wish?' *'Perfect loving relationships with many
people including a perfect partner.'*

Defining the second wish can sometimes be helped by
suggesting that there are twenty-four hours to the day, eight
of which we spend sleeping, eight eating, chores, socialising,
we still have eight left. Finally a client mentions that the
remaining eight would be spent working. Often the *work* is
seen as a way of merely passing time in order to get money
to pay bills, making money. Very rarely deeply satisfying,
often caught up in the rat race.

'If you have three wishes, of which you have already spent
one, why not have the second as *"The perfect work that develops
and uses your deepest talents and skills?"'*

(No one has ever argued with that wish, although doubts
may be expressed at that point as to it being a possibility.)

Third wish. Silence often follows while the first two wishes
are still being contemplated. 'Let's think about this. If you
found the perfect loving relationships and the perfect work

say in Cornwall, and you lived in Belfast, what would you have to do?' It's amazing how many people say 'travel'! 'What, every day?' Eventually the word 'move' is aired. 'Well if you move what will you have to find?' Again, after a pause. 'A house.' Me: 'What's a nicer word than a house?' At last *'A home.'*

So the third wish has to be *'The perfect home in the right place.'* Obviously it has to be in the right place near the relationships and work. A perfect home does not have to be a castle or a hovel, just the right place for you.

Now comes the challenge. 'Do you have all these things?' The answer is usually 'no', or if someone has one correct wish, they don't have the others. Actually if one aspect of our wishes is not right, usually the others are out of balance in some way.

At this point I am forced to say 'Well if all your wishes are loving, as they are, because if you have all the loving relationships you wish, that's nice for other people, because they can then have them with you. If you find the work that develops and uses your deepest talents and skills, the world will be a better place for you having lived. If you are not in the perfect home for *you*, someone will be in *your* perfect home, and you will be in *theirs*.'

'So, why haven't you got what you most want? Read on to find why not.'

Here's the next challenge, because I then have to say 'we have just proved that everything you would like is loving, and a little while ago we proved that life is also loving It stands to reason then that everything you would most like must be here somewhere. It is also on your unique vibration or electrical frequency since we are all unique, as has been proved by science. It would not be correct for anyone else to have it. In other words it will be wasted if you do not claim it.'

Your three wishes will automatically include everything you most want, for instance: the perfect work would include, if it is *perfect*, having enough money; the same applies to relationships and home.

Q: 'So, have you got everything you most want?'

Ninety per cent or more people, as I said earlier, will say 'no' to this question. You do not have to ask chapter and verse at this point as to why their answer is in the negative.

Of the remaining percentage, who think they have it all, even though they are coming to see you for stress problems (!), it is usually a fairly simple to ask if they had an opportunity to improve existing relationships, work, home, what would they improve?

They will invariably come up with a desired improvement, which will allow you to remind them that perhaps after all, at this moment in time, their lives are not *quite* perfect.

It is important to reassure them that no one is minimising or criticising anything at present already existing in their lives.

On the other hand it is now that we recall that if everything they most want is here somewhere, and the Highest Power there is will never take it away, because the Highest Power is perfectly loving, and life is also already loving; can they give a reason as to why they have not got everything they most want?

This may take a little time, trying to tease out the reason why, in words with which the client feels most comfortable.

For example 'I am not good enough to get what I most want.' or 'it's not safe to get what I most want.' 'If I get what I most want, someone will take it away.' 'I'm afraid to get what I most want.'

I have to remind a client that they have just told me a big whopper, because they have already been successful, have done the most difficult and dangerous thing they will ever attempt, so how can they come up with such fibs?

In asking the other person to tell you when this most difficult and dangerous event occurred, teasing out the correct response takes quite a lot of patience and tact, but finally the answer emerges. 'At my birth.' Of course, as we discussed earlier, we leave the safe place and cannot return, come along a time of confusion to go somewhere we have never been before, and don't know if we will make it. We have to put all our eggs in one basket. 'It's like diving off the top board in a swimming pool in a fog, not knowing if there's water in the pool!', 'Did you make it?' 'Yes.' 'So congratulations, you have already succeeded in your *greatest life challenge,* so the negative statement you gave needs to be corrected, for anything else you wish to do will be a lesser challenge.'

'On the other hand probably something happened at your birth after you made such an almighty effort, which may have given you the impression that you had failed.' (I refer to the possible birth trauma which could have been experienced by the baby earlier in this chapter.

'Your first introduction into life is when you made your foundation erroneous thought about life because, as we have proved, life is already loving, even if the energies at your birth seemed unloving. You thought you had failed then, and somehow the failure thought has been spoiling your life ever since. The negative energies were not *life*, rather the limited way in which your birth may have been handled by people whose energies were not totally loving. Even if yours were. *But they did their best.*

'Remember you came into life carrying the highest electrical frequency of love, and so were victorious despite what seemed to be opposition.

'You have to forgive them, and also yourself for the incorrect thoughts you have had about life not being loving.'

I have discovered that the negative reason or thought someone gives as to why they have not got what they most wanted, often seems to mirror the negative first thought at their birth experience, and this erroneous thought conceived at the vital time of entry into life, has been called our *Personal Law*. If it was profoundly negative, this law has to be reversed by words and action, otherwise it will remain as a perpetual unconscious block in our lives It is an incorrect thought about life, and as long as it is there in our mind at any level it will remain as a saboteur to our being all that we may be, limiting our potential and confidence.

As we heal our breathing this very powerful negative thought usually surfaces fairly soon. It is amazing how often it mirrors the Old Personal Law a client has produced to explain why they have not got what they want in life, even although we have scientifically proved that they can!

The purpose of this exercise is to bring this old life-destructive thought to the surface, and reverse its negative power, which has been preventing the client from achieving their potential.

Here is a way to begin to *reverse our Old Personal Law* in easy steps. Change is best achieved in gradual stages.

WE HAVE TO CREATE A PLAN, EVEN IF YOU HAVE NOT YET COMPLETED THE PLAN

Let us think of one of the commonest negative laws. 'I am not good enough to get what I most want.'

'*What never ever? Think of what you have already achieved.*'

A: 'Well, sometimes I *am* good enough to get what I most want.'

Q: '*Could we up-grade that statement, say for instance?*'
'A little more often I am good enough to get what I most want.'

'OK!'

'Quite often I am good enough to get what I most want.'
'OK.'

Q: 'Very often?' ''   ''   ''   ''   ''   ''
A: *'All right then.'*
Q: 'Most of the time?   ''   ''   ''   ''   ''
A: *'OK. I'll go for it.'*
Q: 'ALL THE TIME?'   ''   ''   ''   ''
A: *'YES!'*

The above last sentence actually represents what we really did at our birth, we got what we most wanted, which was? *Life.* You will never want anything more passionately. Did you make it? YES. So you have already been successful in the most difficult and dangerous experience of your life, and nothing can ever be so difficult. Let us now write your NEW PERSONAL LAW.

It is now safe for me to be good enough to get what I most want *all the time*.

As we embark on the journey to correct our breathing pattern, and also our thoughts, changes happen in our lives, and we need supportive help on the way, which may not be available from family and friends, particularly as they are not travelling on this solo journey, and can't be expected to understand what is happening in our newly created lives. The preceding pages are to give you *your own* supportive help on this journey.

However, down the ages there have been wise men and women, spiritual leaders, philosophers, who have written down words which can stand the test of time. These words in a simple form represent truths which are irreversible. They can form a scaffolding of trustworthy support as we go through the transitions which accompany our breathing changes, as we move through the exciting time of 'letting go of who I am, in order to be who I have not yet become. I did it successfully when I was born, I am *now ready* to claim the prize of being all I can be.'

We can call these wise words *affirmations:*

1. I can have *everything*, and I deserve it.
2. All things I seek are now *seeking me.*
3. All my ships sail home to me *over calm seas.*
4. All my heart's desires have been placed there, *in order that they may be granted.*

FINALLY

5. If the Highest Power and intelligence has already put into the world for you everything you most want, whether or not you have yet got it, it's time you were grateful.

'Praise and gratitude are love in action.' - Leonard Orr. Let us address this Highest Power. The client is encouraged to write down the following as a letter of gratitude:

NEW PERSONAL LAW

Dear Highest Power God, Friend, energy, loving being [The client must choose for him/her self the form of address that their hearts feel right with.]
I *now* give thanks that the perfect loving relationships, the perfect work which develops and uses my deepest talents and skills, the perfect home in the right place, *which are mine by right,* for my own prosperity and the greater good, are now released and reach me under grace in a perfect way.

This chapter will probably require you to read and think it through several times. I wrote it to support anyone who is healing their breathing, which can seem a lonely process sometimes, but so well worth it. I hope the 'penny drops' as it did for me.

Here's a good thought to finish with:

IF YOU REALLY WANT TO BE HAPPY,
NOBODY CAN STOP YOU.

Sister Mary Tricky

Chapter 23

THE NOSE

A FEW YEARS AGO I would never have believed that I could feel so passionately about what I suppose would be called 'the right use of the nose.' Until fairly recently as far as I was aware, the nose was just an appendage on the front of the face, occasionally to be cleared. When I was a child I used a handkerchief to blow my nose, probably embroidered with a flower motif in one corner. I still have a few of these within, what was called in my childhood, a *handkerchief-sachet,* one of my first achievements in my primary school sewing class. It was worn acoss one shoulder, and hung to the side. A good place to hide the odd sweet. My father used to use a dozen or more large white cotton handkerchiefs each week, which my mother boiled on washing day. As a nine-year old amateur I had the job of pulling out the corners and creases, and ironing into exact immaculate white squares for his working days in his office. Nowadays most people use a tissue.

The proper use, science and function of the nose is one of the most vital health lessons we could learn, and I believe *need to learn.* In the past few weeks, having once again been confronted by the abbreviations IQ, I realised they invariably apply to *intellectual* intelligence, whereas increasingly I am concerned that universally we seem to neglect another more important EQ measurement. That of *emotional intelligence* which, I am positive, must precede intellectual intelligence, or the latter is a hollow column of meaningless figures. Nose science develops the use of emotional intelligence.

At eighty, it is only in the last twenty years I have realised that in breathing correctly, we are meant to breathe in through the nose, *and out through the nose*. This matters so much to me nowadays, that I watch with horror the actors on TV who seem to spend their time breathing out through the mouth in any exclamation of negativity, while my emotional EQ is registering the amount of additional polluting CO_2 they are discharging into the atmosphere by exhaling in this way. To me these days exhaling through the mouth seems as ridiculous as putting food up the nose in order to eat!

I do understand that we *can* use the mouth to get air in and out of the lungs, but believe that should be only in an extremity, just as only in an extremity we see someone being fed through tubes in the nose in a hospital.

Someone who is hyperventilating breathes in and out through the mouth, because they are locked in a state of fear and panic. When we *over-exercise*, we bring mouth breathing into use. *I am not sure if we are meant to over-exercise!* You can easily recall a memory of an athlete who is constantly over-exercising in competitive sports bending over in respiratory extremis and using the mouth for breath recovery. I do not have a great deal of sympathy for competitive exercise to try and prove oneself superior to someone else. I believe it is morally questionable to want to prove myself better than another, in any form of man-made test.

I note how many competitive athletes seem to develop later life-threatening health problems, and that the so-called competitive life-style does not necessarily ensure a longer life span or freedom from later life ill-health or disease.

Cricketers may be the exception! I am sure that many will disagree with me on my comments in these last lines, but I speak from observation.

There are many beautiful ways to exercise the body which

do not impose competition, or the unnatural strain of oral exhalation.

Nature never seems to run like mad, except possibly when she is reacting to man-made excesses. She then has no option but to bring herself back into balance in apparently violent ways such as natural disasters.

The astonishing discoveries which I have made concerning the nose have come to me *despite* rather then *because* of my therapeutic training.

In my training as a psychotherapist, or any subsequent training I have undergone, any mention of the nose has been noticeably absent. My discoveries and training have come from working with many people in breath repair, the unintentional re-emergence of my own emotional IQ, and gems of information which mirrored my own findings, from too few writers who understand the language of the nose.

This true science of the nose seems to be rarely understood, because medical science and treatment appears to be involved with intellectual IQ, and not its connection with the emotions. Again the concern with symptoms rather than cause.

If a highly-paid medical professional concerned with the nose does not breathe correctly themselves, as some do not, I cannot see how they know how to prevent the symptoms of the patient from re-occurring.

I remember someone well-known to me who was treated as a young person for what are called nasal polyps (a growth protruding from the mucus lining of the nose). From what I recall of the emotional environment of that highly intelligent young person's childhood, his relationship with his father had been disastrous. I now believe that the growth of his nasal polyps was the result of breath-holding from fear of his father during his childhood. In holding his breath from apprehension, the suppression of the circulation of nasal oxygen would, I suppose, have created the build-up of surplus energy tissue.

Despite the operation to remove the physical problem, as a man, he spent his whole life affected by the emotional trauma from his childhood, and his eventual death mostly from alcohol and nicotine abuse despite a highly successful intellectual career, reflected I believe the *nasal* tragedy of his emotional life.

It seems appalling to reflect that in the boxing world, the main aim is to render your opponent helpless by one of several lethal blows, and the one to the nose is most vital. What an occupation, to encourage the one organ of the body which was invented by nature to convey the life-force to the lungs to be so abused. Obviously such an injury will quickly limit air to the lungs, and therefore loss of energy. Use of the mouth as an emergency supply is restricted by the gum-shield. How obscene is this parody for gruesome entertainment, almost a hand-me-down from the time of the Roman gladiators! While the audience screams and gloats.

Only a few writers have spoken as graphically as I would wish, on the right use and function of the nose. One or two span several generations, from Yoga Ramacharaka, who spoke of 'mouth breathing as being the most disgusting form of breathing known to man', and Tania Clifton-Webb who runs a breathing practice in New Zealand who, in her recent book *Breathe for Success,* speaks of nose-breathing as 'Nature's Second-best Kept Secret'. *Secret,* because I believe that intentionally or unintentionally our intellectually motivated medical hierarchal IQ treatment of its responsibility to the masses, has withheld from those masses the secrets of health which, if understood, would deprive the medical and pharmaceutical world of much of their livelihood. For those masses would then recover the true secrets of health known from within. The secrets of healthy living are thrown at us ad nauseum, in various forms of media coverage, but what is withheld is the single most important health information that of *correct* breathing.

Unfortunately many health educationalists are not healthy breathers themselves, particularly concerning the emotional IQ implications of correct nasal respiratory function. Nature's No. 1 Law of Health.

I have lost count of some yoga books, health books and health teachers who will tell you that you must breathe in through the nose, and out through the mouth. I disagree with this, which I believe to be erroneous, and against the laws of Nature.

Now try this little exercise. Find a quiet room, and stand upright comfortably. Think of slowing down all your reactions, then try this breath experiment without haste and with awareness. Listen to what is happening in your body, especially the lungs as you: (a) Breath in through the nose, and out through the mouth. Then: (b) Breathe in through the nose, and out through the nose. Do notice that when you breathe as in b, do you discover that there is an impulse to draw the next breath in from a lower part of your lungs?

Repeat this little exercise several times, until you understand that there is a subtle difference between (a) and (b).

I have come to call (a) *carnal breathing*, and (b) *spiritual breathing*. When you really study this subject, you are apt to come up with new verbal inventions to describe the art of respiration. This often happens when I attempt to describe aspects of breath use.

They don't teach soldiers correct breathing from what I can gather. The (b) method, would make it much harder to go out and kill your enemy, you might even refuse to do so, your conscience would not let you. To be a fighter you have to have a lot of held tension, in order to discharge it in aggressive action. The (a) breathing method encourages us to suppress loving emotion which complicates the issue when you have to summon tension to kill. To breathe correctly makes it impossible to kill. On the other hand when man is eventually civilised enough to discover other ways to disarm his opponent by the power of breath and thought, he will be able to utilise higher spiritual means to deflect aggression.

Understanding the fine and full subtlety of nose breathing does not happen overnight, you have to think about months, even years, so be patient. To clear blocked or partly blocked nasal passageways enough to take oxygen straight to the brain means that all the years of suppressed breathing have to be reversed. The thick white substance which has lined the respiratory tubes, because of undischarged nasal waste has to be melted into mucus, runny enough to be discharged via the orifices of the head, nose, mouth eyes, even ears! This can take quite a longish period.

The *melting* effect of correct oxygenation gradually dissolves the wax into a mucus sufficiently loose to be coughed up in the form of phlegm. This elimination process must take whatever time is required.

As a result we become aware of a gradual lightening in the breathing mechanism. It is as if we are beginning to *use* ourselves in a better way. We seem to be bringing in a new perspective in our loving respect for ourselves. We have more energy, confidence, an awareness of a sense regained from our childhood, that of the *joy* of life with which we were born. This has been lost or mislaid in our intellectual and materialistic culture, and we are now reclaiming our spiritual inheritance. The right use of breath (spirit) respiritualises us.

My own process of this rediscovery has been further confirmed in my breathing therapy sessions with clients who had been forced to use mouth breathing as a back-up because their nasal passages were almost blocked.

It is distressing to be with someone who cannot sustain nasal inhalation and exhalation for more than a few breaths, without having to open the mouth to draw in extra oxygen.

Living examples of being unable to use Nature's law for life, which cannot be disobeyed without eventual loss of health.

The frightening number of people who suffer from sinus problems, and who are dependent upon medication to clear, but probably damage, the delicate membrane lining of the nose, are proof of this appalling problem in our midst. From those I have met, their long-standing mental and emotional symptoms include constant worry, under-achievement, poor relationships, negative thought patterns, and general health problems. The one constant symptom was inhibited nostril breathing.

I vividly recall a key-speaker at a health conference many years ago, speaking of sinus problems as *'blocked tears'*. A truism prevalent in all stratas of society, as the symptom of blocked breathing, the precursor of the blocked tears stalks our streets. *The tears are always those of the child within.*

Time and again as a person re-established correct nasal use, there was a noticeable reduction in stress symptoms, and an increasing ability and insight into ways to solve their difficulties *without my help*! Nothing else had happened other than the re-training of the breathing instinct and correct nasal use, which led them to solve their own problems.

I remember learning about the five basic instincts as a schoolchild. The one attributed to the nose was 'smell'. Why breathing for life was not taught us as the prime nose use I do not know. Surely smell is the *secondary* use of the nose.

Re-training in correct nasal breathing, which warms the air and catches dust before it reaches the sensitive membranes of the lungs, draws up a more adequate supply of oxygen to the brain, and in exhaling through the nose, we seem to excrete a more refined volume of waste CO_2 from the base of the lungs. Once again, try it and see. Stand easy, breathe in and out through the mouth, and then try the same action through the nose. Different as chalk from cheese.

If you have not been in the habit of using the nose properly, it may be a little difficult at first. As you bring lazy nasal muscles into use again, the result resembles trimming the hedges of an overgrown lane, which has restricted human access for some years!

A better intake of oxygen, opens up brain-cell information, which needs that extra sparkle of oxygen to open up new life, just as a plant sends out fresh green shoots. As Karen Roon says in *The New Way to Relax*, 'like giving water to a dying daffodil.' You notice this particularly when you are assisting a child in improved breathing.

As you become more nose aware, try watching the people on TV who are speaking, discussing or trying to answer questions in the various programmes. You may observe them (a) rubbing the ends of their noses as they give an indication of worry, (b) tapping the side of the nose as a sign of keeping something secret, and (c) taking the top of the nose between finger and thumb in trying to work out a problem. Over the years, like the hands and feet which are the outposts of the physical body, I have realised that the nose is really an outpost of the connection of the lungs with the brain and our feelings. Rubbing the tip signals a degree of worry, tapping the side seems to trigger a breath-hold in the diaphragm area, a holding-in, (of a secret) and the slight squeezing of the top of the nose, indicates trying to solve a problem, drawing answers from the intuitive right brain.

Some writers refer to this area at the top-centre of the nose between the eyes as the 'third eye'.

The tip of the nose does, I believe, have a direct connection to the lowest area of the lungs, which when filled correctly, stimulates what is known as the sacral (sacred?) area or *second brain*, the seat of wisdom and feeling, between the pelvic bone and the navel.

When this occurs, the up-rise of the breath from that

lower point oxygenates the higher brain area, a strategic ignition activator for the harmony of mind/body/spirit.

I began to think that each tiny part of the nose has a connection with a specific part of the lungs and brain, and right use triggers infinite possibilities to fresh ideas and creative ways to use our potential. Something I would like to study more fully.

For me the most inspiring factor which has emerged from all this has been the emergence of my own and a client's spirituality. This has nothing to do with any religion, but a sure knowledge and acceptance of a Power greater than our own, which can be trusted. This awareness gives us the insight and courage to resolve former apparently insolvable life problems.

I seem to have spent quite a lot of time in the last years in the occupation of *musing,* which is perhaps an under-rated word. When did you last use it? It's not one I use very often, but it describes a period of silent communication with the self. No doubt all creativity arises from a period of musing.

When someone is stretched out nice and warm and comfortable, breathing away steadily, I sometimes cast a detached look at them, and realise that at a very deep level they are involved in an intense inner search. I believe that person is *re-inspiring* themselves as inspiring levels of their persona are revealed to them through the re-oxygenation of brain cells through correct breathing, which have held important core information now being restored to consciousness.

Have you ever observed someone whose nostrils are not equal, in that one side seems more open than the other? The narrower the nostril, the narrower the outlook. Wide nostrils I understand indicate a person of rude health, but of course there's a happy medium. Too wide can indicate a coarseness of outlook. When you observe a disparity of nostril width, It indicates that we are drawing up less oxygen up one side.

Remember the left nostril feeds the right creative brain, and the right nostril the left logical outgoing side. I have noticed that a number of correct breathing sessions seems to help re-balance the size of the nostril width, which also assists in re-balancing the two brain hemispheres.

Disparity in nostril width can mean over-stimulation of one brain hemisphere at the expense of the other.

To me learning the subtle language of the breath and nose has revealed as much information about the nature of man as the Encyclopedia Britannica!

The clients who come to us teach us so much, I am eternally grateful for the amazing insights imparted to me by people, some of whom I have now known for many years. You cannot teach what you do not really believe yourself. Much of what I have learned has come to me from what I can only call the People's University of Health, which is the wisdom already unconsciously known to us all, but so rarely imparted through our established centres of learning who ignore its vital educational importance.

I believe it is the old wisdom which we all know, which if it came into being, would regenerate the race and the world. Disease would become a rarity as Ramaharaka said. In ignoring the old wisdom, the medics and scientists have lost the way, and if we listen to them, mankind will never reach his potential, which has to be his spiritual potential *never mind if there's life or not on Mars!*

You hear of scientific experiments using stem cells from the lining of the nose which seems to affirm, without telling us why, that there must be something special about those cells, linked to our primary essence. Running the oxygen over them correctly must have very specific implications for our health as we breathe correctly, or incorrectly.

For me the science of the nose carries with it the full development of instinct, intuition, and the harvesting of the power of the creative brain. I am positive that as animals have a full range of sensitivity from the use of the organ of the nose, so humanity has probably lost the function of that same area of sensitivity by an insensitivity which veils from our awareness much that would delight our days.

At the beginning of this chapter I mentioned the work of three writers. In *The Science of Breath*, Ramacharaka refers to an outbreak of small-pox on a naval vessel. Of the deaths which resulted, all were mouth breathers, and not a single man who breathed correctly through the nose died.

If this assessment was applied in connection with the scourge of modern day diseases, I wonder what the researchers would find. What about MRSA? Swine flu?

In his book *The Healing Power of Breath*, Jonathan Daemion refers to the fact that nostril breathing stimulates the sinus cavities on its way to the brain, and a special essence within the air then stimulates certain areas of the brain into higher consciousness.

If we breathe out through the mouth, this consciousness is diminished, so that any shadowy impulse received via the brain is unlikely to be transformed into action. Since all action is the result of what we believe to be true from our consciousness, we have the choice by correct breathing as to whether our actions stem from a higher or lower impulse!

Tania Clifton Webb's very much up-to-date book on breathing, called *Breathe to Succeed In Every Aspect of Your Life* has made an enormously valuable contribution to the effect of correct breathing on our modern life-styles.

The title of her second chapter is called, as I mentioned earlier, 'The Nose - The Body's Second-best kept Secret' (*Breathing* is the first). What a great title. It refers to the fact that mouth breathing is an inefficient gas exchange, and she states that nose breathing increases oxygen intake by ten to twenty per cent.

The brain needs well over thirty-five per cent of the oxygen we take in (some say more). When correct, the process of exhalation excretes seventy per cent of our waste material in the form of gas. This excretory process is meant to be via the nostrils. I believe, although do not have documentary proof, that there is an area at the back of the throat over which the exhaled air has to pass, which acts as a *'catalytic converter'* and performs a purification function, in the same way that a filter by the same name on the exhaust pipe of a car reduces toxic fumes.

The incorrectly filtered toxic breath waste from the lungs carries infection, as it is a pollutant, which contaminates, and is probably the biggest carrier of infection in our hospitals. How many decades do we have to go through before all health-workers have to pass a breath-test? Health and Safety officers take note? Try it for yourselves!

So you have the choice between carnal or spiritual breathing.

BE AS NOSEY AS YOU LIKE ABOUT THE NOSE,
IT WILL PAY YOU DIVIDENDS BEYOND PRICE.

Chapter 24

THE POWER OF
THE BREATH

WHEN I BEGAN MY THERAPEUTIC WORK, I thought that it would be a good thing to accumulate as many qualifications and certificates in complementary health (as it is known) as I could. After a while my aspirations changed. At that time everyone seemed to think that massage was the answer. Somehow I cannot think of massage as a therapeutic tool, despite the expressions of euphoria one sees on the face of someone who is on the receiving end of the treatment. What happens then? Another massage in a week or two, and so on and so on. For some reason I have never been interested in giving or receiving massage, but have given this process some thought.

Touch is, I admit, a very important part of communication, but if we are regularly so tense that only massage can relieve the tension, it is as if we are looking for the touch and stroking that we should have received as a child. If we did not receive this, perhaps that is why we are constantly seeking that touch, but that need was supposed to have been received in childhood. No other adult can fill that need once we are of an adult age. To me massage can put the recipient into a needy child role with the masseur as the parent. I have strong doubts that any therapeutic activity in which a repetitive parent/child scenario can help the child within the adult to mature. I may be wrong in this opinion.

I hope my words will not give offence to anyone who gives or receives massage as a purely social activity. No doubt I have trodden on some toes already!

There are many other forms of complementary help available, all of which require two people, but I often wonder if someone was shipwrecked on a desert island, how they could help themselves with no one else around to give them therapy. Or when we are alone, with no one else available, how can we restore ourselves to balance?

When I began to experience the power of the breath personally, and realised that parts of my own nature which I can only describe as the hurt child were beginning to surface, it was as if I was being given an unseen tool from within myself to move through these levels of incomplete maturation, which I had not realised existed within myself.

None of this growth was secured easily, again as Jung said 'there is no growth without pain.'

On the other hand the energy for the healing of the pain came up from within, at the same time as the experience of that pain as it left me, and I realised what was happening.

I knew then that I had to *re-grow* myself, and this was true for anyone moving through the same process. I also had to do it myself. Only someone who had also gone through the repair of their respiratory pattern, which also involves mind and emotions, could perhaps share and interpret what was happening to me, but they could not do it *for* me.

I began to understand how the wonderful energy and power of the breath can actually recharge into action, glandular and cellular changes essential for full maturation, the plan for which is stored within the blueprint of each individual psyche. It could only be converted from a dormant state to cellular enlightenment by the action of spiritual oxygen moving through the physical, mental and emotional levels of personality. Like a benevolent virus which knew its precise work with the accuracy of an invisible laser beam.

It occurs to me that as we correct the breathing process, the lungs act rather as an internal self-masseur as the muscles around the lungs then release their tension, and we feel the full benefit of relaxation. An identical process to an external massage, but inwardly generated, the effects of which are clearly felt as the muscles gripping the lungs relax. Circulation is improved, with the racing brain slowing down, through correct breathing, thereby inducing the resultant feeling of peace and calm. If the brain does not relax, nothing beneficial has happened. This *correct* breathing is a genuine deep internal self massage. Why pay for something you can do for yourself?

Some years ago I was speaking at an alternative health conference in Glasgow. Following my talk I was demonstrating one of the only two touch therapies I use from time to time, in this case the Metamorphic Technique, a detached way of gently using the hands to stimulate an area down the spinal bone of the foot. There is no aspect of expectation of results in this work, in which the therapist is merely acting as a catalyst, and the life-force within the client creates change *at the right time*.

A young woman was brought to me, who seemed to be in an unstoppable process of weeping. Eventually without conversation I indicated that I could work with her in the Metamorphic process, and she seemed willing to be a recipient. Very soon the weeping stopped, and we completed the session in silence.

This lady asked to see me privately, and came to my consulting rooms. On the second occasion of meeting her, she again broke down in tears. I did not attempt to obtain much information from her, but felt that it might be helpful to introduce her to an exercise in correct breathing.

She seemed to find this helpful, and we spoke more fully about her present life, in which she did not outwardly appear to have many problems, being happily married with two children. However she still seemed to bring with her a feeling of great sadness.

Because she later became quite interested in my respiratory work, she developed the ability to maintain the correct breathing mode for quite long periods, always declaring herself to feeling much calmer and more stable as a result. On a particular occasion I was sitting quietly while she was maintaining her breath re-training, stretched out on a mat with a blanket.

I began to notice a strange odour in the room which became more invasive, and which I eventually interpreted as resembling anaesthesia. I had no idea where this could have come from, but subsequently mentioned this to my client. She told me that she had had a very difficult birth, and her mother was in labour for a long time with no apparent progress. Her mother was in such distress that she was given an anaesthetic just before the birth, not, I understand, recommended practice, and we could only conclude that the same smell in the room was the excretion of anaesthesia which had been trapped in the baby's lung tissue at the time of birth.

This lady also said that she had not been anaesthetised at any other time in her life, which could have explained the presence of its distinctive odour.

Sometimes it is very difficult to interpret the original cause for a client's symptoms, but I believe that a baby can pick up and absorb the maternal emotional state at the time of birth, which in my client's case was one of feeling/near to death. I do not believe her relationship with her mother was very close as she grew older, but certainly I could sense a feeling of relief in my client, subsequent to this episode, which I could only interpret a regaining use of former blocked lung-cell tissue, which opened out vibrant brain information which had been dormant since birth. Her air of sadness disappeared naturally.

In one of those isolated snippets of information of which we all hold hundreds in our brain memory, I recalled reading of the vital importance of our first conscious breaths. They must I suppose be connected with our initial impressions of life. The earlier we go back, the more vital are these impressions. To be without them even at an unconscious level is to be without the connecting information that makes some sense of our first experience of life as we emerge from the womb. We can feel uprooted from life and therefore aware of a distressing floating insecurity of loss which keeps us from being able to enjoy being alive. We seem to be permanent carriers of an unknown grief.

I know of no substance other than the energy of correct breath, which can achieve the miracle of repair in order to regain self-wholeness, and I believe there has to be a great leap in collective understanding for us to realise that we alone are the only ones who can breathe for ourselves in order for self-repair or health-healing to take place.

Without any disparagement of the medical profession, it has its limitations of understanding in respect of the art of breath healing, which cannot be achieved by drugs.

As my client regained the use of full correct breath, and the excretion through her blood-stream of the toxins which had been suppressing the vibrationary health of primal cells, she began to live a full creative life, and the tears were a thing of the past.

I recall another client in a professional career who had been diagnosed with a brain tumour, which had been operated upon, but post-operative lesions required further operative procedures. These entailed the insertion of a very fine needle up through the groin, and the body, and eventually into the brain to achieve what I understood was a sealing process.

Quite naturally she was apprehensive at the thought of the operation, but when she came to see me subsequently, she had some interesting information to impart.

Apparently after an operation, it is normal procedure for a physiotherapist to physically apply pressure to activate the elimination of remaining anaesthesia from the lungs of post-operative patients. In respect of my client, the physiotherapist was amazed that in her case there was no anaesthetic to eliminate. By correct breathing she had naturally excreted the anaesthetic from her system! There was no other explanation.

Only correct breathing properly eliminates waste material from the system. Anything less ensures that we remain clogged-up with the poisons of these harmful toxins which eventually usually results in a health crisis of some kind.

THE POWER OF THE BREATH IS EXACTLY THAT, A GREAT POWER, WHICH IS UNIVERSALLY MISUNDERSTOOD IN OUR SO-CALLED CIVILISED SOCIETY.

A different kind of intelligence needs to be developed, and we are running out of time.

The intelligence we need to retrieve from the core of our being is directly connected with that core. It is to do with the loving child in our central being, the child who risked everything in one great endeavour to bring itself into life, who left the safe place, came along a time of confusion to go somewhere it had never been before, did not know if it would make it, and yet had to put everything into that great effort plus the 'extra mile'.

It did not seek to please anyone, ask anyone's permission, and in gaining life broke through the barrier, in order to be successful in the most difficult and dangerous challenge it will ever undertake, to gain life. Yet more than that, to use the power of the breath to carry out the unique task it came to perform, to leave the world a better place.

Is mankind achieving that object? From the parlous state of our unique Universe it would seem not.

In pondering on what we need to do in order to save our Planet, we have to retrieve the courage we used to bring ourselves into life, to leave the safe place of our individual search for selfish gain for an artificial security, which recent financial chaos has proved to be no security. We have to make an ultimate collective decision to leave behind the false womb of material gain in which we have been cocooned, to risk all in order to save our precious Earth. We may not know if we can, but as long as we are content to remain as puppets to materialism, we shall lose it all anyway.

The effort will have to be Herculean, but we have been there before and we made it. We earned the right to breathe, as a baby we knew the power of right breath, if we have given away that birthright, we can get it back again. I sincerely believe that it is only by the power of correct breath that we can save not only the Earth but ourselves.

In her book *We Can Heal Ourselves,* that great writer Louise Hay speaks of something far more precious than money without which we could not exist. She tells us that our breath *is* the most precious substance in our lives, and 'we take for granted that at the end of each inhale the next breath will be here.' From what I can gather of the increasing pollution which is fatally affecting so many forms of natural and plant life, before long our next breath may not be assumed to be available.

Louse Hay suggests that if we trust the Power that first gave us breath, to supply all our needs, everything else we need will also be supplied, but we must use it *correctly.*

It is because we do not value that breath, we misuse and abuse it, and take it for granted, that we are in the middle of such horrendous problems. Yet by the right use of correct breath, I am truly positive apparent disasters could be averted. All our needs will get supplied. I have proved it. Correct breath leads to correct thought, which leads to correct action and results.

There is still time to trust the Power of the breath, but I believe it has to be the *correct* breath, anything less than that carries the limiting power of fear, and artificial substitutes, which are only shadows of reality, and can only come to nothing or less than nothing.

We had the power to bring ourselves into life, that knowledge correctly used would help us to save Mother Earth. It supersedes science as we know it.

President Obama of the USA, spoke at his election of the people 'breathing with one breath.' In the context of healing the earth that is exactly what is needed, but only the correct breath is good enough, *for it carries the highest power.*

WE HAVE TO LEARN, BEFORE IT IS TOO LATE,
HOW TO USE THE HIGHEST POWER, TO SAVE
OURSELVES AND THE EARTH.

Chapter 25

MAGNETIC NORTH

I THINK I HAVE ALREADY SUGGESTED at some point in this book that you 'suspend your disbelief'. A little later in this chapter I would like to introduce you to a very interesting experiment which you can conduct by yourself in your home or garden. Once it has begun to work for you, you can demonstrate it to your friends. It is not however a party trick in the usual sense of the word, but a graphic example of the wonderful way in which the world of nature responds to nature within us, and as such should always be treated with respect.

Let me tell you how I was introduced to this fascinating exercise which I will call a phenomenon which is neither occult nor psychic. I have found that sceptical people will take a little longer to allow themselves to respond, but when they do, you may notice a change in their apparent cynicism, and even a sense of pride, almost of relief that they had discovered that there was a whole new world out there worthy of exploration, which has nothing to do with intellectual training, the computer or business world.

Anyway to cut to the chase as they say. I was with a group of people in a classroom of an old school in the centre of Glasgow, which we had converted to a stress centre, primarily to teach relaxation and correct breathing. A therapist on a visit from Australia was giving a talk. I forget what was the main theme of her subject, other than that it was relevant to the mainstream of our work.

At the conclusion of her talk, a period of discussion led

to her asking us if we had ever experienced the power of magnetic north. As far as my own understanding went, it was a compass point mainly used by helmsmen navigating ships at sea, but our speaker called for someone to be prepared to act as an example. She produced a small compass from her bag, and instructed the volunteer to stand relaxed in an open space, and holding the compass, to face magnetic north. The first volunteer who was a female who then handed back the compass.

She was next asked to think of a very simple question, to stay facing magnetic north *but not to allow her mind to register the answer.* The question was a simple one in order to make the experiment as basic as possible. In this case 'am I a woman?' Obviously the volunteer and all of us knew the answer, but the object of the experiment was to assess the effect of the mental impact of the energy of her reply on her physical reaction.

After several attempts in which, as might have been expected, the slightly flippant influence of the surrounding audience was a deterrent to the experiment, a more serious atmosphere prevailed. The volunteer was then able to give undivided attention to her inner response. Suddenly, as the simple question was repeated, we noticed the volunteer start to lean forward as if propelled from behind, towards the direction she was facing, that of magnetic north. She was not creating an artificial response, and we were all aware that she had had no option other than to physically respond to an energy linking her answer to that direction. Of course the answer in her mind had been the simple word 'yes.'

The other half of the exercise then followed. The next question was, 'are you a man?' Naturally everyone knew the answer, but were not prepared by the quite dramatic physical response to the question. The volunteer started to lean back! i.e. *away* from magnetic north. It really was an amazing 'no' reaction! She did not move deliberately.

What followed then became more and more interesting, as the lecturer suggested that the volunteer then asked herself one or two other questions, to which the answer was not already known to her. This took several minutes while we all waited with baited breath.

The expression on the volunteer's face turned to that of a sense of wonder. She then told us that she had asked herself several questions and was amazed at the response from magnetic north. We of course had only been able to note which way her body swayed as she allowed herself to go with the flow of some part of her which was directing her whole body. Obviously directed by an area of the brain which was acting as an indicator. That part of the brain was not directed by her intellect, but apparently by intuition, and she was positively affected and impressed by the answers she received.

I read recently some remarks of Einstein (source unknown) in which he suggests that 'as humans we exist in a field of energy, the fourth part of which he called our connection with *Universal Intelligence* which science will never be able to measure, and which it would be wasteful to try and validate to the traditional scientific community.'

I believe that it was this part of her brain that our volunteer allowed herself to contact, which then produced the fascinating reactions we observed.

Naturally the ten or so people who were present were all interested in trying this, what I now call our *fourth dimension* exercise. Eighty per cent reacted in some degree to magnetic north, a few quite dramatically, the remainder did not react, not I am sure because the reaction was not within them, but their own tension and I believe dominant intellectual brain could not release control at that time. I heard later that several were able to reproduce the phenomena at home; perhaps it was difficult for them to 'let go' in front of an audience.

I suggest that if you want to try this experiment for yourself, go out and buy a compass! A small one can be purchased quite cheaply, and if you continue with the practice you will allow yourself to develop the intuitive part of your brain, which our perhaps over-scientific and intellectual culture has allowed to atrophy. I believe with possible future dire results, if we do not acknowledge Einstein's *fourth dimension.* I am sure that it was his own use of this faculty which has established his permanent reputation as the genius he was.

Without qualifying as a genius (!) in any way, I believe that I have only been able to write large sections of this book from a contact with an intelligence not my own. My experiences as a dowser, and above all correct breathing, have given me an awareness which I prize above all else in my life, and which can never be bought. Obviously I am not the only person to learn to live by this inner law of the natural intuitive fourth dimension.

I believe that it is only by the universal retrieval of this neglected faculty that we shall be able to regain the knowledge we so desperately need to reverse global pollution.

When you become completely familiar with the use of this fascinating reaction, you may find that your response to any question you may ask your inner mind will become more pronounced, and you may have to step forward in order to keep your balance.

The reaction you experience is reflecting the fact that your old wise brain knows the answer to anything you can ask it, and the magnetic north phenomena is one way by which we can retrieve information which our conscious mind cannot answer. Keep your questions simple to start with, and gradually you will learn to respect this extra dimension of your life. Daily we are faced with problems, in which we search our brains for an answer. A simple yes or no answer to an unresolved problem can be a great relief in helping our decision-making process, especially when regular use proves your new skill to be valid.

Try to avoid attaching a success or failure label to your growing expertise, you are learning all the time, one good tip is to try and make the mental questions as concise as possible. Above all try and breathe correctly and stay as calm as possible while you are looking for an answer.

This experiment may be the first time you have considered the power of your intuitive mind, the only other apparatus required for this particular process is a cheap compass.

After all, if sailors can navigate a great ship by the power of magnetic north, why should we not also take advantage of the same process?

Simple questions we can ask once we have given ourselves a trial period by getting results to queries to which we already know the answer might be, for instance:

(a): We can try to estimate when someone in the family will arrive home.
(b): If a particular food is suitable for you.
(c): How best to programme your day.

Whenever I have a problem with an answer from magnetic north it is because I have asked a question which is too 'woolly'. If you want an answer to something which may or may not happen today, make sure you include the word 'today' in your question. What is right for today may not necessarily be right for tomorrow.

While of course we can demonstrate the magnetic north phenomena with a group of friends, we must always treat it with integrity. Eventually we can use it in a very discreet and unnoticed way even in company. A slight leaning in one direction need not be too dramatic, our internal dialogue is always silent. If you are relaxed and facing the right direction, you can experience magnetic north without the need of a compass, and get results while sitting down, although it is better to stand if you can. You can appear do this work quite casually, in a way that is invisible to the onlooker.

This special dowsing technique can add extra pleasure and satisfaction to your life as long as you are alive, I would go as far as to say that it is rather comforting to feel that we have an invisible friend through our magnetic north discovery. Developing this sense of an unseen but real dimension, could add quality time to your days.

I believe its use has a reassuring effect on our sense of life's great mystery, to the extent of lengthening our lifespan, through an enhanced sense of wonder at life's mysteries. Of course that is something I cannot prove. On the other hand, it is rather comforting to feel that we have a constant wise friend who never lets us down.

Obviously the nearer we are to Nature, the greater chance we have of a longer and happy life. That wise old lady gets great pleasure from those of her children who stay true to her, she needs them as much as they need her.

Remember Science is only about what man has been able to prove *so far,* about our wonderful Universe. Don't disregard the fact that a new-born baby probably already senses and responds to the most advanced natural scientific laws more accurately than intellectually orientated Nobel Prize winners.

In my personal world only *intuitive* scientists (who can also get results from the magnetic north experiment!) will be allowed.

By the way, to be completely flippant, wouldn't it make good TV coverage to see a Parliamentary vote being decided by the Members using the magnetic north experiment? Or some conference room full of learned professors carrying out the same process before debating a topic with global implications? After all dowsing is just finding out the truth, what could be wrong with that?

I now realise that I experienced my life-changing out-of-body experience referred to in the chapter of that name, when I was certainly facing north. Magnetic north I cannot say with certainty.

If, after trying for some time to achieve results with the experiment described in this chapter, you arc still unsuccessful, do not label yourself a failure. Give yourself a break of a few weeks, even months. In that interval try and read and if possible practice some of the basic concepts of correct breathing and relaxation, until you feel that it has become part of your life. Read a humorous book, get out in the fresh air, love yourself more. Ponder Nature. Then quite casually without worrying about performance have another try.

THERE WAS A CERTAIN BISHOP,
WHOSE NAME I QUITE FORGET,
WHO SAID THE REASON FOR FAILURE IS,
'YOU HAVEN'T SUCCEEDED – YET.'

Source unknown

.

Chapter 26

THE OUT-OF-BODY
EXPERIENCE

THE SUBJECT OF *the out-of-body experience* is usually portrayed in the media in a way which is accompanied by an over-dramatic background build-up of sonorous music, occult graphics, and suggestions of ghostly activity, quite hilariously observed by anyone who has actually undergone such an experience.

Very often years may pass before a person realises in quite a matter-of-fact way that an unusual past experience almost forgotten but brought into consciousness by a mundane present situation, was actually what could be termed an out-of-body experience.

Anyway what exactly is meant by that phrase? I can only tell you of my own version of that happening, which was one of the most if not *the* most powerful, wonderful and important of my life. I must have been in my late forties when it occurred. I have never since reached such a sense of heightened awareness, but it was a pivotal turning point of my life. Perhaps what was revealed to me *was* enough to last me for the rest of my life.

The 'happening' occurred during a period of my life when I was at my lowest ebb, indeed wondering if I could even *bear* the rest of my life. One life crisis after another had happened to me, and things looked so black that there seemed no way forward, certainly no way back. I had to find some new way to make meaning of my existence.

At that time my parents lived nearby in our little village, and my mother who was ill was being treated by a GP from a nearby small town.

I have always been fortunate in possessing a strong constitution, when a visit to a doctor was a rare event with years intervening, and then only for a minor matter. However the problem on this occasion was mental stress caused by my apparently unsolvable life crisis.

When the doctor was visiting my mother, I asked her if she could subsequently visit me as I lived nearby. She suggested a course of tablets for depression, saying that it would take several weeks for them to work, and I would have to take them for six months. I must not suddenly stop taking them, or I would 'plummet'. What a graphic word. It seemed to burn into my brain. Anyway I got the prescription made up at the chemist and started to dutifully take the dose as dictated on the bottle. After a few days I felt that my brain was starting to work in a funny way, and began to feel a little uneasy. However I thought that anything was better than the nightmare in which I was living.

About three weeks later alarm bells began to ring, and the word 'plummet' kept coming into my brain. Something was telling me that medication was not the way. But how to prevent the ominous experience I had been led to believe was the result of suddenly stopping the tablets?

However I *did* stop but very gradually decreased the dose, until in about three weeks I was no longer taking the tablets. Even so, for about six weeks I experienced some degree of what the word *plummet* meant, it was not a nice experience, and my mind was for this period under two very negative influences, my personal circumstances and the withdrawal effect of the tablets. A kind of nightmare.

My parents and family were not aware of the life-crisis in

which I was immersed.

The words 'out-of-body experience' seem to have emerged in print during the last fifty years, and from time to time you read of someone who has had this experience.

It is interesting to look back in time and see how long it takes for new ideas to filter into an era of history, until it becomes an accepted norm. Such has been the case with the stream of wise and often spiritual books which the cynics label at best New Age, and at the worst occult. I remember it seems only recently such books could only be obtained from under the counter in the local library, where they also kept the books containing sexual content and therefore not suitable for the open shelves!

Having for the past thirty years avidly read books on alternative health and spirituality, representing in the main, truths which for me could not be denied. I also admit that I was once a cynic. My cynicism was soon to be challenged.

I recall a wise woman much more advanced in spiritual matters than I, who said that if I understood her work, she would have '*made it*'. Possibly she saw that the strength of my then cynicism if reversed could lead me in an equally positive opposite direction. She was right, but it took a long time. She did however see the cynic within me.

Anyway what is the New Age? It seems to imply the time when we are moving from one area of history into another You could call the discovery of nuclear energy a New Age, with its awful potential for destruction. We are moving into a New Age as we realise the effects of Global Warming. You could say that every day is a New Age.

At the time I was speaking of at the beginning of this chapter, I mentioned I was at the end of my tether. A prime candidate for a necessary new age of some kind. At the end of my tether was when my cynical mind finally had to concede defeat, and did an enormous favour to my creative brain by condescendingly getting off its pedestal to give nature a try. This is how it happened.

I had returned to my home in the country, after a long day of council meetings, weary, despondent, weighed down with earthly problems. It was a lovely sunny evening, and I decided to take a wooden kitchen chair out to the back lawn, and sit down for a while.

From time to time somewhere in my mind I had been pondering the question of a word called 'relaxation' which various women's magazines were saying could be helpful for stress. Part of my brain was saying to me, 'what a waste of time sitting out here, you should be inside getting a meal together.' Another part of me told me just to shut my eyes for a little while longer.

Something I had read about relaxation said that you should shut your eyes and try to stop yourself thinking. After some of my previous remarks, you can guess how hard that would be. I kept on trying to shut out thought, the first time in my life I had really tried.

Perhaps it was with a sense of no other way left to me that kept me persevering, because what I was trying to do eventually became rather interesting. Some never used part of me seemed to be trying to help me, or was some other energy helping me? I do not know how much time passed, but all of a sudden I felt a great wave of inexplicable calm spreading up the back of my head, and my consciousness opened up, rather like a flower which you see unfolding in slow motion in a TV documentary. That is how it felt. Then it was as if I was in some way suspended above my body, conscious that I seemed to have risen above the tops of the pine trees on the hillside above the garden.

The feeling of unutterable peace, calmness and wisdom was total, I wanted to stay in this place forever, aware of a great power and sense of peace which was infinite.

I felt as if I could fly anywhere! I knew I could soar into boundless space and so much wanted to. Then, another voice inside my head started to draw me back. It was time to get the tea! So I came back.

Going indoors I started to prepare the meal, but it was as *if I was in charge of me again*, I remember thinking about the problems in my life, and they seemed to have distanced themselves into a totally manageable solution which would sort itself out as long as I could retain this wonderful feeling that came to me in the garden Another energy was available to me, but I knew that I would always have to take time to find this special place again which was *within me*.

As I peeled the potatoes, a part of me still seemed to hover above the earth and I felt sad that I'd had to come back. My sense of despair however, had vanished, never to return.

I have never been back to that place again, with the same clarity, perhaps it was only necessary to just experience it, and to know it exists. I have since learned how to shift my consciousness in a way that distances problems which once would have caused me anxiety. Perhaps this place I experienced was what Einstein called the 'fourth dimension', or 'Higher Intelligence'. A place where science can never go, the alchemic wisdom of the Universe.

During the time when I was writing these particular pages, I went for a stroll in the village, and met a neighbour. In responding to her enquiry about the progress of this book, I spoke about the subject of this chapter. She told me of an incident when she was travelling by car with her family in Edinburgh.

They were approaching a traffic light which was at green, but despite this and for *no known reason* she screamed at her husband *'Stop!'* He braked sharply but with evident annoyance such was the urgency in her voice, when a car suddenly speeded across in front of them, apparently ignoring what must have been its own red traffic sign. My neighbour had not seen that car's approach, her cry to stop had come from some part of her consciousness, of which she was not aware. If her husband had obeyed the green light telling them to proceed, there would have been a bad if not fatal accident. Another kind of out of body experience?

A similar incident was experienced by a special friend of mine, Lilla Bek, who was driving down a steep hill from a hospital where she had been visiting a patient. Suddenly an inner voice shouted to her to pull over to the side - '*now.*' She responded instantly and at the same time a car shot down from behind her which would have crashed into her had she not pulled over. Admittedly this particular friend is rather psychic, but the '*voice*', where did it come from? I think in both cases Einstein's fourth dimension.

This same friend told me how when she first started to study yoga rather half-heartedly, she almost gave up because of the resulting pain which comes from stretching unused muscles.

However she persisted with the lessons and on one specific occasion was lying with her eyes closed during a relaxation period at the end of the session. Usually at this point the lights were dimmed, and Lilla with eyes still closed had this thought 'why don't they turn off the lights?' She opened her eyes hoping to catch the attention of the teacher, to find that the room lights were in fact switched off. The light had come from *within her*. It was a significant event which altered the course of her life, and led her to become a well-known author, lecturer and healer, being consulted by countless people down the years who were looking for a right direction in their lives.

Many people who read this chapter will have had an out-of-body experience, perhaps when lying in a hospital bed, or in some traumatic situation. In general society disregards what it cannot explain or see materially, thus denying the existence of a vital part of the jig-saw of human awareness. I believe that we shall have to recognise and call upon it in an hour of need still to come

Without constant access to Einstein's 'fourth dimension' my life would lose its savour and meaning. Its awareness enhances all my experiences. My closest friends can all call on this dimension. I can understand why so many people feel their lives are meaningless if they are cut off from this important part of human consciousness.

THE LIGHT SHINETH IN THE DARKNESS AND
THE DARKNESS COMPREHENDETH IT NOT.

New Testament

TO THOSE WHO UNDERSTAND, NO EXPLANATION
IS NECESSARY, TO THOSE WHO DO NOT
(WILL NOT) UNDERSTAND, NO EXPLANATION
WILL SUFFICE.

Author unknown

Chapter 27

WORK, INTUITION
AND AWARENESS

DURING THE PAST THREE DECADES I have met hundreds of people who came for a therapeutic consultation. I dislike the word patient, and have always favoured the term client, even that seems a bit formal. The focus of all our meetings has been for each person to find *a way back* to the special unique individual at the core of their being. I don't know if we ever *completely* reach that goal, but to regain a strong sense of that true self, can make the resulting lifetime journey worth the effort. That is if we are to justify being given the gift of life.

We have to regenerate that authentic self, just as a plant has to regenerate itself from its roots, otherwise it cannot stay alive. A plant deprived of its correct environmental habitat cannot flourish. It may appear to have died. Yet replanted in its natural habitat, a miracle seems to happen. You can almost see the fresh new growth appearing above the surface again, the blueprint of the original plan is energised, a miraculous re-birth.

So in the human condition. I have seen such miraculous re-growth, one could almost say re-birth. There is a quotation which goes 'give a plant a chink of light, and it will grow to it.' This is quite easy to prove in the case of a plant restored to its right location, balance of sun, shade and soil. Yet we seem to give less importance to recognising each individual as someone who has to find the right environment in order to fulfil their purpose for existence.

Just as the plants in our home will always turn towards the light, so with the human spirit once it has become aware of its own uniqueness. That knowledge is known to every young child, and it is to that light we must return, in order to pick up the clues.

Wordsworth's 'shades of the prison house closing around the growing child,' as represented by our culture, education, and lack of right nurturing required for each individual, too soon obliterates 'the clouds of glory from whence we came.' His prophetic words are as vividly true today, as when he wrote them several centuries ago.

To re-read his words is to comprehend as he did, the contortions imposed upon the young child by the universally accepted stereotypes of our present day child conditioning, known as education.

The unrecognised cry for help is so tragically evidenced by the hundreds of thousands who end up as addicts, chronically sick, or depressed, including the criminal community. 'The evil that you teach me I will execute, and it shall go hard but I will better the instruction.' (Shakespeare's *The Merchant of Venice*) must be vivid evidence of how little we know about the healthy rearing of the young child plant.

Fortunately however deeply buried, the original unique blueprint of each individual remains etched into our deepest consciousness and our awareness of that uniqueness remains a work that is waiting to be carried out. Our original purpose is still to find fulfilment through that work. Whatever we are doing, if it has no connection with that blueprint we will be aware of a nagging sense of incompletion.

However humble the task may seem to be, we are the only ones who are equipped to release that particular part of the cell information which makes up world wholeness, and if we do not carry out that work there will be a gap which no one else is fitted to fill.

The regaining of the knowledge of our life's work may take almost a lifetime. It is seldom painless, and requires great effort to listen to its signal. Yet once re-contacted we now have to use this pearl of greatest price, to give to the world in a loving way our own particular talents, the reason for our existence.

A writer I have been unable to identify once said that 'most people at the end of their lives are sick with guilt at having lived below their spiritual potential.' Is this the reason why so many people suffer from degenerating illnesses as they enter old age unfulfilled?

To re-grow, we need to find the vibration of our own particular wavelength, our homing signal. For me personally, and for so many people who have experienced the liberating power of correct breathing, this knowledge has been re-claimed by the deep relaxation and enlightenment which results.

In his book *The Turning Point,* Fritjof Capra, physicist and philosopher discusses Wholeness and Health. Concerning relaxation, he speaks of it as a 'psycho-physiological process which requires as much diligent practise as any other skill and has to be practiced regularly to be fully effective. Correct breathing is one of the mot important aspects of relaxation, and thus one of the most vital elements in all stress-reduction techniques.'

As mentioned elsewhere in this book, Capra goes on to explain that when we are relaxed, we can then contact our unconscious mind which will release information necessary for us to solve our problems. This can only really happen when the mind is not pre-occupied with the business and minutae of the material world of our daily lives.

I have noticed that when I allow myself to be affected by the cares of daily life, that the moment I start to relax, priorities seem to be sorted out from some part of my mind which already knows the answers for my personal well-being. Everything then seems simpler.

Some of the most rewarding break-throughs in my therapeutic work have come about when I am totally quiet, sitting on the floor beside someone who is in the deeply relaxed state which comes about after a session of correct breathing. The process may take one to two hours, I may have said nothing in that time, but the odd encouraging word, and the effort required to maintain a safe, quiet environment. Yet that period of time can be more profitable than many others which I call *verbal time-wasters*, a talking-only session which some call counselling. I believe that talk alone can never produce the deep insightfulness which comes from the self-relaxed state of quiet intuitive awareness which arises from correct breathing.

I will never forget a comment made by a young Glasgow woman of limited education who suddenly exclaimed as she was coming out of this state of deep calmness, 'what we need are spiritual gladiators.' How true and profound. Sometimes limited education leads to *enhanced spirituality*. Always in harmony with the laws of Nature.

Such jewels of insight flow from a brain whose activity has been enhanced by the power of correct breathing. With all our intelligence and intellectual knowledge, we seem to totally under-estimate the effect of correct breathing on the brain-cell oxygen supply, and that this effect so often takes the form of spiritual illumination.

Spiritual insights can be trusted, obtained in this way, they represent the *re-growth* of the tender new shoots of self-generated human growth and maturation.

The doctor who said at a conference on holistic medicine, 'take away my needle, take away my knife, take away my tablet and I have nothing,' revealed a truly spiritual insight about the training limitations of his profession.

I give eternal thanks that I have been given the gift of understanding *the language of the breath*, a perfectly natural process apparently not yet known to doctors. It has allowed me to assist hundreds of people to throw off physical, mental, and emotional illness without the aid of needle, knife or tablet. They have contacted that inner source which made them ill, and through correct breathing, an even deeper inner source which can be re-tapped by the mind to heal that which is of lesser depth. Once the deeper level has been aroused, it can with the help of two important instincts, awareness and intuition reduce and eliminate the fear and resultant stress which caused the original problem.

Virtually without exception the real problem was this *fear* from childhood which began to suppress correct breathing, and therefore the self-repair information residing in the deep unconscious mind.

It is really amusing to hear someone who has healed themselves in this way, to confirm the saying, 'don't sweat the small stuff, it's all small stuff.' because they have proved it's truth. You can only really understand these words when you have gone through the experience. Another quote 'fear knocked on the door, faith opened it, and there was no one there.' I do not know the source of that saying either.(Many quotes I mention have been given to me 'out of the blue' by others, over three decades) but to grow through the breath correction challenge is to know its truth.

You cannot carry out the work that is your gift to life, until you have freed yourself from fear, because only then is your personal splendour revealed to you, *which you will then allow no one to undermine.*

I find that my whole life is governed by these words, *intuition and awareness*. I see the same way of life, being lived out by so many of those with whom I have had the privilege of sharing therapeutic time, as I have been inspired by others. When I disregard these words, I go off my straight path, as will anyone else who ignores their intuition and awareness.

Fortunately my own lapses these days are short-term, the yardstick that has to be applied is *'what is right for me at this moment?'* Operating from the spiritual-breath guideline you begin to realise that if you do what is really right for you, you cannot do wrong to anyone else. Eventually the situation will work out satisfactorily for all concerned.

Most of the people with whom I have worked over the years, have been in wrong relationships, home and work, and like myself at one time, want their lives to change, *without* changing their relationships, home or work! The practice of correct breathing gives the insights, courage and wisdom to do just that. Usually we think that we have to find the right *relationship* first, looking outside ourselves to find that elusive other one.

Finally and irrevocably we realise that the relationship we are looking for is *ourselves with ourselves.* Once that relationship is re-established, then we realise that it is the *work* we have to find, which represents the truth of who we really are. We took on the gifts and talent of what that work means, when we were born. Relationships follow naturally when we find our right work.

We cannot get away with being false to our inner truth without becoming ill.

Hospitals, doctors waiting rooms, and institutions are full of the casualties of this perpetual silent war we wage, through our physical, mental and emotional violence to our authentic selves.

That wonderful doctor, Edward Bach MB, BSC, DPH, speaks most vividly of this danger in his priceless little book, *Heal Thyself.* He writes 'Let everyone remember that his soul has laid down for him a particular work, and that unless he does this work though perhaps not consciously, he will inevitably raise a conflict between his soul and personality which of necessity reacts in the form of physical disorders.'

During my time of intense change it seemed as if the Universe was sending me confirmation of immortal truths which were coming to the surface of my mind. Truths also experienced by others down the centuries, in the form of poems, articles, books, words spoken by another even in a casual conversation. A few words, a single sentence in his book which matched exactly my own dawning realisations. Dr. Bach has expressed his certainty about the importance of our own unique work. Others have confirmed this in different words which have identical meaning.

They are not my words, but say what I have discovered time after time in practice, with many people who have since found the courage to 'walk their own walk'.

> 'If your vocation is also your vacation, you have
> discovered the secret of life.'
> 'When your work is also your play you have
> discovered the secret of life.'
> 'If you do not follow your heart and your emotions,
> sooner or later you will fall ill.'
> 'If you do not develop that which is within you,
> what you do not develop will kill you.'
>
> *Leonard Orr*

This last saying is not one which I would quote to a client, but it means that the only reason we do not develop our joyful gifts will be from fear. Fear suppresses our circulation, which changes blood cells, and eventually we will develop an illness which will cause our death. It may be quick or slow, but will be the reason which will shorten our life-span.

Death is meant to be a gentle release of life.

I wonder if you have read the chapter in that beautiful book, *The Wind in the Willows,* by Kenneth Grahame, in which Mole and Ratty are strolling along the river bank, after the Mole had spent many weeks staying with his friend. Suddenly Mole is aware of a far-off memory, an instinct, an awareness, an intuition, which fills his thoughts and emotions as a sense of great loss, of some vital part of himself missing. It causes him heartbreak, and he know he has to listen to these feelings, because they constitute the reality of his own dear little home to which he must urgently return. He appeals to Ratty to slow down, to retrace their steps so that he can follow this overriding need to find his own home. Which he does.

It is to this lovely safe home within ourselves to which *we* must return, in order to re-find our core self, and transform our lives by the work we know is our gift of our life's talents. Much of the grief expressed by people moving forward in their lives, tentatively and still with fear of being true to themselves, represents the fear and grief of the small child. The child is facing the overwhelming strength of perhaps unintentional opposition from its parents, surrounding culture, education and other negative factors in its formative years which are blocking its ability to be true to itself. It corresponds to Mole's feelings on the river bank as he remembers his natural environment, which he had neglected, and felt despair that he might not find it again. Helplessness and such a sense of loss.

Many people are living life in a perpetual state of hopelessness, helplessness and sense of loss of their true selves.

Here are some of the words of a lovely young girl, written after her first experience of correct breathing and relaxation.

★ ★ ★

I am on my way back to you
Journeying east through the scuttling dust of the
storm driven desert,
I am on my way back to you,
Flung into the western sky by a force that conjures
the largest ocean,
The dust of other planets on my skin,
Bearing the eternal frozen tears of galactic skies.
Glowing stone given up to space,
In the inevitable curve of flight
I am on my way back to you,
Drawn like the moon to earth myself in you.

Denise

From the time we intentionally begin to correct our breath, we are on this journey back to the *you*, the *you* of your legitimate self, in reality *the me*. The young woman who wrote the poem had suffered intensely in her childhood, correct breathing released the brain-stored memory of her true self, to whom she knew she must return.

Using the awareness and intuition released by the relaxed breath, we re-train ourselves to stay grounded once again, to find the right path for ourselves in the confusion created by negative messages from others, which have been embedded in our unconscious. Messages which say, 'you couldn't, shouldn't, mustn't or aren't good enough.' They are now on the way out, being released, cancelled out by the power of the breath, but for a time it is difficult to ignore them, as our negative/positive balance readjusts. On the other hand there is that other still small voice which says, 'you can, you will, you must, you *are* good enough.'

This is when we really have to learn to trust the still small voice of our intuition, our sixth sense, which becomes as real, important, and *urgent* as our other five senses.

Within the eighty thousand thoughts (approx) which occur to us every day, each thought will have a value choice of two options, either positive or negative. Our choice will be followed by action of either a positive or negative energy. The action taken from a negative thought doubles its intensity, and ensuing reaction. That from a positive thought doubles the good power of the resultant action. Which will you choose? Whatever the excuses we like to make, if we take the negative action, we can forgive ourselves, perhaps that is the only way we can re-train ourselves in the opposite energy. It takes time to discover which is the right path for ourselves.

When we first start to practice listening to our inner voice of intuition and awareness, action must follow based on positive or negative thought. Sometimes the thought is to take no action, which if you really consider *is* some kind of action, for there is always a result based on that thought, which will affect the Universe in some way for better or worse. As Leonard Orr said, 'there is no good or bad, but there are consequences.'

Often at first the choice of action seems unbearably diffi-cult. We can *see* no difference in the result of whichever choice we make, for they appear to carry the same value. This is our testing time, for one decision may carry the risk of going completely into the unknown, and the other may appear a little more clear-cut but only fractionally. It seems unbearably difficult, for something important may hang on our decision. The right decision will lead to success, the inaccurate to the opposite. So we choose the *wrong* one! We are for a time still afraid of going into the *unknown*. This is where we learn the truth of the saying 'don't sweat the small stuff, it's all small stuff.' With awareness and intuition, apparently *wrong* decisions can lead to subsequent beneficial situations. The bonus is growth in our wisdom.

Back to those words whose origins are lost in the mists of time. 'There's nothing either good nor bad, but thinking makes it so.'

Here is a really important law of Metaphysics. If, having done *the best we can,* we still make an apparently wrong decision, the negative consequences are usually much less serious than we would imagine, and that it is because *we tried to do our best.* Life always gives us credit for good intentions, and the *apparent* negative result often leads to a spiritual learning curve.

I believe that gamblers are usually people who for reasons linked to childhood experiences, are unable to face up to the growth process described in the preceding paragraphs. The materialistic gamble seems preferable to a gamble requiring the risk of making a spiritual choice.

Treading the *spiritual* gambling path of intuition and awareness will always eventually lead us to our life's work. It may at first seem hard going, even painful, but through correct breathing to stabilise that growth, our understanding grows about the real meaning of our existence. The fact is that Mother Earth *needs us,* has work for us to do, and will inevitably provide our necessities. It eventually brings back into our life the delight in life we felt as a child.

Maria Montessori, that wonderful teacher and writer on childhood, emphasised that the child *'loves to work',* and unless disturbed by our culture, will develop along the path guided by its innate knowledge of its own personal life's work.

The terrible frequency of the words 'I'm bored.' uttered by so many of our children, is really a symptom of the way in which we have taken away the child's delight in its own existence; it has forgotten what was its work.

★ ★ ★

'WHEN OUR WORK IS ALSO OUR PLAY,
WE WILL HAVE DISCOVERED
THE SECRET OF LIFE.'

Author unknown

'ALL IS THERE; ALL IS PUT WITHIN.
BIRTH TAKES PLACE, AND IF THERE IS NO
INTERFERENCE FROM BIRTH TILL DEATH
THE CORRECT PATH WILL BE FOLLOWED,
THE CORRECT ACTS WILL BE INDULGED IN, THE
CORRECT INFORMATION WILL BE ASSIMILATED.
IT IS THE INTERFERENCE WHICH CAUSES THE
PROBLEMS. TO AVOID THE WHIMS OF OTHERS,
THE WILL OF OTHERS THIS IS WHAT MUST
BE DONE TO FIND THE CORRECT PATH.'

Unknown author

Chapter 28

REST

WHEN I LOOK BACK AT MY CHILDHOOD, it seemed that my parents were always in a hurry, although as I write these words I realise the opposite was also true. They made time at the weekends for excursions into the lovely country-side around the beautiful cathedral city of Salisbury where I was reared. They always had a library book lying around, and latterly I remember my mother had an afternoon nap, short as it often was. I never remember my father napping, except perhaps on a wintry Sunday afternoon. I wish he had done so.

I think the sense of rushing came about from my father's work as an Insurance superintendent, where he was always involved with beating the last year's financial figures, which became a great strain when he had for several years attract-ed more business than his other country-wide colleagues, and no doubt felt he had to maintain his record. Latterly however he began to reap the health problems caused by his twenty a day cigarette habit, at a time when cigarettes were cheap, plus the stress of his work. He eventually developed emphysema, and had to retire several years early.

The impression of hurry came clearly to me first thing in the morning as a child, when I heard my parents' swift foot-steps down the stairs. This vivid memory has remained with me for so many years, my parents' hurrying footsteps on the stairs in the early morning.

I can remember my father constantly saying as he went

through the door, that he did not know how he was going to get through the work awaiting him. My mother's life centred around his needs, they had a quite rigid routine, and of course not being aware or able to understand their adult cares, as adolescents we found some of those routines irksome.

I never remember being able to have a weekend lie-in when I lived in my parent's house. At least not beyond 8.30am, because the bedrooms had to be mopped and dusted every day, even on Sunday. The thing which I found frustrating was when I first had a boyfriend, and was allowed to entertain him in the drawing-room after my parents went to bed. Only for about half an hour, and then very pointedly before they retired to bed, my father would come in, rake out the fire embers, and take them through to the kitchen boiler to top it up for the night! More than a hint to the boy-friend not to stay too long. We used to smirk behind his back!

Looking back I suppose that our lives reflected the social norms of the period between the two wars and immediately after, when the influence of the life habits of the middle and working classes, and a workaholic philosophy, dominated the flavour of our days.

Small wonder then, that I grew up with the sense of an unknown force at my back urging me to hurry. When I caught a reflection of my body language in shop windows always with chest out, followed by my rear end propelling me along! I am sure I continued this habit, throughout my marriage, as a wife, mother, Councillor, in all my activities, almost as if I was telling myself 'however hard you hurry, you'll never get there.' Upon reflection it seemed to be some unknown force outside myself urging me on. People would say 'you're always in a hurry!' Well, what mother of three children isn't? This in the days before disposable nappies and washing machines.

Yet a psychologist once told me that I was a deep thinker. I can't think how you can be a deep thinker if you are carrying around an inbred guilt feeling, that life is an endurance test, and it's wrong to take a rest during the day.

This thought pattern was interrupted at least for a time when for a period before the birth of my second baby, I discovered the work of Dr. Dick Grantly Read, and his invaluable little book on *Relaxation for Childbirth*. At last I found the self-discipline to take time each day to learn to relax. In fact I also taught myself a form of self-hypnosis, although at the time I would not have recognised it as such.

The benefits to my feelings of calmness and peace were astonishing, and I know allowed me to manage my daughter's home-birth in a way in which I was in charge, and was said by the midwife to be the happiest birth she had ever attended. How come then that I appear to have turned my back on this amazing way to ensure that the calmness and sense of peace stayed in my life? Perhaps I felt that it was only to be used in preparation for childbirth, when in reality it is a lifelong process to keep one's life in balance.

I am now astonished at my complacency in virtually ditching Grantly Read when my third child was born, again a home birth. Thereafter my life seemed to take on an acceleration of too much to do, and never enough time to do it.

We moved to a much bigger house with a very large garden, and there was always so much work to be done. I seemed to be always tired, taking a rest during the day, was a non-event, and although my children gave me great joy, there never seemed time to savour the joy. I suppose the influence of my early-life still gave me a sense that I always had to be 'on the go.' Habit and conditioning taking precedence over listening to what Nature was telling me. Because she is always talking to us, ignore her as we often do to our detriment.

Resting when we are tired is an instant self-healing process for happiness, known to all small children, who are near to

Nature. A child responds instantly to its inner signs of fatigue.

For reasons of our own adult timetable and the long memory fingers of historical enslavement of the masses, we soon begin to programme our small children to go past their rest 'sell-by date', because we want go somewhere, meet someone, all the reasons why it would be inconvenient to have to let a small child stretch out and sleep when its nervous system dictates. For the child's nervous system is a barometer not to be ignored, yet ignore it we do

Look through the small window often set in a primary school first year classroom door at about 2.30pm, and you will see the thumb sucking, drooping heads, stroking of the earlobe, the comfort signs indicative of the child having reached the end of its ability to remain alert.

We impose on small children a working day almost equivalent to that of an adult, particularly when you take into account the travelling time dictated by the distance of school from home, often after school activities until collection by working parents.

I remember one much-loved teacher when I was about eight years old, insisting that we rested our heads on folded arms for some time every afternoon. She knew the importance of a child being allowed to opt-out of the educational routine from time to time.

I am not surprised that I had a life-crisis in my late forties. Many people do. If we do not listen to the still small voice which speaks very clearly to us when we are deeply relaxed, we are ignoring the correct sign-posts for our life's path and will find ourselves off-course, having lost our way. Often from childhood on we are *tuned out* of thinking that we must rest when we are tired.

Other people may think we are very successful, but we know differently.

The bad-temper, irritability, aggressiveness we meet every

day on the streets, in shops and business are usually the result of lack of rest, inadequate sleep, the result being as one writer put it that 'we see everything through emotional magnifying glasses.'

A few days ago I was filing away some papers, and found an article minus the top third of its content, but the word 'rest' caught my eye, and instead of scrapping another odd bit of information I realised that the article was a gem, in that it confirmed what I have been trying to say in this chapter, the importance of the nap or rest. The writer of the article was Tom Hodgkinson, Editor of a magazine called appropriately 'The Idler'. I had heard of it but not read it, shall have to rectify that! Sadly the mid-day siesta in other parts of Europe is being discontinued, do we have the EEC to blame for that? Commerce over common sense.

When we continue to work after feeling tired, we become much more accident prone. 'Tiredness kills' they say on the roads. Researchers into horrific motorway deaths realise that it is fatigued, rather than intentionally criminal drivers who cause so many accidents.

I believe that future awareness will force us to understand that to try to deal with the intricate life-style we have chosen when we are tired, might well be considered a form of unintentional suicidal criminality, for suicidal criminality it is. We are disobeying Nature, and look where that is leading the world. This little publicised aspect of ignoring fatigue as if it was unimportant, has the same lethal effect in its repercussions on so many lives in a more subtle way when we are not even actually driving. When we ignore the need to rest, we see life as the cup half empty, the cup full mind-set can only be sustained when we are free of fatigue.

'Take rest, the field that is rested gives a beautiful crop.' As with the field, so with you and I. You cannot write from the heart unless you are rested. It is the invisible food which needs to be consumed to bring the nervous system into equilibrium.

Several years ago, because of the need to complete some very important work, I managed for some months to find the self-discipline to get up at four in the morning. Once the first painful effort was made, I found that my body clock woke me up at that time, with a sense of urgency to be working.

I found this to me at first Herculean effort soon began to pay dividends, not financially but in a valuable form of me using the life-force with a feeling of power instead of feeling pushed by time. I actually found I had more energy, and was conscious that decisions were made with greater precision. On the other hand it was necessary to go to bed by eight o'clock, and during the day I had to find time for a couple of cat-naps which completely refreshed me again. I felt I was keeping to Nature's timetable, and realised the reason for that timetable. To make the most of time as invented by Nature.

This experience which lasted for almost two years, gave me a great sense of satisfaction, not only of being able to overcome my lazy self, but also the realisation that in those early morning hours my brain was able to function at optimum energy.

I have a great friend who rises early, and therefore retires early. I always remember her saying 'I can't wait to go to bed with God!' I know now what she means, there is no greater peace than knowing we have used the hours of the day to our best ability, it's as if you drop into a beautiful space of peace at the end of the day when you go to bed.

Perhaps this early awakening does not appeal to you (it did not to me!). I had to metaphorically take myself by the scruff of the neck, go to bed at eight o'clock the night before, set the alarm clock, and train my mind to re-orientate itself. Amazingly it very soon did. You know the mind can be re-orientated. Waking at dawn is still part of rural life. They have been described as the 'absolutely quiet hours'. I came to call them *monastic hours,* and understood why the monks and nuns in monasteries and convents rose so early, and also the value of early prayer and meditation. In reading of these early hours kept by many religious orders, at which I used to shudder, I now understand and empathise with the concept of greeting each morning with thanks at the early start of the day.

I have often thought that we won the last war because Winston Churchill always took a rest during the afternoon, which enabled him to harness his mental energy to much greater effect, and increased his stamina for long and intensive meetings, with the effort to think clearly at times of great crisis.

We are so intrinsically part of the natural world which exists by unalterable laws, and have to understand and prioritise why we need to rest, rather than deferring to a slave mentality which drives us on as inexorably as if we were indeed slaves. Except that the cruel slave master is ourselves.

I believe that when we persist in driving ourselves, despite rest and sleep demanding our co-operation, we offend Nature, who never requires any of her creations in the natural world to so abuse itself. The resultant negativity in thought and wrong action, is usually at the core of many accidents, the energy surrounding us is harmful to others as they pick it up and become adversely affected and infected.

A virus does not have to be a physical one to affect others. What they pick up from us, they pass on until a whole mass of people may be affected, because *we* are over-tired and therefore negative. Do not under-estimate your personal power. There is a saying that some people may warm a room or freeze it. I am constantly aware of that truth.

We can destroy the beautiful energy of life which surrounds us, as surely as if we smashed a valuable ornament. We are responsible for the state of the atmosphere which surrounds us.

With all our intellectual ability, we still have to publicly acknowledge that there is a *global priority to obey the laws of nature*, with the laws of man coming in second place. The energy of Nature which we need to revere and respect exists on an unseen plane, it is almost impossible to stay in tune with it when we are fatigued. Babies, animals and plants are completely sensitive to that energy, our *insensitivity* to its voice, is responsible for most of the turmoil we see around us.

Shakespeare as usual comes up with the right words about the virtues of sleep.

> Sleep that knits up the ravell'd sleeve of care, the
> death of each day's life -
> Balm of hurt minds, great Nature's second course,
> Chief nourisher in life's feast.

> Shakespeare - *Macbeth*, Act 2, Scene 2.

These words have only impressed me with their depth of awareness, since I learned the joy of giving myself right rest, although I learned them some sixty-five years ago at school, from a loving teacher. I'm glad I don't have to carry Macbeth's guilt in order to painfully realise their truth!

Elsewhere in this book I have mentioned a very special book *The Aquarian Gospel*, which came my way unsought, but which contains so many gems of wisdom. It was written by a man called Levi, an American medical doctor, a profound Christian and was apparently written in the absolutely quiet early morning hours between four and six.

When I was hand writing the first draft of this book, it was with the early morning time-span in my mind which I realised would allow me to write from a more creative brain energy source. I did not manage this every day but was able to regain the feeling that I was in charge of time, rather than time being in charge of me.

With the image of the healing power of rest in my mind, comes the saying, 'never stand when you can sit, never sit when you can lie!' As I get older, and often have to stand for quite long periods of time waiting even in banks and post offices, I find that I am no longer hesitant about asking for a chair. The lack of such a necessity in big stores is I am sure lack of imagination, but would be a great help not only to older people but to mothers with young children.

I feel concerned about the staff in any workplace who are forced to stand for many hours each day. One or two super-markets supply high stools, but in the main there seems to be a lack of concern shown by management who would feel indignant themselves if required to maintain the same stance for hour after hour.

I recall some twenty years ago when I dislocated my shoulder after trying to reach out to hang wallpaper from the top of a ladder. The ladder tipped one way, and I tipped the other, and I could feel an ominous ripping sound. After driving one-handed to a (fortunately) nearby large Glasgow hospi-tal, I arrived in Casualty. I was required to stand before the usual glass fronted reception window, and answer the usual endless questions, while a part of me was ready to collapse, and another part thinking how inhuman the process was. I did think of slowly sinking to the ground in an effort to indicate my near-fainting condition. A dislocated arm is no joke.

Nowadays I would have requested a chair in a firm voice! Never stand if you can sit, never sit if you feel like collapsing!

I believe it is insensitive for any owners of public property not to provide a seating provision, to allow customers to sit down when necessary. The time when older people and others are required to wait endlessly while assistants try to cope with the complicated computer processes which seem to accompany every transaction in order to reduce the company overheads, costs the customer time, money and stress in addition to the purchase.

I can imagine the howls of protest that would arise, if the customer took an equivalent amount of time to produce the money for the goods purchased.

Being sensitive to other's need for rest could be the 'open sesame' to a great cultural revolution in happiness, goodwill and health on all levels. We must start with the children, we say they are never still, hyperactive, that is one of the *symptoms* of lack of rest, never being able to be at peace. The symptom is hyperactivity, energy out of control.

The gateway to my strong feelings on the subject of rest evolved as I corrected my breathing pattern and became kinder to myself. We have to start with ourselves or how could we pass kindness on?

Without thinking, when we are tired, we pass that fatigue on to others in the form of short-temper, criticism, perhaps open aggression. It then becomes a sickness symptom.

A truly National health service would become a money-saving service if it pointed out more of these truths. Guilt from a culture inherited from a master and serf ethos flavoured with the long shadow of Calvinism, and the worst aspects of the industrial revolution, leaves many feeling guilty at resting unless it is during the hours of darkness.

Is it natural to go without a proper rest period for sixteen hours at a stretch?

We forget that when we are relaxed and resting, the mind often solves effortlessly a problem which may have stumped us for hours in the waking state.

I am sure that the present trend for late-night social activity particularly in younger people, is reflecting the need to be free of the left brain demands of our society, when the only release from that anti-Nature vibration must be found during other hours in the twenty-four, as if we have to have *some time any time* to be ourselves. The discovery so often through mind-altering substances of a short cut to our true self, which then proves not to be a reliable short-cut. So desperate is the need to find an oblivion of some kind to be free of the man-made pressure of our culture.

The science of healing described elsewhere in this book, requires that for healing of any kind to take place, a state of calmness needs to be attained by the healee. That is Alpha rhythm. The healee's constant high Beta rhythm will have caused the problem. The healer therefore must be in a higher state of Theta (Einstein's fourth dimension?) for the electrical vibrational change to take effect. It is only then that Nature's constant state of Alpha can permeate the cells, the building blocks of our bodymind.

We all have the healing process encoded within us, or it could not be re-awakened. That is what happens in any form of healing, freeing the encoded vibrational level. In general our Society does not yet understand the science of healing, yet I suspect in times to come the level of our separation from Nature's rules may be beyond the capabilities of any existing health service to provide a solution.

I notice the media lately seem to love the word *pandemic*, the global outbreak of some incurable virus. Being out of touch with the laws of Nature and her correct breathing is an *unrecognised pandemic* in which we are permanently engulfed, and goes ignored. There will be a great need for healers in the future who abide by the laws of Nature and can by their very presence help to change the anti-Nature mind-set of a stress sufferer who is out of synch with the Rule of Rest. Lack of rest causes us to see everything through emotional magnifying glasses, which en-masse can cause hysteria and chaos. On a global scale the results are unimaginable.

Some people will accuse you of laziness when you say you

have to go and rest. Forgive them, but take no notice.

Rest and sleep are the same sides of the coin. Rest brings alertness, lack of rest brings apathy and laziness, lack of direction.

In therapy you have to think up various ways to help solve the problem. The approach depends on who is the client. I find it very effective when talking to people in the business or financial world, to describe fatigue as being in overdraft in their rest bank balance. When we start to pay back that overdraft, it can only be through breathing correctly. Rest and relaxation, are the only coinage permissible. Anything to do with the accumulation of money for its own sake is a direct route to heart and stroke problems.

Until the rest debt is paid off, we cannot even be solvent in the energy Bank. Too many people are actually bankrupt from energy loss, which is the way I describe the modern disease of ME or chronic fatigue syndrome.

At this moment we are in what seems to be a never ending financial crisis caused, I am positive, by left brained individuals who by an incorrect thought process, are emptying the world's spiritual breath coffers. Forgive them, have compassion, they are not well.

I see that there is a drastic increase in the numbers of billionaire and millionaires. What will save the world is a big *increase* in the number of respiratory (breath-orientated) *spiritual millionaires, billionaires, yes trillionaires as well.* What wealth!

Nature will not allow herself to become overtired, sooner or later the imposition being placed upon her resources could cause her to rid herself of the non-spiritual virus threat posed by mankind. Yet we have the solution encoded within us.

'TAKE REST, A FIELD THAT IS RESTED
GIVES A BEAUTIFUL CROP.'

Chapter 29

THE STORY OF THE
AQUARIAN GOSPEL

IN LOOKING BACK at our lives, I expect that like myself, you can see in hindsight events which seemed insignificant at the time, yet we now realise triggered off very important turning points in our lives.

If you read these pages, you will realise how the understanding of correct breath has changed *me*. *The precise breath* has been the most important turning point of my life, yet that miracle almost crept up on me unawares. It took the discovery of a book, *The Aquarian Gospel of Jesus the Christ* by Levi Dowling, to crash into my consciousness and help me to realise that what I was discovering about breath and its spiritual meaning, was what *Jesus was trying to tell us.*

A meaning without the trappings and almost obstructive layers of pomp and ceremony by which man has distorted His life, which has caused a diversion from the simple path of His message, which really has nothing to do with religion, but everything to do with spirituality.

Some years ago I was involved in starting a charity in Glasgow which was concerned with the relief of stress. Great changes were happening in my personal life, as I was stumbling along a fresh life-path concerned only with trusting my intuition. I was only then beginning to realise that ignoring my intuition seemed to lead me into disharmony.

The fascinating world of dowsing which is based on

335

scientific intuition helped a great deal to encourage me, as I also discovered my own latent skills in that direction.

I met a number of interesting people in that formative period, when I had to answer the challenging question within. 'Am I willing to let go of who I was, in order to be the person I had not yet become?

On two separate occasions I was in the homes of new friends, and for some reason noticed a book lying around. It may have been a lull in the conversation, or my host had gone out of the room, but my attention was drawn to the book's title which was *The Aquarian Gospel of Jesus the Christ*, by Levi Dowling.

Apart from quite a concentrated childhood acquaintance with the Bible from having been educated in my primary years at a Church of England school, where regular teaching of the Bible and Christianity was an important part of our timetable, I had only infrequently opened a Bible since.

Then for some inexplicable reason this book called *The Aquarian Gospel* was lying around in the living-room of yet another friend. In idle curiosity I opened it for the second time, not even realising that this *second* time was in itself quite a coincidence.

Anyway the book seemed easy to read, the words flowed creatively and the print size was easily read. Not in minute script as in many Bibles, which is a bit off-putting for easy absorption. I was attracted to the text, for it contained familiar extracts from the New Testament. I wanted to read more, but the social nature of the visit prevented that, and I did not refer to my interest in the book to my friends. On the other hand when I got home, the thought kept re-occurring that I wanted to read the book properly. And at my leisure.

Funnily enough when I contacted each of the friends in whose house it had been lying about, one person couldn't even remember it, and the other had apparently returned it to the original owner.

Frustration kicked in, at that time the resources of the computer world were not available, I was not publisher friendly, and did not know the publisher.

Despite the set-back I could not ignore the need to find the book, and eventually discovered it through a publisher called Fowler, now regrettably swallowed up in the world of mass corporate publishing. I learned that Fowler published many books on subjects in which I was becoming deeply interested. The existence of a certain small number of 'enlightened' publishers at that time in the late eighties must have been due to the spiritual interests of their management board, and sadly many other titles in their lists are not being reprinted by the *'big boys'* who took them over. This in an age when the spiritual dimension in publishing is so sadly lacking, I believe to our national and international detriment.

The way I eventually received the book was by another remarkable coincidence. Some friends in Edinburgh, many in the second halves of their lives, and in diverse professional occupations regularly came together to read and discuss 'New Age' books.

This was at a time when such books were kept under the counter at the local library. The group had received two boxes of 'New Age' books from a Trust in England, which I then contacted in the interest of my own newly-fledged charity. Two tea-chests of books finally arrived at my flat. Tea-chests are rarely seen nowadays, but were much in demand then, in the days when tea arrived loose in such boxes, minus the tea-bags! The boxes were prized by removal firms for packing the small items. Are there any left?

Anyway, when our two tea-chests arrived, lo and behold, within one was the Aquarian Gospel. Divine coincidence? You tell me.

I pulled the book from the tea-chest with a profound

sense of pleasure, not realising at that point how important that book was to become in my life. The reason soon became clear. It arrived at a point, when I had been correcting my breath for several years, and had felt the profound spiritual changes which had uplifted and improved all areas of my life, and those of so many of my clients. This understanding had permeated my work as a psychotherapist, and I had begun to include the teaching of correct breathing as a major part of my therapeutic work. I felt *I owed* this to my clients, who I realised without exception, *all had incorrect respiratory patterns.*

There was another reason for this inclusion. I discovered that people who had often come to see me full of tears, were beginning to smile again, were working their own problems out, and required fewer therapeutic sessions. They saved money! More importantly they had gained an appreciation of their own worth, and time and again stated that they did not think they would ever become so stressed again having discovered correct breathing.

On physical, mental and emotional levels they had really healed themselves. As is the case with anyone who becomes stressful, the knock-on effect of a stressful family member, also spreads depressively amongst family, work and friends, like the ever widening ripples when a pebble is thrown into a pool of water.

★ ★ ★

As I sat down to turn the pages of *The Aquarian Gospel*, the words 'Holy Breath' met me time and again. They were spoken by Jesus, in many different situations. I could not ignore such words, particularly in the light of my growing certainty of the importance of correct breath as the vital factor in any good therapeutic work.

Without this catalystic element, I did not see the purpose in many so-called therapeutic mind-centred processes.

Increasingly I was being approached by therapists either in the orthodox or complementary professions who were themselves suffering from stress, and the extra teaching dimension of improved breathing brought them back into balance. You can only help others to re-balance if you are balanced yourself. (Well, more or less!)

I do not see how the medical profession can ignore the urgent importance of this work. It has allowed so many 'sick' people to gradually withdraw from medical drugs, in co-operation with their GP, yet I see such an irony in requiring co-operation from anyone who does not understand the work, or apply it personally. If there is any blame, it must fall on the medical training establishments, and their historical patriarchal reputation, which has gone unchallenged for so long. I have heard that the medical profession is in the power of the big drug companies, but others who have done more research than myself have already published important information on this issue.

My growing awareness of how breathing is the vital factor in health transformation, not only physically, but mentally and emotionally, since they are all inseparable, has led me to much interesting reading in recent years.

I discovered that the word breath means spirit in several ancient languages, Greek among them. Where had the vital understanding of its importance become so trivialised, as indeed it has? Again I came back to the fact that when you breathe correctly you will not become anyone's slave, and you only have to look at the global history of the nations of the world, to know how important slavery has been in the 'growth' of many nations.

From the way in which the word slavery is generally understood, to the slavery of the way in which women and children are treated in so-called developing countries. To a wider field by the self-induced slavery in which millions are caught up in the slavery of blocked potential, ill-health and housing ghettoes. *What I call left brained societies,* who enslave their inhabitants in such subtle ways.

The slavery of personal non-fulfilment enslaves the victim and those who victimise.

Over the ensuing years from my first discovery of the *Aquarian Gospel* in the house of an acquaintance, I have come to realise that within its moderately few pages lie a pattern for man's emancipation from his present misery. It has nothing to do with religion, but everything to do with spirituality. Each day I open it at random, and read a chapter, indeed I feel uneasy if I have not made daily contact with its sane and sensible comments on the Holy Breath, which surely has to be the correct breath

The writer Lynn McTaggart published a book some years ago, entitled *What the Doctors don't Tell You.* I can't help thinking that there is another book waiting to be written entitled *What the Religions don't tell You.* The theme would be on breath and spirit. The only unifying element which could create universal spiritual harmony.

If life gives me time, I would like to write another book, which describes all the occasions in which Jesus spoke about the Holy Breath in the Aquarian Gospel. This would not be a religious book, but would tell of the ways in which the breath is used to teach us how to live in that state of higher consciousness and spiritual intelligence as a way for the human race to free itself from all the self-made afflictions which blight its existence. Breath is the alchemic key.

As I began to realise the unique power of the *Aquarian Gospel* and breath, which I now also think of as *Holy,* another book emerged from the tea-chests. It was entitled *On the Death of my Son,* by a lawyer called Jasper Swain, who lived in Pietermaritzburg in South Africa, in the mid twentieth century.

The book tells of the tragic death of Swain's son Mike in

a fatal car accident while two cars were on the way to a family celebration. The son and a young female cousin were both killed outright by an out of control oncoming car. The young man, Mike, was gifted mentally and physically as a golden achiever. The grief of the family can be imagined.

Before the funeral Jasper Swain received a brief note written by an unknown woman from Port Elizabeth some hundreds of miles in the south of the country, asking him to visit her. In his grief-stricken state of mind he threw the letter down, but after the funeral he was very unsettled and happened to notice the letter lying. As something to occupy his mind he decided to visit the letter writer, and eventually arrived at a farm, where he met the owner who said 'my wife is expecting you.'

On meeting the lady he was astounded and at first sceptical when she told him she had been speaking with his son, and eventually through the process of her gifts as a medium, he himself was able to converse with him. Before long he seemed able to *contact* his son direct without any intermediary.

Having many years ago become aware of the gifts of mediumship, without becoming involved directly, I can accept all that Jasper Swain tells of his subsequent talks with his son, and what existence was like 'on the other side.' The communication was entirely wholesome and matter-of-fact, with no occult overtones. Mike the son told his family not to grieve, the souls or spirits of the two young people had left their bodies immediately or even before impact.

He said that the grief of those left behind hold back the development of the so-called *dead*, who have work to do in their next and more pleasant existence. The regular interchange between father and son, gave great comfort to the family, and entirely changed their thoughts about death.

Jasper Swain spent many subsequent years talking and

preaching about his experiences.

If you have read biographies of many famous statesmen it is surprising how many of them have sought and received advice from mediums in times of crisis, even political and military figures.

Jasper Swain did not seek this help, it was given to him unsought.

In my work I have met a number of people who had lost sons or daughters by illness or accident. It can seem the worst sadness, if our children are called back before us.

So many have been comforted and heartened to read this book, which of course always had to be offered in a sensitive way.

My former sister-in-law was a well-known journalist on consumer affairs on a South African newspaper. I had always wanted to write to Jasper Swain to thank him for his book, and the help it had been to a number of people. Unfortunately I delayed doing so but eventually asked my sister-in-law to investigate the book and its author. She did so, and I was sorry to learn that Swain had died, but his widow confirmed its authenticity, and the many people to whom it had brought comfort.

What I would like to share with you is a conversation between Mike and his father in which Mike said: '*Dad, beg, borrow or steal if you can a copy of the Aquarian Gospel. It was written in the earlier part of the century, but it will come into its own in the* [19]*70s. It is a very important book because it is uncorrupted text.*'

So there you are. I unexpectedly saw the book in the house of a friend, it came to me in an unexpected way, and was confirmed unexpectedly through another unexpected book!

'Coincidence is God's way of remaining anonymous.'

All through this period I felt I was being given clues as to the direction of my work, a dawning realisation that if we seek and trust, we find, often unexpectedly. Our thoughts possess an energy for good or ill, which attract a similar energy back.

Above all I have been given a deep and satisfying understanding of the spirit of the breath, an invisible working tool which when used correctly, can bring our lives into blossom, or when ignored, stunt as the sharpest frost. We have been given that greatest of blessings - free will.

The story of the *Aquarian Gospel* was written by an American doctor called Levi Dowling, who was a medical missionary. It tells of the life of Jesus between growing up and starting his ministry, when little seems to be known of his travels. It was recorded from the Akashic records, the *'imperishable records of time'*, on the invisible energy of thought, and written in the 'absolutely quiet hours' between four and six in the morning.

THE MIGHTY POWERS OF WORLDS UNSEEN
DO NOT SEND FORTH THEIR HELP 'TIL MAN
HAS DONE HIS BEST, THEY ONLY HELP
WHEN MAN CAN DO NO MORE.'

The Aquarian Gospel

I have no doubt that sometime in the future we shall need the unadulterated wisdom of this special work on the life of Jesus.

Chapter 30

THE TEARS OF THE EARTH

'CLIMATE CHANGE' is the 'in' word these days. It is repeated so often, that we are in danger of ignoring its urgency. It just goes into the back of the mind like the words *violence, addiction, insanity, poverty*. If any of these do not directly affect our lives, they only exist as words. We are able to understand that diseases such as cancer do not appear overnight. The severity of their symptoms may seem to break surface in a dramatic way. Yet they are the outward semblance of a seed which has often taken many years to germinate before our immune system has become too enfeebled to resist its stranglehold.

Surely we are intelligent enough to realise that global disturbance symptoms have been germinating for many years. However their insidiousness is no less acute and threatening to mankind's future existence than the individual appearance of the virulence of a poisonous cancer. By and large we are more concerned with our own personal agendas.

In any attack by a virulent and noxious energy on a living organism, the strength of that organism to resist and overcome depends totally on the strength of its auto-immune system.

Sometimes when an individual is under threat from personal disaster of any kind, they receive a 'wake-up' call of some kind. Perhaps a friend or loved one can help them to overturn a behaviour pattern that could end in self-destruction, perhaps a minor illness under investigation, leads to the discovery of more serious symptoms which can be arrested before they become fatal.

I believe that the many symptoms which are being shown to us from air pollution, ice-meltdown, the loss of a high percentage of the world's bee population, and so on, are early-warning signs which cannot be ignored. Forget the cynics, there will always be cynics. I would take a wager that the cynics who are saying that Global Warming is all pie in the sky have a profound over-dominance of the left cynical materialistic side of the brain.

We are unable to prove which of the upheavals which have occurred in various parts of the earth since the phrase 'climate change' became household words, are natural disasters, or caused by man's abuse of her treasures. All the same it seems obvious that many scientists believe that the latter is responsible for many, quite enough to warn of the chaos awaiting us if we do not change the way in which we nurture the Earth.

Many people vaguely think that there may be something *in* the warnings which are coming to us from many directions, when we are presented in human terms with the results of tsunamis and other eruptions, which cause loss of life and misery to thousands. Because they are not happening in our own back yard, the possible links to climate change are tucked casually back in the corners of the mind, as we check the football results or read the latest glossy magazine.

There are no alternatives to the laws of Nature. I remember when I was in the middle of labour with my first child, that it came to me that I was in the grip of a great confrontation with nature from which *I could not back out,* and for which nothing in my experience had prepared me. Even although the pain was all consuming I could not as in other situations change my mind. I had to go through with it, give in to the Nature I had been taught to distrust.

At the present time I believe that we are being confronted

by an all consuming challenge, when the actions of nature will *force* us to take on understanding the *pain* of the Earth. Then to be prepared to take responsibility to go through whatever it takes to give birth to a whole new way of being. To exist in obedience to the laws from which there is no escape, the laws by which mankind will have no option but to obey We cannot go back. They are the irreversible harmonic laws of Nature.

When I was a child at school, I was given the understanding that mankind had to *conquer* Nature, as if she was *against* us. An enemy as surely as an opponent in war. I wonder why we always talk about Mother Nature and not Father Nature? From the *blame nature* message I received as a child, it sounds just like another instance of putting the responsibility on the feminine gender! A carry over of our macho culture.

Now there seems to be a turn around, we are starting to realise that Nature requires our co-operation and respect, which is at least a step in the right direction.

Many years ago I was in the throes of a potentially personal disaster, some might call it a psychic attack. I had not then learned that when you start out on your true spiritual path, you often seem to be faced with a personal crisis which requires all your strength to survive on a spiritual level. I had to raise my spiritual courage quite a few notches in order to find the strength to move through that time. Looking back, I now give thanks that I was given the opportunity to find a courage for which my life up to that point had not prepared me.

It taught me that our thoughts alone can affect a situation, we can *choose* our thoughts, and also the value we decide to place upon events which *seem* to be to our detriment.

Time and again I have been able to be of assistance to those who have sought my help, just because I had gone through that earlier agonising (to me at the time) experience. It taught me the great truth of the saying which some might call slang. '*Don't sweat the small stuff, it's all small stuff.*' Or one which will be familiar to most, 'There's nothing either good or bad, but *thinking* makes it so.' Such statements can be of great help when we are going through a personal crisis, even if they are sometimes dismissed as *platitudes*.

The situation between ourselves and the Earth is not however small stuff. A well-known therapist, Caroline Myss, spoke of her own life crisis, implying quite graphically, 'When the Universe comes to call it kicks you up the backside!'

The Universe is indeed calling on us, and the call will not go away, ignore it and the kicks will indeed be painful.

When I was going through my personal crisis, it was not so easy to drop into sleep, because *in my opinion* I was suffering badly. At one time my agony of mind was such that I thought of Jesus on the Cross, and realised how paltry my own problem was in comparison. That realisation brought me a little nearer to the understanding of His courage, when I was looking for courage to face each day. This was not a religious experience, as generally understood, but from that time I was given the strength to overcome. When you are under what could be termed a psychic attack, when your own character is being undermined, you discover the spiritual truth that *you cannot attack back*. However you can defend, so there is always something you can do. To attack back weakens your position. When you do not choose the eye-for-an-eye rule, somehow life itself seems to introduce solutions you would not have dreamed could have occurred.

On one particular occasion I was lying awake at about two in the morning in a deep meditative state, after my personal crisis had been resolved.

I thought I heard a voice calling to me, like that of a small child. The voice said, 'I'm holding on as long as I can.' I must have slept then, but when I woke up I remembered the voice, it was still so clear in my head. There was no doubt in my mind that it was the voice of the Earth, with the innocence, beauty and courage of a little child who is weeping. The experience opened within me a great love, compassion and understanding for our Earth, and how she is being abused by man.

There is a wonderful book which came to me some years after the above experience. The book is called *The Voice of the Earth*, by Theodore Roszak.

Within its inspiring pages I came upon a paragraph which reminds us that our deepest links are not with our parents, they are with Nature. The words confirmed unspoken thoughts in my own mind, when I had been seeking to find solace for those who have had a terribly abusive childhood. It is hard to understand how such trauma can be healed because the early formative links of love with their parents had never been established.

We may believe that it is now too late, but we *can* form or re-connect the *deepest* loving relationship with Nature within ourselves. Roszak says our relationship with Nature is deeper then our relationship with our parents. I have seen it happen time and time again, particularly with those who have corrected their breathing or life force. It had been brought into being by Nature, as if we had re-connected to a wisdom of which we were aware *before our conception*, and so the scars of parental abuse can be healed and eliminated. Our relationship with Nature is deeper than with that of our parents.

To see this happen is such a satisfying experience when you are a breathing enabler, because you know that person is *healing themselves*. The oxygenating breath opens up brain cells which understand this perceived wisdom of our deep ties with Nature. In addition such people can be a catalyst to help others. There are hundreds of thousands who need this help.

Jung said that you can only heal others to the level that you have suffered and healed yourself, You have to have walked the walk, the intellect can only be in the way.

My personal experience of the voice of the Earth has led me to my life's work, it was the voice of Nature within which could be trusted, and discovered in its most profound aspect through the correction of spirit breath.

To discover and be certain as to the nature of your life's work is a great joy and privilege. It restores an on-going sense of life being an exciting adventure, full of humour and surprises .You can't plan the journey in detail, if you are ready to read the signs they will be shown to you.

Other chapters of this book refer to the Law of vibration, the function of the two brain hemispheres, the electrical 'gears' which influence thought, emotion and behaviour. These have also been scientifically evaluated, (if you need scientific proof). You will recall that these *gears* function within the following electrical frequencies:

BETA. *15-25 vibrations per second.* Constant Beta activity leads to stress.(*i.e. Beta Blockers? Drug medication.*)
Correct breathing can avoid reliance on medication.
ALPHA. *9-15 vibrations per second.* Produces a sense of calm, joy, peace, love.
THETA. *5-9 vibrations per second.* Meditation, Healing, Higher Intelligence.
DELTA. *0-5 vibrations per Second.* Sleep.

It has been scientifically proved that the vibration of the Earth's magnetic field (called Schumann Waves) is at Alpha, a loving energy (the loving voice of the Earth). It never changes, and the Earth has to stay on that vibration to maintain the stability of the Universe.

It seems obvious that a predominance of Man's beta left

brain fast activity could be seen to be in opposition to the Earth's Alpha magnetic field which is of course that of Nature.

Calculate the effect of global violence, wars, nuclear explosions, commercial greed, greed of all kinds, anger, revenge, addictions, the sum total of man's inhumanity to man. All of these must manifest as a high-beta vibration. It is easy to understand its effect on the childlike beauty and innocence of the Earth's Alpha core energy field. After all the earth has been given to man as a gift, and we are destroying that gift.

The unchangeable laws of magnetism which control our collective destiny, simply mean that what we send out returns to us. If we send out harmful energy, it is like touching an electrical switch with damp hands, we shall receive a shock. If we bounce a ball it bounces back, if we throw a stone in a pool of water we see the ever-widening ripples. All our actions whether positive or negative have the effect of ever-widening ripples on the earth's atmosphere. The Earth has to stay within an Alpha frequency, so any of our actions which oppose Alpha have to be returned to us or they harm the Earth.

Einstein remarked that the most important question man has to ask himself is *'is the Earth friendly?'* He must have been aware of the *unfriendly* way in which we treat the Earth, and question how long She can put up with us.

The Earth does not wish to harm mankind. However She has no option but to excrete or get rid of the poison in many forms with which we abuse her. She has to survive, and if Her rules are broken, surely there must come a time, when She will have no option but to give the impression that She has turned upon us. I am positive that some of the recent global disasters represent the energy of magnetic return by which Nature is trying to heal Her man-made wounds.

There is a story in *The Aquarian Gospel* by Levi Dowling,

in which the disciples challenge Jesus to tell them how evil could come about if God made the world, and God is all-good. To which Jesus replied that everything made by God is good, but sometimes two goods mixed together produce disharmony. This is an interesting way to describe what we call *bad*. You will know of people who are married, both of whom are good people, but who when coming together produce disharmony, and the marriage is a disaster. They were not meant to be 'mixed' together. Separated they thrive, and perhaps find partners of equal harmony.

Everything in this world originally comes from Nature, including the materials for nuclear bombs. It is in the mixing of earthly ingredients that man makes his fatal errors, for if his mind-set is not loving, the magnetic energy return from such disastrous mixes will be chaotic and disastrous.

It takes a lot of understanding to grasp Nature's philosophy, and I have a great deal for which to thank my wonderful clients, who have brought their lives out of chaos, to a state of harmony, by mixing together the good ingredients of their individual talents which return to them as a bonus straight from Nature. Nature does not only consist of that which is seen to be *growing* in visual terms, her actions are on an unseen level of vibration. It is then automatically attracted to any of Man's creations which are on a similar positive vibration.

To breathe correctly with the breath of the Earth, changes disaster to healing. What works with the microcosm in terms of one human being, will also work with the macrocosm as represented by the population of the Earth.

In the *Aquarian Gospel* Jesus talks of two people walking along a road, 'one will be taken, one saved.' I am sure the one who breathes correctly would be the one to be saved!

The co-partner with Nature's laws.

I believe that man has the power to create a colossal healing positive vibration which could help the Earth to heal herself as she knows quite well how to. She would then I am sure send back remarkable and undreamed of benefits to mankind in return. She would be unable to do otherwise. Think of the elimination of wars, human strife, famine, is there time for us to comprehend our power? We have an immense potential to help the Earth to heal herself, so that its beautiful soul like that of a hurt, loving child need no longer feel that it is just 'hanging on'.

Disaster can happen in the twinkling of an eye, so can its opposite. Which shall we choose?

The Earth does not wish to harm mankind, how can she if she is on a loving vibration?

It takes only a few grains of sand to tip the scales one way or the other. To the onlooker the weight on each side of that scale may be exactly similar, *but* just a few grains can change the balance.

Nevertheless the Earth will have to ensure her survival, and if mankind stands in the way of that necessity, she will have no option except to do what it takes for her survival, *whatever the consequences to the human species.*

Under sufficient negative pressure all living organisms will suffer a breakdown. The colossal and unimaginable pressure we place upon the Earth's harmonic balance by our beta-orientated systems must go step by step nearer to the breaking down of the Earth's ability to regenerate. It might not take as much of a change in attitude as we imagine to tip the balance in favour of regeneration. But only if we show willing, to recognise that the Higher dimension mentioned by Einstein has the power to multiply our efforts, by whatever is needed. And will.

★ ★ ★

I AM CERTAIN THAT I HEARD THE EARTH
WEEPING, LIKE A LITTLE CHILD. HAVE WE
THE HUMILITY TO REMEMBER HOW TO NURTURE
A CHILD? FIRST OF ALL WE MUST NURTURE OUR
OWN CHILD WITHIN, ALL IT NEEDS IS LOVE
AND CARE, AND SO DOES THE EARTH.

Chapter 31

GLOBAL WOMAN,
GLOBAL MAN

AS I GET OLDER AND LOOK BACK, I realise that the time when *I* was a child is now looked upon by today's children as the *Olden Days*. This I recall was a phrase I used to roll round my tongue with a sense of importance when I was about eight. It carried a feeling of ancient mystery. Olden Days for me then would probably have been in the 1880s. I am therefore writing these words from an ancient perspective! A decade is measured in terms of ten years. I realise how much of what is known as social change has taken place since I was born, and how old-fashioned, photographs look from the years of my infancy.

They say that human nature never changes, but to some degree it must, or what is known as social change could not be a valid phrase, otherwise we would all be wearing skins or living in caves.

The only certain thing in life is change, so things must change for the better or worse. Despite all the horrors of modern 'civilisation', when the beast side of human nature is seen so graphically on television, and read about in the papers, I still get a sense of a great struggle going on in the collective mind of men and women. Often as we grow spiritually, it looks as if we were moving two steps forward and one step back.

In the Western world, no doubt the emancipation of

women has had a great effect on social change, yet obviously a change in women's role could not happen without that of men changing also, even unconsciously, and at first very unwillingly!

Therefore what is emerging is what I call a new Global man and woman. There is no clear dividing line between the old and new, the old does not let go willingly, just as we can find it difficult to convert from positive to negative thinking.

During my years as a full-time therapist, I was privileged to share time with thousands of men and women of differing nationalities and religions. They were suffering from stress, often under appalling internal and external pressure, with no known means of relief, apart from drugs, either medical or illegal, cigarettes, alcohol, or projection of their stress on others. Internalised, the stress eventually developed into illness.

The most successful and natural way I know of to help someone release themselves from such nightmare prisons, is to free themselves from their *respiratory prisons*. For without exception that is the major observable physical symptom even while they are talking about their mental pain, whatever the nationality. There is no geographical boundary to correct breathing, nor has there been since language evolved from the mists of time. The most important work of my life has been to learn to read what I call 'the language of the breath.'

After I had begun to absorb this fascinating natural science, I discovered *The Aquarian Gospel of Jesus the Christ* by Levi Dowling, which contains many wonderful references to the Holy Breath. I read the following words: 'Man may read the signs of wind and sky, but he cannot discern the signs of Holy Breath, but You shall know.' I felt as if I was being spoken to personally, as the signs of Holy Breath began to be revealed to me, and also to the men and women who came to me suffering from stress. I did not often mention the book, but the 'signs' or spiritual helpful truths which helped them with their problems appeared to come into their consciousness as their breathing improved.

Listening to scientists of either sex talking knowledgably, or forecasting cataclysmic climate change, I note their often blocked breathing and stressful voices, and wonder in terms of the above quotation, how *could* they in that case have access to the real truth?

Language may have evolved from countless tribes, but the internal organs and brain vibrate to the same basic natural rhythm, the lungs also. They all only function correctly when the auto-immune system is vibrating to the rhythm of Nature.

Time and time again, irrespective of nationality or religion, I have seen the same reduction of stress and its symptoms whatever the causal problem, when a client becomes involved with breath correction. The miraculous thing that also happens is that the person begins to express thoughts concerning solutions to their problems that could only have come to the surface of their minds by a new (to them) wisdom, which certainly had not been expressed to me or by me, in our earlier discussion about their difficulties.

The only interpretation I could place upon their words was that this wisdom had come from a great Universal Higher Wisdom which exists at a subliminal level in the unconscious mind, which had been 'speaking' to me ever since I had begun to correct my own breathing. It was also beginning to resonate within any other person involved in the same process.

According to the man-made rules and customs by which my clients had been indoctrinated since birth, this new thinking often clashed with their national laws and traditions, and could cause some confusion. Such confusion will not disappear until my clients like myself, have had time, sometimes quite a long time, to sort out the new self from the old, eventually realising that the new knowledge imparted by correct breathing cannot be disregarded, and new priorities for right living have to be established, whatever the religion.

I am seeing with great joy an east/west mind fusion of kindred spirits emerging, based on the true understanding of correct breathing, creating what I hope could eventually become an invincible new world order for peace.

Despite my awareness as a woman, of how much needs to change before we are truly an equal sex society, I have been constantly reminded of how far we have advanced when contemplating the sexual imbalances in other cultures. My mind constantly returns to the fact that where there is respiratory imbalance there will always be an environment of fear, control, violence and repression.

Interpreting the signs I have noticed of respiratory limitation in either sex which cuts across national boundaries, there are two significant misuses of the breathing pattern. In women the constant factor is a holding in of the lower stomach at the base of the breath impulse, so that the lower, larger base of the lungs is not filled. This is the prime cause of hyperventilation and constant fear, because as a result the upper respiratory area becomes over-inflated, which does not compensate for the restriction of the lower lungs. Such a pattern results in over-excitably and hypertension.

In women it is hardly surprising that this constant under inflation of the lower lungs leads to circulatory problems in the lower pelvic area, gynaecological problems and, I believe, it is the main contributory factor in cancer in the reproductive area.

In males the lower lung area is often over-inflated, with a powerful restriction of the upper lung area, as the diaphragm muscle is held in to prevent the air going into the upper lungs. This creates a strong tension in the muscles around the heart, with subsequent risk of heart problems. The suppression of the full and natural respiratory movement not only leads to heart disease on a physical level but to an inability to express real affection. Cold-heartedness is the outward symptom. You can't block the heart physically without blocking the emotions. Such symptoms in any nationality leads to the same illnesses.

Correct breathing, leading to spiritual growth will, in any nationality, inevitably lead to similar thinking trends about the real priorities of life as seen from a loving perspective. No indoctrination takes place, racial, political and religious boundaries all seem to dissolve in a community of brotherhood and sisterhood, while still keeping the highest qualities of racial characteristics and personal individuality.

I believe that it is from this alchemic fusion that global woman and man will evolve, if there is yet time for this evolution.

When the upper or lower respiratory pattern has been impaired from childhood, there will always be a corresponding physical, mental and emotional immaturity.

The information in the above sentences is applicable on a world-wide scenario. I have noticed for some years that you can apply your knowledge of the correct breathing pattern to world leaders as they appear on television. It is easy if you have that extra dimension of awareness gained by breath training to know their fear levels, if they are telling the truth, and the quality of their integrity. This information applies to any nationality.

There is a science of the eyes. If a politician is asked a question, and the eye focus shifts to the right before answering, you may be suspicious about whether they are telling the truth. They will probably be telling the truth they think you want to hear. Alternatively if their eye focus shifts to the left before they reply, you can be fairly certain that they *are* telling the truth. The left eye is controlled by the right creative brain, and the right eye by the critical, analytical hemisphere. Read Chapter 32 about The Eyes.

There is an appalling lack of know-how of such simple body/mind language by people who are reckoned to be intelligent, or who are interviewing for high-power jobs.

Knowing your political or global opponent's psychological make-up from the truths told by the breath which never lies, could help a great deal in settling differences in another unique way. As a therapist it can help enormously in finding the most helpful way to communicate and shorten therapeutic communication time. What works in a one-to-one situation also works on the global level.

All world dictators who rule by fear, because their breathing is distorted, will see 'reds under the beds' and feel the need to shore up those fears by aggressive tactics. They have a desire to subjugate others in order to feel safe. Such leaders, and those who are led by them, will eventually meet disaster in some way. Unfortunately such leaderships can take all too long before their basic weaknesses are revealed, so cunning are they at disguising the cracks in their armour.

If I could be granted one wish, it would be that all world leaders breathed correctly!

International disputes would then be solved easily and effortlessly. Within the home so would domestic friction, with its appalling effect on children. Any male/female imbalance would disappear naturally. You cannot have world harmony and good relationships, unless the world's breath is true to Nature's laws.

People who breathe right call in an extra dimension of brain energy from the power of unseen worlds, not yet known to science, and can diffuse negative energy in an environment. I have heard that a person can freeze or warm a room by their very presence. A truly global man or woman will always warm the area round them.

You may think my dreams are unrealistic, but world changes and increase in man's natural spiritual intelligence can happen overnight. World health is an acknowledged aim; you cannot have world health without correct breathing, even although those who take responsibility for speaking on behalf of world health are shockingly silent on the subject.

At present, irrespective of nationality, we arc all suffering from the strangulation of relationships between men and women. We in the west view what we see as too submissive the head-covering of female heads in the middle or far-east, because to us it represents female subjugation. One can understand that decades ago when society was even more predatory, such covering might have been seen to be a way of protecting women from would-be abductors. I see the habit as simply unhealthy, preventing oxygen from reaching the scalp, which I believe to be a health requirement.

I can understand how those from the east can see some of our western feminine excesses of dress and unnecessary flaunting of sexual flamboyance, as distastefully as I do myself!

It is very exciting to see some countries begin to emerge from a male-dominated society, where women are beginning to enter the political arena in ways previously undreamed of.

The lower breath holding distortion in women has always appeared to me as a Western version of the former terrible Chinese habit of foot-binding, designed to hobble women from self-expression, seen as a threat to male supremacy. Breath holding creates a 'hobbling' effect on a human being. I wonder exactly how and when the foot binding custom started; there must have been a first occasion. All such practices have an origin. You may have heard of the idea that all victims attract their predators, the law of supply and demand in its worst sense. When you think of the influence for good or bad that a mother possesses, where have we women gone wrong, for all men have mothers?

Training in correct breathing reverses the fear and violence syndrome. Over a period of quite a short time, a world-wide *epidemic* of right natural breath use could, I am convinced, bring about an epidemic of right thought and action.

Sensitivity to others' needs, the loving nurturing of our children, could reverse global suffering, with a re-balancing of the best qualities of male and female attributes. A natural sequence to such a revolution would be that poverty and starvation would fade away.

Who can forecast the time period for such a dramatic change in our downward spiral, which can only be reversed by a world-wide respect for each sex by the other? This may be seen by some to take centuries, but as energy trends gather momentum there comes a time when this momentum becomes unstoppable.

The future of mankind is only ensured through healthy birth by healthy women supported adequately by healthy men. For this to happen there has to be a reversal of the all too often symptom of the female lower-lung suppression death impulse, for that is what it is. How else can one evaluate the non-use of the ability to expand and contract the largest life area for the continual flow of the life force? This is a vital necessity for a healthy pregnancy. Lower breath constriction produces womb constriction. No wonder there is the need for so many Caesarean deliveries, not to mention forceps, inductions and interventions present at so many births.

The freeing of the heart respiratory area in the male would also free the male to express and feel his love for himself and others, particularly during the so-important period of pregnancy when the a vital factor for the woman is a sense of loving protection from her mate. We see this in the animal world. Is man lower than the animals?

An emergence to global man and woman can only come about from a deep and respectful observance of the laws of nature. As we increasingly become aware of the damage we are creating by the indifference we pay to these laws, we must surely begin to realise through our own apathy the extent of the power we have relegated to only a few people, who between them hold most of the financial responsibility of how that power is used. Looking at the trivial priorities of the way the financial energy is used in the raping of the earth's resources, it reveals that there is an assumption that these resources are limitless, whereas we are discovering daily that some natural stores may not be able to be replenished. It is a form of cancerous leaching of the bone-marrow of the earth.

As with the macrocosm so with the microcosm.

An assumption of the continuation of present financial and power priorities can no longer be assumed by any who hold unnatural power, because it repeats the mind-set of those who treat the Earth as a mother without respect, expecting her to come up with solutions long after we are meant to have assumed the cloak of maturity to make right decisions for ourselves. Only a human mother who is afraid allows her children to believe this, and a woman who is afraid will keep her children immature, assuming the role of the endless provider. Those who assume unnatural power will have to accept a profound change in their priorities. Nature will force it upon them.

I have mentioned in another chapter the name of Elizabeth Kubler Ross (a wonderful psychologist who was one of the first people to enter the concentration camps after the war) and her never-to-be forgotten words, 'the most important word you have to learn to say to your teenage children is 'No. No.'

Our Earth Mother has begun to say 'No.' We have to listen and grow up. She has her limits.

The change must start with woman and man simultaneously, the adult woman communicating that her role in relation to the adult man is not that of a mother, nor can she regard him as the eternal father provider (the Adam and Eve syndrome).

In gaining respect for each other's role, we also begin to use the Earth in a more mature way. Respect extends to every aspect of our lives, including our unborn child and its needs which, as a priority, includes an adequate supply of oxygen for full growth. That oxygen can only be provided by a fearless mature mother who breathes correctly.

Obviously for all of us life begins at birth, and our vitality and health at that time depends on the health of the mother during the gestation period. A woman who from childhood onwards has restricted correct breathing by the constriction of the diaphragmatic muscle is not likely to give birth easily. Caesarean section, forceps, epidural and other artificial aids are the path by which the infant enters the world, often in a state of unrecognised but life-long shock.

The woman who holds in her diaphragm and lower stomach when she breathes, creates as one imaginative writer puts it *'a body like a cadaver in* Vogue *magazine.'* The financial strings of the fashion magazines seem to be held by men. This is the body image which our daughters are encouraged to emulate in our age of 'enlightenment', which we see in the emaciated models in fashion magazines. To me it represents another form of the Chinese foot-binding in a modern context.

The unnatural births I have described from a human body so repressed, produces a new human generation plant also damaged physically, mentally and emotionally.

Sons grow up with repressed mothers, daughters with unemotional fathers, unable to really love themselves or their children. Many children with childish parents spend their childhood protecting such parents. Their offspring feel guilty for daring to seek their own pleasure because that would leave their parents behind, who are unable to cope alone, having been immature parents during the whole of their children's lives. This parental vampirism is all too common. Immature parents enjoy an artificial period of power which lasts only until their children leave home, and then because they have so few resources to fill their days, try to hold on to their adult children, by a form of guilt and emotional blackmail. 'Look what we have done for you, you owe us...'

At an emotional level such children suppress a deep growing anger which strengthens as they develop; it may not be expressed verbally, but emotionally they represent time-bombs which will eventually explode in ill-health in some form, or anti-social behaviour when under extreme stress. So the cycle continues.

Such family units produce neither Global Woman nor Global Man, because the laws by which they live are not the laws of nature, and in fact are in opposition to those inexorable laws which govern us. These are not negotiable, and we disregard them at our peril.

In nature the weakest plants do not survive. The human race is no exception. Eventually we can no longer propagate from the weaker plant; the same is true of man, the weaker strains die out.

Remember that Yoga Ramacharaka in his book, *The Science of Breath*, stated that 'one generation of complete breathers would regenerate the race, and disease would be looked upon as a rarity.' I believe this is possible, and could be possible within the forseeable future. All it would take would be for Governments, governing authorities, civil servants, health and educational specialists, religious bodies, to step off their podiums, platforms and pulpits, study how a little healthy child breathes correctly, and do the same themselves. Humility is required of course. They would then become truly living examples to the people they serve.

What amazing insights they would gain in rediscovering about how simple life really is, how full of fun, joy and love. How easy to solve problems. How easy to stay healthy, how easy to move the mountains, which will have to be moved before we have on earth a race of Global Men and Women. Mountains can be moved in a nanosecond when we obey Nature's laws.

The laws of higher power and nature *have* to reach down and support us as we go through a quantum leap of change if man is to fulfil his destiny and survive what may be to come, if we do not listen to Nature. We have to learn to heal and save mankind. The Earth would then heal herself. Heaven on earth for Global man and Woman.

As the doctor said, 'Take away my needle, knife and tablet, and I have nothing.' Those who profess to provide health must learn about the fact that if they heeded the laws of Nature, the needle, knife and tablet would soon become virtually obsolete.

Not so long ago the average man who saw his role as head of the house, and the average woman who saw herself as his submissive inferior, would have felt that they had nothing, if these false roles were taken away.

It may be that the ordinary man and woman will need to step into their global roles *without* the help of the professionals, because I do not think there is much time left. As they establish the laws of correct breath, the magnetic laws of life will respond to them, it cannot be released until they have stepped out of the old role model which has lost its role anyway. Its garment is outworn. A new relationship must emerge between woman and man, based on natural love and respect, the by-product of right breathing.

I think that woman may have to take this first step on her own initiative as the begetter of life, but I see the necessary change beginning to happen in the hearts of many men also, a small stream could soon become a great river.

IN THIS CASE THE RIVER OF LIFE
CREATED WITH THE COMBINED ENERGIES
OF GLOBAL MAN AND GLOBAL WOMAN.

Chapter 32

THE EYES

FOR MANY YEARS of my earlier life I suffered from what I can only call tired eyes. A feeling of physical and mental strain. Later in the day, having to force the eyes to operate, to stay open, even a feeling of slight staring, feeling threatened by life and people, although no one else seemed to notice. A feeling I can now better interpret as a sense that the world was not necessarily a friendly place, and I had to be on guard.

I now realise part of the feeling must have come from being brought up during the war, but even after it ended, always being active, of not having the right to rest during the day, for that would be laziness, *not* my parent's way of life.

Our English culture has a lot to answer for in this respect, compared with our European neighbours who have a tradition of the mid-day siesta. Where did we absorb the notion that we are machines?

This feeling of always being on guard, which also translates as defending oneself from others, even if not being attacked, is also very tiring. Trying not to let others see who we are, as if who we are is not very nice.

After many years, having frequently heard about the word 'relaxation', I finally decided to 'have a shot'. I put in slang a process which was to become one of the most important and valuable aspects of my daily life. Looking back, I procrastinated for many years, at last being reined in to the new behaviour like a bucking colt. Someone must have been

369

looking after me, for no one actually *persuaded* me to try the art of relaxation.

The first benefit I noticed after tackling this new skill in my typically Piscean lackadaisical way was that my eyes felt better, the world a friendlier place. It did not occur to me at that time that this was meant to be a naturally permanent condition. It seemed *unnatural* from the normal strained and tired self which was at that time my permanent state of being. What a sad state in which to exist. I didn't think I realised I was in a perpetually unhappy state, just this frequent feeling of strain.

It was when I began a training in psychotherapy and hypnotherapy that I began to take the relaxation reflex more seriously, and to realise I had the *choice* to make changes, which gave me the conviction that I had the *right* not to feel eye-strain. The course required regular training in placing oneself in a relaxed state in order to experience the state of self-hypnosis. The continuing new habit of being in a more relaxed level began to be a constant condition, as if the scales were being at last tipped in a very interesting way which enhanced my enjoyment of life. My eyes felt so peaceful. I remembered I had discovered this process when I was expecting my second baby, but I mistakenly thought that it was only to be used for birth preparation!

When I was 16 and undergoing a routine school health check, it was found that I had an astigmatism in my eyes, i.e. one favoured long, and the other short-sightedness. I was supposed to wear glasses all the time, and I remember going into my father's office tearfully imparting the tragic news. I clearly recall the negative feelings involved at now being short of perfection, because I was a keen member of the school lacrosse team, and advanced gym class. How could I throw myself over the vaulting horse, or charge down the lacrosse pitch at full speed with such a hindrance as specs stuck on to my nose?

During the next ten years I went through about eight pairs of spectacles. Often I would read without them, they were always getting lost. Highly energetic physical activities were also part of my work as a farm secretary. Every moment I could spend away from my desk in the physical work of the farm which I loved, meant that my spectacles and their place on the bridge of my nose were the least of my priorities. As far as I could see, my vision was as good with or without the glasses!

In the seasonal demands of nature, seed-time and harvest, caring for animals, the sheer delights of the glorious Wiltshire downs, specs seemed an anachronism, hastily donned from time to time when guilt or office duties persuaded me that I *should* wear such horrible fixtures on my face, particularly when often a lens or side-arm was missing!

The first physical impression I was aware of from wearing glasses was a sensation of pulling of the muscles at the back of my eyes which made me suspicious and mentally worried as to the permanent effect of an artificial visual aid. When I was aware of visual distortion after I had been wearing glasses for a few hours and then left them off, I finally rebelled. I could still see car numbers from twenty-five yards without aids.

My final recollection of my 'specs' era was of a pair residing in the glove compartment of my car, as I say minus lens and side-arm. I must have finally thrown them out. Perhaps my rude health meant that I could disregard the optician's diagnosis, but now at eighty, I can read, write and drive without glasses. Indeed I was talking to a young man of about thirty-five recently, who had to bring his glasses out to read a paper we were discussing. He was quite shocked that at my age I could read the article unaided.

So many of my friends of my own generation cannot even see across the room without spectacles, that I feel privileged and thankful to know a lot more about eyesight and its direct link to brain function than I did when in tears in my father's office at sixteen.

I find it distressing to look at school class photographs of children of about eight years old, and to notice how many are wearing glasses.

I am a profound admirer of the work of Rudolf Steiner, who believed that children should not be introduced to the kind of education which involved reading and numbers before the age of eight, and before then the use of colour, creativity and nature are all that are required to encourage and open up the child's natural curiosity and need to learn and work, which to the child is also its play. Very much so before the age of eight.

A formalised education which requires concentration on small letters or numbers requires a pull on the eye muscles on a brain not yet mature enough to operate in this way, which then inevitably produces unrecognised eye strain, resulting in artificial aids such as glasses at an early age.

In other chapters of this book I develop ideas about brain function, including the fact that the muscles at the back of the eyes control a third of brain activity. Presumably when these muscles are over tense the brain becomes over stimulated. Constant over-stimulation of an infant brain must have a detrimental effect on the eye muscles, tissue of the eye, and its still immature development. The child may require spectacles while still in the early primary years.

Conversely when the brain is relaxed, the whole body is relaxed, and there is no strain on the eye. Brain relaxation does not imply laziness, the brain may indeed be very active within an Alpha electrical frequency. Other people will be pleasantly affected by the relaxed change in that person's personality.

The fact that brain function of a child under about eight

years of age fluctuates between Alpha and Theta frequency (love and meditation) is the reason why we feel such affection for children, who are of course much nearer to Nature than ourselves. As I say 'straight off the production line.' A lovely poem by Michael Quoist called *I Love Children* contains the words 'for I know of nothing more beautiful than the eyes of a five-year old child.'

In the course of my work I have learned that one side of the body is controlled by the opposite side of the brain, the cross-over occurring at the eyes, so that the left eye or brain controls the right side of the body and vice versa It amazes me that so few people know these kind of facts. Knowing them, if you have a relative who has suffered from a stroke, you will be able to understand whether and why their creative or verbal skills have been affected. The left side of the brain controls the functions of objectivity, speech, science, maths, analytical and critical thought. The right brain hemisphere is concerned with emotions, creativity, intuition music, art.

I am sure you will understand that it is important for the two brain spheres to work in harmony, or balance, and that over-use of one side of the brain, will then impose a strain on the eye which controls that brain area. It should be easy to understand why formal left brained learning imposed too soon on a still forming infant brain will result in the deterioration which results in artificial aids to eyesight in the form of glasses.

If you belong to those who feel uneasy as I once did to see a small child of three or four sucking a dummy, think again. Yesterday, upon noticing a little boy enjoying this comforting occupation, I suddenly realised that the child was totally correct in his instinct. Looking at his eye focus, I realised that he was meditating, a natural necessity for a small child confronted by the many unnatural aspects of our culture.

In some countries the child naturally suckles at the breast

even until the age of about five, not necessarily for food, but the legitimate comfort required by a small organism who spent nine months only recently within its mother's body. It is not surprising that there is a need for a few years to return to the safely and comfort experienced at that time within the womb. The little child is legitimately trying to maintain contact with Wordsworth's 'clouds of glory' from whence it came. Perhaps next time you see a child enjoying the ecstasy of its dummy, have a look at the magic in its eyes, as it reverts to the beautiful centre within. A taste of Heaven? Just popping back to the 'clouds of glory'.

I don't know how much analysis has been done on eye weakness in a small child's eyesight, and whether the left or right eye is most commonly affected. As a culture we seem very loath to admit to any faults in the way we educate children, and its effect on eye strain.

It is time that we viewed with great concern the way our educational system seems to be evolving with its over-emphasis and demands on the functions of the left brain resulting in an over-materialistic and analytical way of life and thinking. It treats the creative activities of the right brain as the poor relation, even although the spiritual and intuitive functions reside there, the areas of highest priority by which we steer our lives in any satisfactory and fulfilling way.

I came upon a very potent comment in an old article about Ghandi, the Indian spiritual prophet, who spoke of 'the call of the spinning wheel as being the noblest of all. The spinning wheel is the reviving draught for the millions of our dying countrymen and women from galloping consumption. I claim that in losing the spinning wheel we lost our left lung. The restoration of the wheel arrests the progress of the fell disease.'

You may feel confused when reading these words, as I did at first. Then the penny dropped! I realised that in referring to the loss of the left lung, Ghandi also realised that the left lung is controlled by the creative side of the brain, and the lack of the universal hand-spinning creative activity in most homes led to the deterioration of the left lung through lack of correct oxygenic function. In his time Ghandi had seen the artistic and creative skill of spinning, overtaken by the industrial and mechanical production of cloth, so that the calm and reflective focus of the mind involved in spinning had been lost to India, overtaken by a left brain way of mechanistic manufacturing of the enormous quantities of cotton goods required by the population.

Equivalent and parallel arguments may be made for similar situations in our over-industrialised Western culture. We may also have sold the left lung, and function of the right spiritual brain for financial gain. Of course it is only in recent years that my understanding of Ghandi's words would have made such an impact on my imagination.

Our current undervaluation of the poor relation right side of the brain is probably behind the present financial world crisis. Education, training, computer over reliance, have become the priority of what one might call the civil-servant mentality, for to get into the civil service I believe the emphasis is on left brain function. This, as Ghandi said, depletes the left-lung and its breathing efficiency, which we deprive of adequate oxygen by a limited respiratory pattern, and therefore right brain function. Loss of a creative way of life.

I can understand why the philosopher and educator Rudolph Steiner advocated that children should not be introduced to intellectual subjects until the age of eight, for he knew that the right close-to-nature hemisphere side of the brain needed to be nurtured and strengthened before being introduced to man-made intellectual concepts deemed necessary, but frequently not spiritually sustainable. In which case their use will come to nothing. Children need to be able to trust their inner awareness of what is spiritually correct, and not false and fleeting.

In my experience children educated in Steiner principles do just as well, and frequently better when entering mainstream education at eleven. Our over-rated 'intelligence'?

Assessment based on learned facts does, I am sure, do untold harm to the sensitive plant of the small child. It represents to so many a pressure from which they block off, become afraid at not knowing what is asked of them, and their breathing becomes restricted with mental blocking. Their tension can result in bullying or being bullied. Children become violent and out of control, rebel in the only way they can, and we call them naughty.

The withdrawal of corporal punishment (thank goodness, perhaps we have made *some* progress) meant that something has to take its place as a way to maintain the possibility of an educational environment. Over the years an enormous amount of humane and thoughtful measures have been introduced by educational specialists in an effort to try and fill the gap caused by the inability to deal out corporal punishment.

I recall one client who came to me and told me that when she was a tender five-year old just starting school, she received the belt on her first day. For what? For wearing white knickers to school instead of the regulation brown. It was a Catholic school.

The ancient Celtic people had a saying that 'only poets should be teachers. Why? Because knowledge not taught from the heart is dangerous.' Perhaps teachers with a breath-right heart centre will be able to resolve the discipline problem in our schools. Looking back at my own school days, we knew which teachers liked children, they did not have discipline problems.

When someone is in contact with the heart I have noticed a sweetening of the expression of the eye, and an improvement in breathing.

I believe the educational hierarchy is stuck in a quagmire of its own making, teachers and pupils alike suffering from rampant bullying and stress. You cannot get a good atmosphere in a classroom, if neither teachers nor pupils are breathing correctly.

The answer is simple to me at least, but what seems simple to me seems impossible to many of the people I have spoke to who are *experts* in the educational field. When a lovely senior biology teacher came to see me to discover if I knew more about breathing than she did, the list she gave me would I feel be an ideal additional aspect of student teacher syllabus throughout their years of training. Her list was headed 'What correct breathing has given me.'

1. Enormous reserves of energy.
2. Perfect control in the classroom.
3. The ability to think.
4. Poise.
5. Complete confidence.

How many teachers would give anything to be able to say such words with truth? A school containing teachers with such training could be a blueprint for the whole education system with, I am positive, a reduction in eye-strain as one of the many by-products.

I believe the national curriculum must eventually contain correct breathing and relaxation training as an essential part of educational requirement. Education must be seen within a much wider context than intellectual attainment. As long as we see education as fodder preparation for an industrialised society the present problems will continue. I heard a lovely quote recently. *'Children learn through the loving eyes of their teacher.'*

The inclusion of the study of correct breathing and its enormous effect on all biological functions would, with practical training, provide a new dimension in the understanding of true science which the scientific world has still to embrace. I notice a high proportion of scientists require eyesight aids.

To me such ideas represent a fresh breath of life, so desperately needed in an educational system which has become bogged down by its emphasis on the trivia of intellect, the amassing of facts, without drawing out the wealth of genius trapped within so many of our children, by a culture where I have discovered respiratory malfunction and inevitable brain-oxygen starvation to be the most common symptoms in all illness.

As I was writing these words today, the television was reporting that heart and circulatory problems are the most common form of illness. You cannot get circulatory problems if you breathe correctly, heart problems are usually the knock-on result of poor circulation, so it all comes back to correct breathing.

A vital inclusion of breath re-training needs to be introduced in all aspects of our national life. It would reduce crime, addictions, and I believe that within one lifetime Britain would become a world leader of a new kind, envied and hopefully emulated by all other nations. This for reasons which do not have an industrial/financial/scientific basis, yet we could emerge as a joyful nation, able to be self-sustainable. I suppose one might call it a spiritual revival, for within such understanding, anything is possible. Breath means spirit, it has nothing to do with any kind of religion.

The introduction of correct breath would reduce crime, addiction and domestic misery like snow melting in the sun.

People who have discovered the simplicity of joy, of seeing Heaven in a grain of sand. A symptom of clear vision.

In returning to thoughts on eye function and health, you will I am sure know of the old saying that 'the eyes are the mirror of the soul.' You may have also experienced the change in your own reactions when meeting the eyes of a violent, sad, or joyful person.

There is such a lot of energy projected into the world, or indeed on other people from the energy from our eyes, which is of course a measure of the energy in the brain. It can freeze or heal us. We unconsciously avoid hurtful eyes, and feel drawn to the warmth of its opposite.

Words from A. E. Housman's poem *A Shropshire Lad* had a profound effect on me at the time I was writing this chapter. Housman talks of his earlier years in the country when everything of nature all around him represented 'homely comforters'.

> But here in London streets I ken,
> No such helpmates only men
> And these are not in truth to bear,
> If they would another's care,
> They have enough as 'tis I see
> In many an eye that measures me,
> The mortal sickness of a mind
> Too unhappy to be kind,
> Undone with misery
> All they can
> Is to hate their fellow man,
> And 'til they die, they needs must still
> Look at you and wish you ill.

How many people do we meet who seem to look at us and wish us ill.

The look that seems 'to wish you ill' is, I believe, the initiator for much spontaneous violence on the streets. If you meet someone with apparent violence in their eyes, and your eye focus is at all aggressive, the trigger for spontaneous combustion is there. It took quite a leap in my understanding to realise that those with the hurtful eyes are so unhappy that compassion is the only emotion possible in order to defend yourself. Compassion in your eye contact is not weakness, but it can protect you, and help to defuse the non-love projecting from someone's gaze, for you then pose no threat.

After I learned to breathe correctly, and my eyes no longer felt strained or my brain tense, it also led to me being able to love and approve of myself. The other wonderful result was the increase in my love for small children, and a sensation of empathy. Never trying to make a child *like* me, but to wait until a child approached *me*. The child seems to realise that you are in a similar world as themselves, which gives them confidence.

They respond to loving eyes, which make no demand on them.

I do not in any way wish to infer that I have solved all problems, or believe myself always to be right; one is always at the mercy of one's own personality weaknesses. On the other hand I like the me I have become, rather than the me I was thirty years ago! To be able to relax simply by mentally releasing the tension from the muscles at the back of the eyes. It provides a wonderful always available visual ability to stay calm, and not be upset by events which used to upset me, which I notice send other people into extreme and unnecessary over-reaction. Please don't get the impression that I think I am perfectly calm in all situations, but I do know how to reverse negative feelings.

This habit of inner-eye relaxation creates a fifty-fifty brain balance, so that whatever trauma is happening in the outside world, its effect can be tempered by contact with the real natural world within which is infinitely wiser than any man-made activity. When the inner perception is only twenty-five per cent, thus increasing outer awareness to seventy-five per cent, tension and distortion occurs. We become vulnerable to other people's moods, subsequently tense and fatigued more quickly.

Some of the points I have raised in this chapter you may have noticed in other chapters. An overlap frequently occurs when writing about the breath, since it affects all aspects of our lives.

Below are extracts from a wonderful poem on the eyes of a child by Michael Quoist, from *Prayers of Life*. I cannot think of a more beautiful example to enhance what I have been trying to say.

> But above all, I like youngsters because of the look
>   in their eyes,
> In their eyes I can read their age
> In my Heaven there will only be five year old eyes.
> For I know of nothing more beautiful than the pure
>   eyes of a child
> It is not surprising for I live in children
> And it is I who look out through their eyes
> When pure eyes meet yours, it is I who smile at you
>   through the flesh.
> But on the other hand,
> I know of nothing sadder than lifeless eyes in the
>   face of a child
> The windows are open but the house is empty
> Two eyes are there, but no light
> And, saddened, I stand at the door, and wait in the
>   cold and knock.
> I am eager to get in

And he the child is alone.
He fattens, he hardens, he dries up, he gets old
        Poor old fellow.

What more can we add to these words?

There is nothing more fascinating or more humbling, once one studies what I can only call 'The Science of the Eyes' to observe a sleeping baby. Your own awareness of the link between breath, spirituality and the eye, gives an almost x-ray awareness that even although the baby's eyes are closed, the child appears to be in touch with a higher world of perception, far away, as if it is once more contacting in sleep that same process which showed it how to grow from a single, cell to an infant within the womb. To me it conveys a spiritual perception, to which I believe we must return, in order to re-connect ourselves with that great wisdom before it is too late.

I read once that if you look at the eyes of a person in a photograph, and focus on eye expression only, that expression reflects the feelings experienced by the baby as it emerges from its mother's body into life. Newspaper photos can be illuminating in this respect. I do not make a hobby of this fact, but the setting of the eye within the socket can give quite a lot of information about character. I have found this confirmed in my therapeutic work. Deep-set eyes indicate a personality which seems to be locked away and hard to contact, a need to retreat from life at birth, while staring or rather protruding eyes can indicate a bucolic nature, quick to explode. With the former it takes all one's skills to make easy communication, while with the latter it is necessary to choose words with care, for even an ordinary comment may cause objection. Both indicate the state of brain stress function. To me such extremes seem to imply that the deep-set eye wants to hide or retreat from life, while the staring eye has perhaps met extreme fear at the time of birth.

Our eyes are the welcome or unwelcome sign of who we are to other people. If we are a parent whose signs are negative, they are also negative to the child, the loving child whose feelings about what life is like, whether it is friend or foe, can be affected for life by the impact of our gaze. Of course we damage our own child within, before we transfer that hostility to others, including our children.

I think this is why I feel so concerned at the recent trend to have the child facing away from the mother in its pram so that it cannot see her, while it is being pushed about. It is then so much more vulnerable to the impressions it receives from strangers and the world around it, especially in busy cities. This may often mean a visual threat to a the child not yet mature enough to deflect such challenges, whih have gone unnoticed by the mother.

We therefore have to reflect love from our eyes, this is not grovelling for acceptance, flirtation, or looking for approval. Indeed such reflective love is an impregnable security power. The loving eye protects the sender, indicates a deep peace from within, and can change an atmosphere from hostility to peace within seconds.

There exists a fascinating science called Iridology which can analyse the state of the iris of the eye, and show up the scars of past illnesses and our general health.

Iridologists speak of the texture of the iris in the context of quality of materials, i.e. silk, linen, cotton, hessian. These days there are, apparently, very few people with a *silk* iris, due to the quality of our over-intellectualised civilisation, and sparsity of a truly natural life. Silk eyes belong to a healthy and spiritual person living close to Nature. Linen irises, the next finest, are getting rarer, with the majority of people in the cotton and hessian range. Not so surprising considering the chemical pollution in the air, chemicals in our diet, and our uncivilised 'civilised' way of life. The quality of the iris material indicates vitality. I don't know where man-made fibres fit in, no doubt at the lowest end of the spectrum.

It was Jung who said 'the eyes of suffering see the furthest.' I have noticed this to be true, as many courageous souls have grown up and out of the misery of a miserable childhood to make it to the stars. They can act a beacon to others who are still stuck in the throes of stress, hopelessness and depression.

REMEMBER THE BEAUTY IN
THE EYES OF A CHILD.

Chapter 33

THE HEART

The heart that breaks open
can contain the whole universe.
Source unknown

Ponder in thy own heart,
and in thy Temple, and be still.
New Testament

The heart has reasons that reason
cannot comprehend.
Source unknown

ARE YOU warm-hearted, cold-hearted, big-hearted, hard-hearted, kind-hearted, heart-weary, broken-hearted, glad-hearted, soft-hearted, generous-hearted, down-hearted, good-hearted, heartless?

Think about the above words, and how they may have come into being.

I wonder why we say mean-spirited as the opposite to big-hearted? Perhaps the hard-hearted inevitably become mean-spirited. They are probably *'mean-breathers'* too.

We refer to all the above as feelings either emanating from ourselves, or an impression received from someone else. Why the heart and not another organ? Well we do have lily-livered, gob-smacked, gutless, legless. The origin of such words are lost in time, but they do come from some source of profound understanding as to how our feelings affect the body. All our responses come from the brain, via lung breath accuracy, the source of thought creation, which then affects our actions, emotions or feelings. Our feelings are, I believe, dependent on the effective flow of our blood-stream round the body as a result of our thoughts. Fearful thinking causes blood-stream block, and stress.

Actually the heart does not really *feel* at all, it is merely an enormously important central organ designed to regulate the flow and circulation of the blood, and responds to our thoughts and feelings.

When the muscles surrounding the heart are tense, there is naturally a knock-on squeezing effect upon the heart, restricting circulation of oxygen to the blood cells. The media announced recently that the highest sources of ill-health are heart and circulatory problems; they forgot to mention, apparently are not aware, that this can only happen when correct breathing is suppressed, an activity within our voluntary control. Any suppression affects the whole system, and represents a threat highlighted by the precipitating negative thoughts and feelings of the individual, whether child or adult. This ultimately becomes a threat to survival. Such a set of reflexes permanently held, requires someone to concentrate on an often supposed threat, the source of which is not understood.

A survival threat requires our constant attention and energy, so that we do not have time or energy to give to others, a situation which can make us appear cold-hearted.

By contrast when we are calm and relaxed, the muscles also give up their tension, including those around the heart. Circulation reverts to normal, the warmth in our blood-stream spreads around the body, and is felt in the heart, the epicentre of the circulatory system, as a warm-hearted sensation.

It is so easy to forget that the heart acts as a barometer of our thoughts and feelings. If they are 'hard' and very negative we shall appear hard-hearted and indifferent to other people's needs. Before we project our thoughts and feelings onto others, we have to hold them in our own consciousness first, or we could not project them. The archer has to fit the arrow to the bow before it can fly.

The opposite awareness to loving thoughts and feelings may 'load our bow' and be experienced by others as hard-heartedness.

We may observe that people with known heart problems often seem to be generous public benefactors, and so it may appear, but when we feel under great pressure or indefinable threat we feel less of a person, and think we have to placate or please others in order to feel worthy again. Generous cash bequests may attract public approval which restores our feeling of tribal safety. It is said that public advertising of our bequests nullifies their effect. 'Do not let the left hand know what the right is doing.' (*Aquarian Gospel*). It takes spiritual wisdom to know that the anonymous bequest is one which attracts spiritual rewards.

Spiritual generosity is the one which really helps the Universe. It is never visual but its energy can move boundaries, with a priceless spiritual bonus involved. Its use will still lead to prosperity, for it creates a secure framework in which healthy growth can take place.

A gift from a warm-hearted as opposed to a cold-hearted source will grow in value, for there are no strings attached of unmerited approval, obsequious gratitude, or hidden agendas involved. The modern back-slapping process which continually undermines a healthy society.

The heart cannot function efficiently without efficient circulation, which by default cannot function efficiently without correct breathing. Fear, and all its many manifestations is the one factor which upsets the correct breath, and the opposite of fear is love. There seems to be an apt saying for every occasion; they are not platitudes, but reminders of the limitations we place on unalterable truths by the narrowness of our inadequate thinking.

Research carried out some years ago in a chest, heart and stroke hospital found that of one thousand patients taught correct breathing, some ninety-five per cent responded so favourably that their symptoms disappeared in most cases, or were drastically reduced. Why then do we hear so little from the medical profession, and health publicity about this vital link between correct breathing and a healthy heart? Surely right breathing is heart-lifting? From several decades of observation I have noticed that very few health professionals breathe correctly themselves. This is an observation, not a criticism.

A National campaign to teach correct breathing would, I am sure, greatly reduce the workload of the medical profession possibly to the point of wholesale redundancy, so that the continuation of what amounts to a National Ill-health Service would seem unlikely to continue in its present form. Of course they could train thousands of health service staff and send them out as community breath teachers, but it is also vitally important that this work needs to be understood and personally demonstrated by the high earners at the top.

One spin-off from such a national respiratory training scheme would be a dramatic drop of violence in the community, a drastic reduction in all addictions including sexually addictive behaviour. (See other chapters of this book.)

The newspapers might be forced to write about more heart-centred news stories instead of so much crime and violence. Boring? Never. The addictive habit of searching out for the 'nasties' would fade away, become rarer, and new habits would form, causing the media to join the wholesomeness culture, which would eventually become a great alternative addiction. Boring? Never! Wholehearted? Yes.

I used to keep two big Advent Calendars in my office, the ones where you can open a little window each day until Christmas Day, and find a chocolate button behind.

After their chocolate-button use had finished, I kept the calendars and called one the parent, the other the child. Imagine, behind each window, instead of the chocolates were the fruits of the spirit, love, kindness, forgiveness trust, humour, etc. The baby comes into the world with all its windows open reflecting the gifts of the child's beautiful spirit.

If many of the parents' windows are closed, so that the parent has shut off some of its spiritual gifts, how then is the tender vulnerable child to keep all *its* windows open? One by one they close and shut off, the heart eventually also becoming closed. It takes a lot of later life spiritual joinery to persuade the adult who was once the tender child, to open those closed windows once again.

Without the qualities of love, forgiveness, trust, joy continually shining out through the adults' windows, the child will think it is wrong to keep its own windows open. It only has the adult to teach it about the world. So it closes off its heart, why not? It cannot bear to face repeated hurt to its soft-heartedness.

Parents with limited heart activity usually breed heart-damaged children, a condition they call gene-inherited. I call it behaviour inherited, behaviour which can be changed within a generation.

Thank goodness the alchemy of the combination of breath, spirit, love and mindfulness can open the closed windows of the heart again. Correct breath is the alchemic key.

'The heart has reasons that reason cannot comprehend.' So the saying goes. What does it mean? The left analytical side of the brain will always demand a reason for everything that happens, so that it can analyse and make the answer *tidy*. Most of our problems arise from ignoring the intuitive instinct, a function of the right hemisphere. Not so tidy.

Many of our most inspiring actions arise from the intuitive right side of the brain where our true self resides, and if we were honest about where our intuitive actions come from, we might in all honesty say '*something told me*.' (That *something* is the non-provable instinct from the right brain.) An answer which is not acceptable to the left brain which demands logic and proof. Our earlier training and education which has been based almost solely on logic and proof, may eventually find the spontaneous messages from the intuitive brain unacceptable, as they go against the training with which we are have been 'stuffed'. So we close off the access path to the magical light-hearted side of the brain. What a bore.

This blocking of the creative access path is where, it seems to me, our analytical and intellectually-based educational system has gone too far in sealing off the child's creative gifts at an early age. Many clients suffering from stress have told me that the one subject they enjoyed and were good at was art, which was dropped from the timetable due to having to be 'streamed' into a maths and science-based curriculum.

In an educational journal published some years ago, and using words which are still pertinent today, Bob Carlisle, a former lecturer in Physical Education at Aberdeen College of Education stated:

> In the face of this call to develop children as persons, it seems important to me that we recognise just how depersonalising our schools, our society and our relationships are. It seems to me that our schools are overly intellectualising, and that this bias which begins in the nursery school turns

good secondary schools into academic factories, and many teachers into custodians of an examination system, with many children refugees of the same system. For those who cannot cope at an obvious personal level, a heartless scientific psychiatry dominates our hospitals.

Heartless, heartless, heartless.

R. D. Laing, that brilliant Scottish psychiatrist, wrote the following words in one of his articles, 'They have been prepared very efficiently to become hooligans by the sheer weight of a system which values academic success highly, and all other aspects of education hardly at all.'

He went on to say, 'A child born today in the United Kingdom stands a ten-times greater chance of being admitted to a mental hospital than to a University. This can be taken as an indication that we are driving our children mad more effectively than we are genuinely educating them. Perhaps it is our way of educating them that is driving them mad.'

I have quoted elsewhere that the Celtic people insisted that only poets should be teachers. It was their belief that knowledge not passed through the *heart* is dangerous.

If knowledge is not taught through the heart, the core of love, from where else is it being taught? *Wherever else* spells danger and harm to the child, whose one priority need is loving and warm-hearted parents and teachers.

> The evil that you teach me I will execute, and it
> shall go hard but I will better the instruction.

Shakespeare - Shylock, from *The Merchant of Venice*

From the frighteningly high figures on mental health breakdown which are regularly placed before us by the media, the non-loving exam and assessment based education with which we are indoctrinating our children is indeed bettering Shylock's words. See also the reports and results of research into violent crime statistics, addictions, and sexual perversion in our society.

Are we a heartless Society? When I was being re-trained in correct breathing by my own instincts, studying the all-too-rare appropriate books available, and discovering the higher unconscious 'fourth dimensional' power once referred to by Einstein, I reached a place within me when I realised that my heart was functioning in a different way. My heart felt warm, and from that warmth vital insights and strengths suddenly came into flower, from a place which had not been available to me for many years. Once experienced, I knew it had to be guarded like a precious jewel, and not allow it to be lost again.

This expansion of the heart has been experienced by many others to whom I have had the privilege of teaching correct breathing. It is so sad to recognise that until the breathing is corrected this wonderful experience is blocked from our consciousness. Children need adults whose hearts have opened, as theirs *are* opened.

A fully functioning heart means that you want to pass on that warmth not in the form of sentiment, but why not a hug where once you would have felt embarrassed? Naturally you still have to know that a hug may not always be possible, but the loving sharing energy that lifts the heart when a hug is naturally exchanged is worth more than gold. I believe that all loving exchanges raise the Earth's vibrational field. An unchallenging hug represents the expression of a mutual love of life. Words are unnecessary.

As my own heart opened I had to release any sorrow in my life to which I still clung.

I met many people who had allowed their hearts to open, despite great tragedy in their lives, and to feel the loving wisdom and compassion which emanated from them. This phrase would constantly come into my mind: 'The heart that breaks open can contain the whole universe.'

The heart of the child which has suffered and become *heart-broken* can be healed and mended by a heart-healed adult who has 'walked the walk'. Walking in a big city, you become so aware of the adult children with heart damage not discernible to the medical eye. The mending of all the broken hearts has its effect on our global family, we need so many people who can empathise, contain and heal a broken-hearted world. Again remember the words of Carl Jung: 'You can only heal to the level you have suffered yourself.' As you heal your own pain with the help of sprit-breath, you can truly help others, because you have been there. As they say, 'Worn the T-shirt.'

'Ponder in thy own heart and in thy temple and be still.' (*New Testament*) Our noisy culture will have to take time to do this. I believe we will be *forced* to do so, by events now happening and others still to come which will rock society to its core.

Until we ponder in our hearts and in our temple, (the temple of the heart) and become still, to listen to the deep thoughts of that heart, which then bring about the fresh shoots of our healing, and our ability to help the heart of our poor suffering Mother Earth.

So take time to listen to your own inner Temple, it is there, and so worth entering; correct breath will take you, you can do so any time, anywhere. Living from the heart is the only safe place to be.

'THE HEART THAT BREAKS OPEN CAN
CONTAIN THE WHOLE UNIVERSE.'
THE HEART HAS REASONS THAT REASON
CANNOT COMPREHEND.

The human heart can go to the lengths of God.
Dark and cold we may be, but this
is no winter now. The frozen misery
Of centuries cracks, breaks, begins to move,
The thunder is the thunder of the floes,
The thaw, the flood, the upstart spring,
Thank God our time is now when wrong
Comes up to meet us everywhere,
Never to leave us till we take
The longest stride of soul men ever took,
Affairs are now soul size,
The enterprise
is exploration into God
Where are you making for? It takes
So many thousand years to wake,
But will you wake for pity's sake?

Christopher Fry

Chapter 34

ALONENESS IS NOT LONELINESS

ONE OF THE MOST BEAUTIFUL GIFTS I have been given as a result of obeying the laws of correct breathing (well, most of the time), is the ability be alone with myself and to revel in that space bubble of meditative thinking which is the opposite of loneliness. This receptive state which seems to draw in universal wisdom gives a sense of enchantment to the hours that follow, only comparable to the days of childhood when I used to spend hours at the top of the garden making mud pies. These would be coated with a fine sprinkling of 'icing' scraped from the plentiful supply of pieces of chalk lying around our Wiltshire garden. A state of sustained and absorbing creativity.

Naturally as the stresses and strains of what other people thought I *should* do and what I *must* learn, closed the prison doors on that creativity, the ongoing sense of despair and loneliness which *tainted* my post-childhood years often seemed overwhelming. I used to long for *some other person* to relieve that loneliness, while some deep inner voice told me that I did not need to be *needy* in this way. Small wonder that relationships and friendships seemed so vacuous.

In breaking up this grey cloud of nothingness which clouded my life like a grey mist, I eventually realised that no one I knew provided a solution. There was a solution *within* me if I could only find it. Now I know from several decades as a therapist, that feeling separate from one's sense of identity in this way is a common problem with thousands of people, and produces enormous suffering.

As I grew up, I began to realise that my solution lay within, even if at that time I could not find a way out of the resulting loneliness. Somehow I recognised that the sadness, fear, loneliness and worry belonged to the *hurt child* part of my nature. Despite this constant frustrating spiritual drain on my life, naturally it was not all doom and gloom. Another part of my consciousness allowed interest, fun and a sense of vital self-identity to break through. Often this lasted for days, but then returned a feeling of having to carry a great weight of guilt and unhappiness around as if I was not *good enough* to feel happy, or indeed did not *deserve* to be.

Now I know that like many people I have met since, this guilt is not because of having committed some great sin as the world knows it, but of living a life which was not *authentic to my true self*. The real sin as *I* now recognise it, was against the Power which gave me life, my true identity. The responsibility for the harvesting of my own gifts and talents whatever they were, lay with me. For what else had that life been given to me?

The negative periods did not last all the time by any means. As I started my own process of creative introspection I began to ask myself why these creative spaces were not more long-lasting? If this *sense* of loneliness in my adult life could disappear temporarily, what was stopping it from disappearing for good?

It was only after I began to breathe more correctly, and not because I realised then that it might improve my mental and emotional blocks, that I realised something was happening to those mental and emotional limitations. At first I did not trust it to last, then I had the problem (a not uncommon one) of accepting that such a simple invisible process could be so powerful. That was my naïve and unenlightened level of thinking at the time, which today seems to me so ignorant and laughable. Little did I know then that what I would eventually learn about breath (spirit) could eventually fill a sizeable bookshelf!

Of course it took even longer to be able to say the word *spiritual* without feeling self-conscious. Nevertheless my increasing feelings of being centred, happiness, joy and vitality had to come from somewhere. I began to realise these sensations could be relied upon to be a permanent reality. I was recovering the happy child who enjoyed making mud pies!

The lonely state was an artificial illusion, and I had the tools to eradicate it.

The invisible air I breathed became a living essence, which I learned to respect and love. It occurred to me that our present problem with Global Warming has arisen because of our global lack of awareness and respect for the vital oxygen spirit of air. I truly believe that the most urgent and important problem we have to face, is to help everyone to personally regain this respect by corrective breathing, a self-healing process. Then the earth would repair herself, because if we have the power to damage her, we also have the power to heal her. In other words our poor breathing which encourages limited thinking and actions which hurt the earth could reverse the process by correct breathing. It did with me, why not everyone? Including the living organism of Mother Earth.

You can go on correcting your breathing whether at home or work; you don't have to lie down if that is not possible. You tune in to your very own internal cosmic radio station, which when obeyed, tells you how to walk on your own path. You have access to your own comforting inner adviser who dispenses healing advice on problematic situations. For all problems there are in general two possible solutions. Each of these solutions may seem equally plausible until you search internally, and see the tipping of the internal scales. One side may be balanced only fractionally lower than its opposite, but that fraction tips to the proper solution. You have then begun to regain the magic formula or panacea 'to see life clearly and to see it whole', the fruit of the intuitive faculty.

Access to this inner adviser banishes our loneliness, the loneliness of the hurt child who has been crying out but ignored. Our immature adult is still saying, 'I'm small and lonely, nobody loves me, I'm afraid.' Yet the mature adult cannot permit a hurt child within, or the adult can never mature. To breathe correctly is to relax and feel loving, directing that love back to the internal hurt child so that it breathes a great sigh of relief and says to itself 'Now I am safe, I am looked after again, I can go and play.'

It is so delightful to regain this sense of the joyful child within the adult, that relationships improve naturally, first with ourselves, friendships are enjoyed, you no longer need someone to make you feel OK, you know you are already OK. People are attracted to you by your raised vibration of love which is infectious.

At a critical momentous period of my life when I knew that I was faced with going it alone, facing loneliness but fearing it, Lilla Bek, (healer, writer and spiritual adviser) a very wise soul I am privileged to call a friend, who had faced the same situation in her own life, said to me, 'It is only when you are on your own, that your guides, your helpers seem to be present, so that even the silence is *pregnant with possibility*.' I have always remembered her words, their truth did indeed change the course of my life, and they have helped many others facing a similar situation. The new possibilities revealed by the 'pregnant' silence enabled me to become an *authentic* me.

Since then I have rediscovered that 'bliss of solitude',

spoken of by Wordsworth in the last verse of his beautiful poem *To Daffodils*. I have the loving friends who could never appear in my life while the lonely child who felt sorry for itself needed someone to fill the gap of a loving parent. In this role we make ourselves vulnerable to over-parental people who can be over-controlling. A mature adult will never allow themselves to be drawn into this kind of 'friendship'.

The renewed delight in being one's *authentic* self, re-discovered through the power of breath, lights up an inner guiding star which seems to be attracted to you by the power of coincidence. People you realise you were meant to meet appear in your life, however briefly, where each may have a message for the other, like ships that pass in the night, or berthed alongside for some time. The enhanced sense of soul meeting soul enriches the sheer pleasure of the wonder of life, the energy around you infuses the surrounding atmosphere with an unseen positive vibration, allowing the permanent energy of love which Higher Power has already created all around us to be absorbed. We have removed the block between it and ourselves. So beautifully described by Francis Thompson in his poem *In No Strange Land*:

> The Angels keep their ancient places,
> Turn but a stone and start a wing,
> 'Tis ye, 'tis your estranged faces,
> That miss the many-splendored thing.
>
> But when so sad, thou canst not sadder,
> Cry, and upon thy so-sore loss,
> Shall shine the traffic of Jaob's ladder,
> Fixed betwix't Heaven and Charing Cross.

Can this release from loneliness only come to us after we become fully mature? I do not think so, the virus of loneliness can be released at any time, but from my experience of sharing with thousands of people, this virus always has its roots in childhood. It can only be permanently overturned when we regain mastery of our breath. It may be improved by various methods, some claim a *little* improvement as a *cure,* but when you are trained in the language of breath, you will recognise these limited claims.

Returning to my own childhood experiences, I remember my Mother telling me at quite a young age that I was born with the cord round my neck, and was a 'blue' baby. This is not an uncommon experience but she went on to tell me that the doctor at this home birth had told the nurse, 'never mind the baby, look after the mother.' At that time I didn't register the implications of such words until I began to look into my own adult negative thoughts about life, but they must have thought I wasn't likely to survive!

Did I pick up the thought that 'I don't matter' at that primal experience? At the time I was born, the ideas of a certain Dr. Truby King from New Zealand were in vogue, and his researchers were looking for mothers-to-be who would be under the instruction of a Truby King nurse after the confinement to 'train' the young infant. For the first few months of my life I was exposed to the Truby King method of baby rearing which decreed that babies should be treated like machines, fed every four hours, toilet-trained from day one, not lifted if they cried, their whole routine dictated by a rigid clock-like efficiency.

This without taking into account that each child is an *individual* from day one, with different needs, not least the need to be held close to the mother particularly after a difficult birth. The baby at that stage *only* has its mother to comfort and reassure it. I think the sheer *shock* of a traumatic birth may affect a baby for months and years, long after its birth. The apparent total neglect of its natural and unique emotional and nutritional timetable can trigger a double shock, perhaps permanently upsetting its attitude to life. Even without Truby King's inhuman, cold-blooded rules, I think the seeds of bulimia and anorexia are probably sown in the frustration felt by many infants in the denial particularly in the early days after birth, for whatever reason, of its *right* to natural emotional and oral satisfaction. Fortunately I never suffered from these problems, despite Truby King! I think after a few weeks, my mother threw his methods out of the window (metaphorically). She fed me on demand.

Some years ago I was reading an account of an interview with the world-famous writer Doris Lessing, who revealed that she also was the product of the Truby King rearing method, whose parents inflicted this callous regime upon her early days. No doubt with the best of intentions, in the same way that we unquestionably follow a new fad. To be persuaded that your baby would soon be trained to be non-demanding, (a non-person?) must surely be a temptation to those who wish to have a child with minimal disturbance to an established routine. That is not how Nature works however. A baby responds to its natural emotional and hunger signals in the only way it can, noisily and lustily! Doris Lessing strongly felt that her Truby King start in life had caused her needless unhappiness in later life. I share a complete empathy with her feelings.

Fortunately, I believe that my mother was probably intuitively unable to tolerate what she probably felt to be a wrong way to treat her baby, and must have dispensed with the services of the Truby King nurse before her three months were up. Deep within me I have a feeling that I was subsequently happily breast-fed. I do believe however that some damage had been done to my primal experience and attitude to life, which left a fear layer in my early consciousness. I am sure that this layer contributed to the loneliness of my childhood, and extended even into the first half of my life. The interesting thing is that the later gift of breathing revelation has given me such joy, knowing how one can reverse such early primal shock. Passing on this training to others makes me ask myself if I could have been able to gain such insights without my earlier unhappiness!

I am now in my early eighties, and can only imagine how many babies were damaged perhaps permanently by the inhuman life foundations laid down by the Truby King process, creating later-life misery in many ways. Too late now to research the casualties, they will be untraceable. I am glad to be able to record my own life story and speak on their behalf.

The long-lasting effects of birth trauma, our lack of comprehension and inability to pay enough intuitive attention, time and thought to early infant needs is in stark contrast to the way in which many so-called 'primitive' mothers keep their babies swaddled to their bodies in the early months. The babies do not seem to cry because they feel secure, they are suckled on demand.

I have spoken with many midwives, and know from numerous first-hand sources how many babies in Western society are born by mechanical means, the appalling level of Caesarean deliveries, inductions, suction, epidural and breech births. How many women feel repugnance at the thought of breast-feeding? How increasingly unfitted women's bodies seem to be for the act of childbirth?

The high heels that precipitate the body at an unnatural angle for carrying a child, the implication that narrow waists and hips are desirable, that the modern woman's body should resemble, as one writer put it, 'a cadaver in *Vogue* magazine'. Are women allowing their natural role to be dictated by a fashion market whose methods are not really so far removed from the Eastern fashion of binding female feet? Are we becoming little more than dolls manipulated by our inner loneliness and desire to please, to submit ourselves to married lives which are doomed from the start because the partners are still lonely, never having discovered the beauty of *aloneness*. Both have married because they need to be 'looked after'.

The results of so much of our rearing methods in the first five years deplete the respiratory process, resulting in so-called *mature* adults, who are nevertheless *immature*, being affected by fear, tension and stress, addictions of all kinds respectable and not so respectable. Yet married or about to be parents. So the cycle continues.

Despite all this, each one of us is unique, we each have our own grand plan, the talents given at birth, encoded in our core cells, waiting for the magic formula to unlock the magic. The spiritual breath to heal the negativity. Deep down we all desperately want to find this chalice.

Many people I have now met have found its true meaning through the healing of the breath, and in so doing, accepted the responsibility for being their true selves, a gift which imposes the ability and *wish* to be alone and yet not lonely, so that the messages from within can be decoded and acted upon. Often perhaps with other people in joint creative activity, yet the centre of the plan can only be rediscovered in the aloneness and courage by which we birthed ourselves and hopefully can now regain. Reborn in this present existence in a blaze of glory which has also marked the harvesting of our creativity.

If we do not find the key to harvest our gifts, we shall die unfulfilled. I remember hearing of a well-known actor who in his last hours said that his only regret was that at the end of his life he realised that he could have had *everything*. A tragic reflection that may be common to many as they enter that *between* land of moving on from this world into the next.

All that had held them back was fear, the holding in of the breath. All that had been needed was to *rediscover* the breath of spirit to learn again the delight in being alone, and find in correcting our breath that we are never lonely, but instead have direct access to our own unique and magical gifts.

I suspect that all the disharmony, violence, addictions, sickness, obesity and sheer unhappiness in our society has come about from our fear of aloneness.

WITHOUT THE BREATH WE *SHALL* BE LONELY,
WITH IT WE BECOME *ENTRANCED*
WITH ALONENESS.

Chapter 35

WOMAN'S ROLE

AS I STARE AT THE TITLE of this present chapter I wonder if I haven't bitten off a bit more than I can chew. For how can I deal with woman's role in one chapter? In thinking about what I would like to say from the centre of my heart I may appear narrow minded and a fuddy-duddy to anyone embarrassed by heart-centred speech.

From the perspective of my considerable age, I imagine it as if I was looking down from a great height, and see the habits, customs, fears and thought patterns down the ages concerning the male/female relationship. I must discount as incorrect in *Higher Power* any relationships created from a fear base, because they will be incorrect in natural law, and must eventually lead to chaos. Springing as they do from incorrect thoughts about life, life can never support them, so they fall by the wayside, in the process causing much human grief. This applies to whatever part of the world in which you live.

We enter the 21st century bringing with us any incorrect man-made rules which go against Nature, left over from previous centuries about the male/female role. The roles our culture accepts as female will decide that of the male, and vice-versa.

We possess the supposed advantage of laws of science available to all nations. The *sensible* laws I mean, because a lot of what credible science says one day may be overturned overnight by another *scientific* discovery. So you have to have

405

your feet firmly placed on the ground to see through to the truth. I refer to the truth as Nature sees it, the only reliable yardstick which is revealed with greater clarity as we correct our breathing.

Having said that, the laws of man (why do we always say the laws of man and not the laws of man and woman?) particularly laws or assumptions about woman, as dictated by various religious, sexual customs and the male sex over the centuries, eventually always have to be acceptable to the supreme rules of Nature, the only true arbitrator. We have no option if men and women are to find harmony together. To put it simply were they created from a sense of love? The Alpha vibration which supports our planet, (and us when we obey these laws), or from strong Beta leading to fear, which is in opposition to the laws of the Planet? Using that yardstick, a lot of the man-made laws of both west and east regarding woman's role appear to be seriously out of harmony with Nature. Of course many of these laws are really *assumptions,* accepted by both sexes often with tragic rigidity, as recorded historically by the amount of sorrow, horror and bloodshed imposed by man *on* woman down the centuries.

So who is responsible for the fall from the grace of Nature down the centuries? I'm not a student of the Old Testament but often think about the story of Adam and Eve when, as Adam put it, 'the woman tempted me'. Poor old Adam, silly Eve. However the blame has been placed upon woman for having created all the problems throughout the ages! Adam clings on to his sense that he is Mr. Perfect while Eve carries the burden of guilt, but why should she? Her guilt should be in allowing him to assume that role.

Eve may have tempted Adam by wishing to have a pretty object which she cannot not and was not supposed to reach, her immature adult like a child wants something it is not meant to have, while Adam's immature adult is afraid to say 'no' in case he displeases Eve. Both sexes must share responsibility.

As we mature we learn to differentiate about what we are *meant* to have, as opposed to what we *want* to have, and find it easy to accept that what we are meant to have will come to us naturally. However Eve was not mature enough to know that, even though she was of adult age.

Adam thinks that he has to please other people in order to be acceptable, another symptom of the immature adult. In the end, both began to dislike and despise each other. Eve became a helpless weakling, and Adam becomes a condescending coward/bully.

Both Adam and Eve bear the same guilt for ignoring Nature's laws of needs and not wants.

Neither man nor woman can regain their genuine and valid relationship until they have released their immature attitude to each other and gained mutual respect. It is only Eve's love and respect for herself that will prevent her looking for baubles beyond her reach, and only Adam's love and respect for himself that allows him to say 'no'. Each has to forgo a habit-formed behaviour pattern in order to love and respect themselves, so they can correctly love and respect each other, the only proper basis for any relationship.

Let us project the Adam and Eve story into the 21st century.

Most of the people in crisis I have met over the years, and read of in the media portray enhanced accounts of multi-divorces and marital life conflict. They tell of the disastrous relationship tragedies of famous people in all walks of life, and reflect the Adam and Eve duo projected in many guises.

In many world religions, this same imbalance seems to be vividly apparent, the inferiority of one sex, and the superiority of the other. This unholy alliance is maintained for questionable religious customs to which they culturally cling. Changes are happening however in such dismal liaisons which we also see in politics, changes which were unthinkable within the memory even of an octogenarian like myself.

However long it takes, the change must happen; love and respect are the only criteria by which we can survive. It is the relationship between the sexes which determines its counterpart within the family, creating a healthy community, and as the ripples spread wider, the nations and the world.

Reference is often made to woman's intuition; this does not make her superior to man, but I believe this is the vital sense she has to bring into being. In the all encompassing act of giving birth the woman has to draw on resources within herself not taught by an intellectually biased education system which goes no way to prepare her for the supreme demands of the most important life achievement, that of birth.

Each sex has its unique potential. The deeper sense of listening to the intuition of Nature within woman creates the strength to cope with the long hours of labour and the final great effort of birth, followed by the subsequent complete dedication and often exhausting early years of child-rearing; inadequately recognised in our macho-orientated culture.

Man's equivalent is his great gift of invention and instinct to provide for the protection of the family. We see it replicated within the animal kingdom. The most aggressive nations reflect this lack of respect for the role of women, particularly the protection of the young mother and infant. They always suffer first when man's need to conquer spirals out of control.

Why is the scale, availability, and financial commitment to the health of future generations decided by masculine-dominated committees? Why are women not fighting for the right to be the major role-player in decisions about birth provision?

I wonder if our dual neglect and negative misuse of our great nature-based gifts, created the present problems with childbirth? Nature's prime law is for correct conditions for the female in which to give birth. Shortage of birth attendants, loss of knowledge of the environment which is required for a happy birth. Women in labour being hauled many miles to the nearest maternity hospital, when anyone who knows about animals will tell you that this is the worst scenario for a female in labour, make so many births a nightmare.

Mothers may desert the baby emotionally if she has no time to create her nesting emotionally safe environment. Physical abuse of the baby also occurs; you cannot interfere with Nature-made laws without serious consequences. We seem to regard birth as merely a clinical occurrence. Some animals like pigs can eat their young when disturbed. Anyone closely connected with animals know that they have to create right birth conditions for safe delivery of healthy stock.

We wonder about complications which we are actually creating ourselves. The high level of Caesarean births are really unacceptable, some for obscene cosmetic reasons. It has been noted that people born by Caesarean section often find it difficult to complete plans and activities, since they did not complete the last stages of the birth plan. This may not be a universal law, but is a common occurrence which I have noticed in therapy.

Guilt pressure lies heavily on women to return to the 'workplace' when the correct *workplace* is the home one where the child is reared, particularly in the first five years. Any saving on maternity services is, I believe, the sign of a decadent society. I understand our maternity provision is very low down in the European league.

Is the inventiveness of man in the field of lethal weaponry the measure of his misuse of his inventiveness? Are we as advanced as we think we are? As civilised? Is correct use of the energy of spirit-life by correct use of breath the key to the hidden secret of love and female/male role re-balance?

We have so far to go, and yet only a few breaths separate us from the understanding that can change our vision, in the east and in the west.

Whatever our nationality, whatever our faith, we shall be forced to study the world-wide problems of limitations in the basic biological function of correct use of air. It is our only life force and its correct use is *the most exact science which can ever be invented. The one we shall have to observe to restore health to the planet. Could such an urgent problem unite the sexes? There may soon be only be one way out to save humanity. Breath education.*

If a woman is fearful, breathing wrongly, made so by custom and religious laws, she will produce a child who is afraid, because the child's respiratory function will mirror that of the mother. A father who is afraid will also project his fear upon the child. Both have mislaid the image of harmony with the laws of Nature, which is our birthright. Both have become distanced from their roles, and the child suffers, which affects the sense of its correct life-role. Intellectual knowledge does not cure the fear habit.

I speak from observational experience of thousands of family patterns. The unrecognised biological malfunction within damaged individuals who breathe incorrectly is as serious as if fundamental engine faults on a jet plane or racing car go unnoticed. We are *that* far removed from understanding the simplest human basic unalterable laws of health. These laws irreversibly determine the role of women, however extreme our adoption of the masculine role, the only role available to us if we turn our backs on our true femininity. There can really be no compromise.

We employ enormous financial and analytical resources to whatever minute malfunction has caused a plane or car to crash, but only a minimal comparable amount of energy and resources to understanding basic natural laws governing the needs of mother and child at birth.

I cannot see how any nation or faith can forever avoid the above ignorance of the life instinct needs known to a child at birth, which can only be suppressed, by fear, greed and all the negative vices which are ignoring the unchanging laws of Nature. Women will have to unite to preserve the non-negotiable rules to create the ideal birth conditions due to the infant about to be enter the world stage. Man will have to understand his own crucial role in ensuring that his child receives only the best earliest environment, rather than the overcrowded production-line methods of many large city maternity hospitals. There should be no question of finding funding for the most important moments of life for mother and child. Our maternity services, and birth-related deaths shame us in the European league.

I sometimes recall with wry humour the story of Lysistrata, where the Greek women went on sexual strike in order to control their warring menfolk. There must be *something* that women can do to bring about a world change in the horrors we hear about every day. I'm not sure if I am recommending a repetition of Lysistrata, but the one process in which women are unique is in giving birth.

The sole factor which changed my nightmare first birth experience to the enlightened experience of my second, was the self-training in breathing and relaxation inspired by a doctor who was before his time. It is a great tragedy that the medical profession generally are so lacking in the knowledge of the implications of this vital preparation for birth. It seems almost non-existent from discussions I have had with expectant mothers.

You may have read about the monkeys on a certain island who found a new way to crack nuts. It was then discovered that monkeys on an island many miles away were also using this new skill in exactly the same way. There had been no contact between the two groups.

I wonder if this silent, intuitive process without violence criticism or challenge might be the way in which women might have to take upon themselves responsibility to create a world revolution, a bloodless universal victory based upon the correct use of the breath the true energy of life. Of one thing I *am* sure, and that is that the Universal energy surrounding us can and will return that effort with miraculous and unexpected beneficial results. A new World Order? **Yes.** If women can achieve self-mastery in breath, men will be able and indeed have no option, but to 'turn their swords into ploughshares' and find fruitful and satisfying fulfilment in the great creative and natural expansion of their true role, despite earlier childhood exposure to a narrow and limited 'left brained' intellectual framework.

One unique writer has suggested that children born of the union of two people who breathe correctly will inevitably be spiritual and beautiful.

Could there be a spontaneous resolution for women of the East no longer to hide their bodies made by the God of their understanding, from the sun, air and light? The western female to feel no need to over-decorate their beauty, to decide that body hair is ugly, and no longer to undergo the need to carve slices of flesh from their bodies to satisfy what is really an *inner* lack of confidence. No longer for young girls to feel the need to over-expose their bodies for artificial sexual titillation, but to be proud of themselves because of their *inner* glow of breath-related beauty. Correct oxygenation is the highest beauty product of all, which can never be matched by paint or knife. Such beauty is ageless, and its coming into being between male and female would mark the beginning of an age of beauty and reason. An automatic healthy fusion of balanced male/female roles.

When women and men are breath-beautified in this way,

there arises a sense of joint responsibility for the health of Mother Earth which could illuminate the world.

It may take the highly developed intuitive faculty of woman to comprehend the truth of Ramacharaka's words in his book *The Science of Breath* that 'One generation of correct breathers would regenerate the race, and disease would be regarded as a rarity.'

When enough women, and men recognise this unalterable truth there could be a great groundswell of unstoppable pioneering change when the harmonious roles of man and woman are no longer in conflict, and the human race could come into its inheritance. It is time for woman to take the first step out of her self-imposed exile.

A friend told me that the Dalai Lama has said recently that 'it is Western women who will save the World.' A coincidence that I am writing this chapter at this time.

Coincidence? No,

'IT'S GOD'S WAY OF REMAINING ANONYMOUS.'

Chapter 36

EDUCATION
AND LEARNING

AFTER I THOUGHT I HAD FINISHED THIS BOOK, I discovered that I had duplicated the information contained in Chapter 36 in an earlier chapter. I am sure other writers experience apparent disasters of this kind. Of course I could have scrapped the surplus chapter, but then decided that I would create another called Education and Learning.

It is only in these past twenty years or so, that I have been questioning some of the thinking behind aspects of the way in which we decide on the priorities we place on what we think of as educationally important.

The understanding of the physical, mental and dare I say it, spiritual development of the very young child is a highly concise and important area of study, not necessarily left to educationalists alone, but also to those who are completely sensitive to that most precious of working material, the mind of a five-year old child. In some cases four and a half.

The nurseryman knows that his plants will only grow and flourish if he supplies the essential necessary nurturing to his young stock, and that failure at this stage will lead to stunted and unhealthy plants which will never reach their full potential. The poor plants he often discards, but we can't do this with children. Instead the poor stock often kill themselves off a little later in life by addictions of all kinds, and the development of killer diseases. I am writing for those who have begun to realise that illness comes from within, not without, and that infection attacks those with a poor immune system. To be blunt, 'flies only settle on poor meat.'

I am reminded of a story told by a writer who spoke of an outbreak of cholera among sailors in an Eastern port. The only ones who died were those who breathed through the mouth.

We spend untold millions on trying to treat the drug addicts, knowing that we are only reaching the tip of the iceberg, even if the actual treatment is so rarely successful. My blood runs cold when I read of yet another young person committing suicide as a result of classroom bullying. I cannot remember such incidents when I was young, although bullying must have been present. I do not know if it is still experienced in expensive private schools.

We are going through the longest period in history, when the aggressive instincts of the nation are not involved in major wars, even if we must recognise the existence of ongoing conflicts such as Afghanistan in which we are involved. Even so, if our cumulative tendency to violence is not being swallowed and hidden under the veil of military conflict, it has been suggested that the violence in our midst formerly hidden under the instinct of aggression is revealing to us the harm of what we must be doing to young children, for all who are involved in violence and addiction were once five-year old children influenced by the problems of our so-called *adult* society. Children are the first victims on the barbed wire of our 'peaceful' battle lines. They absorb the negative stress of the adults.

Some years ago when I was a regional councillor in the Scottish Borders, I noticed a painting hanging outside the office of the Chairman of the Council. I had at that time become fascinated and involved in studying the functions of the human brain, in particular those of the left logical and right creative hemispheres. I experienced a distinctive shock as I studied the picture, painted by a sixteen-year old girl from Hawick High School. It depicted the left side of the brain as objective, materialistic, aggressive, while the soft colours of the right brain suggested beauty, spirituality and harmony. The two brain halves were separated by a cross.

The caption under the heading read:

> This was my first attempt as expressing my beliefs. I wanted to place a cross between good and bad, particularly at a time when I myself was trying to work out what was 'Good' and 'Bad'. This picture gave me the confidence to continue with the theme 'God and Man'.

Janice Armstrong

Can you understand why I was so moved? Here was a young girl expressing something from her deep intuition which was correct, but had never been taught at school.

Why don't they teach such information at school to help young people to understand more about brain function? When there are cut-backs in education, it is always the right brain subjects which are affected, yet this is the area which needs to be encouraged as a young person is experiencing the pangs of adolescence. It has taken a wise young adolescent to reveal to us the shortcomings in our educational system.

I was later able to buy the painting, and contacted the young painter, now a grown woman. We have kept in touch.

This dramatic picture has become an important feature of my own teaching, for another reason. *Our two brain hemispheres are only in perfect balance when we breathe correctly.* Nature *demands* the human brain to be in balance, and for us to breathe correctly.

We are constantly being told about what we are doing

to Nature, we need to put our own house in order first as individuals. A World Health statistic states that 60% of people in the Western hemisphere have an over-development of the left brain. A danger to the young?

Maria Montessori, that great ambassador for the young child, stated in her book *The Secret of Childhood*, 'No one could have foreseen then that the young child held within itself a secret of life, able to lift the veil from the mysteries of the human soul, that he/she represented an unknown quantity, the discovery of which might enable the adult to solve his individual and social problems.' The picture I have described reveals a solution.

I believe that if we understand the message and meaning in that painting, we would truly realise that the young do indeed hold the secret by which the adult world could heal itself.

If we do not have a balanced brain vision in our educational system, we are rearing yet another generation of addiction and aggression, turning into immature adults. How could they be otherwise, when the educational priorities of our intellectual overdrive are distorting the precious mysteries of sane human survival unrecognised and locked within the young soul, unable to communicate because it has never been communicated *with*.

Some years ago, when I was running a voluntary stress centre in Glasgow I had a vision for the creation of 'The College of Childhood'. It was created to suggest a way in which teachers could be trained to help understand and respect what a child has to teach us, and how we abuse that knowledge. All the staff would have corrected their breathing, so that the atmosphere would be peaceful and loving. Correct breathing, relaxation, and the study of brain function would be taught subjects. Most subjects would be at first self-taught, as dictated by the inherent gifts and skills of the pupils. The real aim of the College would be to revive the loving child aspect of the students, in order for them to later become an adult teacher who could be trusted to respect and bring out the wisdom in each child they eventually taught. Such teachers bring to their teaching the loving eyes of the child within. Someone quoted a saying to me recently, 'Children learn through the loving eyes of their teachers.' That is the purpose behind the idea of 'The College of Childhood'. Nothing else is good enough for the child in our midst. A truly loving teacher will be a better breathing teacher.

When I had three young children, each had a different timetable which matched their age, so that the youngest might be sleeping or need feeding, while the eldest had to be got ready for school, and the middle child required help with dressing, also at the toddler stage where you needed to have 'eyes in the back of your head' to keep up with their toddler stage mentality. As any mother with children at these stages will testify, getting the eldest to school by nine o'clock can involve using more energy and expertise than anyone else in the community can imagine, because children are not *objects*, and their needs must be met.

When I see a young mother trying to get a first year infant to school on time, while holding a recalcitrant toddler by the hand, and pushing a baby in a pram while crossing busy roads, often in heavy rain, I am filled with compassion, knowing how they will have done a day's work before many people will have started. Society still does not support such a young mother, who is doing the most important job of all; all it does is to place a well-nigh intolerable burden on her shoulders, and even question how soon she can get back to work! I believe I have mentioned that in my opinion elephants show more understanding of mother and infant needs than the human race.

When you think of the relatively unimportant issues funded by the State, our culture, having created an educational requirement for mothers of very young babies to deliver other very young siblings for a nine o'clock school start, might consider providing a pick-up transport service for young school-age children whose mothers have to drag several children across town not once, but twice a day to the detriment of the natural needs of toddlers and babies. I lived near enough to the rural school when my children were young to just about cope with this problem, but it was a nightmare period even so.

You may say that we cannot afford to provide such a service, we can provide plenty of others not so urgent, even in these times of financial crisis. Young children cannot protest for their needs, young mothers have no time. The purse strings are not held by women, even although as I write, some sensitive journalist is stating that it is women who will bear the fallout from our present financial crisis.

All small children up to the age of six or more, need a rest period during the day, how is our education system providing such facilities, where are the infant size small 'easy-to-set-up' rest mats? How can a tired child be expected to learn, yet we read of drivel on report cards saying that John or Jean is sometimes unable to concentrate. Can *you* concentrate when you are tired? Most of the other European countries have starting dates at six or even seven, why are we so hard on our children? Get the mothers back to work? With redundancy running at an all-time high and getting worse, there do not even seem to be jobs enough for the men. Child-rearing is a full-time job for the first five years. Yes, mothers need a break from 24/7 care. Many fathers these days are carrying their share, but many are often away most of the week.

The advent of pre-chool playgroups was a great development, started by young mothers, recognising their needs and that of their children for a wider social environment,

I question the understanding of much nursery provision, now talking of more formal education for under-fives, to really understand the spiritual needs of a child. It has its work cut out to take on board such over-stimulation of the left hemisphere of the brain, while the true self located in the right side of the brain is being starved of the sensitive understanding to which each unique personality has the right. That is to develop its natural gifts and skills.

We fail to recognise that the child already has *within itself* the raw material, the skills to build into the right structure for its own unique personality.

Place that child in a formalised educational structure too soon, and it cannot carry out this work of self-build. It becomes anxious, then afraid, and finally starts to restricts its breathing. It starts to have a sore tummy, perhaps be sick. It does not feel right about itself, and becomes separated from its true self in trying to conform to inappropriate pressure. It cannot learn, the fear paralysis creates often lifelong learning blocks.

Go into any classroom of eight-year olds, and you will find that most of the children have restricted breathing. This symptom represents deterioration of the child's development.

Uncorrected, that restriction will lead to all the health and social ills for which we pay dearly in corrective methods years later. Much of that money and effort is wasted and ineffective. We are talking of billions of pounds.

As Karen Roon said in her book *The New Way To Relax*, '*teaching a small child to breathe correctly again, is like giving water to a dying daffodil.*' How many of our *educationalists* are capable of giving water to that dying daffodil?

It is important to remember that what the State thinks is necessary in the education of our children, is often in direct opposition to what Nature thinks is right education. Fact cramming child educational factories from five to eighteen will never ensure that the coming generation will in any way be fitted for the crucial decisions which lie ahead for the human race, and our section of it in particular.

I remember reading about a school in the north of England, I think it was run by the parents. Twice a day the children were given a period of ten minutes for quiet and meditation. Apparently this school came first in all the county-wide school competitions of various kinds. Eventually it was asked not to participate for a period. If they are going to appeal for more parental involvement in schools, it seems these sentences hold a very important message.

The unique picture on the opposite page was painted by Janice Armstrong, a gifted 16-year old former pupil at Hawick High School. The picture was not inspired by her education, but the heightened intuition of a sensitive adolescent of the two hemispheres of the brain, and what they represent. Left - materialistic, analytical, and logical; Right - creativity, beauty and intuition.

World Health Statistics show that the Western hemisphere has a 60% over-dominance of the left brain, which is also anaytical and critical.

When we breathe correctly, the two brain hemispheres are in precise balance. The following is the enlightened comment by the artist on her painting:

This was my first attempt as expressing my beliefs. I wanted to place a cross between good and bad, particularly at a time when I myself was trying to work out what was 'Good' and 'Bad'. This picture gave me the confidence to continue with the theme 'God and Man'.

★ ★ ★

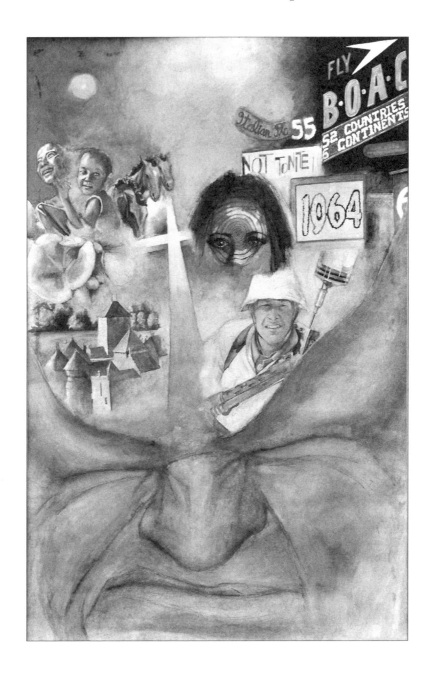

Chapter 37

THE BIBLE AND
THE KORAN

United by Breath

IN COMMON WITH MANY OTHERS, I have discovered that part of my mind is often preoccupied in wondering if there could be a common denominator which could unite the religions of the world in spirituality, so that despite ideological differences, this common denominator would ensure the end of injustice and violence done in the name of religion.

After the last London bombings, my inner voice kept suggesting to me that I needed to find out more about the Koran, having noticed a copy in the office of a Glasgow councillor I had been visiting. In fact that copy was an abridged version, but when I visited my local rural library only the full version was available.

I had heard a political programme on TV where it had been voiced that the Koran held clues as to the justification for the London bombings and other acts of violence.

The library copy of the Koran which I took out on loan was a heavy and lengthy book, made even more so by excellent English text translations, and an enormous number of complicated explanatory notes. As I began to read I was not quite sure what I was looking for, and then I realised that I was looking for references to the breath, because then perhaps I could discover a common duality with similar references in the Christian Bible which talks about 'the breath of God.'

My own favourite Bible, *The Aquarian Gospel of Jesus the Christ* has been a great inspiration to me down the years, because it frequently talks about the *Holy Breath*. In my 25 years of teaching correct breathing the words *Holy Breath* now come to me automatically, without thinking about the Aquarian Gospel, because I always think of breath as Holy.

Time after time a client, who has been correcting their breathing, expresses a profound sense of wonder and respect for what breath has told them, without my saying a word. To use breath *correctly virtually ensures* the dawning awareness of a sense of spirituality and holiness from within.

In all my years of breathing awareness I have heard no whisper of this sense of wonder in any Church service I have attended, or proper respect for this Breath essence which is life. Or in television programmes, quality news articles, very few books, many of which do not make it into reprint because what the media wants is visible phenomena. We make programmes and write endlessly about the solid earth, the warmth of the sun, the mystery of water, we can see and feel all these, but for the essential but invisible element, air, upon which we depend for life, we are appallingly silent. Silent about the *correct* use of our *primary support system,* even although we cannot survive more than a few minutes without the life-enabling essence of air. Is it because so many people assume that because they are breathing at all, they are breathing correctly? Or that enough clean air will always be available to us? Think again, whatever your religion.

I have therefore been wondering what the great religions have been saying about this, and so far have met with little success, although Buddhism and Sufism are very much aware of its presence.

I haven't studied many other religions in depth, but feel very concerned that my own Christian Bible has little to say on breath. There seems to be a brick wall about breath and Spirit meaning the same thing. Spirit is after all what it is about, and its interpretation is the word Breath. After all if we use Spirit wrongly, surely we must use breath wrongly. By inference, wrong breath equals wrong Spirit.

Jesus said 'I am the Breath of Life.' I haven't found any eminent theologian who has taken this wonderful statement at its face value, and really understands what it means. Does any Christian church teach people to breathe correctly, and in so doing correct their Spirit? Let me know if you find one.

The way we individually use air will, I predict, in the forseeable future, supersede our obsession with the food we eat, particularly as in large parts of the world millions survive healthily on a few basic staples. The amount of air that is available for our use in the vast depths of the atmosphere, is the air we pollute which could become unusable, and represents as Al Gore states in his DVD *An Inconvenient Truth*, the equivalent depth of a layer of varnish on a very thick piece of wood. In other words it is pretty thin. We are contaminating that layer, and that includes the members of most of the religious faiths, whether Christian, Moslem, Hindu, Jew, or any other man made religion. Having said that, most religions admit, maybe grudgingly, that their God is a God of love.

Will there come a time when as a biological species we will *all* will have to be united in a universal in-depth study of the correct way to breathe? All negative action on a world scale comes originally from a negative thought created by one person, which develops into negative action and attracts negative people, sometimes millions of them. Correct breathers are unable to tolerate negative thought, because that is a form of poison, so the problems of man are the negative macrocosms formed by one negative microcosm. I believe that correct breathing can and must eventually unite the races and religions of the planet, because it will be understood as our only means of global survival.

It will be initiated by those individuals who have rediscovered this right use of love. A positive macrocosm will then be produced by a positive microcosm, in the same way that right breath constitutes right action and attracts others like itself.

We often take our nearest and dearest for granted, we can no longer take our air for granted. There is no other option open to us. Just as two former foes may be united in a common cause greater than themselves, in order to survive, will the air of *spirit* and its ability to preserve mankind be the common cause which will force us *all* to come gasping in supplication for its benediction? *If only to save the children.*

Maybe collective awareness of possible global self-asphyxiation could bring us all together before an ultimate crisis. *If only to save the children.*

Surely this collective study and respect for what gives us life, an invisible loving force, could unite us all in a natural spirituality, where love uncontaminated by dogma from any man made religion becomes the common bond.

So far, in my study of the Christian Bible and the Koran the word breath is sadly lacking, but there are references to spirituality which has its Greek root origin in the word respire, i.e. to re-spirit through air. Would it really take a quantum leap for all religions to understand and study together the deepest meaning of the word spirituality sourced by the only true use of the common life force which unites us by a mutual God?

In the opening commentary of the Koran by its translator I noticed in the second paragraph on page ten 'In the application of spiritual truths to our own times, we must use every kind of knowledge, science and experience that we possess.' What a wonderful statement. It allows growth in so many ways, hopefully the understanding of correct breathing! I wish our Christian Bible contained such an up-to-date suggestion. Being previously ignorant of the words of the Koran, I was however surprised and inspired to see many unexpected references to the birth, life and teachings of Jesus the inspirator of the New Testament within its pages.

In some of the chapters of *The Aquarian Gospel of Jesus the Christ*, we read of Jesus travelling to many far-eastern countries in the years between maturity and beginning His ministry. A period of which we know nothing from the material in the orthodox New Testament. When you think about it, He must have embarked on an intensive preparatory period. From other documents I have read, He apparently studied many religions, had respect for all, and in His travels was harmoniously affected by numerous other religions, including the Moslem and Hindu faiths.

The Universal language of breath is an exact science, one which our science of today has yet to study, in its depth beyond the physical. To do this, to experience its full mental emotional and spiritual scientific depths, scientists would have to change themselves, which is the most courageous thing we can do. ('The most courageous thing a man can do is to be true to himself.') It is an individual personal adventure, which for anyone trained in the super intellectual world of present day scientific limited experience, represents travelling out of the comfort zone of the science lab. I say this because I have not yet met a scientist who can reproduce the correct breathing pattern.

On the other hand to travel to the *core* of breath reveals the non-fear state of love which in a group of people of diverse religious faiths scientifically experimenting in correct breath, could create an ever expanding common brotherhood of spiritual faith.

Such a microcosm could be replicated in a world macrocosm. At a time when we demand the strictest accuracy of measurement, blind trials, placebo groups, timespan, replication and countless exactitudes, scientists who have solved the complexity of space travel have never yet had the courage or intelligence to explore their own inner space revealed by the alchemic formula of correct breath.

Science is unfortunately over-dominated by the left hemisphere of the brain, yet I submit that scientists of all races and religions will never achieve the ultimate potential of the right brain, which contains the mystical experience of the meaning of life, unless they have personally understood the great Science of Breath. Only then will they have fully experienced life itself. An impossible experience unless precision guided by the accuracy of the spirit of air, whatever our religion.

Correcting one's breath is a lovely way to reveal to oneself just how wonderful we are. Having said that, it can seem a bit painful too, but a necessary pain, of revealing to us things we find rather objectionable about ourselves. Thank goodness this happens, as our faults then come into our minds as they *are on the way out.*

Putting it gently, we all limit our potential if we limit our breath, whatever our religion, and therefore our perfection! It's amazing how much wool we can pull over our own eyes in thinking that we are always right. This is the egotistical self. We are always right to love ourselves completely. How else can we love someone else if we do not love ourselves first? The egotistical, *always having to be right self*, reveals itself in a discussion by telling the other person that they are wrong, and that we are not supposed to love ourselves. I remember arguing this point with a minister of the Church who declared vehemently that we must not love ourselves. Yet Jesus told us to love our neighbour as ourselves, giving permission for us to do just that.

Leonard Orr once said that there is 'no right or wrong, only consequences.' Think about that. How do we demonstrate that someone else is wrong? By pointing or shaking a finger at them. When I was going through my ego-clearing period, obviously still not then completed, I realised that I had the nasty habit of sometimes shaking my right forefinger when in conversation about a controversial topic. When we do this, we are invoking the opposite left bossy side of the brain, the criticising, analytical side, which is communicating to the other person in a parental way, i.e. 'I'm right, and you're wrong.' This is likely to provoke hostility from the other person not conducive to an amicable outcome. Watch religious or other debates, particularly political, on TV, to see this in action. I found it quite interesting to recognise this habit in myself and to have to work to reverse it. The mental reversal of this habit encourages us to listen more, and to acknowledge that the other person can be right too, a hard fact for the ego to swallow, but a habit well worth cultivating.

Transferring my attention to my own personal errors, I began to further study and recognise the finger-pointing habit when watching these political and religious debates on the television. It was amazing how often it occurred. From personal hard won experience I found myself realising that the person who did the right-finger point had a lot of humility to learn, they thought that only they knew the right answer to a problem. The attitude was bossy and parental, and by the law of inverse therapy was also a bit childish. A mature adult never points the finger.

Try this exercise on yourself, or by watching whatever political or religious leader or guru you admire. Study them. The person who doesn't *have* to be right, is more likely to be a more suitable role-model, and is in fact more likely to *be* right! Question the power motives of the person who often points with their right forefinger. You don't want a bossy religious leader, they invite extremism.

Any group which advocates violence as a remedy will usually have a higher proportion of right forefinger wavers! Body language knowledge of this kind is a useful yardstick, until you have learned the sure-fire loving language of the breath, the most trustworthy sign I know.

Devotees of many religions interpret and adapt their various religious books from a perspective the writers of such epistles never intended. All too often twisted to suit their own 'truths'. If the followers of any religion, believers in the Bible or Koran, really interpreted the wisdom of their creeds in the way the writers intended, the mention of the word *spirituality or the Spirit* would ensure that word and that word alone together with corrected and natural breath would break down the finger-pointing attitudes. Attitudes which ensure divisiveness rather than the core spirituality of right breath; which is the golden cord which could bind us universally in the brotherhood and sisterhood of love. Correction of the breath is the secret of the golden cord.

If the advocates of the Christian Bible and the Muslim Koran and in fact all religions started to study the language of the breath together they would start to use the words 'spirit, love, forgiveness and mercy,' and act on them. Right action for all would follow. What other words do we need for mutual understanding of the real meaning of the word *Religion?*

Chapter 38

BACK PAIN

DESPITE BEING AN OCTOGENARIAN, I am fortunate never to have suffered from *back* pain. Well maybe the odd twinge now and again with one exception, as you will soon discover. This despite the fact that according to my mother my birth was pretty traumatic. Having the cord twisted round my neck and appearing rather blue, I mention in another chapter that the attending doctor said 'never mind the baby look after the mother!' Quite a recipe for rejection. Probably my little spine was in quite a state of tension. It could have provided a great foundation for later back-ache, but as I say I have been lucky in the back-ache department. However, with the one exception referred to above, the little pains I have experienced have made me aware that they always related to a difficult situation in which I was involved, from which at the time I could see no escape. Hence my spine tensed, and pain resulted.

My growing understanding of the Power of Breath, and work as a therapist, has brought me into contact with hundreds of people who had problems of acute anxiety and stress, who also reported that they were under medication or treatment for problems of back pain. Indeed since a large percentage of our population experiences the same symptoms, I can only imagine what an enormous cost their treatment must be to the National Health Service. From what I can gather, only a proportion is successful.

Obviously I am not a chiropractor, nor qualified to issue

prescriptions even if I had wanted to, but one persistent factor continuously emerged. When I re-taught a client to breathe correctly, the symptoms of their back pain improved and in most cases disappeared. Obviously some people had undergone surgery for the problem, and bits had been removed, which made it difficult for the healing pattern to re-run the progressive natural cycle contained within the structural breath blueprint.

In my own case I came to understand the wonderful alchemical power of oxygen to heal, some forty years ago. I was helping my husband to lift a number of pine tree trunks some twelve feet long from our field to a roadside gate for uplifting. We alternated the lifting of the thick or narrow end over some pretty uneven ground. I must have twisted or sprained some vital muscles in my lower back, for a day later I experienced agonising pain over my right lower hip. In fact it confined me to bed for several days until gradually the pain went away, and I thought that was that. Unfortunately the pain returned several months later, and recurred at roughly yearly intervals, being quite severe for several days.

After I began to understand the healing power released by correct breath and oxygenation, I began to consciously and deliberately *breathe into* the pain as it arose, and exhale as if I was removing it. Gradually the intensity and frequency of the attacks began to diminish and I realised that I could actually *prevent* the discomfort from peaking by quickly beginning this healing *injection* of oxygen until the pain disappeared. It was an interesting and salutary self-teaching process in learning about Nature's great healing balm by sending a healing electrical frequency to the problem. It over-rode the lower pain frequency. After all that is what Higher Power is all about! Obviously the improvement of *spiritual-ised* oxygen energy to the area assisted cell regeneration.

I mentioned earlier that my birth had been difficult.

Very often such a situation seems to pre-programme an individual to suffer from a variety of physical complaints later in life. I must have been pre-programmed with a strong constitution, or maybe the physically active childhood I led allowed me unconsciously to iron out the spinal 'blips' from my birth. I was fortunate to grow up in the 1930s when children from quite an early age took it as natural that they went for long walks unaccompanied by adults, at least after the age of seven. I grew up in Salisbury, an ancient Cathedral city with easy access to the nearby downland countryside. My elder brother was eighteen months older than myself, and we often walked seven or eight miles on a Saturday, perhaps with several of his friends. Before long they became tired of a younger sister lagging along behind and would contrive to lose me, so that at the tender age of seven or so I would trudge home more annoyed with my brother and his gang than worrying about the long walk.

Then there was the high park wall at the end of our garden where I would spend long periods of time doing endless handstands and backbends, or on the parallel bars in the park, hanging and twisting around by the arms from the maypole. Qualifying for the extra gym class at senior school; captain of the under-fifteen lacrosse team; and a short spell in the West of England lacrosse team after I left school, continued my athletic activities.

Finally I spent eight years as a farm secretary in the beautiful Wylye valley of Wiltshire, and later in the magical border country between Herefordshire and the Welsh border. In that capacity I was never happier than when I was out on the farm involved in all the various tasks of an eight hundred acre mixed farm and its routines. From milking to tractor driving, haymaking to harvesting, in the days just before the combine harvester made that particular job less back-breaking. I was strong and healthy, even for a dare transferring a couple of two hundredweight sacks of corn from one trailer to another, a feat which I now shudder to contemplate. Of course during those days when the Women's Land Army was still in existence, women were carrying out tasks which they would formerly have considered impossible. Anyway as a result I was extremely fit, and a strong constitution has enabled me to avoid the aches and pains from which many of my contemporaries suffered after the age of forty and rearing a family.

Even my good health however could not have cured all the personal breathing limitations which I had to repair through conscious correction, after the subject of breathing properly became the passion of my life. It was then that I began to realise how intrinsically the act was so closely linked with the mind and emotions. This self-educating process coincided with the greatest challenge of my life, that of overseeing the restoration of an old vandalised four-story inner-city school in the late eighties, as a stress centre. At sixty I could run up the 102 stairs to the fourth floor without being breathless, and took a naughty pleasure in innocently escorting out-of-breath officials twenty years younger to the top of the building.

With a budget of less than £30,000, instead of the £250,000 quoted by another organisation, we achieved what I now see as a virtual miracle. We had a wonderful team of hardy volunteers. Until then I was what might be classified as a kept house-wife. The work was back-breaking, and hands-on. Looking back one could call it heartbreaking, only the absolute certainty of the urgency of teaching as many people as possible to breathe properly (most of the population), sustained my spirit. I took up this challenge at the age of fifty-eight, only my earlier country inherited physical strengths, with the mental and emotional insights gained through my own personal experience in healing my breathing gave me the energy, patience and faith to help bring the project into being. The work was with people suffering from stress; *all stress sufferers breathe wrongly and badly.*

Profound insights, which came to me during the next fifteen years, from working with thousands of stressful people who were also poor breathers, convinced me:

(a) of the enormous need for many thousands of basic breathing teachers;

(b) that teaching people to breathe properly again is giving them a healing tool for life.

In other words very little help was needed in traditional therapies, either orthodox or alternative. Teaching correct breathing is hardly an alternative, since it is the core process of life for which there is no alternative... tell me if you can think of one. A high proportion of stress sufferers also suffered from back pain, which seemed to improved dramatically as their breathing improved.

Back pain improvement for so many of these people came about without any manipulation or massage, it happened as a *result* of a number of sessions of training in correct breathing, with the client also daily practicing improved lung use between sessions, generally about 20 breaths at a time several times a day, until the improved habit became second nature. Sometimes a person would experience a period of temporary discomfort as unused respiratory muscles became supple, but without my prompting would say 'Oh, that must be part of the healing process.' What we came to describe as *a release*, i.e. a release of tension. If you refer to the chapter in this book about the Healing Process, you may understand this natural healing method better.

Despite going through this period of healing pain, it became evident that the mental and emotional symptoms for which someone had sought my assistance also began to improve, often without any direct therapeutic counselling guidance from me. Briefly the stress symptoms appeared on the surface of that person's life but as a recognisable process of release or letting go, while on a parallel level the problems for which they had asked for counselling began *to resolve themselves*. At the same time my client was increasingly aware of limiting ways in which they had been making decisions and acting upon them. These also began to change. The most noticeable symptom being that they were facing up to life with a greater degree of courage and less fear. Standing tall also lessens back pain. The other common factor reported was a conscious improvement in the breathing pattern.

Naturally the more acute the original respiratory limitation, the more pronounced the symptoms of the healing process, and also the length of the period of recovery, but when one considers the long period of time during which the problems had been incubating, the reversal of the problem on all levels required an appropriate period of readjustment. As a firm believer in miracles, I have also seen miracles happen.

I have come to associate the location of the area of back pain with a limitation of the full respiratory inflation in the lung area directly opposite where the back pain is located. I have never read about this in any other literature but having met many people who had gone through intense periods of back manipulation for their problems it was evident that their therapist did not seem to be aware of this coincidental symptom. When and where the breath is withheld, there must also be a withholding of oxygen to the human frame the bone structure at the core of our framework. Bone, blood, muscles flesh and skin are all composed of cells, each one requiring adequate oxygenation, the same material in a different density, like vapour, steam, water and ice. I believe that restriction in some part of the lung has a knock-on effect on the part of the spine which correlates to that lung area. This restriction takes the form of oxygen starvation, and as the circulation of the blood is restricted in that area, the cells do not receive adequate oxygen, so the bone begins to deteriorate. Pain is experienced, which is Nature's warning signal that all is not well.

There is another way of looking at this process, which has to do with the connection between the brain and the spine, the latter being the pathway down which are transmitted our thoughts and feelings. Whenever we hold in or restrict our thoughts and feelings because of fear or negativity, we restrict oxygenation to the brain, in particular the part of the brain connected to the corresponding area of the lung and the link to the nervous system enclosed within the spinal sheath. Remember all breath holding implies negative thinking which de-oxygenates the brain and body cells.

It took me several years to understand this process and innumerable internalised question and answer dialogue sessions relating to this connection between breathing, brain and the effect on the spinal column. Also to the fact that the engine of the brain can only function effectively if it is used as it was invented, i.e. if the respiratory action arises from the lower belly, that point between the pelvic bone and the navel which conveys to the upper brain a vibrating electrical movement. It acts like an emotional computer message which cancels out fear, and allows the alchemy of love to underpin all our thoughts, emotions and actions.

I sometimes imagine the body resembling a puppet dangling from strings attached to the head, which controls the brain spine energy mover which operates the strings. These respond to each spinal impulse like the arms of a crane or earth digger perpetually moving in response to the electricity generated down the brain/spine motor or combustion engine. Unlike the combustion engine however, humans have a primary emotional or spiritual brain, located in the ganglions of the sacral or sacred area situated, as I mentioned before, between the pelvic bone and the navel, which influences the upper brain according to respiratory accuracy.

When the breathing mechanism is unencumbered with limitations from fear, we can send subliminal information of great wisdom to the upper brain, so that the puppet string movement is decisive and fluid, rather than awkward and jerky. If I see a person's movements resembling the jerky mode, I visualise them as a puppet whose strings are being wrongly handled, because of fear, in this case of course as breather and breathed. The person is playing the role of puppet and puppeteer. Still playing out the part imposed on them by the damaging influences of their formative years. On the other hand it is never too late for us to loosen the puppet strings and reverse our victim role by correcting our breath.

The only puppet master I respond to these days is that of Higher Power which never pulls the strings too tight! The healthy new-born baby also reflects non-tightened strings, giving the truth to the title of the book by Bronson Alcott (father of Louise Alcott) *How Like an Angel Came I Down*, saying that a new-born child brings with it spirit and wisdom. In repeating once again that all held fear tightens the strings or restricts lung activity, a healthy new-born child is the most outstanding example of great courage we shall ever encounter. It has come through the act of birth, the most dangerous and difficult challenge of our lives, since we only have one chance, and have to get it right.

Unfortunately a very difficult birth, or subsequent early childhood trauma can lead to a separation of this vital lower respiratory connection, and cause the source of this move-ment to rise incorrectly from the higher part of the stomach and lungs. This involves constriction of the primary lower impulse, which is pre-ordained by Nature, and goes against Natural Law. The yet immature child has an internal fight either to obey this law, or the great fear it is now experiencing from whatever cause. The baby thinks it now has to respond to this fear for it exists within the very surroundings within which the baby is living, and with which it thinks it must co-operate in order to survive.

In such or similar situations we become separated from our core source of truth, begin to live an untruth, and block our true spiritual impulse from reaching the upper brain. Subliminally we then start to live an existence out of harmony with Nature which causes the tightening of the puppet strings from early childhood. This tightening is experienced as stress in the brain, which, unresolved because the means of healing is blocked, leads to the permanent tensing of the back muscles and eventual pain.

I believe that it is very wrong to hold a new-born baby up by its feet, in some sort of triumphant demonstration of medical expertise. I remember seeing a distressing photograph of a new-born infant handled in this way where you can graphically see the little spine in acute tension. The expression on the baby's face reflects this anguish. What an introduction to the world of man! These first impressions are of vital importance, and can become the slippery foundations of our thought dictionary of how we see life and subsequently treat life, ourselves and other people. Our foundation and formative thoughts are that life is stressful, and all our subsequent thinking about life unconsciously refers back to this law we have created about life, *which is incorrect.*

Life or the life energy which surrounds us is always on an Alpha or loving vibration which never changes. The baby has however erroneously formed its impression of life on what happened at its birth, the stressful primal experience created by the mother's tension and the strong Beta-orientated vibrations within the birthing room. The baby responds to the atmosphere of the energy vibrations of the birth attendants, bright lights, noise and temperature change into which it is introduced to the world, so different to the conditions of the womb in which the infant *has grown itself*. Not surprising then that the child thinks that the world is a hostile place, and behaves as such in its subsequent life.

The *fear* trigger activated by the above experiences thus creates a self-fulfilling-role model which damages from birth onwards our primary life function, that of breathing. We constantly refer back to this initial impulse from an unconscious subliminal brain impulse, and our body obeys the command. Potential brain power fails to develop, leading to a limitation of mental, physical and emotional ability. As a result we have an organism which is *taking* too much compensatory energy from the world energy bank, rather than from nurturing the infinite supply from Higher Intelligence.

On a health level the shortage of correct energy supply at cellular level prevents natural cell regeneration, ensuing faulty breathing leads to faulty circulation. The build-up of toxins and accumulative storage of poisons, eventually affects the bones, tissues and skin. I cannot for the life of me see how any kind of medical drugs can reverse this degenerative spiral. Naturally the spine, the main highway for the life impulse, is the prime casualty in this fall from perfection. So many people suffer from lower back pain which I understand from therapeutic sources represents the birth area impulse. Time and time again the clients who come to me for help from my training as a psychotherapist, suffer from lower back pain, and during the recording of their case histories, reveal a traumatic birth experience. Amazing too, is the resultant back pain relief, when respiratory corrective training is introduced.

As the muscular armouring begins to relax, the blood

begins to flow more efficiently through the adjacent blood vessels taking oxygen (air, spirit) in a corrective spiral from the lower to upper brain. Wonderful changes then begin to take place within the client which become permanent, as if the cellular blueprint has been enabled to correct its original plan. Naturally the length and severity of the problem dictates the speed of recovery, but in many cases it is as if the precipitating factor of the back pain is forgotten like a bad dream, as an individual's personal life is transformed on all levels, not only health, but creative work, relationships and so on.

Nature will always hold the prescription for the repair job not obtainable from the chemist or doctor. Remember Nature's laws are 'set in stone' and there is no alternative prescription. World culture, in its scientific and technological egocentricity has been treating Nature's laws in a very slovenly way during the past hundreds of years, and I believe that Global Warming represents our appalling superficiality in this respect.

The wonderful alternative New Testament, *The Aquarian Gospel,* refers to the human body as a harpsichord where the strings can be too tight or too loose. Remember my earlier reference to the puppet suspended from the spine with arms and legs operating from its movements.

Naturally with so many people leading a sedentary existence in this computerised world of 'work', we do not have the experience of our forefathers who would have had to adapt to lifting weights as part of their lives. Of course many of them operated at the other extreme from our present 'easy' existence as they slaved in over-heavy manual jobs. We have yet to devise a life-style where our work and leisure creates a perfect usage of the human body and mind, co-ordinating from a perfect respiratory pattern. I think that will lead to an end of back pain, and we shall be less prone to accidents as we are in control of our mind/body/emotional balance. Perhaps that is what Heaven is all about, but I believe we all have a right to this way of living our lives in *this present existence*.

Only as recently as 150 years ago countless workers died as a result of the overuse of the body in weight bearing work, as the Industrial Revolution trivialised human life with the easy replacement of manual workers as they wore out. Nowadays I believe the exact opposite is causing an increase of cancer-related and other illnesses through the wrong use of the body and mind in computer-fixated work requiring little movement, which creates minimal conditions for the clearance of toxins, and an easy replacement of 'drop-outs' from stress-related illnesses, by fresh supplies of computer whiz-kids who are ready to fill the gap. Yet even in this day and age, our various life-style needs require us to lift weights (Ikea flatpacks?) and general poor muscle tone so often means that the back cannot take or adapt to such strain. The result is often weeks and months 'on the sick'.

I am lucky to have had an 'earthed' grounding from my youth, and have always felt in touch with the world of Nature often in manually related activity, indeed at 80 can still bend and place my palms flat on the floor without bending my knees (don't try this movement except in easy stages!). I am sure that this suppleness has come from breathing correctly, an internal yoga movement which pumps oxygen constantly into the muscles and maintains *tone*.

The love of Nature and the information she has revealed to me of her scientific invention of the Correct Breath has been restored to me in the second half of my life. It is a source of sorrow that most educators and scientists do not understand this process or apply it personally. If they did I am sure that the scientific world would be less mesmerised by space travel and cloning, but use their great gifts to *really* understand Global Warming, as I believe it will have to be understood in order to avert potential disaster. It would be a bonus if they also took time for breath correction! That still, small voice of utter inner calm would tell them how to go about it!

Although I have enjoyed good health all my life, like most people I have come through several periods of intense stress, which revealed to me the close link between breath, mind and body. In my case the physical manifestation of that fear stress always resulted in some kind of skin eruption. When the problem was resolved the skin problem always resolved itself too.

I once read an interesting article which suggested that in esoteric terms the bones represent the mind, the flesh the thoughts, and the skin the emotions, giving credence to another saying that 'where no tears fall from the eyes other organs weep.' There is nothing like personal experience to consolidate another piece of wisdom that 'the eyes of suffering see the furthest.' My several life crises, once resolved, taught me so much not only about myself but about the need to live my life by the irreversible laws of Nature. When I obeyed these laws the Planet allowed me to heal the disharmonies in my own life. This came about when I first of all obeyed the law of correct breathing, the same law which applies to all the inhabitants of this Planet.

I may seem to have rather digressed from the title of this chapter on back pain, but I felt it necessary to give a little background about my own personal life experience on the understanding of health. Having come across a number of wise sayings in my studies, the one which seems to fit the back pain problem states 'as the twig bends so does the tree.' Nowadays I see so many people with back problems who lean like the bent tree. Knowing about breath and the corresponding relationship between body, mind and emotions, I say to myself, 'I wonder *who* is leaning on you.' In observing those who come to me for help with stressful lives, there is almost always a near relative or friend who is leaning or 'parasiting' on them. Almost always the *habit* taken on board by my client was established in childhood when they were psychologically leaned on too heavily by an immature parent who used the child to give them a sense of artificial power handed to them 'on a plate' by the act of parentage. When through corrective breathing my client was able to throw off this weight on their psychological blueprint, the back problem usually went too. Those who had parasited did not like it, but sometimes they then *grew up*! They had to straighten their own spines, in order to stop leaning on another person.

Many years ago I met (and in retrospect was destined to meet) a wonderful psychologist then in his nineties called Dr. Arthur Rowbotham. He was a passionate devotee of yoga, and anyone reading these pages who has studied this art for some time will recognise his name, as that and his spirituality lives on. I remember him telling a group of students how in his eighties he was involved in a near-fatal accident involving a bus. According to him he broke almost every bone in his body, and twice when in hospital was declared dead, and taken to the mortuary. Twice those in charge realised he was still breathing and he was returned to the ward! Eventually he recovered, a miracle for a man of his age, or indeed of any age considering his injuries. Dr. Rowbotham declared without hesitation, that it was only his conscious application of the healing power of the breath that enabled his recovery. I can understand how he did that.

He studied at the Vienna School with the eminent early psychological pioneers Jung and Freud. Despite their genius, from reading and research of their work, with great respect I do not think that they seemed to understand the Higher Healing Intelligence of correct breath as did my friend Dr. Rowbotham.

Recently I discovered after a long search, a book by Captain W. Knowles titled *New Life Through Breathing*. He was born at the end of the 1800s, went to sea for three years, and developed tuberculosis of the lung, probably from the hardships of such a career at that time. He was sent to Canada for the purity of the air, and met a GP who taught him some specific breathing exercises. His TB disappeared after a few months as a result. Coming back to this country in 1914 to start a career, he was caught up in the Great War, spent two ghastly years in the trenches, and was awarded the Military Cross. Sheltering in a bunker with his platoon, he was badly injured by a shell which killed outright his nine comrades. He himself suffered severe shrapnel wounds, and lost his right hand. In the nightmare period before he was rescued he attributed his survival to his awareness of using breathing to stay alive during that horrendous time, and to heal himself afterwards.

When Captain Knowles returned to this country he spent some time in establishing a successful career, but the need to teach what he had discovered eventually became a priority, and he established a School of Breathing in London, sharing his knowledge with some 40,000 people, military personnel, sportsmen, football teams and the ordinary man and woman. The foreword to his book was written by a great sportsman of the middle twentieth century, Lord Wakefield of Kendal former, MP and captain of the England rugby team of the day, whose name is inscribed in the rugby Hall of Fame.

It is so vital that the ideas and work of men such as these is recognised, but it will not be understood by the medical world until all in that profession, indeed anyone involved in health (and education) understand and restore their own correct breathing pattern. What a saving to the NHS as the use of needles, knives and tablets dramatically reduces. Of course this is my own independent opinion!

447

The wonderful work on breathing within the area of childbirth will be mentioned in chapters discussing this most vital of life experiences. In this connection I must mention the work of Betty Parsons CBE. Betty trained an estimated 20,000 pregnant women in the art of relaxation and breathing including, I understand, HRH The Queen and other members of the Royal Family. I believe her book on the subject is not now easily available, but her training tape was discovered by one of my colleagues in a bargain box. Betty Parsons strongly insists that her work is not only for childbirth, but also for life. Is this why our present Queen retains such a strong impression of vitality in her early eighties?

When I was expecting my second child, I had decided on a home confinement, as I had vowed to give birth under a tree as they do in more 'primitive' countries, rather than repeat my first experience of childbirth in a local maternity hospital now closed. I had realised that the emotional support so sorely needed by a first time mother was probably less supportive than that given to a pet cat or dog. It was clinically frigid and uncaring.

Anyway, between this disaster and my next confinement I had discovered the work of Dr. Grantly Dick Reid another pioneer in correct breathing for natural childbirth. I taught myself better breathing, and was able to put myself into deep relaxation which made an amazing difference when my daughter was born. *I* was in charge, with no one patronising me as if I was a non-person, and *they* were in charge of my body and baby. We even made a tape of my daughter's first birth cry, one of my most treasured possessions. The visiting midwife said that it was one of the happiest births she had ever attended. This from a highly trained midwife from the Elsie Inglis maternity hospital in Edinburgh.

The important factor during the labour period was the deep relaxation, and internal instructions from Nature to breathe and make use of my spine in order to obey her internal instructions brought into consciousness from my breathing.

I have heard from many women that they felt their post-birth back pain problems came from not being able to respond to Nature's instructions, which seemed to be in conflict with those given by their birth attendants. An acute muscular tension resulted in which they seemed to be 'locked'.

The wonderful work of these breathing pioneers seems to go unrecognised by the medical profession generally, but I rate their insights and dedication higher than so many of the applauded so-called 'break-throughs' in health care we read of weekly, but which do not seem to lower the disease and addiction statistics. It is as if we have to go for the complex and by-pass the obvious which seems too simple, because we make the mistake of taking for granted that which we cannot see but which gives us life. Breath.

Perhaps that break-through cannot happen unless all doctors, nurses, health and education professionals are taught to breathe correctly. The effect has been likened to a dose of laughing-gas, so that's a free side-effect, not to be under-estimated!

It is a reflection of my own immaturity at that time not to understand that this better breathing and ability to completely relax was a proper natural skill for all life-experiences, and not just for giving birth. If I had, I could have saved myself subsequent painful wrong decisions about my life-path, and the equally painful experience of reversing that pain. Well it seemed painful at the time, now I realise that I would not have been without that priceless experience, for it allowed me to grow, and be able to empathise and assist thousands of others to trust themselves.

I suppose it was not trusting myself that made me forget and ignore for many years what my childbirth experience eventually taught me, that the way to internal balance and tranquillity, is to give only about twenty minutes a day to breathing correctly, which induces relaxation, mentally, physically and emotionally. The knock-on result is brain and spinal suppleness with a highly decreased risk of developing back pain problems. The twenty-minute training eventually turns into a permanent natural breathing habit.

The existence of another common back pain symptom is frequently observable on the streets of our cities every day. It is what we call 'coat-hanger' shoulders. You are walking behind someone and notice that the person in front of you seems to have their shoulders permanently hunched as if their clothes were hanging off their shoulders instead of fitting the body. To maintain this *holding* position the chest must be held in a concave position making it almost impossible for the top of the lungs to inflate. If you try to copy this position yourself, you will become aware that the emotion which accompanies this posture is fear or apprehension. Permanently set in this way must make life a living nightmare, and the holding of the breath will severely limit oxygen intake, produce curvature of the spine and its permanent tension. Small wonder that such people constantly complain of upper back pain as the muscles in these areas are in perpetual tension. Lack of oxygen and tense muscles will create ongoing pressure on the bone structure of the spine, eventually resulting in bone erosion as the bone-cell tissue is unable to be renewed.

The younger the individual, the more likely it is that improvement can take place, by the introduction of correct breathing training and relaxation. Eventually the client realises that the weight they have been carrying across their shoulders, like a heavy load, is beginning to feel lighter, and as time goes by one notices a straightening of the posture. Mental and emotional enlightenment eventually accompanies the process, and a person will begin to realise that they have in effect been 'carrying' the burden of the traumas of their childhood on their back, usually the fears of their parents which a sensitive child seems to absorb. Self-understanding is the biggest help to the continuing straightening of the spine as increased oxygen, and release of tension allow the bone-cell tissue to be repaired. The younger the person, the better the prognosis for improvement, but it is not a quick process. It can however break the cycle of back problems being passed on down the generations.

Have compassion for the person with the coat-hanger back, in later life they will always be only too ready to take on other people's burdens, even although they have not yet resolved their own. No one can carry another's burdens, but you can help someone to release the unnecessary burdens that so many children carry. When you know the language of the breath, you understand the invisible problems of the immature parent that a child often shoulders in order to survive in the only home it has known, for it knows that it has not the ability to find another place to stay. Often the parents do not know that they are putting this load on the shoulders of their children, but the addictive *power fix* that parenthood brings can be used in an appallingly overt and destructive way.

I am frequently reminded of a slip of paper I used in a group setting, in which we discussed the messages which we had received from our parents. This particular sentence read 'however hard you try to please me you never can, but keep on trying.' To me any form of back pain represents some degree of that adult oppressive message, absorbed by the vulnerable child, the tender human plant.

★ ★ ★

The child who bears its parents' fears
Down all the empty years,
In stunted souls and bodies
In man-created oceans
Of unnecessary tears.

Eventually the soft spinal bones of the growing infant, no longer able to stand upright in its own power path, start to develop out-of-precise alignment, and the distortion from perfection begins.

In speaking of back pain, this chapter is referring to stress-based back pain, not back injury, although of course correct breathing always helps the healing process.

As I complete these pages I repeat how often I have observed the close link between the location of respiratory muscular tension easily noticed when someone is stretched out, so that breath-holding areas can be seen, and the parallel site of reported back pain, i.e. if the respiratory restriction is at the base of the lungs, the back pain is at the *base* of the spine. Respiratory restriction at the top of the lungs appears to produce *upper* back pain. By restoring correct breathing in the respiratory activity to the *base* of the lungs there is invariably a reported lessening of lower back pain. I have observed a similar reaction that when breathing improvement to the upper lungs is activated, *upper* back pain is relieved. This action resembles the release of a stretched cord which has been held too tautly.

There is an additional reason which I have noted for constant lower back pain, which I have proved to be accurate in my work with breathing. When I see someone in a therapeutic case-study I always enquire about birth trauma. It is very often that a person born by Ceasarean section, epidural, breech or forceps delivery reports symptoms of recurring pain at the base of the spine.

If you think about the cycles of enormous energy that a baby has to activate in order to free itself from the birth canal, you can perhaps imagine what happens when this accumulated energy cannot produce a result, and the forward movement cannot take place. Medical intervention intervenes, but within the baby, the trapped energy which was to have propelled the baby onwards stays unexpended, and is *trapped* within a muscular holding of unexpended primal tension of high intensity. This tension and resultant back pain can be removed by the client themselves, by intuitive corrective breathing therapy over a period of time. Sadly therapists are few and far between in this field, which requires a deep empathy with the natural movements of the labour process.

If you think about this interrupted birth process which may seem necessary to the professionals, you can imagine the enormous strain placed upon the baby's spinal cord as it tries to emerge from a blocked passageway and then attempts to deal with the intervention of other alternative birth options. Such interventions may seem like an attack on the baby's life. How is it to know any differently?

Birth is the most difficult and dangerous experience of our lives, and at some deep unconsciously inspired level the consciously voiced thoughts of so many people I have worked with whose birth has been by other methods than self-induced, has been that for no known reason that person has all their lives *felt a failure*. The child is so attuned to nature and the *correct* way to come into life, that *not* to activate this process correctly represents a deep sense of having taken the wrong path.

Correcting the breathing pattern or vibration back to its natural rhythm may take a number of sessions, not necessarily at frequent intervals, perhaps over several years, but as one client put it, 'I feel as if I am coming back to *me*.' In this self-healing process from back pain, no one has massaged or manipulated the client's back, or recommended a special diet. All that is needed is for the therapist to know the process and to be quietly and unobtrusively *there*. Very frequently by consciously breathing correctly yourself in a quiet breathing session, you can assist someone to bring about self-repair from back pain. I know, clients have told me 'I heard you breathe, and it helped me.'

In concluding this chapter, which has turned out to be rather longer than I had originally intended, I realise that I could have written a whole book about the subject!

Back pain however is one of the most common human afflictions, and I feel it has been important to share not only my own thoughts on the subject, but many years of personal experience of positive outcomes.

Chapter 39

TERRORISM

WHENEVER I SEE a newspaper photograph of a man with what is commonly referred to as a 'pot belly' it always conveys a very direct message to me formed from several decades of working as a psychotherapist, particularly with regard to the language of the breath. This language honed to quite a precise skill will always tell me that that person's heart is blocked, i.e. a powerful restrictive muscular band around the area of the diaphragm is preventing the easy filling and expansion of the upper lung area. This obviously causes a restriction in circulation in the heart area thereby raising the risk of heart illness.

Interpreted from the emotional viewpoint, the symptom is seen as that being *hard-hearted* to themselves or denying themselves love. They may be millionaires, surrounding themselves with material comforts but these are so often *substitutes* for love. They may 'seem' to be bluff and good-hearted, but again to the trained eye this symptom is often a camouflage for a heart that is hurting, physically and emotionally.

What has happened is that the emotion of love has been suppressed, revealed by a breath disruption in the correct and natural expansion of the upper area of the lungs. This causes a rigidity of the muscles of the upper chest area which are meant to be supple, allowing the full expansion of the lungs from the lower to the upper lobes, so that the healthy flow of emotion is not trapped. As Plato (*yes, Plato!*) says in talking of incorrect breathing, 'The accumulation of degenerative white phlegm often happens because the natural expansion of the lungs is intercepted by the central barrier of the diaphragm.' In other words a block is created, which not only upsets circulation of blood and oxygen in the veins, but also the circulation of healthy emotion, essential for a healthy and happy heart.

The opposite dysfunction also occurs, perhaps more often in women, where the stomach is held in so tightly to conform with unnatural fashion habits and its ignorant lack of understanding of nature's laws. Here the lower area of the stomach is unable to expand because of tense muscles holding it in, to give an illusion of slenderness, so that again tight muscles prevent the healthy expansion of the lower and largest area of the lungs. A denial of the natural life instinct.

I have occasionally noted photographs of supposed religious leaders and gurus who have been accused of inciting violence and terrorism among their followers, and have observed how many of them have exhibited the enlarged lower stomach syndrome. The psychological traits of heart-blocking mentioned above seems to me to be a symptom of the need for power without a heart, which is such a danger to impressionable young minds.

In fact alarm signals go off in my mind whenever I see this enlarged lower stomach expansion in anyone in a position of power in politics, business or indeed any other profession.

We demand so much information in paper-based facts and statistics, without being able to read the symptoms of unhealthy minds in physical misalignment. These inevitably carry accompanying mental and emotional limitations, observable to students of human behaviour; not very reassuring to see in someone in a position of authority, who demands our approval.

I see in such symptoms a desperate unrecognised need for corrective breathing training for all religious, political or business leaders who suffer from this enlarged gut problem, because there is such a need for them to open the heart. Apart from which, they have a much greater risk of suffering health problems in that vulnerable part of the body. The increase in prostate cancer symptoms is no accident.

In order to loosen the grip of the self-imposed terrorist mentality, the heart has to open. I passionately believe that corrective breathing training is an essential ingredient in the curriculum of our education system, particularly in multi-faith schools. In fact in all schools, because I am convinced that such teaching could drastically reduce the serious bullying factor, which causes so much misery to thousands of children.

This training work could help to keep open the naturally open heart of the child of any nationality a process which, if maintained throughout the primary years would, I am sure, drastically reduce the addiction problems which in some cases have already begun before the change to senior schools, where addiction can become a serious common factor. Racial animosity would also I believe become a much rarer occurrence.

Obviously such teaching would best be given by teachers themselves, or their own tensions could impinge on the children. I have taught this process to many teachers with positive results, and I believe the classroom atmosphere created by good breathing habits would become so much more relaxed, an ideal environment for enjoyable learning. What would also be learned would be something more important than the three Rs, where skills would develop without pressure. Discovering a class activity which would bring calmness and peace to our classrooms must surely be rated as the highest priority in the world of education. Such a goal must also be attained by those who make bureaucratic demands on teachers and the whole system changes. Also in the potentially damaging emphasis on unnecessary exams and critical assessments throughout the school life of the child.

I am sure that the knock-on effect on our national educational environment would be a world inspiration. The effect could be global, effecting better future relations between nations, inspired by the children of today. They have become mature adults with peace and love in their eyes. It has been produced by an education system which enabled them to retain the wisdom and joy of life that was their birthright into adulthood. It would be wonderful if parents were also brought into this process.

I believe that there is *no* alternative to correct breathing that can lead to a really good outcome, because *incorrect* breathing arises from negative thinking. Yet in classrooms globally I could fairly safely predict that well over 80% of children over eight years old have restricted and incorrect breathing. This creates a hotbed for tension, anti-social behaviour, bullying and violence. Human fodder for groups inciting violence. All who are destructive today, were once children with love and trust in their eyes.

When I re-teach someone to breath correctly, one of the things which gives me such joy is that after a few weeks, when I meet that person again, there is a new calmer light in their eyes, and they give you a sensation of peace.

The unifying factor which is present between those who breathe correctly is that their relationships do not become corrupted by fear and suspicion, there is no need to hide aggression under a cloak of non-religious religions, whose faith is based on a God of hate and subversive power.

From a personal experience, whenever I have been in a group of people of different nationalities and faiths who all breathe correctly and naturally, there is a sense that we all belong to a greater faith than diverse religions, are bound by a collective force which can only be described as love.

There can be difference of opinion, but a consensus is finally reached agreeable to all.

I know I am looking at a scenario yet to happen, but it must happen, this is as yet an unwritten formula in the natural world. There is an energy form yet to materialise, but that is how all energy eventually comes into being. I remember learning a poem as a 10-year old. (I still remember all the poetry I learned as a child.)

> For I dipped into the future, far as human eye
>   could see,
> Saw the vision of the world, and all the wonders
>   there would be,
> Saw the heavens filled with commerce, argosies
>   with magic sails,
> Pilots of the purple twilight dropping down
>   with costly bales.
> 'Til the war drums throbbed no longer, and the
>   battle flags were furled,
> In the Parliament of Man, the Federation
>   of the World.

High Flight - John Gillespie Magee, Junior

This poem was written before the advent of the aeroplane, embodying prophetic words, the last two lines still to materialise into being.

From the groups of diverse nationalities and faiths of whom I have had experience, which represent a microcosm of the global population, could evolve the greater macrocosm of all, united by the power of correct breath. Anything which can be created by a single thought can materialise and come into being; this is the principle behind all evolution. Calm and loving thoughts arise from correct breathing.

'I'd like to teach the world to sing,' runs the song, let us teach it *to breathe first*.

Extremist states of mind then cannot find a foothold, the clean laser beam of correct oxygenation sweeps away the foetid stagnation of negative and unhealthy thought/action which without the cleansing power of air/spirit spreads like a cancer within any community whatever its size.

When the false leader who no doubt breathes badly and whose personal internalised anger from a source allied to childhood injustice, attracts a loud and magnetic powerful aggressive energy, it is all too easy to attract others of similar damaged personality. Perhaps we could suggest a course of breath re-training!

No one can stop thought. I rejoice that I can visualise the most important thought available to me which is the inclusion of corrective breathing for parents, teachers and children in all educational programmes. This enlightened provision must come from an enlightened educational establishment.

Thank goodness today I hear that there is an acknowledgment that young children need less formalised tuition and more play. How much more education do the educationalists require before they have the intelligence to notice how many of the pupils of all ages cannot breathe properly. Which means that they cannot play properly. Those who do not breathe properly cannot learn effectively. Is our nation really pro-life in respect of the children in our care? Can this ever happen until we learn that the first priority of being alive fully is to be able to breathe fully? An educational priority.

The children in our care increasingly come from many nations and religions, what better demonstration of the melding together in one caring community than to understand and put into practice collectively the loving art of breathing together correctly. A golden opportunity uniquely available to us in our schools which I truly believe must all be community schools dedicated first of all to the nurturing principle of using correctly the energy of life, before children can learn happily. The learning bonus would be amazing. If we have the courage, the fruition of such a courageous step would be natural self-discipline, self-determination, self-education, with schools and communities brimful of ideas, excitement and creativity.

Our collective abuse of the life-force which is given to us freely, and which we continually ignore, could dissolve like snow in sunshine as we retrieve our human birthright of physical, mental and emotional balance by the most vital science of correct breath. Its spiritual implications are unfortunately not understood even by leading religious leaders, certainly not the scientists. Certainly not the mainstream religions I have studied.

NO BULLY WHO SPREADS TERROR CAN DEMONSTRATE THE ART AND SCIENCE OF CORRECT BREATH!

Many potential terrorists may be born and educated in this country who, as young adults, become attracted by the fiery rhetoric of trouble makers, a freedom available to all in our democratic country which prides itself on free speech. Those who breathe correctly are not taken in by such hot air, the better you breathe the less you can be taken in by the power hungry. Those who breathe correctly are never power hungry.

Change must always come from the roots, and that applies to any nation. The best of our national way of life must be preserved, but only the best. I believe that the leaders of every nation must eventually understand the language of correct breath. There was never a better time for this to become a global priority as we begin to understand with increasing horror how we have polluted the ozone layer, our life-line. Such a terrible threat would not be on our doorstep if we had preserved the humility to study the small child and its natural and correct use of oxygen. Humility is the key-word here. Humility, which leads to enlightenment.

As the forces of terrorism and possible global catastrophe force themselves upon our awareness, trivialities must lose their clamour for our attention. We still have time. The word breath means spirit, and the collective spirit must prioritise.

I prophesy that when we prioritise breath, terrorism must fall away. The energy surrounding our beautiful Mother Earth was seen with such unexpected spiritual awe in exquisite colours by the first astronauts. They realised just how special is our planet, too special to be tarnished by the ultimate selfishness of terrorism in all its forms, whether in the home, workplace or society.

May their inspiration come to assist us as we prioritise the nurturing of our children and the Planet with healing breath.

Chapter 40

WATER

I RECENTLY RETURNED from a holiday in Portugal near its Eastern border with Spain. The sun was wonderful, just what I needed. As one gets older, there is a deep intuitive awareness of an increasing vulnerability in the bones, an understanding of how easy it could be to sustain a fracture, particularly in the lower limbs. In Portugal I can *feel* the heat reversing this awareness, as the warmth seems to seep deep into my body.

One of my grandmothers had Italian blood, and I always attribute my ability to enjoy really hot sun without discomfort to this genetic strain, and having a head of hair declared by my hairdresser to be the thickest in his experience! I also seem to be impervious to the sunglasses syndrome. Luckily my eyesight does not seem to have deteriorated since I was at school, again better personal oxygenation of the brain due to correct breathing does, I am sure, help eyesight. The eyes are part of the brain, and tension in the muscles behind the eyes blocks oxygen circulation to the brain, and tissues of the eye.

This heat-resistant energy stood me in good stead during a recent holiday when I sat on an upright flimsy kitchen chair for virtually three days in the blazing sun on a Portuguese hillside, totally absorbed and fascinated while a local dowser or water diviner walked over the garden ground of my daughter's cottage, and apparently casually pinpointed with the aid of a swinging pendulum, a source of water over which a bore-hole was to be sunk Two days later the drilling rig arrived and an ample supply of water was found at a depth of 150 metres. A well-trained and good-humoured team of young men carried out the boring, laying down apparently endless lengths of piping, until we saw a damp grey sludge begin to seep round the bore-hole, which gradually became clearer until a spurt of clear water indicated that the spring had been located. There was never any doubt in all our minds that the water would be found, all based on an apparently casual swing of a hand-held pendulum. A non-scientific gadget powered by no engine other than the electricity in the mind of the dowser. It is said that a good dowser breathes from the stomach.

The dowser's brain had sensed through the amplification of the pendulum, the presence of a considerable volume of water many metres below the ground, and its accuracy was confirmed in the arrival three days later of a heavy drill-mounted tractor, a large yellow transformer, and three lorries carrying the 3-metre lengths of steel piping to screw down the drilled hole. These were later replaced by heavy blue polythene tubing, through which the water would be drawn up by a ground-based pump.

One of the most impressive factors in all this activity was that it was based upon a leisurely wander over the area by the dowser with no paper, pens, measuring instruments, or modern technological devices apart from a swinging pendulum. This stroll by a casually dressed local man resulted in three marking stones weighing about a kilo each being placed in a little pyramid over a certain point. He had also estimated the depth at which water would be found, and the purity and volume of the water. It was to these three stones that the modern drilling rig with all its accessories arrived, to commence an operation costing about 6,000 euros, which, considering the equipment involved, professional fee, labour and powerful pump, was a not-too-expensive investment.

During the three days of the drilling, I sat watching mesmerised on that kitchen chair in the sun, and eventually when the job was finished we had a small celebration involving two bottles of cheap champagne and an ample distribution of lager. The resultant slight confusion in my head was due to the latter rather than the hot sun! I don't usually drink more than one glass, but there was a question of thirst involved even as an onlooker in a temperature in the upper 70s.

The ample supply of pure tasteless water ensured a supply of about 2,500 gallons an hour, considerably more than was actually needed, but it also helped to provide an irrigation system for the cottage garden, and the large vegetable plot which was then able to be planted.

The Portuguese water operation was of course accompanied by considerable interest, of elderly gnarled locals, many of whom had their own bore holes, also found by a dowser, and the banter about depth, volume and so on formed a background audience as the team of perspiring and muscular young workmen laboured in the heat.

As the drilling team and heavy equipment trundled off to another site, I felt that I had experienced one of the most exciting events of my life, not the least the reminder of the use of dowsing or intuitive gifts most of us possess, but never use. Unfulfilled potential, the use of the intuitive faculty, has no limit to the amazing ways in which it can be used to gain Nature's co-operation. Correct breathing amplifies its limitless power.

The intense interest I felt in this search for water comes from my own hobby and researches over several decades as a dedicated dowser, latterly in the human health and energy field. Once I discovered that I had the ability to locate water, I realised I was to use the gift in the field of health without any dowsing instrument other than my mind. Occasionally I used a pendulum, a commonly used dowsing instrument. It took me some time to re-orientate my mind from the search for water, to that of healing. I have not for one minute regretted my decision, as it has led to such satisfaction in helping many to restore themselves to health.

The experience of the use of man's intuitive gifts triggered off subsequent thoughts which had been circulating in my mind for some years. There are a few interesting facts which I would like to share with you. When I became interested in dowsing or water divining, I was also a local authority councillor, and at that time to display an interest in such *occult* subjects as water divining was to be considered an '*odd bod!*' Imagine my relief when I discovered that an official of a Water Purification Board, of which I was a member, was also a dowser. He would locate broken underground field drains where pollutant effluent, perhaps from silage spillage, was being discharged into the river, and obviously saved the local authority thousands of pounds in expensive exploratory mechanical investigations. He was invariably accurate.

Through my research I discovered that millions of gallons of water are lost daily through broken underground cast-iron water pipes laid many years ago, which supply the population with the precious liquid. I suppose many of these pipes have reach the end of their days, as they were laid well before the last century and just crack when their time is up. Only an unnatural level of water loss in a given area can indicate that something is wrong, and then the leak has to be located, not always where the water may burst through.

I formerly lived in a village, where I remember an enormous cast iron water pipe carrying water from the Border reservoirs to Edinburgh erupted on several occasions in the road through the village, creating an impressive plume of water which rose high into the air, and caused a traffic diversion for several days.

We are constantly urged to save water, even to reducing the frequency of toilet flushing, yet the waste of water from cracked underground water pipes must put such savings into a fairly minor category. I do not waste water. As I turn on the tap, I am constantly reminded of those millions of the world's population whose lives could be saved by even a fraction of the water we consider our right to have available for daily use, and give humble and respectful thanks that my supply allows me to enjoy. unthinkingly what so many consider an unheard of luxury.

When I was living and working in a big city near a large housing scheme, you could be sure that a very hot spell of weather would guarantee that all over the city in such schemes, small boys would find a way to unscrew the fire hydrants which had to be kept unlocked at that time, so that fire-engines could source an immediate supply in the event of a fire.

I remember ringing the local Water Authority to report water spouting some metres into the air from a tampered street hydrant, wasting thousands of gallons an hour, which I could see from my office window. After contacting the Water Board it was often several hours before their van and engineers arrived to stop the flow. In the meantime, crowds of local small children under ten, mostly boys but with a scattering of admiring girls, would dash in and out of the powerful sprays in a form of primitive dance. They were probably innocent in their own eyes of wrongdoing, but the heat and need to become cool in a congested housing scheme had set off a deep natural craving for the healing power of water. I supposed that the delay by the Water Board in arriving to turn off the water was because such problems were being experienced all over the city, or perhaps it was better to wait until dark, when the children were not around to turn the water hydrant on again!

I saw this phenomenon on a number of occasions when

I lived and worked in the city, and its replication in other housing areas, as I passed through on my way to my Border home. I wonder if it happens all over the country? The sheer force and power of these eruptions was quite impressive, the waste of water colossal. I have a feeling that the water authorities and the fire department may now have come to a coded locking arrangement, known only to themselves, for these vulnerable but essential hydrants.

From my dowsing information I learned that only *one ninth* of the earth's water is above the surface, a scientific fact, but a dramatic thought to mentally absorb.

The earth is a living organism, and as such I believe has its own auto-immune system. When the auto-immune system of an individual is under attack, all the other systems of the body begin to deteriorate and eventually break down. I believe that the auto-immune system of Mother Earth is under threat. Possibly the acute climatic conditions world-wide in recent years are an indication that all is not well with the Earth's self-healing ability.

The composition of the human body is created from a divinely-inspired exact mix of the elements of earth, air, fire and water, and our health depends on the maintenance of this precise formula.

The Earth must also maintain her own unique balance in order to stay on the Alpha frequency (Schumann Waves) and keep her precise position in the planetary system at the vibration of Alpha. I shudder to think of the effect of the countless underground nuclear explosions which have been imposed on her sub-structure during past decades. Their external power may have been constricted by virtue of the below the ground claim, but the atrocious sub-surface heat generated by such activity might best be understood by imagining a powerful foreign body being activated deep within the human anatomy. Does the fact that it is deep within the living organism render it harmless? I don't think so.

Nature must heal herself if man is to remain a permanent tenant on her surface. I wonder how much of the planet's underground water has had to be diverted by her as a coolant, in order to defray the toxic poisons of underground nuclear explosions, and heal the man-imposed wounds. In general the interior wounds or disease of a human come up to the surface in order to be thrown off. Are the climatic extremes we are experiencing partly due to the Earth trying to excrete the noxious energy from her internal man-imposed abuse? In particular underground nuclear tests?

Are the drought conditions in the Eastern hemisphere due to surface water drying-up, due to the earth requiring this water to heal herself? She can spare no regard to the needs of man, for we have had no regard to *her* needs, and she must be healthy if *we* are to maintain life, even if much of human life may eventually be at risk.

When I came back to Britain from the dry heat of Portugal there was a torrential outbreak of rain within twelve hours, and I noticed how beautifully green the countryside appeared. A sign of health, I gave thanks.

I brought back from Portugal a little bottle of the first water drawn from the bore-hole. It had no taste, and appeared completely clear and tasteless, even weeks after. The great drill had pierced through layer upon layer of the earth, stone and rock, from the golden sandstone to an eventual slate-blue rock. Then the water was found.

The mind of man was able to locate and source the water of life. I believe he has the power to help the Earth to heal herself, can he suspend his ego to listen to the voice of intuition within which will tell him the way...He must listen to what his breath is telling him...

HAS HE TIME?

Chapter 41

SEX AND SOME
REFERENCES TO FOOD

WHEN I STARTED WRITING this book five years ago, I was seventy-seven, have now hit the great eight-0. After writing it painfully by hand, and even more painfully learning computer word-processing, I come to the chapter you might feel least appropriate to my age, that of Sex.

I understand that the three most powerful instincts are the maternal, self-preservation and reproductive (sex). I do not in any way underestimate the power of the latter, nor the problems of keeping it under control during the years when it is at its strongest, mid teens to early thirties. During those years the more tense we are, the stronger may seem to be our sex drive, with a need for satisfaction sometimes at any cost to another person. Tension relief sex gives little relief, since our basic tension almost immediately demands that relief once again. Sex as a result of such an *appetite* leaves someone feeling unsatisfied and often depressed, even if the crave has lessened.

All tense people breathe wrongly, and are more likely to use sex in a wrong way, like binge eating.

Someone who is fairly calm is less likely to 'use' sex as an addiction, and more likely be able to enjoy its beauty in the right way, at the right time, and with the right person.

It therefore makes sense from a sexual perspective to breath correctly and discover the way of calmness, which is more likely to lead to more meaningful sexual relationships. Satisfaction then involves the mental and spiritual as well as the physical, leading to a sense of wholesome well-being.

As the chapter headings came into my mind, intuitively day by day, their contents came into focus in my mind, as if I was then ready to address that issue. So here I am finally writing about sex in my ninth decade!

I am sure you have heard the saying, 'if youth only knew, if age only could,' which might reflect the unspoken thoughts of many older people, as they ponder the highs and lows of their earlier lives, particularly with regard to their love relationships and sexual partners.

Satisfaction of the sexual appetite and the satisfaction provided by food can seem to be the two priorities of our memories of youth; the former giving way to the latter as we grow older.

Today's emphasis on food often reminds me of our much loved and respected GP, who delivered two of my children, and remembered the exact dates of their birthdays, even years later. When we moved twelve miles away to a more rural village, he said that he wanted to keep us on his books, because he loved the high hill road he would have to travel to visit us. It gave such a wonderful view of the valley of the River Tweed. On a moonlit night a most beautiful sight, with the river winding like a silver ribbon below.

He got the chance with the home birth of my baby daughter at midnight, but she pipped him to the post by ten minutes. Still he got the drive! Sorry, I deviate. In the light of NHS bureaucracy these days, I wanted to share such a GP gem with you.

Returning to the main focus of this paragraph, our doctor's attitude to food has always remained in my memory. He said he never bothered much about food, as long as he had access to bread and cheese. I share the bread and cheese pleasure with him, and funnily enough read recently that it was the staple diet of my favourite Saint, Kentigern or Mungo of the Borders and Glasgow. Both humble and simple men.

At present both nationally and internationally, we seem to have an over-absorption with food and sex. Both important appetites with which we seem to be over preoccupied.

They both need to be restored to a wholesome and acceptable place in our lives as *spiritually* based appetites. Their disharmony exists as starvation in many countries, along with horrific sex-related diseases. Given the stocks and food stores of the affluent nations, and our obscene waste of food there need be no world hunger. The misuse of the sexual instinct is also there for all to see, not only in the AIDS epidemic, but in all too frequent reports of paedophilia and pornography.

Regarding food. The present over-concern with what we put into our mouths and stomachs is revealed as a national and international addictive over attention to edible substances. Much of which has been proved to be less than beneficial in terms of health.

On the other hand we have the other extreme of those who are so over-conscious of nutrition, that one can get bored hearing them dominate a conversation with their food fads, over-precise diets, and warnings that unless we eat such and such and avoid the other, we are in extreme anger of early demise. The words of our old beloved doctor often come into my mind on such occasions, and his simple preference for bread and cheese.

I have found that the most loving and interesting people I have met agree with the saying that 'it's not the importance of what goes into your mouths, as what comes out.' They thoroughly enjoy their food, and appreciate its importance, without belonging to either of the two extremes I have mentioned.

I must concede, there is a positive advantage in our increasing awareness of the essential balance of proteins, fat, fibre, vitamins, minerals and carbohydrates in our daily diet. This is the first time in history that there has been a national attempt to educate the whole population in food values. By contrast it does seem distasteful to me to watch and hear the anger and blasphemies emanating from some TV programmes, where the food is considered so precious, but the verbal vibrations given off by the chef would render any dish they made for me to be sullied by a less than pleasant energy. Anger and uncouth words should not be present where food is prepared. As living energy food can pick up vibes from negative people. It may look pleasant and appetising, but a sensitive person will not be nourished by it. Incidentally animals know exactly what kind of food they need. Are we less than the animals?

The statement 'if something isn't spiritual it isn't.' applies to food and its preparation. Food lovingly prepared nurtures in more than the accepted way.

This spiritual rule applies to any action we take, every way in which we use our energy, every thought we have. It also includes the sexual dimension. Anything that is not spiritual can have no positive effect on life. By spirituality I mean thinking and acting from the deepest truth within yourself. It does not mean belonging to any religion. I don't think it matters to God if you have a belief in any particular religion. In applying the above yardstick to anything we do, if we breathe correctly we possess an invisible sure-fire compass that is safe to steer by, you don't need to know your destination, it will be shown to you. The way may seem sometimes difficult, but it is also often delightful, chuckly and hilarious, don't kid yourself that Higher Power has no sense of humour. An alchemy becomes available which evaporates apparent disasters, those words constantly come to mind, 'don't sweat the small stuff, it's all small stuff,' as we are given the right and acceptable solution to our problems. If we don't choose this path, we will find some incorrect alternative to avoid facing up to our true spirituality, and go backwards instead of forwards. We never stay still.

Misuse of sex and food are two of the commonest erroneous *solutions* to spirituality avoidance. I am not speaking of spiritual sex or food satisfied from a spiritually chosen need. We all have to eat, and reproduction is a natural instinct. No one can deny the power of these two instincts: (a) to stay alive, and (b) to reproduce the species. I do believe however that good food, and good sex should be beautiful experiences.

I have read that before empires crumble their demise is frequently accompanied by orgies of greed and sexual depravity (the Nero complex). The British Empire as such has certainly become a fact of the past. I hope I don't sound prudish if I see all around in our culture, the signs of gluttony and depravity, the wrong use of sex and food. Such signs surround us, in cities, towns, rural areas. We are bombarded with shoddy press and media titillation with a sexual or gastronomic content, totally in conflict to a wholesome life-style, but totally geared to the profit market.

Our appetites for sex and food are meant to be allied and subject to the beauty, discipline and laws of nature which beats to the loving Alpha rhythm, yet on all sides our senses are being constantly assaulted by the opposing obscenity of trivia which must cause confusion of standards to the younger generation for whom we bear responsibility. They are being endlessly assaulted by the rhythm of perpetual, Beta the stress and disease-making vibration, which appears to portray an over-indulgence in sex and food as the right way to exist.

The ever rising presence of sexual diseases and obesity in our young must be a profound and urgent sign that change has to happen in how we deal with those two basic life appetites of food and sex. The motivation for change can only come from adults.

We have all the intellectual knowledge we shall ever need about the physical construction of the reproductive and digestive systems.

Excessive consumption of food might seem to be the primary reason for obesity, and the knowledge that weight loss *can* be achieved by a reduction in food-consumption, but we know that all too often when weight loss is achieved in this way, there is soon a return to the original obese condition. The *cause* has not been tapped.

Giving ourselves excessive food is a second-rate form of loving ourselves, which as a therapist I have found invariably directly relates to a less-than-loving parental relationship in childhood. Such a deprivation, also constitutes a spiritual withholding, a non-material starvation, which represents insecurity and vulnerability. It creates an urgent need for a compensatory alternative for the child's primary security has been violated. To a child food also represents security, and so eventually it sees no alternative than to draw to itself a material form of security which it perceives unconsciously as the only defence possible. to provide some sort of satis-factory protection.

Just as with food obesity, I believe we are nationally in a sexual obesity crisis, where the wrong use of an all-powerful instinct needing to be recognised and respected as such, is being debased and abused. The shocking disease statistics, and stark figures revealed by computer records of child sexual abuse and paedophilia numbers, are an unacceptable proof of a national collective malfunction. Without the colossal problem of Aids.

As individuals we have to become ill, physically or emotionally, in order to recognise that our minds and bodies are sometimes trying to speak to us. Our intellect may understand the problem, but it is only the spirit that can find a permanent way out of our distress.

One heartening factor in all this darkness is that many people are finding a way, *The Way* to heal themselves, despite the needles, knives, tablets, and often second-rate counselling offered by the NHS and other caring services. These are not yet ready to accept that the only solution has to be a spiritual one, they do not have the words or the training, or in most cases have not walked the way of enlightenment. Otherwise they would be enlightened. I have met so many people who have experienced healing of food and sexual addictions and enlightenment through correcting their *breathing,* despite years of expensive and unsuccessful exposure to the professionals trained in their intellectual halls of learning.

These people represent beautiful points of light now illuminating others, because they have self-healed through the power of correct breathing, pulled themselves out of their own spiritual health crisis, and now know *the way.* The need for food and sex reverts to Nature's laws of balance.

For many who have self-healed by correct breath, the use of their sexual instinct had been previously out of control, with multiple sexual encounters, and the conviction that this was the only way to feel successful or good while being forced eventually to admit the hollowness of their existence.

The sexual hollowness in which millions exist reminds me of one of the most unusual and interesting books referring to the primal life instinct. Many years ago I discovered an old book which contained no author's name, but was written by a lady. I say lady, because the descriptions in this book made numerous references to a life-style applicable to almost a century ago, in which only this word would have been used to describe a female writer. She was no modern woman in any sense of the word. The book was called

Your Hands can Help to Heal You, probably a forerunner of many books on this subject now on the market. Yet this is a book with a difference. It contains almost visionary insights about the fullest implication of correct breathing, which I have read nowhere else.

The book tells how the author, a private governess and educational coach, discovered over a period of years that she was able to heal herself of a number of quite serious physical illnesses by the placing of her hands over the afflicted area and using her breathing to bring energy to the area. The result was that healing took place, without medical intervention.

A chapter entitled 'What I Have Found So Far', discusses her convictions in the following words:

> I found too that the movement of breathing arises in the centre of our body just behind the sacrum. (My friends at the School of Dancing in the South of France first introduced me to this centre.) This is a wonderfully liberating breath, its position (breathing centre) near our sexual organs is, I believe why humanity suffers from an overdose of what appears to be sexual urge [*see diagrams on pages 72-73*]. We are, in reality prompted, influenced and moved by this region of this centre of our body, and we mistake this urge as coming from the nearby sexual region. When we have regained the consciousness of breathing from this centre, we will be liberated from the over-attention to sex, and from the misery, sorrows and misunderstandings that it creates.

I have found words of such common sense in no other present-day book, despite its publication early in the last century. I believe that science and its marvellous discoveries have masked by their very intellectualism, vital and sensible information which if properly understood could cure many of the social and addiction problems which are globally destructive. It would take an intelligent, unbiased and intuitive breakthrough by the scientific mind to comprehend, and a universal understanding of its truths.

Of course the non-commercial aspect of air as a solution might not be an attraction to the pharmaceutical industry, because air is free. If they could commercialise it, they would.

The younger generation desperately needs a different yardstick from the attitudes and images presented by press, TV and constant barrage of commercial advertising, if we are not to perpetually advocate ad nauseum the abuse of food and sex as a desirable norm. Not to protest is to comply.

We have more or less moved out of the oppressive Victorian era of excessive prudery in relation to all things sexual, in those days seen as a rather nasty and furtive act. The pendulum now seems to have swung in the opposite direction, where anything goes, anything is acceptable, but most of the semi-pornographic material bombarding us from all sides seems to be produced by those with a sniggering-school-boy attitude still mentally stuck in defiance mode against our Victorian forbears. As if they were getting away with being naughty, and still giving the impression that sex is coarse and not to be mentioned.

Our attitude towards sexuality still has to mature; why do we think maturity needs to be boring and without fun?

Any day of the week the evidence of immaturity is revealed in the media; nude photos in the desk of a senior official which leads to dismissal. Page three nudes in national newspapers which must have passed some censor, (how and why?) and the pornographic films obtainable through TV channels. Always debasing the female, which by default debases the male.

No one would wish to go back to Victorian attitudes towards sex, but we still have to enter the golden era of knowing how to appreciate such a beautiful process in a

wholesome way. It was created by Higher Power. I am no
Mary Whitehouse, but we have yet to learn how to re-train
the devil that we have created, and the right joyous use of its
awesome power.

As we become sexually active, there are numerous choices
we make in the way we handle this so-powerful urge. As
adolescents we read of the hardened paedophiles, prostitution
providers and users, the rapist, the supposed abstaining
priest, multi-sex gymnasts. We also see as a contrast happily
married young or older couples. The one common factor
is the power of the urge, and the way in which it seeks satisfaction in the expression of such a power. The emotionally
immature, whether business man, priest or woman, will seek
immature outlets, whatever their so-called respectability in
the community. I have found that wherever the breathing
pattern is badly deficient and limited, the sexual outlet
chosen will be some form of deviancy which goes against the
laws of Nature, even if not seen as criminal.

We often think of sexuality as arriving at puberty, but this
is really the outward manifestation or ripening of a process
which has been going on since birth. Obviously from a basic
point of view the prime purpose of all the different species
is the regeneration of that species. That being so, it must be
accepted that every day of our growth is sexual.

Each day from day one adds its own meaning to this jig-
saw. We don't suddenly become capable of sexual activity at
the age of twelve or thirteen, the energy of nature has ensured
that each of the thirteen times three hundred and sixty-five
days of that formative time constitutes an important minute
growth spurt into our cellular reproductive system. You
might thus say that we are a sexual being from day one.

Any intense trauma experienced by a growing organism
during its period of growth inevitably threatens its survival,
and unless the absorbed shock is able to be reversed or thrown

off, that shock will be trapped within the system and cause a block in maturity, including sexual maturity. Never noticed by the carers of the young infant or growing child, it creates a stunting shock of limited or severe degree, affecting the organism in all parts of its being.

The resulting affected growth upsets the ability of the growing infant to carry out its purpose according to the perfect laws of nature, including sexuality.

There is still the need to function, to biologically complete growth, but because of the block, that function will be less than perfect. Usually the malfunction is not picked up by those in charge of the child, in fact even if noticed, there would be a lack of knowledge of any corrective action.

Given even the barest knowledge of the harm done to little children in our society, the malnourishment of body, mind, and emotions, the violence, addictions and perversions, we must acknowledge that something far wrong has happened to those who are involved in such diseased activity.

That *something far wrong*, I am one hundred per cent convinced, would have occurred in the early years of life of most of the people, described as addicted to food or sex. It will have been caused by early deep shock or trauma. It has resulted in the inability to experience the natural joy of life and loving. This block also exists on a national scale, and part of its symptom will be the deviated energy of natural sexual or anal activity. When energy cannot find a correct and natural outlet, it takes another path, but because it is blocked energy it will take an unnatural alternative.

Please do not assume that I think everyone with blocked or stagnant energy always uses it in a deliberately aberrant way, but the other alternative is its inward mutation in some form of physical or mental illness.

Our society creates sexual monsters from childhood onwards, they do not suddenly present themselves as adults.

Within our cities, towns and villages walk hundreds of thousands of individuals with disturbed sexual function, such unhappy people, whose misery could be greatly alleviated by corrective breathwork. Such work brings the instincts and hormones into a self-regulated discipline, and releases the creative instinct which can change lives and even lead to a more normal sexually satisfactory life. I know, I have seen it happen.

Having said that, those who walk among us with immature sexual time clocks, who Society labels as evil, and receive lifelong labels as outcasts of society, are still human beings usually once sinned against. I loathe the sin, but increasingly understand how the sin originated. The sin is a collective sin, an inability to understand our own nature and the nature of man. 'The proper study of man is man.' We have hardly turned the first page, so obsessed are we with materialism and the god of Science. We need to divert some of that energy into the study of man and his nature, in relation to the natural science of breath.

I have hinted that sexual balance can be restored, and remain convinced that it can be done by restoring the correct function of breath. You ask how I can be sure. I am sure because I have worked with hundreds of people over several decades, whose personal life-styles included a variety of unhappy sexual choices. Many involved the need for repetitive sexual release totally unrelated to a happy relationship. A sexual addiction. The pattern can be seen in both sexes, and seems to be the only known way to resolve tension. In all these cases, the teaching of correct breathing eventually restored a more wholesome balance in sexual need. I have never yet found a situation of sexual imbalance *which was not accompanied by a respiratory imbalance.*

The body is a powerful engine, and when the engine is unable to function correctly, it can be brought back into harmony by expert knowledge, just as the expert breathing knowledge residing within each individual can be re-primed to restore smooth function.

The apparent out-of-control sexual organic function then seems to be returned to a harmonised pattern by a balanced vibratory action of correct respiration. I have seen it happen so many times, together with the restoration of physical, mental and emotional harmony which is the natural result of correct breathing recovery.

Sexual abstinence can then be an attainable choice, where creativity is unrestricted until the right partner arrives, which seems to happen naturally when a person is functioning in balanced mode.

I am positive that many unsatisfactory marriages are entered into for the questionable satisfaction of legalised sex, which constitutes a form of legalised prostitution. The participants are invariably spiritually incompatible, an undercurrent of conflicting personal vibration gradually intensifies, and divorce usually follows. The time factor in this unholy alliance is usually influenced by the unspoken thought. 'Where else can I go for sex and how can I do without it?' Risking going out into the unknown without the security of the *sex at any price* blanket is to risk going into a physical and mental downslide which could end in depression, another name for blocked creativity.

Correct breath will avoid this downslide. I am not suggesting that changing such relationships is easy, it is not always easy to change long term habits, but we can rebalance our lives much more effectively if we are not controlled by the nameless fears and tensions of restricted respiration.

Creativity is the recognition and expression of our true selves in a beneficial creative form, whatever form that might take. Sex for the sake of sex is merely a comfort stop to avoid the risk of being our true selves. The appropriate term for that activity is carnality. Don't get me wrong, spiritual sex can be hilarious, is beautiful and immensely satisfying, leading to enhanced joy in being alive. Of course the other name for spirit is breath, and those who breathe correctly are more likely to enjoy life-long harmonious sex-lives.

During the period when I was daily integrating information about the importance of corrective breathing, I became more and more aware of the need for training schools in the subject. There is a bottomless potential for such student educational facilities, and the need is urgent.

I gradually realised that all my stressful clients automatically became students of breathing, and in that context they became their own teachers. All that was necessary was for them to re-start the respiratory mechanism which was already programmed at birth to be their internal teacher, for it was linked to that Higher energy which gave them life. Intense subsequent interest in the process led to the discovery of a virtually total lack of Educational training courses on correct respiration, our primary function, without which all else is subservient.

The dialogue between the carnal self and the true self was rather like this: – *Carnal self:* 'I can't, give me this, give me that.' *True self:* 'Yes I can and I will trust that I will receive help, but I have to take the risk first, of listening with trust.' The Correct Breath gives us courage to take the risk, to trust that breath to attract sexual harmony into our lives, to trust 'going without' sex for a time. Then amazing things start to happen, in the form of inexplicable coincidences and opportunities which as another writer put it 'no one would have dreamed could have come their way.'

The wise inner voice also gives hints about improving our breathing bit by bit, never too much at one time. Eventually however we recover the true and urgent instinct to inflate the lungs with each breath from the base of the body between the pelvic bone and the navel. Then taking that expanding movement up to the lobes of the lungs in one eventually easy movement, without muscular tension preventing the expansion.

This natural movement dilutes the unnatural urgency of the out of balance sexual drive.

While still present, that muscular tension indicates fear in mind and emotions, and a temptation to revert back to the quick-fix of carnal casual sex.

As the self-stabilising power of correct breath and inner-listening kicks in, the individual makes many important and positive decisions about putting their lives back on course, *without external counselling telling them how to do so. An internal counsellor has been discovered.*

Another interesting fact that has emerged during this period of re-balancing has been that the client often decided to become vegetarian (i.e. not eating anything with a face!). Food binging then became a thing of the past. A growing interest in natural food, fruit, vegetables emerged, again without my prompting, leading to the solution of weight problems.

Just as the unconscious mind recorded the thought patterns which separated us from our unique central core of our own truth and integrity, so correct breathing unlocks the necessary information that restores to us the intuitive skill of right thought and action.

When you take right action for yourself through the recovery of this self-wisdom, you cannot hurt anyone else, because you are listening to your heart, your core of love. Naturally some people to whom we have appeared as a caring parent or helpless child which allowed them or us to assume the helpless or parental role, may not like our changes, accusing us of a variety of neglectful behavioural actions. Do they have a problem with you being true to yourself, or do they *need* you to vampire upon? You are not responsible for the changes they may have to make in order to be true to *themselves*, and if they choose not to, it is not your problem.

We cannot have healthy sexual relationships until we are true to ourselves, standing up straight, instead of leaning-on or being leaned upon. You are not allowed during this process of change to feel sorry for yourself or others, but you must have compassion.

The imbalance in so many relationships leads to increasing disharmonies, often internalised, conflict and stress, deceitful ways to escape the consequences of wrong action. Eventually such disharmony can result in unnatural behaviour, health breakdowns, food addictions, sexual perversions, abuse.

In seeking for a release from deeply unhappy partnerships, millions of pounds are spent on numerous solution searches, counselling, health consultations, anything but the one process which would work its silent healing on the participants. None of the literature which I have read about sexual problems has suggested that correct breathing could possibly help to resolve them. The trouble is we see the problem in its enormity, when the intellectual mind needs to wrap itself around the fact that what works for one, could work for the majority in most cases.

We have to face up to the fact that millions are suffering from self-imposed oxygen starvation, in the same way that we can starve ourselves of food. Yet our sophisticated society has been indoctrinated to be blind to the magnitude of a simple solution to an horrendous global problem. No one suffering from Aids can breathe properly. It is not the Aids that produces the breathing problem, but the breathing problem which weakens the immune system and creates the susceptibility to diseases such as Aids. The breathing problems exacerbate the drive for tension release, *temporarily* eased by sexual activity, as I described earlier in this chapter.

With correct breath as with no other instinct, 'To hear is to forget, to see is to remember, to do is to know.' Don't undervalue these words until you have healed your breathing.

The *doing-ness* of correct breathing has to be experienced, retraining and diligent repetition of the exact pattern over a period, as much as any other skill. With this repetition comes dawning understanding, interest, natural enjoyment of just being yourself without props provided by others. Addictions such as food or sex lose their influence. We are already equipped by nature to do this, and as we progress we unravel Nature's most beautiful secrets.

In her book *The Secret of Childhood*, Maria Montessori records:

> As civilisation has evolved in favour of the adult, a child is left without social defences. To him were reserved only the material, moral or intellectual resources of the family into which he was born, and if in his family there were no such resources, the child has to develop in material, moral and intellectual misery without Society feeling the smallest responsibility for him.
>
> The State, so rigorous in demanding official documents and meticulous preparations, and which loves to regulate everything that bears the smallest trace of social responsibility, does not trouble to ascertain the capacity of future parents to give adequate protection to their children, or to guard their development. It has prepared no place of instruction or preparation for parents.
>
> As far as the State is concerned, it is enough for anyone wishing to found a family to go through the marriage ceremony. In view of this we may declare that Society from the earliest times has washed its hands of those little workers to whom nature has entrusted the task of building up humanity.'

The above words were written many years ago. In view of the way we treat children these days, the figures of neglect, cruelty and abuse, regularly recorded in the media, are we much further forward some ninety years later?

As the sentencing judges give vent to a rational and understandable hatred and venom on the sexual offenders we isolate, condemn and tag, all we are still doing is to continue to remain ignorant of the basic laws of the natural growth and true needs of the child.

The terrible symptoms of society's disregard and ignorance of the healthy sexual growth of the child appear in the courts of our land daily, or are hidden in the dark houses where horrendous sexual abuse of *countless* children never comes to light. Until we understand and accept our collective responsibility for ensuring our children can breathe without fear, the symptoms of the results of diseased breathing will multiply, and so will sexual aberrations and obesity.

Returning to obesity, if you observe the movements of a really obese child or adult, it is obvious that they reflect a deep internal imbalance. Some say that the layers of fat represent a desire to build a protective wall around the personality, as the true self is feeling so bad about itself, that it must hide away and not be seen.

In our apparently limitless and expensive dedication to the word *research,* I believe it has now become the alternative to the cheaper use of our natural intelligence that Science seems to have side-tracked into oblivion.

For various reasons unless it is to protect present medical procedures of over-intervention in natural birth I cannot understand why researchers do not use their intelligence to compare statistics of obesity with the historical facts which must be available. That is the birth story of groups of children brought into this world by Caesarean section, forceps, breech, epidural, premature delivery, etc. Whether they were breast or bottle fed. How soon the cord was cut after birth, time spent in an incubator. What were the respiratory patterns of the parents?

I think such research figures would produce startling results as to the source of the obesity, and the concentration on overeating would be seen as a symptom rather than the cause.

Breathing is the primary function of the body. We can live for weeks without eating, and for days without drinking, but when we stop breathing for a few minutes, we stop living. And right here is the most neglected spot in the entire health field. Why is that so? First ignorance, second the claim of science that man lives on what he eats; and third no one has yet found a way to commercialise air and breathing.

To an intelligent unprejudiced person who can and does think, the information contained in this work may seem simple.

But it is the fundamental simplicities that are always so difficult to accept, because they are so very simple, and, therefore unbelievable on that account.

Man's Higher Consciousness - Professor Hilton Hotema

★ ★ ★

HOW WE USE OUR BREATH IS THE SIMPLEST
SOLUTION OF ALL, TO CURE OUR OBSESSION
WITH SEX AND FOOD.

Chapter 42

CANCER

I HAVE JUST been re-reading a book by that wonderful woman Louise Hay. For those who have not read any of her books, it would be well worth the effort to purchase one. Most of Louise Hay's books include a glossary of all the common illnesses, and the negative mental mind-set which precedes an illness. An opposite positive mind-set is suggested before the illness can be reversed. Louise Hay has proved personally that an altered mind-set cured her of cancer, so her work must be taken seriously.

The mind-set which seems to accompany cancer is 'deep hurt, secret or grief eating away at the self'. The healing thought-set to reverse the condition is 'to lovingly forgive and release the past. I choose to fill my world with joy. I love and approve of myself.'

In my experience Louise Hay is always spot-on. In fact whatever the illness, I think love and approval of oneself is a necessary factor in all self-healing. We may recall someone we know and loved who had been diagnosed and died from cancer, and disagree with Louise Hay. People who are sick can often put on an *apparently* cheerful even angelic appearance, which hides their true feelings, and deludes their carers.

Numerous media channels tell us that bowel cancer is the second most common form of the disease. It does not surprise me. We are told that at some future date all people over a certain age are to be issued with a testing kit, which could pick up symptoms of a possible health breakdown from bowel cancer. It can take ten years or more from the first minor signs of cell malfunction, to the diagnosis of a life-threatening attack. We frequently forget this fact.

Often when I watch interviews on television, I can hear the tension in the speaker's voice, indicative of tight throat muscles, a tension which originates in the lower stomach muscles, and can also be observed as a tight holding-in at the area of the solar plexus, which is said to be related to the throat. I have never met anyone with tension at the solar plexus level, immediately below the rib cage, who did not have a 'tight' voice, and eventual health problems, including cancer.

The 'gravelly' voice of the hero in many novels, is not to me the sign of strong masculinity, but that of a repressed child.

It never fails to surprise me that I can now pick up the slightest nuances of voice tension, and know which bodily muscles are involved. Although I am not particularly musical, the skill resembles the ability of a musician to pick out a wrong note in an otherwise harmonious performance.

I am not a singer, nor can I play a musical instrument. I love beautiful music which often resonates in my mind during the day. It is distressing to hear the human voice producing a sound like a knife scraping an enamel plate, which is all too common in modern entertainment. More so, when I know that the person who is vocalising such disharmony is severely restricting their breathing, therefore their blood circulation and cell oxygenation. The pre-requisite for cancer.

The fast beta-speed of sound, which passes for much modern music, has a vibration which is in opposition to the vibration of nature and to that extent has to me a *cancerous* sound.

Muscular tension in the lower stomach area is a very common symptom. It amazes me that health education authorities fail to give out public advice about the kind of physical symptoms which can lead to bowel cancer. For instance I have consistently noticed a poor breathing pattern which I believe to be the most important clue. This appears to be invariably disregarded in medical check-ups. You hear endless criticism of unhealthy life-styles, I think the most unhealthy life-style is incorrect breathing.

If this most potent danger signal is perpetually overlooked, it is small wonder that frequently a person is diagnosed, with only weeks or even days of life left.

The means of prevention are always within our grasp, yet is medical training too much centred on a needle, knife or tablet as being the only weapons in a doctor's armoury? Elsewhere in this book I spoke of a doctor at a conference say those very words, with some bitterness. 'Take away my tablet, knife and needle, and I have nothing.' This is no criticism of doctors but a deep regret that medical training has receded so far from a natural diagnostic ability which needs to be the first and most important aspect of medical skills. Distorted breathing is the ever-present factor in cancer sufferers.

Correct respiration is, I believe, the number one diagnostic skill essential for a really good doctor, but doctor training in this aspect of health is virtually minimal. I have this information from a doctor involved in research in a well-known teaching hospital.

Correct respiration sets the 'needle gauge' for perfect health.

When the doctor I have quoted spoke of having nothing to offer his patients apart from needles, knives and tablets, I believe it is because he knew there was a vital 'something' missing from his training. This something is, I am sure, the spiritual aspect, for in my experience when the spirit is not present the body degenerates. The word *spirit* also means breath, and by the same criteria unless the breath is joyfully present, as in correct breath, the body degenerates. Because seventy per cent of bodily toxic waste is excreted from the out-breath, incorrect breathing results in us becoming toxic to ourselves.

I have quoted elsewhere the fact that three per cent of our bodily waste is excreted as solids, seven per cent fluids, twenty per cent perspiration, and as mentioned above seventy per cent through our exhalation. Therefore if the main orifice for the discharge of respiratory waste is inefficient because of poor breathing, all the other discharge outlets are affected because of lack of oxygen, the factor which acts as the catalyst in the elimination process.

A biological factor in nature is that, when oxygen is not present in plant life which includes human beings, rot or a fungal friendly environment sets in, and by inference cells cannot stay healthy. The speed and intensity of that deterioration depends on the presence or non presence of oxygen, and efficient excretion of CO_2.

Do not forget that the trigger for the intake of oxygen is controlled by the brain through the power of thought and breath. I am suggesting that cancer, like all illness, may be brought about or healed by the power of thought. Thought comes in two levels, positive or negative; negative thought depresses the breath, and positive thought expands it. That is how Louise Hay healed herself.

The brain therefore has to re-train the body to respond to thoughts of correct oxygen use. Breath or oxygen also means spirit, so we have work to do in re-training the lung muscles to then allow the lungs and the mind to accept spirit-breath and send it round the body. If breath, spirit or oxygen circulates round the body correctly, it gets into the deteriorating areas and breaks up the toxic rot, allowing it to be excreted, and healing repair to begin.

I fully believe that cancer, particularly in its early stages and even when more fully advanced, can be totally cured. In fact it has been proved time and again that miraculous cures have occurred. The medical profession does not appear to publicise such cures, but I think that it is time that we removed the feeling of horror of the fearful black cloud that surrounds the word 'cancer'. I am reminded of the phrase that 'It is not what sort of disease a person has, but what sort of person has the illness.' In my vocabulary breathing poorly is not a result of disease, but disease is the result of breathing poorly.

I have spent many years working with stressful people, quite often suffering from bowel malfunction or chronic constipation. My involvement was as a psychotherapist, but in almost all cases the re-teaching of correct breathing brought about an amazing improvement in the bowel problems. Oxygen or spirit is the great healer. I say that deliberately. Oxygen may be administered from an outside source other than by a person's respiration, and give a temporary boost, but like an alcoholic drink the improvement is temporary. If breathing is not functioning correctly, the problem returns.

I believe that without the normalisation of the respiratory function, many of my clients would have ended up as cancer patients. Yet where are they teaching cancer patients to breathe properly? Millions of money is raised from countless public efforts in aid of 'research' to produce yet another miracle drug, when the miracle drug is already free, on tap, yet the medical profession is not professional enough to know how to administer it, i.e. teach it.

The best use of a doctor's time may not be hours spent in the operating theatre, when the same amount of time teaching patients to breathe correctly as prevention, might have made an operation unnecessary, saved the use of the knife, needle and tablet, and probably ensured their disease-free future.

Many of the people who have come to me for help had been seeking NHS help for years, were on numerous tablets, yet it was only the correct use of Nature's gentle healing medicine, correct oxygen, which allowed them to finally become drug-free.

This healing inner touch of the fine energy of the breath goes where no needle, knife or tablet can penetrate, and bowel problems become immediately responsive to its influence.

I remember once again an extract from a book *Diary of a Friendship*, by that under-rated genius Wilhelm Reich, who said, 'in sudden fear we all hold our breath for the moment, some children have a lifetime of catching their breath and holding it. The sign of a well-reared child is its ability to breathe fully, it shows that it's not afraid of life.' I have never yet met anyone with any form of cancer who breathes correctly, so why is this not publicised by the researchers?

In my contact with those with cancer, (or any other illness physical or mental), I see the *child as an adult* still holding its breath. In holding our breath we restrict our highest potential, we can heal that restriction on our potential by freeing our breath. What abundance of potential desperately needed by the Universe lies imprisoned within the trapped lung tissue of those who hold their breath?

Cancer of the uterus, the prostate? The answer is *study the breathing pattern*. Any cancer, anywhere? *Study the breathing pattern*. Naturally of course we have to watch our own respiration at all times. Who is to teach you? Not many in our Health (?) Service are able to. Choose the healthy young baby who has not been born by elective Caesarean, breech, epidural or forceps delivery. *These* will probably already register a primal respiratory birth shock for those who can read the signs.

I have a news cutting which mentions the high instance of respiratory problems in young babies. I suspect that many others will go unnoticed, resulting in later-life illnesses. The mothers of many such babies will probably all exhibit restricted breath patterns themselves.

The life-destructive imprint of the fashion industry is to hold in the stomach which also means holding the breath. An abuse created and perpetuated by the immature aims of that industry whose leaders, I notice, also restrict their breathing. If they breathed correctly they would probably find higher outlets for their great creative gifts. They could even suggest better career choices even in the fashion world to the skeletal-like young bodies they persuade to display their flash-in-the pan extravaganzas.

At some point in early life, invariably in very early life, I believe those with later adult limited respiration have experienced fear, trauma or shock, which has not been able to be resolved by adult observation or understanding, so that the shock of the fear can be released. It is therefore trapped. Over the years this oxygen denial leads to muscular (mental) tension, impaired circulation, (also circulation of healing thought). Finally add the certain knock-on effect of cell mutation from oxygen starvation. The still prevalent cultural pressure not to show emotion or feelings provides the cement topping to the blocked energy.

Limit the vital force of life which has chosen you for your own unique way to express that force, and what is left but premature life termination, which inevitably ensues if we choose to block our personal life-force expression?

We can no more expect an engine to function without the fuel needed for its propulsion, than a human being to function without sufficient fuel, breath, the fuel of life. Society concentrates far too much on people who have food problems, without realising that all who have food problems first of all have breathing problems. Resolve the breathing problem, and the feeding or diet problem will solve itself naturally. All animals know what kind of food they require, they don't need other animals to tell them. Are we lower than the animals or less intelligent?

We are controlled by far more sophisticated rules of correct function than any space-ship, the trouble is that they are also so simple that we ignore them at our peril.

Whatever your social standing, wealth, or whether you are seen as a 'genius', limitation of the vital life force by oxygen starvation will inevitably result in disease. Cancer figures represent to me the number of people who are restricting their life force. What will it gain us if we are successful in the eyes of the world, yet die by the long-term suicide choice implied by breath anorexia?

The laws of combustion of the human engine are inexorable and unchanging. Restrict the breath and the human motor's function begins to malfunction.

I have just been watching a TV news coverage about a famous entertainer who has been operated on for breast cancer. From the candid camera of the TV screen I saw how she held in her breath. A factor apparently unrecognised by the *specialists*? All the fame, money and adulation could not guarantee freedom from this scourge.

Last week the name of another well-known celebrity hit the headlines for the same reason, last month another.

The frequency of disease of the reproductive system of male or female is often quoted. Cervical and prostate cancer is a nightmare for thousands. When you can read the oxygen deprivation 'signs' of the human body neither problem comes as a surprise.

As regularly as we read of another well-known person succumbing to cancer, so we also read of a cancer drug 'break-through'. Usually that's the last you hear of that particular miracle cure. Remember all drugs affect the brain, and the physical function controlled by that part of the brain. Also the circulatory link between them. All drugs have their side-effect, some more lethal than the original disease. It has often been reported that many people die from the side-effects of their medication rather than from the disease which the medication was supposed to cure.

Sometimes we read of an inexplicable recovery from cancer. Many who read this book will be familiar with the life and work of Louise Hay, mentioned earlier, who is admired by many thousands for her writings and workshops, all the more important, because she healed herself of vaginal cancer after being told by doctors that she only had months to live. She eventually interpreted the mental thought processes behind illness.

Her words are full of the positive thought patterns needed to reverse negative thoughts and behaviour which she realised were responsible for her own illness. Her full recovery marked the remarkable career which has also been inspired by her understanding of the pivotal part played by the mind breath in all illness.

We owe a great debt to pioneers such as Louise Hay.

So many people I have met who have asked for help with stress problems, have also suffered with physical afflictions. Time after time the physical problems began to improve as the breathing improved, the better circulation of oxygen to the cells being the healing factor. Often deep introspection into a prevailing life-style is required, many, in common with Louise Hay, involved earlier child abuse.

Guilt, lack of confidence, negative thinking, are as lethal as a poisonous snake bite in how they affect the physical system. They may take longer to take effect, but lethal they are. How we feel about ourselves as a person is such an important factor in our health, otherwise that health is constantly being undermined.

A person can be the belle of the ball. Always laughing and

smiling, doing good deeds, the life and soul of the party (often within the family such people are morose, uncommunicative, critical of others). The outside world, which is easily fooled, does not see the inner negativity, misery, lack of confidence, fear, never being really true to oneself. Often such a person dies what I call an angelic death, having projected their misery on their family, while being the sunshine martyr to the visitors. Am I being cynical? I don't think so, just observant. I have spoken to so many of the exhausted close relatives. Beneath the apparently split personality lies a frightened person, who has never faced up to their fears, or looked for the right sort of help. Unfortunately the right sort of help is so rarely available. Behind the facade lies the distorted breathing.

I repeat, behind all cancer I see *restricted breathing,* a reluctance to make friends with our true selves. Louise Hay's personal healing programme involved healing her breathing, and a detoxification process, which resulted in the doctors declaring her cancer-free after six months.

I remember reading about a woman who could give an accurate character analysis from a photograph, particularly the focus of the eyes. They say that if you have a person's photograph, and cover everything up except for the eyes, you get the impression of the baby's expression as it enters the world. I find this a useful therapeutic pointer, but more dramatic for me is to see a head and body photograph, because to the breath-trained professional it is possible to see where the breath or life-force is suppressed. This is sadly common in the young and glamorous men and women who we have chosen to entertain us or top the charts. Whatever their talents, all too often, their speaking voices are strangulated, they breathe out through the mouth, exhibit nasal breath block, and hold in the lower-lungs. The perfect symptoms for diseases such as cancer to develop in later life.

In women it is so often breast cancer. For many men, cancer of the prostate.

This then is the reliable formula for the development of cancer:

Restricted breathing = tense muscles
           = restricted circulation of the blood
           = lack of oxygen to the cells
           = malfunction or mutation of the cells
           = patches of eventual fungal growth due to oxygen
              starvation to larger and larger groups of cells.

These then create an anti-life energy force of their own, which is likely to result in cancer. The end result is breakdown of the organism, as communication between brain and body becomes separated, i.e. brain and body can no longer communicate in a friendly and natural way. The life-force is eventually withdrawn, and *lifelessness* ensues.

Cancer operations which remove cancerous growth remove the symptoms but not necessarily the cause. If the respiratory mechanism is not self-repaired, and because of that the auto-immune system strengthened, there is all too frequently a subsequent outbreak of cancer a few years later.

Changes in breathing lead to changes in thought and behaviour, which have to be life affirmative. The illness can often be a wake-up call for someone to look beyond the needle, knife and tablet to make friends with the real energy which regulates our health.

Once that friendship which was close to us in childhood is re-established, miracles can occur. Read Louise Hay.

Some years ago I attended a cancer conference in Coventry. The participants were mainly members of cancer groups from all over the country, together with doctors and other health professionals. This was at a time when so much information about breathing was falling into place in my understanding.

The talk that still stands out in my mind after more than twenty years was by a young mother who attributed her recovery from breast cancer to breathing training and relaxation, which she had received from an enlightened therapist. I still have a taped copy of her talk.

An article on breathing I have also kept for many years concludes that 'improved oxygenation however attained, will ensure that rogue cancer cells do not develop, and could be a significant factor in the prevention and treatment of the disease.'

Are we going to allow yet another generation of young girls to emerge into womanhood denied the preventative health education which could then ensure what I would prophesy as a dramatic drop in breast cancer?

The same process applies to our young boys, where healthy expression of feelings and emotion are still frowned upon in the cultivation of the macho image, and the idea that boys don't cry. So the upper lung area is suppressed as is also the heart emotional area. The fountain of energy created by full breathing rising between the pelvic bone and the navel is blocked at source, at the base of the body, risking later development of prostate cancer.

The three most powerful instincts are survival, maternal, and procreation of the species. As our culture continually denies recognition of the spiritual dimension, so we deny the spiritual meaning to our instincts, and degeneration of life inevitably results.

The word 'cancer' always reminds me of the saying

'WHERE NO TEARS FALL FROM THE EYES,
OTHER ORGANS WEEP.'

Chapter 43

HIGH BLOOD PRESSURE

THROUGHOUT THE YEARS I have heard from so many people who have reported a normalisation of high blood pressure after correct breathing re-training, that it no longer surprises me at all. They have also gained a new understanding and interest in their health. What does surprise me is the apparent lack of comprehension among the medical profession of what seems to me the obvious way to reduce this problem. Drug medication appears to be the order of the day, and yet even the medical pundits admit that virtually all drug medication has side effects.

Naturally I have never advised clients to come off their medication once they start to breathe correctly, but the fact is, there is now a growing aversion to medical drugs because of the side-effects. My clients gradually reduced their medication with the co-operation of their GP. When they are finally drug-free the medical profession take the credit, while paying no heed rather than a paternal figurative pat on the head when their patient tells them that it is the correct breathing that has enabled them to come off the tablets!

Recently I read a news article which told of a vaccine which tricks the immune system into neutralising a hormone that triggers the narrowing of blood vessels with ensuing increased blood pressure (it is likely to be about five years before it goes on the market!). Apparently about 125,000 strokes and heart attacks are caused by hypertension each year.

I assume that does not include the thousands and thousands of people who suffer from undiagnosed hypertension over many years, before the symptoms explode into disaster.

The staggering figure is quoted of apparently 25% of the population suffering from high blood pressure, the NHS spending about £866 million on hypertension drugs last year.

When I am approached by clients who suffer from stress, and often when taking a case history, they mention that they have a problem with high blood pressure. I always ask them to show me how they usually breathe, while standing, sitting and then lying down. Then we have a short discussion about the location of the lungs within the cavity of the body, in particular the situation of the lower and upper part of the lungs. I ask them to tell me where the largest and fullest part of the lungs is situated. Only about 20% of people give correct answers. I have even found student nurses are often incorrect, and a lot of them smoke, which I find quite distressing. Smoking almost automatically results in lung problems. I used to work near a nurse-training college, and it was alarming to see how many would be outside during break-times puffing away. Adjacent doorways deep in cigarette ends.

At this first interview I demonstrate the correct breath personally, and see if the client can copy this movement at least for a few breaths. Often someone says that they a bit dizzy, which usually happens after the first time or two, and reflects the effect of a little more oxygen on the brain. Incorrect breathing leads to brain starvation of oxygen, so it is not surprising to notice this symptom which disappears after one or two sessions. Depending on the client's ease of ability to breathe correctly, which often brings into use muscles which have not been used properly for a long period, I suggest that for homework they try practicing between 5 and 20 breaths once or twice a day. Preferably lying down comfortably with a reasonably heavy book placed over the lowest part of the abdomen to increase awareness of the importance of taking air into this lower and largest area of the lungs first.

I encourage them also to place a hand over the upper chest area at the same time, in order to notice its expansion as the upper lungs are then filled. Also only to breathe within the rate of a 5-20 recommended inhalation with which that they feel comfortable.

I make a relaxation training tape, repeating the information about the importance of correct breathing. Because I have been using this process for many years my brain is in a natural state of meditation most of the time, with the result that my brain rhythm is in an electrical frequency of Alpha/Theta. This helps the client to relax when the same vibration comes over on the relaxation tape.

Funnily enough I understand that a small child reflects a similar frequency pattern. I think this represents a state where we are 50/50 focused between our inner reality and the outer world. I believe that this same frequency maintained globally by the majority of people would dissipate most of our global problems, including the harm our culture is doing to children. It is the hyper-frequency of perpetual high Beta energy which causes harm to Nature, and also to the child who is so closely part of Nature.

The slowing down of the brain's hyper electrical frequency creates a feeling of calmness, the ability to think clearly and effectively, with right action directed from a feeling of love.

The result on someone with high or low blood pressure, causes a relaxation of muscles, improvement of blood circulation, natural clearance of toxins which is an important factor of correct blood circulation, as well as brain balance. The drop in high blood pressure is achieved naturally and becomes long-term, because sensible education is part of the process. The newspaper report that up to 25% of the population suffers from high-blood pressure represents a horrendous indictment of our stressful society and a reflection of its dis-ease.

From what I can gather the teaching of correct breathing is not part of medical training and from my own observations very few doctors breathe correctly, or can diagnose that symptom in their patients. Yet that is the prevailing symptom in most of the clients who have usually self-referred for breath training after years of dissatisfaction with a medically drug-induced life-style. You cannot teach what you do not practice.

If the medical diagnostic apparatus indicates that someone has a breathing restriction problem, I find that most patients are then put on a drug regime. This side-tracks the medical understanding and build-up of in-depth knowledge of the subject.

The fact that patients with depression or related emotional symptoms also do not breathe correctly is continually overlooked. The emphasis seems to be on the symptoms while the cause goes unremarked. As the doctor remarked 'take away my drugs, needle and knife, and I have nothing.'

I read a report recently that in the USA there are many thousands of respiratory therapists attached to hospitals and GP practices. This provision does not seem to be available in this country. In any case the link between breathing, mental health and emotional balance is so inextricably linked that I am sure a very special kind of respiratory therapist is required, indeed a new discipline. Those sufferers who try to discover someone who works in this way, discover that it is like looking for gold. The paternal 'pat on the head' by their GP is ironical when long-term problems disappear through respiratory correction, often like snow in quick thaw. Respiratory correction merits much deeper recognition by the medical fraternity. Teaching correct breathing is a precise art, encompassing as it does a deep and visionary expertise.

This is no superficial process, it requires as much respect as fine surgery. I can't wait for the day when the stranglehold of the 'easy drug solution' is loosened. The pioneering work of the late Dr. Claude Lum MB, FRCP, FRACP at Papworth and Addenbrokes hospitals, Cambridge should be studied, and his research with thousands of patients with high blood pressure, and chest, heart and stroke problems. He treated thousands of patients with these problems with correct breathing training, and recorded 75% free of all symptoms at twelve months, and 20% with trouble-free mild symptoms. His work requires intense study and international recognition, and I feel privileged to have met him, if only once. His wise and benign presence indicated a true physician who *lived* the breath. He also practised yoga.

The quick and easy issue of addictive medical drugs 'hook' an individual as surely as the sleazy drug culture we profess to despise.

I have never discussed their early life history with a sufferer from high or low blood pressure without both of us coming to accept that the origins of the problem invariably lay in an early distressing family scenario usually still denied by the family, which was the source of the problem. This had blocked communication on a healthy emotional level, leaving the growing child with a suppressed time bomb of blocked frustration seething within. Later even remotely similar situations will provoke a rush of emotional adrenalin held back by the childish fear of healthy communication. These result in an energy block in blood circulation, often leading to explosive behaviour damaging to relationships, *including the person's relationship with themselves.*

High blood pressure produces someone who is known to be constantly *on the boil,* or obviously suffering from suppressed irritation. The surrounding atmosphere is either explosive or charged with tension, in family, work or social situations, frustrating healthy creativity and pleasurable communication.

I believe that the early symptoms of blood pressure may also be sown in the womb or at birth. Much disturbed human behaviour is explainable, but impossible to prove. Working from therapeutic intuitive understanding creates a climate of trust and confidence, within which respiratory healing is expedited.

The *internalisation* of blood pressure symptoms creates a time bomb within the system. Due to emotional blocks the individual *implodes* the stress, high tension affects the flow of the blood, and vital internal organs become erratically oxygenated, particularly the heart, which can eventually lead to a heart attack. The latter is the eventual knock-on symptom of those who are constantly exploding. I mean of course irrational explosion, not the healthy expression of the many minor daily irritations to which we all give vent, and as quickly recover, as we let off steam in a healthy way.

Those with blood pressure problems may use other people's energy quite unintentionally to help keep themselves in an equable state. Behind all such relationships lies a balance of emotional blood-sucking and immaturity. It is difficult to sustain good relationships if the blood, and therefore the brain pattern of your companion, is in a constant state of turmoil.

I remember a former client with problems of high blood pressure telling me that his wife and family found him much easier to live with after he commenced breathing correction training, and family life more peaceful. The *knock-on* unhappiness effect on those who live with someone suffering from high blood pressure must be colossal.

We all have to accommodate the flak from other people's minor emotional limitations, as they do our own, but this strain of trying to cope with the symptoms of a friend or relative with a blood pressure problem can be a real burden. Time and again I have met a client with this symptom where the restricted breathing so obviously apparent to a correct breather is never discussed or recognised. The medication which is dispensed to chemically induce a better blood flow can never address the primal cause, which un-treated, remains as the constant initiator of the explosive problem.

Some of the physical effects of blood pressure problems are disruption of the acid/alkaline balance in the blood, lack of oxygen to the brain, digestive disorders, narrowing of blood vessels, increase in adrenalin the stress hormone. High blood pressure has been compared to an over-heated engine.

Once again we must return to the original cause of this over-reaction. Over and over again I have traced the problem to the powerful rage and fear which was unable to be expressed and therefore blocked by the child. In that situation the normal means of harmlessly releasing extreme emotion in a compassionate and understanding atmosphere provided by nurturing adults, was unavailable at an important developmental stage, particularly before the child had an adequate vocabulary to try to express its frustration.

Emotional pressure builds up within the child, but it has realised that no one understands, so the pain is stored within, layer upon layer as the years pass. The insensitivity of the adults is so often unintentional

In the first eight years or so the child has a built-in immune layer to protect itself against hurt, but when no breakthrough of understanding is reached by the adult, and the child's immune protective years are over, it may become a bully or a coward, be aggressive, or invite aggression.

The impact of respiratory re-training on a pre-teen child can act like a cooling breeze, the bully no longer needs to attack, and the frightened youngster finds a confidence which no longer creates a victim role. A young person between the age of 8 and 12 is still so close to nature within themselves, that corrective breath training by an understanding adult can achieve far more than numerous counselling sessions, and the impact will be long lasting. Blood pressure problems are unlikely in later life.

The end result of continual high blood pressure without natural release treatment such as that provided by respiratory re-training, can be fatal, as the heart and brain can no longer sustain the strain which resembles an overheated engine being constantly over-driven. The 25% population quoted by the media as high blood pressure sufferers is a truly frightening figure, all too often treated as a purely physical disorder, without mental and emotional support being given to the sufferer.

The 25% given is likely to be only the tip of the iceberg of those with potential symptoms.

The need for this support may be more understood than I have so far experienced amongst the health professionals, but the means to do so are considered too costly or time-consuming. Nevertheless I have seen time after time the vast improvement that occurs after six months of breath therapy. Comparing it to a lifetime of regular medical check-ups and medication, with all the side-effects, I have no doubt as to the preferential treatment.

The fantastically sophisticated procedures and knowledge by which we have learned to replace a faulty heart do not seem to be able to take on board the simple laws of teaching good respiratory practice, which should be available universally to act as a preventative brake and thus save enormous sums being spent to save a very few people, many of whose life-span still remains tragically short. Do our heart specialists lack the intelligence and vision to tackle the 25% at risk in our country, or is the simplicity of the remedy impossible for them to grasp?

I read once that it is not a question of what kind of illness a person has, but rather what kind of person has the illness. Probably all illness can be included in this statement.

Our crazy culture which worships intellect, concentrates this priority in the way education is delivered *to* children. They are sitting ducks and have no say in how we impose our priorities on them. In this process they become victims, increasingly unable to nurture themselves creatively and emotionally, as they are programmed to do by nature. Often the child who is too eager to please becomes the brightest in the class, the intellectual pincushion, accepting all that is pumped in from teachers and lecturers. You frequently see them, the 'yes' people, qualifying for the top jobs for which intellectually they are all too highly qualified, but their 'top job' may still leave them emotionally immature. They may often have power over a work-force of thousands.

The strain of keeping up a 'boss' front, eventually leads to a building up of inner tension the true responsibilities of leadership cannot be produced, because these come from the creative side of the brain, which was neglected because of the left brain intellectual demands of analytical and critical thinking of their educational training. Eventually the inflexibility of their mindset precipitates an explosion which occurs either outwardly if there is someone on whom the boss can safely unload the tension in the form of bullying behaviour, or internalised combustion which self-harms. High blood pressure is the most frequent eventual outcome.

Many people have either succumbed as one of the 25% victims, medically recorded, suffering from high blood pressure, or belong to the hidden pyramid of people either experiencing the early symptoms, or cooking them up. It is amazing to me how many escape.

A mature culture values intelligence, but it has to be tempered with spiritual and emotional maturity in order to comprehend the *cultural* problems of high blood pressure. No Super IQ rating or Double First University Degree can protect us from the emotional demands of the top job which comes with the contract, and it will not mention this hidden factor. However prestigious and financially rewarding the power position, our *emotional maturity* decides on the level of our blood pressure.

Worshipping the economic God of commerce and industry does not give us a passport into the hard-won arena of physical, mental and emotional health.

Sudden deaths on the golf-course or in sporting activities are clues pointing to the undiagnosed deterioration of health among the business exercise executives. Statistics of fatalities of this kind among young people are becoming worryingly common. Such instant fatalities are invariably preceded by years of unrecorded strain and respiratory limitation.

An increase in blood pressure problems and heart attacks in women within a wide age range has been recorded.

Young mothers are caught in a no-win situation trying to cope with the entirely natural needs of a young family, while often having to defuse the work-related strain imposed by an unnatural work framework on their husbands. Possibly women are more likely to internalise the symptoms of high blood pressure than men. For either sex the stress which is not healthily resolved, creates a knock-on strain on our three in one system, first mentally, then emotionally and finally physically, the material substance of the personality. The final illness is not always diagnosed as blood pressure, but I am convinced that there is no illness which is not primarily triggered by a problem in the pressure of blood circulation, and its partner, hyperventilation.

★ ★ ★

Has anyone carried out a sizeable research investigation into high blood pressure in the under 18s? The results could be revealing. Corrective respiratory training without drug medication would, I am positive, reverse the symptoms in a very short time.

BETTER STILL, SUCH TRAINING
WOULD BE FOR LIFE.

Chapter 44

ADDICTIONS

TWO DECADES AGO I wrote a little book about drug addiction, after several years working at the coal face of one of Glasgow's first voluntary drug centres in an old former workhouse beside the River Clyde. At the time I was a Councillor and Chairman of a social work committee in another region of Scotland. I was serving on a Children's Panel Committee, a way in which children in trouble or need were dealt with in a non-court setting by trained volunteers from the community, social workers and a legal assessor called the Children's Reporter.

I had begun to feel uncomfortable about the facilities available to children who were glue-sniffing, above all *why* the sniffing? At the time I had begun training as a psychotherapist, and became interested in brain function. Eventually I used to drive up to Glasgow to one of the first 'hands-on' drug centres, from my Borders home or a committee meeting, a 160 mile return journey several times a week, such was the intensity of my need to know.

The Centre was run by the Franciscans. It was my first experience of Glasgow, Catholicism, and drug users. Most of the latter were in their teens or early twenties. It was a tragic but sometimes hilarious experience, at no time was I afraid, at no time was my car vandalised as it sat without an alarm in the lane beside the Centre. The experience changed my life, and caused a quantum leap in my understanding about addictions of all kinds, for in addition to drug misuse we also saw many people with alcohol problems, addiction to medical drugs, and naturally virtually everyone smoked!

Such were my limitations at the time, that I did not see smoking as the addiction I now see it. Perhaps the fact that my father had been a heavy smoker persuaded me into an acceptance that I now find unacceptable. In fact I find it hard not to gag if I pass a smoker in the street who exhales virtually in my face as I pass by. My instinct recently is to blow the smoke back into the face of the smoker, except that it could be seen as an aggressive act, which I cannot condone. It is said that we must never attack, but it is ok to defend. I cannot work out if my returning the smoker's repulsive, harmful exhalation is a form of defence or attack!

Those two years, working at the coal face of the drug problems in Glasgow, formed the hub of a great learning curve of understanding about the source of addictions. I fell in love with Glasgow, its humour and tragedy, at a time when my personal life was at its lowest ebb. It helped me to empathise with the suffering, face up to solutions, and forced me to move on in my own life, a like meeting like in human pain. My own pain had nothing to do with material addictions, but when you take that work down to its root, any addiction seems to me to be based on fear, involving substitute habits of self limitation.

We cling to powerful negative thoughts and entrenched ideas which become a false foundation, until some life-crisis topples the building erected on an insecure base.

It is said that there is only one way to personal growth, it is like learning how to pass through the eye of a needle, there is only one way for us all. At the time it may seem too hard to bear, but facing up to that necessity is the experience which has to be faced by all those addicted to substance misuse or misuse of thought energy. This probably includes most of us in the Western world, also those in middle and far-eastern cultures. Any habit which substitutes an alternative life-style to the true path of the spirit is an addiction.

In becoming so closely involved with the tragic/comic face of Glasgow, and its walking wounded, I became unalterably convinced of the damage we do to our small children, the tender young plants who are the sole inheritors of our culture, the health of whom determines its survival. These walking wounded were once such small children. The only escapism which seems available to them are forms of addiction which alter the chemical nature of the brain fluids and cells, but from which there is no control over the symptoms of results. The short-term results form a dependence on an artificially created feel-good factor which in the long-term produces gradual health breakdown. It is hardly necessary to mention the sub-culture of vice surrounding the drug-scene, because the non-availability of a fix produces a manic desperation which may stop at nothing to ensure a fresh supply of toxic nirvana.

Culture has created a block on a young child's birthright, and its sense of wonder at the beauty of life which, when carried into adulthood, ensures an adult who will contribute nothing to the holistic health of the nation. It ensures the deterioration of that culture. No degree of economic wealth can reverse the disease.

The lessons I *had to learn,* you may consider really quite simple. They concerned the way we breathe, and its effect on balanced brain function. They revealed to me the appalling retribution we attract individually and collectively when we base our priorities on materialism. In so doing we fail to recognise that the same loving care and attention we have to give to a plant to bring it into blossom, governs the same unalterable laws we have to observe in order to raise healthy children.

I learned at that run-down old drug-centre, that everyone

matters, everyone is unique. Unless that uniqueness is recognised and nurtured in childhood, the child will grow up with a hollow and unfulfilled emotional centre, a sitting target for the drug that promises an instant but deceptive fix for the broken heart of the child within the adult, who has lost the path to joy.

We now have no alternative but to consider the needs of the global collective family.

In so doing we are being forced to contemplate the deep divisions between the cultures of East and West. We blame the East for the supply of the drug cancer encroaching on Western society, while we see and hear through the media horrific carnage inflicted in non-Western cultures by lethal weapons created originally in the West. An ironic swap of killer drugs for killer guns.

In Shakespeare's *Merchant of Venice* we read Shylock's dramatic words 'the evil that you teach me I will execute, and it shall go hard but I will better the instruction.' Words which seem to sum up neatly the East/West dilemma in which the world of man is locked, a nightmare which he has created.

Are we admitting that we know of no way, in which we can *reduce the need* for drugs? Some better way of living by which we are no longer in the power of drug-producing countries? If we are incapable of rearing non-addictive children, what are our survival chances?

To understand the source of the addictive disease, we have to ignore the nature of whatever *form* the addiction takes, because it merely constitutes any choice of behaviour or substance chosen by an individual in order to feel good, who cannot feel that emotion naturally.

★ ★ ★

THERE IS ONE UNALTERABLE FACT CONCERN-
ING EVERY PERSON WHO SUFFERS FROM ANY
FORM OF NEGATIVE ADDICTION, AND THAT IS
THAT THEY WILL ALSO BE SUFFERING FROM
RESTRICTED BREATHING. BECAUSE OF THAT
FACT THERE WILL ALSO BE AN IMBALANCE
IN BRAIN FUNCTIONING, WHICH MEANS THAT
ONE HEMISPHERE OF THE BRAIN WILL BE
OVER-DOMINANT.

i.e: The left analytical side of the brain is usually dominant,
preventing the right creative 'sense of self' side from being
able to express itself.

Whatever the specific imbalance, the nervous system will
be aware of this at some deep level, and struggle to redress
the balance by whatever means it can find. In the drug world
a temporary fix will achieve this, although there is no control
over natural balance or behaviour. Nevertheless the individual will usually feel a temporary sense of euphoria, not
otherwise available, and because of its intensity, will not be
willing to relinquish this unique if expensive pleasure. So the
one-off event becomes more frequent, and eventually an
addiction.

I remember one young heroin addict to whom I taught
better breathing and relaxation, emerging from his session
saying, 'why do I need to take drugs if I can feel like this by
myself?' Teaching such a process requires considerable skills
and understanding not studied in academic factories.

The important observable symptom in someone whose
left brain is over-dominant, will be excessive verbalisation.
Language is in the left brain hemisphere, and overstrain
becomes evident in over-use of speech caused by too much
electricity in this area signifying some form of stress. Corrective breathing and relaxation eventually restores the disharmony.

The almost virtual lack of understanding among the majority, of information of this kind, constitutes a serious gap in our educational training. Possibly of greater importance than some of the abstract facts which go in at one ear and out of the other in our early education. As I have mentioned elsewhere, 'teaching a small (or older) child to breathe correctly is like giving water to a dying daffodil.' (*The New Way to Relax*, Karen Roon) All drug addicts represent dying daffodils to me, whatever their age, for no drug addict breathes correctly, or has done so since childhood, representing years and years of unresolved stress.

The symptom of excessive verbalisation, referred to above, implies feeling we are in a corner from which we are perpetually trying to extricate ourselves without success. We don't know where the stress in coming from. Our coping mechanism usually involves trying to *talk* our way out of the problem, with resultant fast speech, and brain over-drive.

Our educational over-emphasis on intellectual achievement, competition and power, indicates a complete cultural misunderstanding of the true purpose of life. We nurture these as priorities in young absorbent minds, at the expense of the culture of the right brain balance where lies natural harmony and creativity, a sense of self-worth irrespective of intellectual success. This sense of self-worth and personal identity becomes eroded, and we *grow up* (?) feeling a sense of isolation from the world within and without. We assume an artificial veneer of confidence by which we fool the world, yet within is hopelessness and desperation, spiritual desperation.

One of the symptoms of this spiritually isolated desperation is the continual verbal over-activity which is really masking fear. Never was the advice 'ponder in our own hearts and in our temple, and be still', of greater urgency. The addiction of triviality seems to dominate so much TV time when this mindless chatter, batters the senses in the name of entertainment. There is no space between words, gaps in sentences pose a threat. As if we were trying to defend ourselves, yet the only opponent is our own spiritual vacuum.

In media reporting, the addictive concentration on international terrorism and violence increasingly dominates the headlines. Terrorists who are deliberately misinterpreting the ancient wisdom of much of their own religious teachings, where love and respect for others form the rooting philosophy, quote the decadence of Western society as the reason for their activities. Are we giving them justification?

I have learned that on a personal level we *attract* disasters to ourselves by our own actions. In my own personal life I can nowadays pin-point the addictive actions, inaction or negative thoughts that attract any negative circumstances in my daily life. As with the microcosm so with the macrocosm. As with the individual so with the nation?

It is difficult to disagree with criticisms of the decadence of Western culture. I was born and lived in England for the first twenty-six years of my life, my roots are still deep, but I have resided in Scotland for the last fifty-four. North or south, in all our big cities and most urban and rural areas this decadence is all too obvious. I suppose that for the first half of our lives we accept whatever we see in society as the norm, and do not feel personal responsibility to right the wrongs, or feel we have the power to do so. As I grew in spirituality *unintentionally*. I came into my own power, and saw others do the same. In fact what I write in this book is the use of that power in the best way I can.

Just as all evil in this world starts with the thoughts of one person, who attracts others of like mind, so all the good evolves in the same way. Never underestimate *your* power.

On a global canvas East and West have so much to give each other. Ancient manuscripts reveal that much of Eastern wisdom emanated from the West and vice versa.

Who would nowadays deny the enormous benefits the Eastern practice of Yoga has brought to the West or the more spiritual martial arts, even of communal exercise at the beginning of the day? While the Western mind might recoil from such regimentation, the obesity we see on an increasingly worrying level suggests that more than a reluctant voluntary effort is desperately needed.

Any addiction to decadence, which is really inertia turned rancid, inevitably attracts an addiction to physical and mental destruction. The addictive decadence is cowardice in loving action, yet loving action is the greatest strength available to man, sadly not universally understood. Refraining from using this strength inevitably attracts aggressive domination.

We are in this present age facing an enemy which cannot be fought by traditional and known methods of warfare, an unseen virus of dark energy, and to fight this virulence we have to generate an addiction to moral strength unused by man before this present time.

We have to open this gate of knowledge which until now has been locked within the global psyche. There will never be a more urgent need to find this key. I believe there is still time, but only just. The opening of this non-material door could open a golden age for our planet.

Spiritual addiction is probably the only addiction available to us. The *intent* of spirituality is the only energy which can alter the addictive cancer of violent thought and action. There are encouraging signs all around us as people emerge who are using and trusting such habits as meditation who become addicted to infusing unseen space with loving thought so that the silence becomes pregnant with the vibration of wisdom. Released from human consciousness and doubly potentised by the wisdom of the universe. Universal wisdom *can* be released by the will and breath of man.

The effect of the existing power of those who use spirituality and loving thought cannot be evaluated, but of the people I know who trust this energy, miracles appear to occur in their lives, and I have also seen it happen in my own. I have watched the disasters in the lives of those who do not yet trust this process. The word spirituality does not mean religion, it includes anyone of any or no religion who understands spirituality, and its addictive effect for good in their lives. Remember the word spirit means breath, the intensity of the spiritual power becomes greatly enhanced by correct breath.

Our constant addiction to chatter in order to avoid a silence we cannot tolerate is a symptom of the over-development of the left brain hemisphere, verbal noises polluted by lack of oxygen, an incorrect respiratory symptom common to anyone addicted to living anywhere but within the true self of the right creative intuitive brain.

Such a universal symptom is common with those who come for help with stress. Those who have lost their way, separated from their own authenticity by the addiction of lack of confidence in that truth, sadly often the sole inheritance of the so-called 'educated' child. The endless chatter of speech at a speed limit impossible for creative communication.

Short of asking someone to be quiet in a military tone guaranteed to give offence, all one's verbal skills become centred into talking the client into a comfortable relaxed position, reclining if possible. I am an enthusiastic devotee of that useful saying 'Never stand when you can sit, never sit when you can lie.' A good tip when you are helping yourself or anyone else to relax.

Once correct breathing is established, and a person relaxes progressively, the addictive verbal smokescreen dissolves, and valid thoughts and feelings come to the surface, revealing information essential for the client to acknowledge and understand. Perhaps it is wrong to think of all addictions as negative, there is an addictive need to listen intuitively to what is right for us, a very healthy and essential habit, since all good communication springs from that inner referral point.

I often ponder about the source of accelerated unnatural speech speed, and can only conclude that its origin was in the first important communications exchanged between parents and child. If those communications were of a frequently critical nature usually about something the child could not understand as a wrong, and is unable to respond to because of fear, the child has only two means of defence. Silence or accelerated noise in the form of speech speed, in order to try to protect itself from imagined anger and punishment.

The latter often becomes predominant as the child becomes perpetually motivated by guilt, and creates a verbal smokescreen, or complete silence, the only other retreat in order to avoid expected criticism and possible punishment.

The child maintains its talking defence mechanism on the supposition that 'if I keep talking they have to listen.' It is hoping to postpone the chastisement it expects.

This same *expectation of disapproval* can continue into adult life, transforming each social interaction into an imaginary encounter of dread between an accusing parent and a guilty child.

The opposite of verbal mania is if course the addiction to silence, being tongue-tied, where a child is so afraid that whatever it says will be twisted by the parent into an admission of guilt. The child becomes verbally paralysed with fear, unable to speak at all.

The same tendency carried into adulthood makes social encounters agonising, something to avoid. Possibly the habit of stammering lies between these two extremes, and of course the phobic avoids all human interaction at all if possible. Corrective breathing helps to release the verbal block.

The therapist needs to find the key which can open up the creative dialogue, trying to glean the golden clues, often from sparse dialogue by which the sufferer, from fear, stumblingly tries to express the thoughts and feelings, trapped within for so many years, which have created a poisonous barrier to healthy relationships. Strengthening the foothold of good communication acts as a key to unlocking the padlock of silence.

The great skill of discernment becomes honed as a fine art, as precise as a surgeon's scalpel. This skill resembles a beautiful dance of creative words, to know when to speak or when to stay silent. I believe there is no greater help available to a therapist than to have experienced for themselves the art and addiction of correct breathing. *Then* the intuitive brain releases the right thoughts and subsequent words, creating a calm, relaxed environment, essential for client growth and understanding, and to regain the courage to relate confidently with others.

While speed of recovery must never be the uppermost criterion in a therapist's mind, for me the use of corrective breath training is the one sure factor to re-establish the re-emergence of the drive for self-responsibility within a client, and therefore reduces the frequency of appointments. Again the positive addiction for self-responsibility is another instance of the good use of that energy.

I have found that precision-based respiratory verbal wisdom by the therapist can achieve more in a few weeks or months than a more frequently used formalised intellectual-based counselling or psycho-analytical approach.

The first important lessons in my later therapeutic approach were rooted during those several years I spent as a volunteer professional psychotherapist in one of those first drug addiction centres in Glasgow, under the guidance of several elderly benign Franciscan priests in an old semi-derelict former workhouse. My childhood influences in the Church of England presented no barrier to our harmonious communication. Those years introduced me to the under-belly of the layers of energy within a great city, its tragedies, hilarity, courage and pain.

Having previously had a lengthy association with Edinburgh, which to me represented the intellectual head of Scotland, Glasgow increasingly came to me to represent its heart, but the heart of the growing addictive scene. Surely its broken heart.

Even so the latent spirituality of Glasgow felt to me like a pulse-beat of a great energy which, if harnessed to that potential, could become an addictive force for good, which could influence the world. I love Edinburgh with my head, but intuitively Glasgow possesses my heart, once a run-own city which I hated to visit, its obvious pain had clouded my vision of its spiritual potential.

Despite all the problems of the addictive clients, mostly young people, I learned more about simple human kindness in those two years in that early addiction centre than in all the years of my previous life.

Nevertheless in my role at the time I began to realise the impossibility of being able to make an impact on the great cancer of drug addiction that was closing in on Glasgow and the big cities. Even rural areas were being affected. I remember meeting a University lecturer at a conference on addiction, who reminded me that spoken words are often forgotten all too quickly, but that written words would be remembered. And were more effective. I remembered his words.

The profound impact of my experiences in that early drug centre gave me visionary insights on the source of the addictive experience. These insights led me to write my convictions down in a little book entitled *Love, Drugs or any*

City Like Glasgow. It was also inspired by my awareness of the part that a restricted respiratory pattern had to play on human behaviour, addiction in particular, and the fact that to me the drug craze was just that, a crazed need for the individual to free themselves from the appalling inner tension that an impeded breathing pattern imposes. Like living in a restrictive strait-jacket.

To an addict the natural means to free themselves from this stifling pressure seems unavailable, because they will also have to free themselves of the fear layers of childhood, a process too frightening to contemplate. How easy, or apparently easy, the quick fix, never mind that the means to this nirvana becomes an irreversible restriction in itself, with its criminal financial underworld and blackmailing violent understructure. Eventual health breakdown is of course the end result for most.

The conviction of the need to have written my little book on addiction is as strong now as it was then, the break-through in understanding of the addictive scene as positive now as the urge at that time to write down what I was feeling. Never mind, that general understanding still has to come.

The continuing reinforcement of my clearing vision showed me that most of the young drug addicts were not only breathing appallingly, but that their physical maturation had been impaired. Their hands were often very immature, with very narrow fingertips, the glandular and hormonal changes meant to occur in adolescence seemed lacking. Of course the poor respiration from childhood had limited the energy cycles from completing the change-over from childhood to adolescence. This inhibition of the normal growth patterns still produced a deep unconscious urge from nature to complete that growth. At a level not obvious to themselves, they were, and still are whatever their age, looking for a way to relax the iron bands of tension and stress in order to release the energy required to promote growth, the carrying out of the internal biological plan.

That the substance and method chosen was also likely to unlock self-destructive mental nightmares, and possibly early death, was a secondary factor, compared with the desperate need for *any* artificial journey to regain the long-forgotten memory of *feeling good about themselves, a sensation denied to them by their upbringing and environment.*

Feedback on the effect of corrective breathing and the natural relaxation experienced by former drug addicts now freed from their addiction, has given me enormous satisfaction, and one of the reasons why I felt compelled to write down my thoughts and feelings about my experiences within the drug scene. I was at a period in my life when I had never been so busy, or so short of time. My life was going through great changes, but the inner drive could not be ignored, and had never been stronger.

Many ex-addicts have spoken to me welcoming the thoughts expressed in my book, because it is so relevant to their own experiences. In regaining the identical insights they have acknowledged the truth of so much personal pain from early childhood.

Much that has been written about drug addiction has been expressed by those who have never been at the coalface of the problem, too much concentration is expended on various drug-inducing substances, and the symptoms themselves, but without any practical skills in being able to change the habit of even one addict. The *behaviour* of addiction seems to have such a mesmeric effect, that the actual person who is involved disappears in a numbers game of percentages and statistics to satisfy the addiction of government departments for intellectual information on which to base yet one more endless report.

The source and how to effect change at the source is

never attempted, because the skills to effect change are not understood. It is in the spiritual environment in which our children are being reared, and lack of spirituality or even admitting to that dimension, which cannot be quantified. One scientist expressed the frustration of being unable to read in the atmosphere the signs that are affecting mankind's future existence. His words were: 'If you could only *see* the essence of the threat.'

In not being able to *see,* or admit to, the essence of the spiritual vacuum in our society, we are ensuring the continuance of the drug-addictive virus, and the weakening of our culture. S*pirit means breath*, and it is through the correction of the respiratory pattern that the secret weapon is always available to defeat the enemy of addiction. There is only one way through the eye of the needle of spiritual change.

The easy way out for countless important specialists on drug addiction is to blame poverty, housing and unemployment. Surely the problem is the poverty of *thought* in industry and politics which has created the infrastructure for these issues. I have never heard of the addiction of 'poverty of thought' elsewhere, but surely that is as serious an addiction as any other. You cannot just talk the talk, you have to walk the walk of spiritual insight. Everything else has failed.

Of course addiction is not only about drugs, it is a rigid, obsessive attachment to a person, place or object. Unless a person through deep inner dialogue can cross the fear barrier which has so far prevented them from facing up to this compulsion, compensatory activity will always be present in order to have easily available an alternative way of experiencing the feel-good factor, i.e. feeling good about life.

A young baby straight off the production line of birth knows that life is good anyway, and swiftly remonstrates when obstacles are created by the adults in charge which block its sensation of delight in life. Alas, all too soon Wordsworth's 'prison doors' of our culture close around the growing child.

The child's precious gift of knowledge of the beauty of life is so strong because for the first eight years or so of its life, it is still being breathed **by** the breath rather than restraining this natural correct instinct. Relearning this correct impulse at any age returns to us the gift of childhood, the sheer delight in being alive.

Once we have regained the addiction of feeling good about life, even when all around us is chaos, we start to learn that this new addiction is a beneficial one, for it can by itself start to reduce the chaos, disordered vibrational thoughts and actions of others, which must change in order to conform to the one that is balanced in nature. Correct breath.

I have just had a creative thought while typing these lines! If you go back a few lines on your computer or to adjust a word or phrase, all the words after that phrase will automatically re-arrange themselves to present a more orderly piece of writing. I am thinking that if enough people restored correct breathing to themselves and others, the rest of the population would probably fall into line. A similar invisible process. Addiction problem solved!

I know, because I have seen it work on a small but representative group of people, and been privileged to be a catalyst, not as a counsellor, not really as a therapist, but just as someone who also had to re-learn how to breathe correctly, after suffering from the addiction of lack of confidence for so many years. These days with the ability to share that knowledge through breath re-balance. That is all you really have to do, people do the rest themselves.

★　★　★

My aim is corrective breathing for the planet. So here are a few addictions you *can* be safe with.

I am addicted to loving myself and therefore others.

I am addicted to listening to my intuition.

I am addicted to trusting a power greater than myself, but which is also in me.

I am addicted to trusting that positive thought brings positive returns.

I am addicted to giving myself adequate rest. So much damage is done by tired people who will not take rest.

I am addicted to the thought that if you really want to be happy, nobody can stop you.

I am addicted to the desire that everyone has the right to live and work surrounded by pure air.

I am addicted to having life-affirmative thoughts in all situations, despite the disapproval of others.

I AM ADDICTED TO BREATHING CORRECTLY.

Chapter 45

DEATH BY MISADVENTURE

YOU MAY NOTICE from other chapters in this book that a relatively little recognised Bible, *The Aquarian Gospel of Jesus the Christ*, by Levi Dowling, has been a defining inspiration for me for many years, because it makes so many references to the *Holy Breath*. As you will have noticed (!) breath is really what this book is all about; nowadays I also believe it to be holy. To me our breath, our life-giver is indeed holy, the latter word translated among other descriptions in my dictionary as meaning *morally blameless*. I could not find a more apt if unexpected interpretation, because those who correct their breath find themselves naturally moving into a more spiritual and wholesome life-style, indicating that this morality is *intended* to be our natural state of being.

Most of my present knowledge of the traditional Bible comes from a childhood at a Church of England primary school, where we were thoroughly grounded in a knowledge of this special book. Such learning has never been forgotten; the passages I learned by heart are still fresh in my mind, especially the New Testament. Such was its impact on an impressionable young mind.

The Old Testament was presented to us in the form of numerous stories, so there are quite a few gaps in my knowledge of its many books, but one of the impressions that has stayed in my mind was the longevity of life of so many of the Prophets. Several hundred years was no exception. It is said that the measurement of time in those days reflected a different numerical table than that which we use today, suggesting that these great ages would be totally different if we applied our present-day concept of time. However I feel free to apply my own interpretation, and personally believe that the stature of the spiritual wisdom of such people, could have ensured that such qualities went hand in hand with their lengthy life-span.

In more recent years I have read of people in various parts of the world, mostly in middle to far-eastern countries, who have lived well into their second century, some even growing new teeth, and becoming a parent after the age of a hundred. Well, maybe not the mother in such cases! Even in the Western world the child-bearing age of a number of women has escalated into the fifties. I remember visiting an ancient cemetery in the Scottish Borders and saw the gravestone of a man recording his death at over a hundred and twenty years. In general the upper ages mentioned above were of people who lived a rural existence on a very simple diet. For myself at over eighty, and from time to time thinking of how I might depart from this present existence, I like to imagine a ripe hazel nut gently falling from the branch, the correct time having arrived for that nut to leave its place on the tree. In the world of nature the nut falls to the ground and all being well, regenerates into a young sapling. Reincarnation? The idea is worth a thought.

I try to practice what I preach and have faith that correct breathing will ensure that I do not experience a long period of degenerating disease before I move on. I am beginning to notice old friends and contemporaries enduring various painful maladies in their later years, sometimes dying in medical drug-induced comas. Sadly I had noticed their limited respiratory patterns over many years, but ethically it is not possible to offer to help anyone to breathe better, even one's nearest and dearest unless you *are asked* for help, and if someone *really wants* to experience this life-giving self-help treatment. Otherwise improvement or recovery cannot happen, and you will be rejected as trying to interfere. The *spirit* has to make this choice.

In my own case, I live a pretty simple rural existence, enjoying and planning a garden where only obeying the laws of nature can ensure success. I have been led to apply these rules in my personal life. Planning forward for the next year and no time for finding life boring. Living in harmony with Nature which must also have a proper oxygen supply to flourish, keeps us in touch with our own adherence to internally known natural law and its abundantly fascinating wisdom. Morbidity has no place in such an existence.

Even so, I lived for some years in the centre of one of Scotland's biggest cities, and was able to find Nature's magic in the most unexpected places. I saw the reality of the saying '*give a plant a chink of light, and it will grow to it.*' The path of natural divine law can be re-experienced in hitherto neglected lives.

I have always been impressed by the frequency with which someone responding to respiratory correction will begin to be interested in plants, the growing of cress on a window sill, bulbs, a house plant or two; indeed I have often suggested to a client who has no house plants to obtain one, and learn about its needs. Even if there are a few failures along the way, the nurturing required represents the care and attention we need to develop in order to listen to our own needs. Needs to which in the past all too little attention has been paid, as if we felt such attention was a sin.

This reminds me of a little slip of paper I have used with clients and groups under the heading 'did you receive this message from your parents?' The words went like this: 'However hard you try to please me you never will, but keep trying.' A certain recipe for a shortened life-span. Brain-washing lack of attention to our own true needs, the universal symptom of those who seek therapeutic help.

I have a videotape about the near-death experience in which a number of obviously genuine people give details of their personal memories of a return from death trauma, having been diagnosed as dead. This and other cases I have met with, heard, read about, or viewed on television per-suades me of the reality of other dimensions beyond our present one. Cynics will disagree, but I often find that cynics have a poor respiratory pattern, and may not be able to oxygenate or bring into life that part of the brain which can comprehend the process quite naturally. The exit gate out of this life can often turn out to be a turnstile given certain energy and vibrational conditions.

Profound deep thinking, questioning and eventual certain-ty of the near-death experiences has accompanied my own deeply humbling awareness of sitting beside a client who is breathing correctly. They will be deeply relaxed and involved with the healthy thinking which results from really enjoying the feeling of utter peace which they are experiencing. Count-less times upon opening their eyes they report what I can only term visionary experiences, even seeing figures which they are sure are Angels. Such revelations are often a turning point in their lives, changing a former rather drab view of the world, to one of boundless possibilities and joy. How can I deny the truth of their vision, when I have experienced it for myself?

Living near to nature in my rural retreat, I am forever absorbed by the miracles of regeneration daily in the plant world, and how specific nurturing can bring back to life a plant perhaps pronounced dead, even by a plant specialist.

How can I close my eyes to the now well documented evidence of the near-death experience?

The ability of plant life to regenerate itself must surely remind us that we ourselves are a plant species, admittedly one with a unique *additional dimension*. Nevertheless like all natural species we are composed of *cells* and cells either die or are regenerated. Cells depend on the life-force of oxygen to effect regeneration.

From my own experience of people I have met who have achieved their century, one common factor I have observed is a strong will to live, a certainty that life is worth living. I have to be very careful here in not implying that *a strong will to live* is always accompanied by a strong spirituality, for occasionally people achieve this age by sucking energy from other people, usually near relatives, in a situation which has been going on for many years, and is not a spiritual relationship. An unhealthy relationship, for which each in the partnership is equally responsible.

Quite often the younger in this unholy liaison will die first, worn out by living life as a virtual slave to someone else's vampirism, but at some deep level there will be an unspoken complicity of role acceptance by both, not apparent to others, resulting in neither having been able to fulfil their true life-purpose.

On the other hand, centenarians that I have observed closely often live alone almost to the end of their lifespan. They live simply, are never lonely, have a great sense of humour. Their diet varies very little, contains a right balance of basic essential foods. They have never lived a sedentary life. Almost without exception they possess a sense of peaceful spirituality, and their respiratory pattern is good.

One of the concepts I have embraced contains the words 'if I breathe fully and freely, the cells of my body will continually regenerate, so why do I need to die?' Or as Leonard Orr irreverently put it, 'death is a grave mistake!'

Not having yet reached the ability to believe I shall live for ever (a real death-defying thought!) I still prefer the thought that 'correct breath regenerates the cells, so why die?'

A more acceptable concept rather than the fear and maudlin attachment to death which preoccupies so many in their later years, sadly seeing life as a cup perpetually less than half empty rather than as a cup more than half full. We can maintain the half-full plus philosophy by the way we decide to think about death, until we are ready to move on.

I did not always have these life-affirming ideas and certainties; looking back now, the first half of my life appears to have been lived with little awareness of my true identity, no one intentionally did the robbing, but that was the accumulative effect of my formative years. In becoming insensitive to one's own true needs and uniqueness, we become blinded to the needs of others. We build up layers of negativity and false values to protect us. If that is what our earlier conditioning achieved, we really have to let go of guilt and forgive ourselves. Otherwise we miss the adventure of life, and die by misadventure.

In my former level of insensitivity I did not realise how near my own mother was to dying, when I visited her in hospital where she had been for two years. The three or four visits a week and often fifty mile round trip perhaps desensitised me into thinking that she would be there for ever. On the last occasion I visited her, she seemed to be losing her grip on reality, but I had an important(?) Council meeting to attend. We had never really been outwardly verbally affectionate with each other, but on that evening I told her that she had been a good mother. That sounds stilted as I write the words. No one at the hospital had suggested she was so near the end, but that night she died. However inadequate my last words to her, I have been so thankful I said them.

These days, knowing what I now know, the meeting

would have been cancelled without a thought, but I had been taught that such things were more important than thinking what would be the right thing to do for *me*, which of course would have been to have stayed with my mother as she was leaving life. I trusted those in charge of her treatment to give me warning of her condition. I cannot blame them, nor yet myself as I was at the time.

Nowadays I would have listened to my intuition, have known I must stay to share her last moments, and to have felt the spiritual urgency of helping her make the transition. I am so glad that I now believe that one can communicate from the heart to anyone who has moved on and to express sorrow and love, so that the sadness can be healed.

Now I know so much more that death is not to be feared, I can sit beside someone during their last moments, sure, certain and able to be reassuring that there is a new life waiting.

Despite so much that was good in my childhood, my parents' own upbringing and the fashion of the times did not encourage open affection, or so it seemed to me. I remember when I was sixteen standing beside my father on a station platform, from where I was going away for a week to stay with a school friend who had moved away from our home town. I recall so clearly wondering with some embarrassment if I was supposed to kiss my father good-bye, and how difficult it seemed just to give him a hug. He appeared so remote. Of course he did not know how to respond either. What a great shame, as I look back in retrospect, and think of the ease with which my son and his daughters are able to easily exchange a loving hug of farewell. One very positive step forward nowadays is how many parents and children naturally exchange a hug and say 'I love you' when separating.

I was passing a portly middle-aged man recently, speaking on his mobile phone as he got into his car. I heard him say 'I love you.' I felt quite moved and thought to myself how unusual this would have seemed even twenty years ago.

After my father died, following a minor operation when the anaesthetic was too much for his heart, I found a small lump of coal in his jacket pocket. The pathos was overwhelming, my austere and distant father evoking the power of good luck in an act of such childish faith. Despite his passing on before we could share a better closeness through sharing discussion over this simple action, I felt that we have been communicating in a much better way over the mists of infinity. I have never felt so near to him as when I discovered that little piece of good luck coal.

The poem at the beginning of this book, which is attributed to an unknown Maori, has told me more about life, death and the journey of the spirit than any books I have read.

It has been a perpetual and magnificent inspiration and joy to me and many others for over a decade, how I wish I could have met the poet. Every line conveys an infinity of meaning with great beauty. I am sure that the writer is no longer alive, yet the love and truth of the lines are as vivid as if being spoken to in the present day. Many times I have said a blessings of thanks to the author and been certain that it has been received over the vibrations of ether. Hundreds of copies have been shared with clients and friends.

Since love can never die, I believe we can retain loving communication with anyone who has passed on, for the spirit is to me eternal. An overpowering grief which is still inconsolable after many years is no longer a healthy emotion and implies an *over*-dependency on which many relationships are based.

We often use someone else in our adult life to fill an immaturity gap from childhood, as a substitute parent. If that person dies we are still left with the gap, and the older we are the harder it seems to grow into the maturity we are meant to have achieved by the time we choose a partner. In fact, to many the task is never attempted and we live on in a permanent state of apparent loss, which is not a healthy loss.

I am sure we are meant to go on maturing *all our lives*. The fountain source of wisdom is endlessly available, more significantly when we breathe correctly. Such interesting information is being continually released.

If we pass from this life *having never* moved on from the sad, worried, frightened, anxious lonely child, to me that represents death by misadventure. The wonderful adventure of life lived from our personal authenticity and power has never been experienced; we have not properly used the gift of life.

Our individual sense of the finality of death seems to come in different wrappings, dependent on our respective philosophy or religion. More frequently these days a funeral service is accompanied by a *celebration* of the life which has moved on, with an unspoken awareness among many that death is not the end. If it is not, I have gained a certainty that our spirit returns in another body, and embraces an awareness that we can have another opportunity to experience *the game of life*.

It is said that we choose our own death by the way we leave this life. After much observation I do not necessarily disagree with that. Wise philosophers have suggested that if we reincarnate, we often do so in groups, large or small, because our group spiritual karma makes the decision.

There is a suggestion that when outward disaster strikes, leading to numbers of people being taken from this life, it is because they have a common learning experience to move through, necessitated by their past incarnations, often as suppressor or suppressed. Such a suggestion may seem unbelievable and unacceptable to many. I am only repeating an idea, which is totally comprehensible to some faiths. I can assimilate this concept, but it does not remove us from responsibility or from working out our own life problems in this lifetime. We are all on our individual spiral of life, and I have no right to expect anyone else to stay alive *just to suit my need of them.* I have heard that we all choose the way and time that we die however it may seem to ourselves and others.

It may be possible that present and prophesied coming disasters could force us to see beneath the surface of events, and be projected mentally and spiritually to cross from our present consciousness into the great dividing line between this world and what lies beyond; in order to stay sane and see the higher significance of events at present invisible to our estranged faces.

The death of a child is one of the most anguishing losses we can experience. A Buddhist saying that 'some souls only have to touch the earth' has been a comfort to many, particularly to those who have lost a very young child. It carries with it the implication that this earth is a training ground, and that our many exits and entrances are part of this process of learning to use life in a state of *lovingness.* When we have done all we can, given the state of our body/mind, we can no longer stay in our present life existence, despite our earthly age.

To understand the above concept which may be impossible for some who read this book, in no way infers a limitation of understanding. I can only present ideas and beliefs gained by contact with hundreds of people who have found genuine comfort and release from grief when their minds can embrace a wider horizon. I find it difficult to deny their hard won certainties. Perhaps there *is* no death by misadventure.

Khalil Gibran quotes in his beautiful book of poems *The Prophet* covering the many states of man 'your children are not your children, they are the sons and daughters of life's longing for itself.'

Beyond our attachment to others must always be our sense

542

of attachment to life itself, this debt we owe for the gift of life, its repayment in our lifetime, by the joyful use of the gifts and talents we have been given as a contribution to the healthy evolution of the species. Perhaps our comings and goings, our passing from one lifetime to another, is the journey we are on. We are all at different stages of the journey, death is only another door of experience held open to us.

As I move through the second half of my seventies, and contemplate its natural conclusion, particularly when I meditate, (not in the Lotus position!) I find that correct breathing keeps me in a *continuous* state of meditation, even when carrying out chores, and the daily demands of life. This state of awareness allows me to mentally liaise naturally with the sense of an existence yet to come. Similar to a form of osmosis. Such awareness is happening without intention, and is uplifting. It is difficult to pinpoint the exact words to describe this sensation.

At the other end of the spectrum from our birth, maybe we recover the awareness I am positive is present in the baby's consciousness in the early months, probably also in the womb, of what is behind the words 'trailing clouds of glory do we come.' I am sure that we return to the clouds of glory, whatever the means of our passing.

A couple of years ago a little poem came into my possession, which has since become frequently used at funeral services. So much so that some people may detract from the value of the words, which when often repeated we are apt to trivialise, giving truth to the statement 'familiarity breeds contempt.'

We are apt to trivialise and show contempt for the gift of our lives by ignoring the importance of the ever-present life-giving breath. I believe that all inspiring words are conceived when someone knowingly or unknowingly is using breath correctly.

★ ★ ★

Do not stand at my grave and weep,
I am not here, I do not sleep.

A comforting, formerly unspoken, certainty is being expressed through these beautiful and true lines.

I BELIEVE THAT DEATH IS JUST ANOTHER ADVENTURE ON THE LONG PATH OF LIFE.

MISADVENTURE? NEVER.

Chapter 46

REBIRTHING

MANY YEARS AGO in the course of my research and studies into the Power of Breath, I was more or less dragged by an enthusiastic friend to a group session on Rebirthing.

I had heard about the process and steered well clear of it, as I had read about people rolling about in the throes of regressed birth trauma yelling their heads off. Not for me.

Instead nothing like that happened. I was a very reluctant participant, extremely self-conscious, and determined to maintain an onlooker role.

In hindsight, I now realise that no one had explained the process to me, what to expect, how long it would last, etc. No one touched me thank goodness. I was just stretched out on a yoga-type mat on the floor. I wasn't told whether to use my nose or mouth for breathing. As I lay there trying to breathe deeply, I had what I later realised was a very profound thought. It was that this was the very first time in my forty five plus years that I had given attention to my breathing. This idea struck me as important, as if I had been neglecting *me* for all those years.

After a while I gave up being aware of those around me in the group. Someone (a helper?) was sitting near me, I suppose keeping a watchful eye. Then time seemed to blur, and I began to have pins and needles in my hands and feet, next a quite painful cramp in my hands, with a sensation that my fingers felt double their size. It felt unbearable and yet quite bearable! Before long these symptoms passed, and quite naturally I found myself making a decision to return to the here and now. I thought, 'so that's what rebirthing is all about.' I had several other sessions in a group, and also on a one-to-one basis. Attending discussions, further training, and reading quite a lot about the process, eventually becoming confident enough under supervision to sit beside someone who was going through a 'breathe'.

After buying a number of books on the subject, and being given some very helpful explanatory papers, I developed a profound respect for the work of Leonard Orr, the pioneer teacher of this work in this country. I may say that this was despite my earlier resistance to the process.

Eventually I began to realise from the remarks made by people who talked about their accompanying sensations and thoughts while breathing in this way, that it did seem directly related to their birth experience, which was not all trauma, and sometimes wonderful.

I began to build up a considerable body of knowledge, and above all intuitive awareness. As I sat beside a person I could guess, often with great accuracy, what kind of birth they had experienced, whether Caesarian, breech, forceps, natural. It was possible to interpret from their distorted breathing, comments made while experiencing the process, present general health, and relate these clues to protracted shock still held internally as a negative mental and physical block to growth and emotions from the time of birth.

My personal breath re-training or corrective breathing seemed to reverse these negative symptoms. Apart from improvement in my physical health there was a significant turn around in positive thinking, sense of love, and self-worth. I was in no doubt that all these improvements were the direct result of improved correct breathing. All this achieved without touch, massage, tablets, special diets, counselling, etc., etc. A personal self improvement process. You cannot ignore what people tell you, or what you see for yourself.

My reading on the subject informed me that a number of respected professionals in the study of human behaviour such as the late famous psychiatrist R. D. Laing had investigated, and even personally experienced rebirthing sessions. As a result of his breathing experiences Laing suspected that 'breathing and the rhythm of the heart can be disturbed perhaps for life, by cutting or throttling the umbilical cord while it and the placenta are still fully functionally us.'

From client experience, I fully empathise with Dr. Laing's words, I only regret that during the several occasions when I met him personally, I did not then know that he had experienced the rebirthing process. His comments about the timing of the cutting of the umbilical cord convinces me that it was probably as a result of the insights he gained through his own rebirthing experience.

Many of my own deeply valued convictions have been formed from corrective breathing practice, which is after all using the oxygen process correctly, the force of life. My insights have also included those gained during a period of my life some years ago, when as I have mentioned I experienced a number of rebirthing sessions.

Let us consider other ways by which we humans deviate from the birth blueprint from which we spring.

All around us we see examples of the obesity which arises from the incorrect use of the visible solid material of the fruits of the earth, including the food we buy in supermarkets, suffused as much of it is with chemicals. These latter are still of course created from earthly material, it's the mix which creates harmful results.

The wrong use of water-based fluids is all too evident from media figures on alcoholism, drug addiction, the misuse of the plants of the earth, the energy from the sun by the nuclear and arms market. We ourselves are basically created from the fusion of earth, air, fire, and water.

We concentrate almost exclusively on the human misuse of the elements we can *see visibly*. I am positive if we used the *unseen* element *air/breath/spirit* correctly, that our misuse of the other three would cease naturally, 'like water off a duck's back'.

I do not like the word *rebirthing*, to many it sounds a bit scary and dramatic. All it means is re-learning to use the breathing instinct correctly, until it as perfect as when we were born, straight off Nature's production line. No one had to train us, we were responding to Nature's laws which began in the womb, our mothers certainly did not teach us.

There is probably a global resistance to correct breathing, not yet understood by most people. Those who do understand will never be slaves under other people's control. Far too many people are controlled by other people, or themselves try to control others. It saves each participant in such unholy alliances from taking self-responsibility. Certainly neither will breathe correctly.

There have been a few highly regrettable instances of activities misnamed rebirthing, which have given the process bad publicity, to which the world's media have given maximum drama. One rightly so, in which a little girl seemed to have been tightly wrapped I believe in a carpet, and pressed on by several people, in some misnamed attempt to release bad energy. The child died, a terrible tragedy, the thought of which never fails to sadden and horrify. How could people be so stupid and unenlightened?

To name such a processing rebirthing is an obscenity.

The results of unenlightened research by the majority of the world's media make the words New Age and Rebirthing the equivalent of a red rag to a bull, with plenty of cynics ready to latch on and add fuel to the fire of criticism.

I have every admiration for the medical profession, even

if I believe that it lacks personal training of medical students in disordered breathing patterns. If I had one wish for medical training, it is that students should be given corrective breathing training. I believe they would gain enormously important insights into what ails so many of their future patients. Even if it meant a dramatic drop in prescriptive drugs!

Young medics would also understand from improvements to their own health, that we all have the power to self-heal a vast proportion of health problems without the aid of needle, knives or drugs.

A health expert and writer, Karin Roon, sadly no longer with us who I would love to have met, wrote a wonderfully sane and sensible book in the 1950s called *The New Way to Relax*. She writes that 'a healthy new-born baby is the perfect instructor in breathing and relaxation. It uses all the muscles of its body that are involved in the breathing process, those of the abdomen, sides and back.'

I believe this is all we need to know to re-attain good health, but in general we lack the humility to study the small child as an example. As we repair our respiratory process, we may find it helpful to pay careful attention to our diet and possibly a period of natural supplements, to maintain the energy boost gained from corrective breathing, and to clear toxins as we regain the drive and passion for life which is our birthright.

From time to time I have read journalistic accounts of observing group rebirthing sessions, where people have been rolling about screaming, doubling up in apparent agony, and it is hardly surprising that such phenomena makes great material for cynical scoffing. I do however believe that there was serious and sincere intent behind the apparent bedlam. From research I believe that latter work in this process has encouraged the commencement of the up-breath from the lowest core-point of the body, as Karen Roon says 'between the pelvic bone and the navel.' She goes on to say that when we start our breathing 'above this point it has not yet regained its proper function.' When people are involved in rebirthing practice, and breathing up from this lower centre, it seems to result in positive results without noisy signs of apparent distress. I believe it is because the client automatically becomes involved in a deep thought process which results in a very positive subsequent forward movement in that person's life. A creative reaction, saving many hours of alternative counselling therapy.

I always feel sad when I consider how few doctors I have met so far who are interested in corrective breathing. Those who do are often regarded as mavericks by their fellows. On the other hand, all medical pioneering work appears to have to go through this negative reaction from colleagues, and yet much has gone on to become mainstream practice.

I look forward to the day when journalists, most of whom breathe incorrectly, become interested and concerned about the global implications of universal breath of life restriction by the majority of people. They could make a wonderful contribution to what I believe to be the most serious and urgent health area yet to be addressed, in order for the world's millions to regain the ability to heal themselves. What a boost for Global Warming recession.

Perhaps not enough rebirthing therapists do themselves justice in explaining the reasoning behind the method in a logical and even scientific way, for there is scientific evidence concerning the self-healing results of this work. Of course many scientists spend a lot of time discounting the evidence of other scientists!

However there is good scientific evidence provable by results that restorative work on correct breathing improves circulation, cell regeneration and brain function. It should surely take little intelligence to understand that restricting oxygen to the brain by limited breathing results in impaired mental and physical efficiency. Everyone who breathes wrongly is damaging brain function, the only energy available to maintain life.

Carol Volderman, the well-known TV personality, recently published a book which reported that exam-taking students who chewed gum attained better results than their non-chewing companions. The verdict was that the chewing process improved brain-oxygen. From where I see it, the chewing gum created an oral comfort stop which induced greater relaxation, which *then* resulted in better breathing, leading to a better *supply of brain-oxygen*. A little sad that better breathing was not given any credit for the improved exam results. Unfortunately many documentaries of this kind do not go very deeply below the surface of a superficially dramatic statement.

I have had the good fortune to teach correct breathing, as distinct from rebirthing, to hundreds of University and College students, many subsequently passing their exams with honours. A great number had been on the edge of stress collapse and dropping out, before they started to breathe correctly, with miraculous results. Just a few sessions was all that was usually required.

The intelligence of these students was never in question, but fear and apprehension was upsetting their emotional balance. The regained confidence was brought about by correct breathing training which produced a relaxed state in which they were able to face exams without the fear which had paralysed their intellectual memory.

I recall the words of the pioneering psychologist Wilhelm Reich in a book titled *Diary of a Friendship*, letters between himself and A. S. Neill, Headmaster of Summerhill School. He wrote, 'In sudden fear we all catch our breath for the moment. Some children have a lifetime of catching their breath and holding it. The sign of a well-reared child is its ability to breathe freely, it shows that it is not afraid of life.' Taking this statement into our schools, the 'well-reared' child is often the exception rather than the rule in most of our classrooms.

If you look at the breathing-pattern of school bullies, none of them breathe correctly, their respiratory reflex is that of a frightened child. Can *you* recognise that? Breath is the right use of the life force, you cannot correct it by punishment, but if it were corrected I am confident we would say good-bye to most school bullying.

Although it is well-known that serious lack of oxygen leads to brain damage or death, I wonder why there seems so little realisation or awareness that most people are surviving on a limitation of oxygen, self imposed. I suppose our life-span is determined by our right use of the precious food of oxygen we inhale, and whether we are generous or mean in giving ourselves this vital essence of the gift of life.

We are taught that we have five senses, speech, hearing, sight, touch and smell. Those who breathe through the mouth seem to have a poorer sense of smell than those who breathe correctly through the nose. Since discovering the great power of intuition, I have no hesitation in recognising it as the sixth sense, or as Einstein said 'the fourth dimension.' The power of the intuitive force seems to be greatly heightened by correct breathing. I have noticed that anyone suffering from deficiency in any of the other senses also suffers from incorrect breathing. Maybe breathing should be named as a sense as distinct from smell.

I wonder who first defined the list of the five senses, perhaps it needs to be revised with correct breathing becoming the first sense, followed by sight, hearing, smell, taste, touch and intuition. I feel more comfortable with these *seven* senses.

Seven is a special number anyway. Didn't God form the world in seven days?

It may be that pioneers of the rebirthing movement were so astounded by the dramatic and positive effects observed from clients in the first years of its introduction as a therapy that they did not realise that they were setting themselves up as a target for an Aunt Sally reaction among the critics. Incredulity and ruthless ridicule were merciless. To be fair, most of us, including the media, can only give our approval to something when we have experienced it for ourselves. We are apt to stick to our heart and lung problems, arthritis, aching joints, and a multitude of other maladies, rather than stretch out on a mat and try a little gentle breathing. After all the doctors are there with their tablets for such ailments, aren't they?

Some of the 'easier' therapies, now accepted as normal because someone does them to you (easier too), were at one time denigrated and scoffed at, but are now taught at College. They receive recognised awards, all good stuff, not requiring anything from the client but to lie back, and be done good to.

Correct breathing is not alternative or complementary. It is not a therapy, it is the non-negotiable law of health. I will stick my neck out and suggest that a great deal of so-called orthodox medical treatment could be termed complementary or alternative!

It is much harder to commit yourself to a therapy you pay for, but you have to do all the work! We all like self-improvement to be easy. Yet the reason why I can at eighty still bend, place my palms flat on the floor without bending my knees is because of the spine suppleness which is a direct result of the inner yoga of correct breathing, without having attended a yoga class in forty years. For me the distinction between self-repair of the respiratory function, and much medical drug treatment or counselling is the difference between the *do-gooding* of much drug and talking therapy, and *doing good*.

Breathing belonging to the latter category.

In general the world praises the do-gooder, and does not appreciate the many thousands of unsung angels, who go around actually doing good. The do-gooder does things for other people they should be doing for themselves, while those who do good often have to find a deep inner strength to allow someone to find their own way out of their trouble. The powerful empathy of their silent support is never recognised, nor do they wish it to be.

This last comment is so true if you are working with a person in breath correction who may have many troubles, for which *you* can see the answer. Yet you cannot intervene, even if it seems the easier solution. That person is breathing correctly for themselves, and I know that before long they will solve their problems and be all the stronger, for they have found and trusted their breath to give them the best solution. Not only that but they will use the same problem-solving process in the future.

Only since my own children have grown up, have I discovered the wisdom of the saying 'never do anything for your children they can do for themselves!' The first rule of parenthood. I wish someone had told me earlier. It took me some few years to reverse my own role as a do-gooder parent.

At one period of my life I was privileged to spend quite a few hours every week sitting on the floor beside a client involved and engrossed in repairing their breathing. In apparently doing nothing, it was a great joy to know that I was doing good rather than do-gooding. It was also fun; that may sound flippant, but so often when a client had been stretched out, breathing correctly for best part of an hour, they would start to chuckle with joy for minutes at a time, because they had unlocked their inner sense of fun, one they had thought lost, and began to chuckle with glee. They had rediscovered their inner joyful child and the sheer exuberant joy of living, they thought lost for ever. How could I not share that laughter? Do gooding? Thank goodness no! Doing good? Yes!

You don't need the world's praise when you do good.

If globally each of us could tune in to the precise wavelength of correct breath, I believe we could sort out the problems of our planet before prophesised possible catastrophe. This wavelength of right breath automatically results in the flowering of self-responsibility and the motivation to exist in natural harmony with Nature. Breath correction, however important the process, will only produce positive results if done without the wish for praise or fame.

It was the great yoga teacher Ramacharaka who wrote that 'one generation of correct breathers would regenerate the race, and disease would be looked upon as a rarity.' I was heartened recently to read a book, *The Oxygen Prescription* by Nathaniel Altman, who quoted some more vitally important words of Ramacharaka on 'The Complete Breath', reminding us that the complete breath needs to be seen as one smooth movement, not as several differing parts. This great yoga master describes these differing parts of breath in his book *The Hindu Yogi Science of Breath,* and how constant 'part-breaths' can lead to illness. There are few writers of books on breathing I respect more than those by Ramacharaka.

I believe the word 'Rebirthing' used to describe an important contribution to the understanding of a basic healthy process, may have been correct for the personal understanding of the first pioneers in the work. There are other descriptions of this process which could assist wider comprehension and positive healthy discussion. In any case it is unlikely that the detractors are able to breathe correctly and would therefore have more need of breath correction even if they themselves did not recognise the fact.

From what I have read, those who have treated this

approach with cynicism after perhaps only one session, have definitely lacked the motivation to experience the several self-treatments under relaxed supervision (recommended number about 10) which would enable them to be *qualified* to comment. Those who have persevered have only enthusiasm, due to their improved vitality, calmness, joy, energy, and quality of life.

In prophesying about the importance of correct breathing as having a greater and more important part to play in health, Fritjof Capra, the physicist, states in his book *The Turning Point*, that correct breathing and relaxation will play a much greater part in therapies of the future. Capra goes on to say that 'correct breathing is a skill that needs as much diligent practice as any other skill such as playing the piano.' We came into the world knowing how to play the breathing piano and most of us have been playing the game of life sadly out of tune ever since.

We do not have to overdo or use the breath violently as if we are running in a perpetual marathon; slow and gentle repetitive accuracy can be practiced all the time. In that way we can deal with the demands of the day while staying in touch with the vibrational wisdom of the universe which is at our disposal as we absorb it through the correct breath. It is available whether at work, play or rest. A very cheap and constant inner teacher. The God if you like, of your understanding, who set your inner compass at your birth; all you have to do is stay in touch through your breath with your own unique inner navigational chart.

If we replace the word rebirthing with words such as repairing, improving or correcting the breathing process, I believe it would be more understandable and acceptable to the ordinary person (if such a one exists). This might lead to more enlightened study and observation of our personal rhythm, to look for ways to correct our poor breathing habit, and repair it until we can use it as intuitively and efficiently as when we were first born. Even if we have had a difficult birth which has upset the mechanism, the blueprint is always there and can be reprogrammed.

The lovely gift that breathing correctly has given me, is the knowledge that it is never too late, we cannot change the losses and mistakes of the past. We do not have to, but the insights given to us on the wings of pure breathing can convert all such negative memories to priceless spiritual victories.

When I was first introduced to the rebirthing movement I felt that there was a missing element, but my knowledge at that time was not sufficient to know what that was. Later I realised that early research encouraged the expansion and improvement of upper chest breathing, which I think triggered off the rather dramatic phenomena of extreme and noisy symptoms and gave wonderful material to the critical media on the look out for drama! There is no doubt however that emotions were actually being experienced by the participant, and that they were better released than repressed.

Shortly after I realised the importance of breathing training from the lower belly, the emotions seem to calm down. I am now certain that when we start the breath from this lower point we bring into consciousness a vibrational thought which overrides the apparent distress caused by the emotional and vocal frothing-over of upper chest repetitive breathing or hyperventilation. We are involved with an awareness before sound, which needs to be investigated, and is also very interesting; we do not have time to moan and groan, my advice is always to 'stay with the breathing'.

There is a saying in the breathing movement, 'I am never upset for the reason I think.' Wise thought rising from the lower breath correct starting mechanism acts as a comfort stop to the stress of emotions, which have been activated by a childhood situation not until then able to be dealt with.

This had caused repressed fear, anger and resultant apparently hysterical symptoms. Contacting the prior thought source diffuses and cancels them out, for it contains useful information which seem to help solve the reason for the distress.

In spending countless hours with clients of all ages, occupations and religions, I have noticed a frequent pattern of movement while the correct breathing pattern is maintained, which reminds me of the actions of the baby trying to free itself from the womb. Having had three children, I am confident of my words. What has impressed me is the sense of *determination* characterised by the movement, a sequence of action and rest. When a client decides that they have done enough breathing (which is always under their own control) their following words confirm that they have dealt with some form of birth shock in a positive way, and in the ensuing weeks are able to deal with their lives much more satisfactorily. They always relate this progress to something that they have discovered from their breathing session. Often in discussion, particularly if the birth had been difficult, i.e. Caesarian (not completed the birth process), always having a problem completing a job or project, etc. There is a feeling that some difficult aspect of the birth had been 'ironed out'.

I believe implicitly that damaged respiratory function can only be repaired when the full movement of the impulse is correctly activated, starting from the point between the pelvic bone and the navel, clearly visible to the trained eye, and physically apparent by the strength of the lower stomach muscles when activated.

The above knowledge of *correctness* is surely encoded in the consciousness of the birthing infant, and in using it in the birth movement, it needs those movements to be reciprocated by the birth mother, and understood by birth attendants. The *determination* of the infant to birth itself correctly, too often meets with apparent opposition from the mother's reactions. If she is affected by fear she does not do lower pelvic breathing to help the baby, and birth attendants who cannot breathe correctly either, must find it impossible to empathise with the rhythm of labour. Their combined energies constitute what appears to the infant as opposition, even if unintentional opposition.

This can make the labour protracted and difficult, as the baby is not getting the correct maternal co-operation. Small wonder that although the determination of the baby to get it right results in what *looks* like a 'normal' birth, there frequently remains an after-shock of post-birth trauma stored within the cell memory of the child. It has gained access to life through unnecessary opposition. I am positive from extensive experience in being privileged to act as a detached no-touch relaxed birth attendant to adult breath-repairers, that birth-shock, which I consider to be a major factor in later life problems, can be ironed out by later corrective respiratory repair.

I think unresolved birth trauma, and later-life multi-faceted health problems to be a seriously misunderstood vacuum of research in the world of medicine and science. Sadly they may find it difficult to admit what could seem like medical lack of expertise, or intuitive intelligence. The more scientific our training, it is difficult to acknowledge any lack of under-standing of what could be the very probable cause of disease: ignorance of nature's *free* healing solution of the breath.

During many years of sharing with others the great joy of their primal breath self re-balancing, I have met with few dramatics, although some people say that they have seen Angels! I have no problem with that for I believe our early infant consciousness is very close to the Angel territory, and the white light often seen reminds me of the light seen at the end of the tunnel from someone who has experienced what is known as the *near death experience*.

Working with breathing has given me a tremendous admiration for us all and the great sense of purpose we were in touch with at the dawning of our entry into life; the knowledge of our own direction and, I believe, our contact with a beyond-earthly wisdom, as Wordsworth has said, 'trailing clouds of glory do we come.' I am sure as infants we knew why we had to come, what we had to do, with the knowledge of our ability to use our gifts and talents. For what other purpose did we fight so hard to get here?

We no longer need to feel like stranded whales in the present destructive environment we call civilisation, staying focused on our breath we are always safe.

The lower *sacral* area of the body from where we naturally are meant to commence each breath reminds me of the word *sacred*. Remember that as Karin Roon stated in her book *The New Way to Relax,* that 'correct breathing when we achieve it means that the breath starts from an area between the pelvic bone and the navel.' It brings into mind the basic structure of the Christian church building, where the *nave* and the *sacristy* are named important areas of its construction. Did these early Church builders have a meaningful knowledge of those spiritual respiratory areas of the human body in mind when naming special parts of their Church construction?

PROBABLY.

Chapter 47

WE NEUROTICS

DISCOVERING HOW TO BREATHE correctly again with the resultant benefits of becoming more relaxed, calm and confident, often opens us up to a new life, even if it has taken us *half a lifetime* to rediscover our true selves. It is no good becoming bitter about the apparent waste of years of under achievement because we were out of touch with our core-self. There is a certain truth in the saying, 'the years the locusts took away will be returned in full.' Being given a new lease of life via correct breath makes us cherish that life in a way that perhaps we might not have done had our path been *straight* as in the world's terms.

Regaining the magical information so vital for a magical life, which I am sure we are all meant to enjoy, does cause us to reflect on the impoverished priorities held with the best of intentions by our parents and teachers. If we are parents, we have to allow the gold we are rediscovering to be passed on to our own children, even if it means saying 'sorry, please forgive me, I did my best with what I knew at the time.'

The priceless pearls of wisdom now being released to us from the re-opened window into our true selves, are confirmed by inexplicable coincidences, meeting wonderful people who we feel we have known before, books we now understand, which before have been 'closed' to us. Unexpected sources of amazing wisdom which we recognise have also always been stored within our own psyche. These become more important and valuable to us than any of our possessions.

Some people may suggest we are changing for the worse! Disregard them, perhaps they are no longer meant to be in your life, as other people will come in who recognise and share your new enlightenment.

Obviously all our journeys will be different as we are unique, yet we all face similar challenges. We will have to deal with the anger which often comes to the surface as we feel safe to jettison our fears, fears which have masked the anger we felt as a very young child when the love we brought to the earth was not recognised. It has been buried beneath layers of frightening cultural do's and don'ts. Our educators thought they were vital parts of that education, but they clashed with the rules of Nature, known to us as children, and which child-like we knew was the real teacher to whom we must listen.

Yet we were so small and powerless against the 'adult' world. What they did was to *un-teach* the wonders that were already in our possession, which we did not have the words to express in any way which could change the inflexibility of their rigid adherence to what *they* had been told. Who could blame them?

Untruths about the laws of life or nature still break the spirit of the child in our midst.

When asked what was the most important question for the future of humanity, Einstein answered '*Is Nature friendly?*' (forgiving?) That is why as adults, regaining our natural child, we have to forgive the educational sins of omission which we inherited from our educators, and it is for us to break the cycle of the saying 'the sins of the fathers shall be visited on to the next generation.' Surely these sins are all too obvious in the violence, addictions, greed and lack of spirituality, with which until we listened to the language of the breath, we have unwittingly been in collusion by virtue of our silence.

Whatever our involvement in the raising of the next

generation, that involvement will be worthless unless we recognise and confirm the spirituality already strong and vibrant within the heart of the child. I have quoted elsewhere that '*the Celtic people insisted that only poets should be teachers, because knowledge not taught from the heart is dangerous.*'

Within the education system, the child's individual soul is seldom recognised, we damage the child, it cannot escape from those who it will come to perceive as its persecutors. It knows from its deep intuitive self, the meaning of its own spirituality, and we ignore it at our peril. The perils on so many of our urban streets today are vivid evidence of this. For a child, just one teacher with whom it can resonate from a soul level of understanding can be a life-line for life, even although the time contact may be quite brief.

As adults emerging from the damage done to us as children, we may even feel guilty, but as a result of correct breathing, we again begin to listen to the fresh green shoots of our spirituality. In order to grow we have to jettison our guilt, there is no longer time or space for it. This spirituality has no known religious source; indeed, many religious teachings seem starved of spirituality.

Such tender green shoots need watering by contact with special people, writings, and all manner of unusual happenings and coincidences, which confirm the *rightness* of our new self. Above all our own special person, our true authentic self within.

For a time we believe that the world in which we were reared had been trying to stamp out our identity. Then we realise that the world culture in which we were reared is in some ways not at a very advanced level, and we ourselves must take responsibility for helping to raise the global spiritual progress to a higher level. Brave words you may say, but that's why we are here. This responsibility is like carrying the chalice forward. It does not need to be too onerous, just an acknowledgment of our own part in the work, and trying to carry out that work. We always get credit for trying.

The unseen loving energy of Nature's life force is our strength. You may like to refer to the chapter entitled 'The Power of Thought' to remind yourself of this power.

We cease to follow unquestioningly in the way we were wrongly led as a child, everything is up for grabs. Moving forward on the path of correct breath, the waters part, and miracles seem to occur. They may be small or large, but miracles they are.

One of the corner-stones of support happened for me as I began to walk my own path, surrounded by very little in my life at that time to confirm my dawning breakthroughs in understanding. At that time I was a Councillor in local Government. It became more and more difficult to keep the results of my personal changes under cover, and I was aware that perhaps I was beginning to be looked upon as an oddity. I probably thought so too.

Despite this, people, events, books, articles began to come my way, and reassured me that perhaps I was not so odd after all. In the beginning one or two articles and special books stood out, and became of special significance, particularly because of the context in which they were set, and my growing awareness of the power of the breath.

Two in particular were, to me, of dramatic significance, because they were of religious origin, and it is of some sorrow to me that the religions from which they arose do not appear to realise how great a source of potential teaching they contained, which have not been taken up by two of our main religions. As far as I can see, current traditional church practice does not use, acknowledge or practice the spiritual exercises which are at the root of these interesting references, and even seem to meet with resistance from the 'Establishment'.

I believe in the saying 'when the pupil is ready, the teacher arrives.'

A short article which has stayed in my mind almost as a pointer, appears to me to say to the Church (in this case the Church of England.) 'Why don't you take this idea and carry it to all your Churches throughout the country?'

I cannot remember the magazine in which I read an article entitled 'God and Mammon's Muscles'. It was written by the journalist Peter Brock, and tells of a Church in London in which at lunchtime, for twenty-five minutes, a lady called Christine conducted a relaxation session. Business people and others from all walks of life came in from the street and stretched out on the chancel and altar steps. For a period of time they learned how to relax to induce peace in mind and body. These sessions were started by the vicar who had been an RAF Chaplain, and who as a young man had had a nervous collapse. He attributed his regaining of sanity to the training in relaxation he had received. It had given him the inspiration to start the work within his church to help the many worried and stressed people who fill the workplaces and businesses.

The article concluded that those who attended such sessions came away with a pretty good substitute for 'Heavenly Peace', and I should imagine more so than for many who attended the sometimes repetitive doggerel of traditional Sunday Services. For such peace found in the lunchtime sessions can only be described as spiritual. Peter Brock, the author of this article, concludes by saying 'I wonder why religious bodies don't go in for this applied pastoral approach on a wider scale.' *So do I.*

I don't know if these lunchtime relaxation sessions still continue in this church, I have the name, I must find out. Is the Church too traditional? I think God must have been delighted to see what went on each lunchtime in the church

I have described. A casual visitor to the church might have found the scene of shoeless, jacketless office workers strewn around the chancel steps somewhat at variance with the traditional image of spiritual activity, which traditions I am only too aware of, often produce less than spiritual enlightenment.

The sessions in the church I mention concluded with people often feeling that they had ended up with their sprits *'wrapped high among the organ pipes.'* How many church activities produce the same result?

This one article was for me a trigger to develop my work in teaching relaxation, at a time when I was really needing just such an inspirational 'push'. As a then Local Authority Councillor I was getting to be known as the 'odd one' with my new theories, and it was good to feel reassurance from reading the article on relaxation sessions in a church.

Wouldn't it be great to start such sessions in the Houses of Parliament?

I am reminded of some of the words in the beautiful sonnet by Wordsworth:

> The world is too much with us, late and soon,
> Getting and spending we lay waste our powers,
> Little we see in Nature that is ours,
> We have given our hearts away, a sordid boon.

Separation from Nature breeds neurosis, correct breath heals neurosis.

Most of those who attended the relaxation sessions in the church were not regular church goers, and on the day that the article was written, the attendance consisted of seven men and three women, a possible contrast to the male/female ratio who attend many of our traditional church services.

It is said that 'there is no army strong enough to withstand an idea whose time has come.' I pray that in my lifetime the idea of the power of correct breath to heal the Universe will come, and sweep the dross of our collective toxic thoughts and action away in a miraculously short space of time. It could.

The profound stillness experienced by those who attended the lunchtime relaxation sessions in that church mirror the words of Jesus: 'Ponder in thy own heart, and in thy temple and be still.'

This sense of profound stillness which is the inspirational bonus of profound relaxation, could produce a new spirituality embracing all faiths, in our multi-cultural schools. Teaching children and their parents how to relax naturally, could not only help to prevent later neuroses, but create a spiritual harmony among children, who as adults might create a new world faith based on true spirituality.

Soon after I discovered the article about relaxation teaching in a church, which inspired me to write the last pages of this chapter, I found a fascinating little book called *We Neurotics, a Handbook for the Half-Mad* by Bernard Basset, SJ. I cannot remember how this book came to me, but like many others since, it fell on cultivated ground, whereas other books I have read containing lengthy intellectual references to the same subject matter, have fallen on stony ground!

This dear little book contains the experiences of Father Bernard Basset whose enjoyment of life was continually marred by constant neurotic worry. The book is dedicated to 'those ordinary people we might meet shopping in Marks & Spencer who, in their bedrooms and bathrooms, know themselves to be a little mad.' He attributes his cure to the calm advice of a little nun, short, stout and deaf, who he met on a train. Despite her deafness she could lip-read with amazing accuracy. She had a twinkle in her eye, and a sympathetic manner. In the course of the train journey he confided to her his problem of perpetual anxiety.

The little nun told Father Basset that his only hope was in learning relaxation, telling him that if he really wanted to learn the skill she would teach him. 'Probably it will all be a waste of time, because so few neurotics are humble enough to do more than talk about themselves and their problems.' (Sounds like the old me.) Obviously she was able to impart this information with a great deal of humour, for she caused no offence.

She gave him a little book entitled *Relaxation in Everyday Life*, and went on to say 'Mr. Dawes, you are but one among thousands in this city who face the problem of curing themselves. We talk of people finding their feet, a ridiculous expression. The real task for most people is to find their souls. First step, you must learn to relax. Do not pray for about a month, for God Himself is not at his best until we are relaxed. Just as I cannot help my children at the clinic (where she worked) until they are muscularly peaceful, so God needs a similar condition in the spiritual life.'

Father Basset went home and began to teach himself relaxation, which entailed lying down for at least twenty minutes and gradually relaxing every part of the body. He eventually realised that the better breathing which resulted made him feel as if he was floating, as though he was 'reclining in a green meadow clear of insects and barred to cows!' This book was made doubly readable because of such humorous touches. It was ten years before he met the little nun again. When he did, she spoke about spiritual relaxation, in other words, when we relax, the spiritual dimension will enter the consciousness naturally and inevitably.

In learning correct breathing and relaxation, my own neuroses and worries have long gone, saving exceptional circumstance. Of course you only have my word for it. I do not claim perfection, but I do know that I have found the means to overcome the constant worries of my earlier years.

I thought I was the only sufferer at that time, but have since realised how a high proportion of the people we meet in the street suffer from such problems.

It is so satisfying to introduce at least some of them to the ever available healing power of relaxing breath. I suppose I could say that I am now a cured neurotic. I hope something I may have said in this chapter or book will encourage you to start you own self-healing magical journey. For magic it is. You can also remain half mad.

BE OUTRAGEOUS, THOSE WHO ACHIEVE
MASTERY ARE ALWAYS OUTRAGEOUS.

Source unknown

BEFORE YOU ARE RECOGNISED,
THE WORLD WILL CALL YOU ECCENTRIC, OR
EVEN HALF-MAD. WHEN YOU BECOME FAMOUS,
THEY WILL CALL YOU A GENIUS.

Source unknown

NEVER MIND THE WORLD, JUST BE A
HALF-MAD OUTRAGEOUS GENIUS.

*Experiences of Father Bernard Basset,
a Catholic, who apparently spent much of
his life in a state of perpetual worry.*

Chapter 48

SENILE DEMENTIA
AND ALZHEIMER'S

THE PROBLEMS OF SENILE DEMENTIA and Alzheimer's illness or disease (depending on how you see them,) appear to be affecting more and more people at an even younger age. In my work I have met so many people whose lives have been curtailed by the responsibility of looking after a near relative, often for many years, who have been suffering from such limitations.

I have often given thanks that I have been spared such a decision of conscience which for many thousands has resulted in a 24/7 strain, often shortening their own life span. It is one thing providing this continuing degree of care for a healthy baby, but then there is also the joy of seeing the child develop, with eventually the natural gradual loosening of such a concentrated commitment. To undertake this latter, knowing there is a light at the end of the tunnel, brings a relief from the stress, but looking after an aged senile relative seems a dedication without reward. Of course we are all potentially aged and senile!

That so many people undertake this work with love (a love not visually returned) must surely merit our highest admiration. State-run services are often only available when the carer has reached the limit of coping ability, and must cost the NHS and Social Services hundreds of millions of pounds.

The ability to remain alive when the life impulse in terms

of self responsibility seems no longer present, begs the question which no specialist seems able to answer adequately, of why the body is still functioning when the coping mind no longer seems to be in residence.

In evoking the challenging statement that 'It is not so much a question of what kind of illness a person has, as what kind of person has the illness', you must return to the constant theme of this book and ask yourself the question, 'If a person has breathed correctly for most of their life, would it be *possible* for them to develop dementia or Alzheimer's?' I have to respond and say that I am virtually 100% certain that these afflictions could not have developed, because the brain would have been constantly supplied with its natural food. The brain cells would have been fed and regenerated, rather than starved and degenerated. The food is of course oxygen.

I believe implicitly that the first seconds, minutes and hours after birth are vitally critical in establishing and laying down the correct sequence of brain cell foundation. It has been suggested by Joseph Chilton Pearce in his book *Magical Child*, that cutting the umbilical cord too quickly may disturb the vital oxygen flow essential for this process. If it malfunctions, brain lesions are formed instead of vital healthy oxygenated pulsating cells containing essential life-coping information. Could this missing-link in our natural life growth be one among others which weakens the whole life chain, and its strength to maintain functioning support to the end of the life-span? A chain is only as strong as its weakest link, eventually the flaw in the foundation stone may topple the building.

Never having read any convincing articles which suggest a plausible cause for acute senile mental deterioration, and without wishing to be deliberately provocative, I have observed that many scientists and researchers do not breathe correctly themselves, so are they likely to discover what I consider could be a fundamental cause and symptom of all dis-ease? Respiratory limitation, deterioration of brain cells. This lack of oxygen can prevent an individual's ability to absorb not only that essential ingredient, but the invisible trace elements so vitally needed to ensure efficient brain activity.

Just as an enormous complicated engine will break down if a tiny central cog within its mechanism is malfunctioning, the same process must apply to the human brain. Even a diet apparently containing all the recommended ingredients necessary for health will still be inadequate if the *respiratory* food process is limited, there will simply not be enough oxygen correctly flowing through the digestive system to disperse the energy from the food. It is as if as if you had left the hot tap running and the expensively acquired water is wasted. According to Eastern philosophy air is an essential *food*.

Someone who has breathed correctly throughout their lives, or re-learns the process, will be an individual who has conquered fear, is confident, relaxed, and in harmony with Nature. I cannot believe that they will develop Alzheimer's. Long held fear could be the unrecognised factor in brain deterioration. It is usually the result of contamination by some dominant person from childhood, and even if that person is no longer alive, the mind-set produced by their possessive power could still be affecting our thoughts, emotions and actions. Eventually our psyche seems to lose the memory of our authentic personality. We have lost the way. I know of no other process than by restoring correct breath (or spirit,) to free ourselves from this entrapment.

If we do not live life as our authentic selves, I believe that the ageing process increasingly shows up this internal vacuum, which spreads throughout the brain as cells atrophy from non-use and we become lost in a sea of confusion. Separated by cell lesions from some apparently tiny but essential part of our earliest growth blueprint, this 'wobbly area' could, I believe, be a clue as to why we may seem to 'lose the plot' at the end of our lives. We may not have been adequately *locked into life* at birth, and our correct breathing may have been faulty from the start of our lives. Hence senile dementia.

You may quote me many well-known figures and statistics, but our collective immaturity does not have mature standards of evaluation, or we would not have the social problems of our present culture. A study of the early childhood of many world famous people who develop the ageing diseases referred to in this chapter, will usually give clues of the stress factors contributing to their end-of-life health problems, I believe caused by accumulative incorrect respiration. Often, birth trauma is not recorded.

The loving dedication of their carers is beyond question, but at what cost?

After thirty years in therapeutic work, I have seen countless people who live their lives as perpetual puppets manipulated by domineering others, and a culture which preaches personal development and freedom, but which often freezes and frustrates such blossoming by an over-intellectualised educational system and bureaucracy.

We are beginning to recognise that a frightening proportion of our children have lost the art of play, even if it had ever been nurtured in the first place, indicating an early loss of the natural joy of life which is every child's birthright.

I can think of a famous novelist who suffered from Alzheimer's in later life, whose work was brilliantly intellectual and analytical, but which always left me with a sense of melancholy. I have since realised that for me it lacked a feeling of joy. Who or what blighted that sense of joy I do not know, but I am sure that this constant symptom I observed in the writer's work, ultimately led to the eventual early departure of the personality and development of the symptoms of Alzheimer's. We probably have to look at the creative and emotional right brain to discover the clues for later regression.

An ideal old age suggests to me a time of gentle slowing down which is still full of joy. It may appear as if brakes are being expertly and spiritually applied until a healthy completion of this particular round of earthly existence resembles the dropping down of a ripe hazel nut from its sheath. Well that is how I would like to go!

If you want to avoid ending your days as senile or an Alzheimer sufferer, I profoundly believe it would be worth your while to investigate correct breathing as distinct from breathing techniques or deep breathing. This latter is often wrongly taught by pulling in the stomach while breathing in, energetically expanding the upper chest and raising the shoulders. I say this because countless clients have come to me who have been exposed to this 'technique' method, and subsequently developed symptoms of hyperventilation which, untreated, can precipitate premature deterioration. This was true even of a yoga teacher I worked with some years ago. Some yoga teaching falls short in correct breathing training.

In order to keep the upper brain healthily and adequately supplied with oxygen, it is essential to expand the lungs fully, first made visible by the expansion of the lower stomach between the pelvic bone and the navel, an area often referred to as the lower brain. This *starter* impulse free of muscular restriction allows the air to rise unimpeded through the lungs to the lobes just beneath the collar bone. A sense of joy and wonder starts to filter through at experiencing your authentic and unique self, keeping you securely and safely 'at home' within your innermost centre, the emotional source of which is located in the lower 'second brain', the sacral area.

Nowadays we seem to have an obsession with food, ignoring the fact that those who breathe correctly know instinctively what food is needed, protein, carbohydrates, greens, etc. Such people seem to graze in a free-range way without worrying about elaborately planning their diet. They do not need some 'expert' telling them what they should or should not eat. Again bodily needs are being made known from within. I continually find that wrong breathers feed wrongly, usually addictively, fast foods, over-sweet or over-fat to provide an artificial feel-good security factor, which is immediately and freely naturally available from correct breathing. They do not need artificially stimulating 'comfort' food to experience the 'feel good' factor.

I believe that what comes out of the mouth is more important than what goes in. It is essential to honour and respect our food, but not to worship it as a God substitute as we seem to do these days. Shouldn't it be loving communication that comes out of the mouth? This loving communication via the right breath on a non-verbal level of *ourselves with ourselves,* ensures a continuous internal 'health and safety'existence which keeps the extremes of old age at bay.

Correct breathing is like having a constant compass point within, which just needs perpetual loving attention to stay on course. Such expert steering bestows great rewards on those who travel unerringly in this way. Improved health, reduced fear and anxiety, the ability to think correctly, intuitively and appropriately in any situation, prioritising in emergencies, in other words dancing with situations as they arise. To do this one must always see the cup as half-full rather than half-empty. It works! A great recipe for graceful ageing.

If we do not have correct and natural respiratory skills finely toned, we shall not be able to think clearly and take right action in our daily lives, or in a crisis. We shall delay and procrastinate. As the years go by the cumulative effect of this confused and woolly thinking creates a ripe breeding ground which is likely to develop in later life as senility or Alzheimer's. That is my opinion.

TO BREATHE RIGHTLY IS TO AGE RIGHTLY.

Chapter 49

THE VIBRATION
OF THE VOICE

THE POWER of the human voice is a fantastic power. Like every other human faculty it can be used to kill or cure. Just pause to think who we are. Our thoughts and emotions are conveyed on the vibration of our breath, via the voice. You may think the phrase 'kill or cure' rather extreme, the eyes also have the same potential to damage. The eyes and the voice are all expressions of our identity. Their energy comes from the human brain. Thought, and murderous thoughts even if not expressed in the form of action, can still be lethal.

By the same token how many people have left it too late to tell a loved one that they love them, in other words expressed that love through voice? Instead they did not actually speak the loving words, and perhaps someone died so they never could be said.

It happens all the time. Remember to voice your love before it is too late.

If you have left it too late, I am positive you can still 'speak' to a departed loved one, through silent thoughts, and say everything you wish you had said before they had moved on. Speak from the heart. You can also write the words in the form of a letter, which you can then tear up or burn, your thought energy will have gone out into the atmosphere, and will find its home. Anyway, that is what I believe.

Criticism, condemnation, hostility, aggression, wish to

wound, are brought to us by the vibration of negativity in all its forms, mostly through the human voice. The more intense, the greater the energy which is being projected from one individual to another.

Children are at the mercy of our wish to hurt by thought, our voice will tell them all that is necessary to wound. Even if physical damage does not necessarily seem to follow a harsh word or look. The child is a growing organism, and it does not take a physical blow to stunt growth. The cold wind of Nature stunts the growth of a tender plant, although no material energy can be seen. So too can the child be injured by a word.

The law of vibration is the law of projected energy, which as humans we direct outwards in our behaviour to others, and the material constructions we create. If these go against the law of Nature which is on the law of Alpha, nine to fifteen vibrations a second, and scientifically proved to be the Earth's magnetic frequency, damage will eventually occur. The contrasting frequency of constant high Beta, fifteen to twenty-five vibrations a second, when projected at its highest level, causes inharmonious vibrations and will eventually affect material constructions. An invisible wound has been inflicted. It does not have to be physical, but the invisible can eventually affect the material.

I heard recently that in her earlier political career the voice of Margaret Thatcher came across as sharp and high, and she had to have vocal training to deepen that sound. A high sharp voice indicates anxiety, and although Mrs Thatcher's voice obviously improved in its vibration, it did come across as a little too artificially perfect during speeches; possibly she had not really lost the underlying anxiety.

I have never been involved in the art of chanting, which develops the sound of the human voice in a very impressive way, coming as it does through the deepest levels which can be attained by the human voice. The origin of chanting is lost in the mists of time, but many will have heard usually through taped music, the amazing sound of Tibetan chanting. The collective sound of group chanting creates a powerful energy vibration. Famous opera singers have been known to shatter a glass by the vibration of their highest notes.

Several months ago I read in the media that a riot in some part of the world (was it America?) was quelled by the playing of classical music. I have thought since that such a brilliant idea could be made much more use of, as I imagine police cars swooping down on gangs with Elgar, Mozart or Debussy vibrating from their loudspeakers! It is very difficult to maintain aggression in the face of melodic music, some part of the psyche must respond to the vibration of beauty, and so the brain begins to slow down, thereby beginning to deprive the violence of its aggressive peak.

Mothers-to-be play classical music to their unborn children. I believe it is the vibrational effect on the mother which is conveyed to the child because of the profoundly relaxing effect on her nervous system so closely linked to that of the baby. The sensitive foetus relaxes and receives the knock-on bonus of an improved oxygen and blood supply.

Obviously the other vital factor is the impact on the developing spirit of the child. No one can tell us at what point the soul of the child becomes active, but I believe that in some way it is present from the point of conception, probably before, if we accept the concept of reincarnation.

When I started my work as a psychotherapist, I incorporated the teaching of the art of relaxation through the teaching of self-hypnosis. This was the first time I had consciously used my voice in a therapeutic situation in order to affect the ability of someone else to become calm. Apart of course when my children were small, and I naturally needed to use calming tones to comfort or encourage sleep.

In order to assist relaxation, I knew my voice had to be

sure and authentic, but it was not until I started to talk to a client who was trying to relax, that I realised I was quite *naturally* using my voice and therefore my self in a way that *rose from the source of my breath*. The sound of my voice rose from the very base of the point where correct breathing commences, between the pelvic bone and the navel. It came to me that, from this point, not only the timbre but also the correct words seemed to emanate unconsciously. Additionally the client expressed pleasure with the deep level of peace and relaxation achieved, saying that the sound of my voice had been the vital ingredient. This stimulated a period of very important understanding in the power of the sound of the voice.

While *what* was said was of course very important, the vibrational *sound* level of the voice had been as important, if not more important, than the words. Indeed if I had spoken the same words in a hard, sharp voice, my client would have been unable to relax. The timbre was the key.

I was aware that I needed to breathe quite naturally from the base of the lungs in order to find the rights words, and those words had to be *spiritually precise*, according to the personality of the client, who could be a school cleaner, a teenager or a lawyer. If someone is going to respond and relax to the sound of a human voice, they have to be able to empathise, trust and respond to that sound and the meaning of the words spoken.

The passages of the respiratory system carry the vibrational sounds of the voice, so that when we are breathing correctly from the base of the lungs, the harmonics of that sound are smooth and unobstructed by muscular tension pressing on the vocal chords.

Think of someone who becomes paralysed by fear; their voice becomes paralysed too, because the tense muscles surrounding the lungs also press against the vocal cords, and no sound can be produced.

The sound and quality of the voice therefore is dependent upon the harmonious relaxation of the respiratory apparatus. I have always wondered why the great singer, Kathleen Ferrier, died of cancer, which suggests to me that glorious as was her voice, there must have been some blocking tension which was a causal factor, so that although her trained voice reached a fantastic scale, there was a restriction at some point in her respiratory pattern. I can think of no other reason for her illness, because anyone who develops cancer has some impediment in the respiratory pattern which affects the voice. I do not in any way wish to detract from the magnificence of the range of Kathleen Ferrier's wonderful gifts.

When you own a radio or TV, you have a permanent reminder of the effect of the human voice on the senses of those who are in a way hostage to the imposed sound. When you become sensitive to the vibrations of the human voice and its indivisibility from respiration, you can tell without seeing the speaker, the accuracy of their breathing, and from that their stress level. Time without number, the speech speed of a speaker, particularly on news and advertising programmes is much too fast, of a high Beta frequency, not able to be creatively absorbed.

Why do we think that speed is what we must aim for?

Because such a speed is unnatural, it produces too high an electrical brain frequency, and goes against the speed of Nature. It is therefore harmful to the speaker and the listener. All you can do is switch off the programme, because you cannot be bothered to try to keep up, and also know that you will miss nothing of spiritual importance by trying to adjust yourself to the same unnatural auditory speed as the vocalist. Nothing is lost in spiritual terms, therefore nothing is lost.

The irritating aspect of such vocal speed and tone is that

the sound of such voices is usually harsh and jarring to the senses. Like a knife scraped against an enamel plate.

I wonder where the tradition arose, which implied that *our hero* had to have a 'gravelly' voice in order to be sexy! Obviously it implied someone who held emotions in severe check, and was only able to tell our heroine of his love through clenched teeth, as if the sentiments were being torn unwillingly from tightly closed lips! The symptom of an era when men were not supposed to express soft and loving feelings, and women grovelled and fainted. How hilarious!

Then again the number of voices you hear on television or in daily interchange which denote someone with sinus problems, tell you how many are not breathing through the nose properly, almost trying to prevent the air going correctly up through that organ. Many will be mouth breathers. '*Mouth breathing*', as the famous yoga teacher Ramacharaka said, 'is the most disgusting form of breathing known to man.' (*The Science of Breath.*) The seeds of such respiratory aberration are usually sown in childhood. The child is a vulnerability barometer, like a fine precision instrument, only more sensitive. It is affected by the lovingness or not of its environment.

If the adults around the child are not sensitive to its nature, they become a threat to the child, who has an instinct to hide away. Usually that is not possible. Therefore the child, who knows its spirit is drawn up through the nose via its breath, thinks that if it avoids doing so it will not be seen, and therefore be out of danger. The child assumes others will not then see it, its spirit is as real to the child as its physical form. So begins the holding of the breath, the nostrils become clogged and overgrown causing the blocking of the sinuses with solid mucus, which then hardens throughout the respiratory passages.

The strangulated voices of so many young people in our

culture, become a source of sorrow to me, they denote young people who are cut off from their feelings, behaving so often like zombies, unworthy of having an identity. The repression of true loving sound conveyed by respiratory tension, tells anyone who knows the science of the voice that future illness is being hibernated. These years are the seed bed from which ill-health starts to root itself in future heart and lung problems, cancer, and mental illness.

Voices are melodious, weak or discordant; you change your voice as you correct your breathing, strengthen your auto-immune system, create or avoid future illness.

The sound of a harmonious voice makes you feel good. I remember meeting a young woman recently who had given up a well-paid job, home, and a not very fulfilling relationship. Her reason for giving up what to many people represent a desired security?

She told me that she had decided not to go anywhere, do anything, or be with anyone who did not give her joy. I respected and admired her, knowing that such a state is attainable if you have the courage. She listened to the voice of her intuition.

How sad that so many children are stuck with parents who do not give them joy, because *their* parents did not give *them* joy. You can hear the trapped tears in their voices.

Of course not all voices have an *audible* sound, we have the voice of reason, the voice of conscience, the voice of despair, of hope. The silent sound of the voice arises from the depths of our being.

The secret of the voice is inextricably linked with the secret of correct breath, as with all harmony of the human psyche.

The best use of the human voice is in good communication, by whatever medium.

I think good communication comes naturally to adults whose nurturing allowed their loving child to be heard and understood. The child is taught by example to listen to other people with respect. First of all to respect their own thoughts and feelings, and be able to communicate them *without fear or anger.*

It took me many years to achieve a good level of communication. I suppose it's almost impossible to achieve perfection, but as I gained the courage to communicate honestly and openly I realised it also gave the other person permission to do the same, and our relationship went up several notches.

Good, right vocal communication allows no sense of competition. It does not allow the use of anger, criticism, or patronage. It has to be expressed with love, particularly the sense of love that the speaker has for him or herself; it allows the speaker to tell the other person that they love them, quite firmly, but with no degree of sentimentality or weakness. Indeed it is necessary to tell someone that you love them, with no expectation or need for that love to be returned. It may seem detached but not cold. It means that the love is unreserved, which is the only love worth having.

Often communicating with someone who is openly hostile requires you to be 'as wise as the serpent, but gentle as the dove.' You give no hostility in return, so the hostile person can find no chink in *your* armour of love, and is left with no verbal ammunition. The verbal communication may end, but the hostile person is also left to ponder the meaning of your words. They sometimes change!

When Jesus was talking to his disciples he told them that when he spoke, his words contained a number of levels, in which his listeners would take for themselves whatever was appropriate for their level of awareness. He meant that for some his words had meaning far too deep to comprehend, while others understood exactly. That did not indicate criticism of anyone, merely that we all come to the full comprehension of the truth in our own time. It is said that there is only one way to learn that truth, which is when *we are ready*. Still, the only route is, 'through the eye of the needle' of truth.

There exists what can only be termed a *healing voice*, when the sound of the spoken word even in ordinary conversation produces a calming sound, in which you feel loved, cherished and somehow *better*, even if you could not really understand why. I spoke to someone on the phone recently, who I have never met, and knew from her voice that she was what is known as a *healer*. There was a richness in her voice. I look forward to the joy of meeting and communicating with her very soon.

The law of vibration, ensures that whatever energy we put out will be returned to us, that is as sure as the return of a boomerang. In our culture we look for instant returns. As we grow in spiritual knowledge we do not expect that, we accept that there is always a *right time* which may take years (and tears) to work through.

In Levi's *Aquarian Gospel*, Jesus taught that what is sin for one person, may not be a sin for another who is not so far advanced on the spiritual path. He went on to say 'a little sin in him who walks in Holy Breath, is greater far than sin in him who never knew the way.'

There is a 'boomerang' law which attracts back to us negative events which match the energy of our negative thoughts, actions and words. It works much faster on anyone who breathes correctly, and yet breaks the law of loving voice! It is how we learn.

BY YOUR WORDS [*your voice*] MEN SHALL KNOW YE.

Holy Bible

I hope this chapter has not rendered you speechless.

Chapter 50

HANDWRITING

GRAPHOLOGY

(Or what you see is not always what you get...)

YOU MAY WONDER what a chapter on handwriting has to do with breathing, which is the theme which runs through most of these pages, again, and again, and again. Should I apologise? Never. It may be your flash recall of one of the repetitive statements about breathing which could save your health or life! However, to get back to handwriting.

In my youth I had terrible handwriting, all over the place; it was as if I couldn't be bothered to wait long enough to form the words. I envied some of my friends whose neat writing flowed across the pages in orderly rows. One of my teachers wrote that I was '*capable* of great concentration.' You would not think so to look at my notebooks.

It was because of the conscious changes I made in my handwriting which convinced me that a chapter on this subject might interest you. I cannot now remember what inspired, prompted or shocked me into a short, intense study of the subject, but after buying a book which seemed to leap out at me from a bookshop, as they do, I became hooked on the idea that change your handwriting, and you can change yourself for the better.

Jumping forward a few years from my earlier encounters with handwriting, to my years as a Councillor in local government. I was once on a selection panel for a new Director of Education, and had been earlier impressed by one of the candidates. My mind was finally made up as we studied the then hand-written applications. If ever there was an application which I would have selected, even if I had not met this particular candidate, his handwriting alone would have given him my vote.

Being the only female on an all-male selection committee, I was able to sway the other members by the good character points evident in the handwriting to which I was able to refer, in comparison to the other applicants. I was so grateful for my knowledge of the science of Graphology, subsequent years in office proved that this Directorship had been a good and popular choice.

Some of the points I had noticed were the size, slope, upper and lower case lengths, the placing of the t-bar, etc., and I even believe that my other male selection colleagues were a little impressed that a mere woman knew something they did not!

I have only met one person who was a professional graphologist, they are rather thin on the ground. If I had known that this might be a career choice I would love to have studied the subject as a vocation, but at the end of the war this was probably not an option, and anyway I wanted to be a gym teacher at the time. Maybe I could have combined both!

I had several fascinating conversations with the lady graphologist at a conference I was attending, and although she did not give much away, I gathered that she had been consulted by the police, and I have since heard that they do indeed use handwriting experts as part of criminal investigations. I also understand that some large business companies use handwriting diagnosis as part of the appointment process for key executives.

Anyway change starts at home, so I had to swallow my

pride and study my own scrawl. In studying several books about handwriting analysis the first piece of information which caught my eye was about pre- or fore-strokes i.e. the curve or straight line which many people insert before a letter itself begins.

A long forestroke, whether straight or curved, implies procrastination, always putting off until tomorrow what you plan to do today, being long-winded, taking a long time to get to the point. Dear me, this was going to involve a lot of self-searching. The wonderful thing was that when I left out the unnecessary pre-stroke, I found that I became more efficient, less dithery. It was as if I had no need to delay decision-making. I *felt* more in the here and now. It saved time too, reduced delaying tactics I did not know I was using.

Next in the self-analysis challenge was to absorb the fact that sharp angles in the downstrokes of *f*, *g*, and *y* imply a strong critical faculty. Critical of oneself, but then inevitably also critical of others. Not a trait I admire, but I had it. At least in any paragraph I was guilty at least once. I had to change that, from sharp down angles to what are called completed loving loops. As I cut out the sharp angles, I began to feel more loving. Amazing!

When the down loop is very open going a long way to the left, it implies a bit of us is stuck in the past. Well I wasn't guilty of that.

Then we come to the t-stroke, where the cross is meant to be attached to the upper part of the stroke, and pointing upward and out, forward looking. If the t-cross is separated by a space from the upward bar, it denotes our aims are too far in advance of our ability to carry them out. Where the t-bar points backward there is a possibility of finding it very difficult to make progress. We are stuck in the past to some extent, usually an aspect of our childhood. When the t-bar starts from the bottom of the upright it can signify depression.

About the dot. If the dot sits in front of the letter, again we are too far in advance of our ability to actually perform, or deliver the goods, running before we can walk. If the dot is behind the letter itself, we find it difficult to succeed, and seem to sabotage ourselves. Hanging back. The thing to avoid is to make the dot like an open circle, as if we cannot even trust ourselves to *be here*.

Last of all slope. Slope upright, that's what you are, upright, may seem bit unbending, but can be trusted. Slope to the right, outgoing, meeting people half-way. Too much to the right, you're a doormat. Slope to the left you hold back, too much and it can be a problem, introspection may be present, emotional withdrawal. Some writing slopes upright, forward and backward all in a few sentences, indicating rather mixed-up, indecisive, confused.

Big space between the words, someone who really wants to be on their own. Spacing themselves away from others, very small writing great concentration, too small secretive Large, open writing, easy to know, affectionate, too large, childish?

Oh! I forgot. The height of the upper part of letters such as *l, k, h*. If this stretches up quite high, the person will usually have high aspirations, be imaginative, often spiritual.

When a letter has a lower loop, which stretches quite far down, it usually denotes a person who has strong intuitive faculties and is very resourceful. I think it is interesting to remember that as upright beings our heads reach upwards (to heaven?), and yet our feet are earthbound. We need to reach for the highest, and yet remain firmly centred on the earth.

Handwriting with a reasonable right slant, which also has a high upward stroke, and long downward stroke, usually indicates someone of high intellect, intuition, and spiritual characteristics. A friend to be valued.

I hope you are still with me, or are you writing away to test you own character? Do not worry, I discovered my personality seemed to change for the better when I changed some aspects of my handwriting. I like to think my character improved too!

Many years ago I thought I was in love with an outwardly very attractive man. At one point early in our relationship, he showed me an article he had hand written for a newspaper. I received a shock. Too small backward writing, a big space between the words, and very sharp-angled down strokes, indicating a very critical personality who likes to be alone, emotionally withdrawn, hiding the real self. The real person behind the persona. Subsequent events proved my knowledge accurate, it would never have worked. Saved my broken heart!

They say that a little knowledge is a dangerous thing, but I'm glad I have a little knowledge about this fascinating subject. I have not kept up with current teaching trends in handwriting; in my childhood expectations were not far from copperplate. At least that was the hope, but I think everything changed with the advent of the biro.

A basic knowledge of graphology helps in understanding relationships, not being too judgmental, accepting that you cannot change other people, not even wanting to, although it helps to be aware. It is so true that the proper study of man is man. If we understood each other with greater compassion, I am sure the natural world would look after itself.

It is also fascinating to study the handwriting of famous people. Very rarely what the world would call neat and even, and yet you get the feeling of the urgency of the flow of thought and imagination. The handwriting of criminals is also very revealing.

Please don't look at your own handwriting, groan and criticise yourself. I believe that some of the stresses that seem to put negative traits into our handwriting occur in early childhood. This may seem strange because that was before we were able to write, but it is the brain which sends vibrations to the fingers, and the only thing that happens in the brain is thought of a higher or lower electrical impulse. Electrical nerve frequencies have an effect on how we operate our fingers, hold the pen, and let the writing flow.

It is helpful to realise that we can change things about our handwriting, and it is also comforting to sense that we seem to move nearer to the nice place within ourselves where we feel good to be, and we've done it ourselves. It's cheaper than employing a therapist.

You may wonder where the breath has got to in all this talk about handwriting.

Funnily enough I have seen a client's handwriting change for the better, including my own, as the breathing improves. Maybe it is because we are giving ourselves more time, which allows us to discover increased pleasure in life, including the art of handwriting. The calmness of a relaxed mind flows into all that we do, the more worried and anxious we are, and start to breathe badly, the more our handwriting will reflect that stress.

Above all it gives you a sense of good power, of being in charge of *you*. Treat this chapter with a reasonable amount of light-heartedness, but don't dismiss it. My work with people suffering from stress has been helped enormously from the knowledge of the science of handwriting. I have sometimes suggested to people that they try to adjust some aspect of their writing, but it has to be done in a very careful way, and with no criticism implied. Time after time a client has expressed continuing interest in the subject, and found the tips useful.

Blocks in handwriting such as the ones I have referred to can create blocks in the expression of our loving potential.

Why block your potential?

YOU ARE A FREE SPIRIT.

Chapter 51

HANDSHAKING

WHY DO WE SHAKE HANDS? It's a physical contact, not too intimate, implying 'so far and no further.' It conveys a willingness to communicate, and seems to be the acceptable form of civilized greeting in Western culture. Further East one finds a newly-introduced stranger may touch the heart and head, perhaps accompanied by a bow of varying degree. Again there is the folding of the hands as if in prayer, with the head bowed. Don't the Eskimos rub noses, or is that how they kiss? I quite like the touching of the head and heart, can you imagine it in a British small town?

Anyway there will always be a specific reason for this way in which we are introduced to a stranger, which will be locked away in time and tradition. Maybe defined by religion or mythology, but it determines how we say 'hi' round the globe, as a form of introduction.

Since I became more aware of everything in my life, which had become heightened by correct breathing, this also applied to an increased significance in the way I noticed we shake hands. Shaking hands conveys more than touching the flesh of one of the extremities of the body through our hands and fingers. It also began to tell me a great deal more about the nature of the individual to whom I was being introduced, their sensitivity, and indeed the warmth or otherwise of their personality. Although you may say that only the hands make contact, the hands are also the outposts of the brain, giving an indication of what that person is really thinking and feeling.

There is a form of therapeutic work for which I have a great deal of respect, which is called Transactional Analysis. Briefly summed up it reminds us that we communicate with each other in three ways, as a parent, child or mature adult. For someone of an adult age to continually communicate with another adult in a parental or childish role, assumes that the other individual in this one to one dialogue is expected to play the opposite role, for instance, a parent or child. Obviously a limited *transaction*. In a mature relationship between adults, naturally the interaction between the individuals is just that, mature, there is no exchange of bossy parental or childish behaviour, which involves looking after or being looked after.

This is adult to adult behaviour, wholesome, and likely to result in positive communication.

Of course within an adult to adult relationship we can *play* at being a bossy parent or helpless child, but that is within a humorous playful context, a form of comic drama, in which each participant is not dependent on the other for security.

Going back to the hand-shake, there are three forms of which I have become aware. The over-hearty, where the other shaker is trying to squeeze your hand as if in one of those hand-grip competitions. In fact the grip is quite painful. There is the shake in which you get the feeling that the other person's hand is held out, so that you do the work of shaking, but gives no impression of an intended reasonable contact. A limp fish impression. Lifeless.

You receive a sensation that the other person is not really there, or actually hates physical contact, and I have often thought that *I* am expected to do the shaking. If I did not support the hand I am holding, it would drop limply to that person's side. Has that happened to you? It is very hard to contact that person emotionally.

Then there is the reasonable and normal contact in which

the grip is firm but not too firm, and you feel that the other person is glad to meet you, which creates an atmosphere for further pleasant communication, i.e. adult to adult.

To me the first hand shake I mentioned implies a feeling of control, especially if you are a woman, and the male does not have the sensitivity to realise that bones in the hand can crack if squeezed too tightly! In a male-to-male context there is the macho image of someone implying that they are the boss because of greater strength. Sorry guys!

As for the limp lack of enthusiasm response, you can get the impression that the other person has no pleasure in meeting you, they are either afraid, or have received no adequate physical parental contact in their childhood, to be able to make outgoing physical contact.

Subsequent experience has proved to me that the handshake which gives firm pressure of touch belongs to a person with whom I shall have future adult communication, which gives equal satisfaction to both hand-shakers. This does not imply that I reject the other people with whom I have exchanged a hand-shake, but I cannot change anyone who seems to carry an over-parental or childish behavioural overtone conveyed to me by this initial hand contact. Usually further meetings confirm the initial negative impression conveyed by the not very pleasant handshakes mentioned.

So for me the awareness created by the first contact exchanged by the way we hand-touch another, can save a lot of time in unrealistic expectations. The mature adult is never bossy or controlling, always wanting to turn us into a child so they can look after us. The mature adult is not continually sad, worried, frightened, helpless and lonely, stealing your energy if you let them, you do not have to 'baby-mind' them.

Those who are over-parental or helpless, can change, but from my own personal experience, a great deal of emotional growth is involved, which can take some time.

From three decades of working with people who ask for help along the way, it is amazing how many marriages and friendships are based on the bossy parent/helpless child foundation. It is not a very healthy rearing ground for raising children, who cannot flourish in the immature atmosphere surrounding them. The same formula by which a psychologically unhealthy parental relationship is founded, is apt to be carried on by the children of such impoverished nurturing.

To me the handshake can tell me whether I am going to have to work very hard to avoid being 'taken over' by someone, or work very hard in another way to avoid having to be the person who is expected to look after the other individual. No way can I be drawn into such unreal relationships, been there, done it, worn the tee-shirt! Time is too precious.

A good hand-shake gives us a sensation of mutual joy. A bad one can tell us that the other person is either too much or hardly at all emotionally present Practice your handshake on yourself, like the way you shake your own hand, do it lovingly, and positively, think of how you would really like someone to shake your hand in the same way. Transferring that warmth with no emotional overtones, and your handshake will invite happiness back. No hidden agendas, just a non-verbal way of saying '*I'm OK, you're OK.*'

OF COURSE YOU ARE.

Chapter 52

BIRTH OF A CHARITY

ONE DAY IN 2005 I woke up at 3am, a not unusual occurrence at my age, perhaps unsurprising since I was in bed by 8pm. The events of the day before, although positive, had depleted my nervous energy and I needed to rest to recharge my spiritual battery.

The words of an old friend, an extremely enlightened very spiritual healer, writer and speaker, called Lilla Bek often return to me. I have mentioned this in another chapter. 'I can't wait to go to bed with God.' she remarked at about seven-thirty one evening. At the time I was not enlightened enough to understand the meaning of her words, now I realise how necessary it is to withdraw into oneself, not to continue making continuous effort, but to allow our higher brain levels to make contact with the invisible spiritual forces from which we spring, as we prepare for rest. These can only communicate when we opt out of the daily demands of our culture, and allow the healing energy of a wiser power to permeate our cells, and release our corresponding wisdom.

Whenever I obey this natural need to retire and rest, I always find I accomplish much more when I take up my work again, and in addition I take greater pleasure in what I do.

I wish I had known the truth of the above paragraphs many years ago in what I now think of as my *battling* years, when on looking back I seemed to be perpetually acting out the role of the willing horse. A great insight came to me one day, for which I have been perpetually grateful, that is realising that we *abuse Nature* when we ignore fatigue signs.

Those signs are there as a warning from Nature, which is a force not to be disobeyed.

Thank goodness someone had the sense to put the road sign 'Tiredness Kills' on our motorways. Disregarding tiredness can shorten our lives, as we gradually deplete our tender engines of their sensitive nervous energy. I think the words *'tiredness kills'* might usefully be put up in shops, offices, educational establishments, and places of work, adding the words *stress, burnout, worry, physical and nervous illness*. I am sure that my good health, which I attribute to the result of correct breathing, is due to the fact that when I do so, I relax and can hear that still, small voice. My still small voice led me to the truth in such sayings as 'take rest, a field that is rested gives a beautiful crop.' So it does. As in Nature, so with us.

Anyway to go back to this early morning awakening. I had not woken up because of some nameless worry, which rarely happens nowadays. Instead ideas were being processed through my newly-refreshed brain.

These ideas concerned a world peace crusade, not the kind of peace crusade that involves delegates from all over the world sitting around committee tables with nothing to show for all the talking at the end of five years, but a movement which could quickly spread like a *loving* virus, crossing continents, without the need of passports, its healing virulence infiltrating, infesting and affecting everyone who catches the bug, which needs no antidote.

This virus is the *art of correct breathing*, a secret known to us at birth, but a pearl of great price, mislaid because of its invisibility in a world which only believes in what it can see and hold. This art is consciously practiced by only a few people in each country, but I believe could be the spiritual force keeping the lid on the volcano of global mayhem. This vibration of correct breath I suggest is the only one truly matching the exact vibration of the Earth's great beating heart.

Do you recall some words which were in circulation a few years ago, that a 'handful of people in each city who meditate, can lower the tension and violence in that community?' I truly believe that a greater effect can come about by groups of people who also breathe correctly, the better the breathing, the deeper the meditation. In fact you *don't really meditate correctly unless you are breathing correctly*. Correct breathers are in a state of meditation all the time. You don't have to sit cross-legged for a certain length of time in a lotus position on a cushion each day, although the discipline of a certain period each day, may initially be necessary.

I think all our thoughts and effective subsequent actions need to spring from a continuous meditative state, and only pause when the need for rest is respected. Subsequently we then carry on all our daily activities in tune with the harmony of Nature, and the God or Higher Consciousness of our understanding.

So you want to hear what that 3am call from the Universe was all about? It was about the creation of a world Charitable Crusade *to promote correct breathing*. I struggled for some time with a title, and abbreviations of that title which would be easy to remember, and convey the core sense of its meaning.

The words that seemed to be given to my mind in those early morning quiet hours were 'Breath is Global.' The concept seemed so enormous, mind-blowing, great. I then considered the word Great. So, **G** for Global, then **R** for Respiratory (breath is life). **E** could stand for Educational, because the *re-teaching* of correct breathing would be our aim. **A** to symbolise Advancement, and of course **T** for Trust. The word TRUST is a special word: TO HAVE FAITH IN SOMETHING WE CANNOT SEE.

I believe that the one element which could unify the

world, is correct breath, to imagine the whole world breathing with one loving breath, Is that an impossible dream? No one could stop me conceiving the idea. A big idea?

THE GREAT BIG TRUST.
(THE GLOBAL RESPIRATORY EDUCATIONAL ADVANCEMENT TRUST)

Breath is Global.

> A man's aim should outstretch his reach,
> Or what's a Heaven for?

Have you got a better idea? As I thought about the idea of a Trust to teach the world to breathe correctly I realised the trust God has put on all who understand the meaning of the breath, to do something, anything, everything, to spread the thought of the idea.

Spread the thought, and also the action required, for the sake of our babies and children who must be our first priority.

The way to stop the violence is to rear children who breathe freely, who can feel love, for it is only love which can heal. To teach the populations of the world that they have the power to use the spirit within the breath to heal themselves.

The higher invisible power that can match and amplify every correct spirit breath we take cannot release its healing energy until we have taken the first steps to erase the darkness we mistakenly think is there. Because of this imagined darkness we are frightened to be true to the spiritual core of the breath which lies within each of us. Once trust the breath spirit instead of the fear, and we switch on the great powerful floodlights of global healing. To dispel the darkness which is only the *myth* of our imagination...

The spiritual bank interest account was opened for us at

birth and is never closed to us, no matter how much we are overdrawn. Correct breath is the currency, and nothing less can keep the account in healthy balance.

It was at this point that my mind closed down again, and I drifted back to sleep.

When I woke I had to write down the thoughts which had come to me at 3 o'clock that morning.

While I have been writing these chapters, it has been necessary to wake soon after 5am, in order to use that time when the brain can be clear and free from the clutter of everyday minutiae. Once having achieved such a practice, the rest of the day feels fulfilled in a special way.

We are used to thinking that it is physical activity which tires us, but I have found that using the energy of the mind when ideas are at their peak flow, takes as much energy which then requires a rest period. Our whole culture seems to disregard this natural and simple law, which probably accounts for an enormous percentage of the bad feelings we direct to our fellow beings daily. In truth we drive ourselves, or consent to be driven, as if we are still in a world condemned to slavery. Above all, we tell ourselves that it is necessary. I often recall the simple words of a poem written by a friend in my autograph album when I was a child.

> A little work, a little play, evenings in which to rest,
> Of all the things along life's way,
> Surely these things are best.

They make for contentment too, together with right breath!

The day after I had written the preceding words, I overslept, and woke up at half-past nine, which upset my intention of starting by seven. I considered why I had broken my promise to myself and recalled the events of the daybefore.

It has taken me some years after retirement to do what

many European countries do as a matter of course, take a mid-day nap. As one gets older this is even more important, to recharge the batteries, and even sleep more. I don't think this is degeneration, but in giving ourselves permission to rest, we give ourselves permission to communicate with ourselves at a deeper and more satisfying level.

Our country holds some pretty unsettling records when compared with our European partners, of poor health and maternity statistics, numbers of the prison population.

The stiff upper lip and *work until you drop* ethos is not the best recipe for contentment; the priority of financial success being the only aim, can never lead to happiness.

I recalled that the day before I overslept I had been some miles away, and because of using optimum time in that place I became involved in a number of additional activities. which normally I would have spread over two days. These continued well into the evening, and on returning home late, after a four-teen hour day, I rewarded myself with a dish of raspberries and cream!

Eating so late meant that I did not have a slow wind-down of activity as the evening drew in, and I could not sleep for a long time, partly because the brain was still assisting the body with food digestion, and also because my mind was over-stimulated like an over-wound spring. The day's activi-ties had not been negative, but I had disregarded a timetable which ignored my personal energy capabilities, which meant staying close to nature. Including a mid-day rest of some kind.

A whole day moving here and there, difficult parking, fitting in more than I would have wished because I was in the area, working on into the evening, hurrying home in busy traffic, drinking too many casual cups of coffee, and finally eating just before I crawled into bed.

No wonder my brain found it impossible to switch off, it was still occupied with the day's activities, not least having to process my late meal through my digestive system. We often forget that the brain has to be in operation while it instructs the digestion to deal with the food we have sent to it, but not at a time of night when it was meant to have time off. It (and I) could not close down.

I will pass on one useful tip to you when in this situation. The problem is that the left side of the brain, what I call the doing side, is still over-active. Now you may not know this, but the right side of the brain controls the left side of the body, and the left side of the brain controls the right side of the body.

The right creative side of the brain sets off the sleep impetus. Think of your eyes, and focus on the fact that the muscles at the back of the eyes control one third of brain activity. Try and breathe as gently and correctly as you can at the same time. The aim is to slow down the electrical activity in the brain.

I have found it useful to close my eyes, and imagine that I am relaxing the muscles at the back of the eyes, thus encouraging the sleep initiator in the brain to come into operation and help the brain to relax. Another tip is to close the eyes, and allow the eyes to move back and forwards gently under the closed lids for about a minute or two. This works for me quite often, but not on the night of which I am speaking.

When I woke up the next day after sleeping late, I felt guilty (part of my remaining hurt child) that I had over-worked my nervous system, which made it difficult to relax into rest. So that morning my writing-mode was not in good fettle. Nevertheless when one is aware in this way and acknowledges the misuse of our nervous system, something often happens to compensate for our error, as if Higher Power is saying 'OK, try not to do it again, here's a bonus for you!' I speak of this at length, because you might care to study your own daily timetable and the results you obtain, positive or negative.

The bonus in this case came my way when I switched on the TV to hear the news. Later than usual. A young man of ethnic origin was speaking from his hospital bed, having suffered lower leg amputation from a recent terrorist bomb on the London tube. His words carried no overtones of hate, only faith in himself to survive. His facial expression and wisdom spoke of a depth of spirituality which reflected the shallowness of most of the remaining TV I happened to watch that day. Such a soul is not often captured by the media; anyone watching could not fail to have been inspired. I could see that his breathing was steady despite the shock which he must have sustained, but his voice and eyes also expressed the beauty of his spirit. I was given the privilege to encounter that spirit.

'The eyes of suffering see the furthest.'

Following this moving experience I was intuitively urged to make a phone call, to someone notoriously difficult to contact. I had already tried several times, but in frustration had put the matter on the back burner of my mind. Anyway I also knew I must make contact somehow, and following my intuitive prompting rang again, and made instant contact. I had a rather important message to pass on from another person, and if I had failed to speak to her on this occasion, it would have been too late.

My relief was enormous. My timetable may have been upset but I had been given two instances to feel satisfaction despite my error. In one day two spiritual lessons had been shown to me, one the fact that when we use ourselves in a way foreign to our known right way, and recognise our error, we receive some compensatory insight. Two, when we listen to our intuition and drop everything to act on that voice, we achieve success. Further delay could have caused hurt to another, and I again realised how important it was to listen to that inner voice. There is nothing worse than the feeling that we have let ourselves down by ignoring the inner voice.

Can you understand how I was rewarded with two lots of interest from my spiritual account? The inspiring manner and words of that young man, and the fact that I had been successful at the last possible moment when I listened to my intuition, are some of the lessons we all must learn as we move through life.

I wrote these last few paragraphs in a state of annoyance with myself, but the lessons I have learned have stood me in good stead, in pursuing the steps required to turn the ideas which came to me at 3 o'clock one spring morning into a Registered Charitable Organisation. It has taken other like-minded people who have experienced great changes to their own lives by the correction of the breath to make the ideas an actual reality. There was probably only that period of time when the dream could come into being, despite its simple I would not say humble origin, with no *big names* at its birth. The words come into my mind. 'There is no army strong enough to stop an ideas whose time has come.' 'Great oaks from little acorns grow.' 'Faith is only faith when you have nothing left to hold on to.'

You need a large number of wise supportive sayings when you create a pioneering project, for pioneers have no maps!

So intuition has been the inner voice which has given birth to a Global Charity about something you cannot see. Almost all organisations are about aspirations more easily understood, which can be seen visually, but that does not minimise its urgency at a time when the future of mankind is under question.

I mentioned that it is said that only a handful of people meditating in each large city, can reduce violence. I believe that a number of people who also consciously breathe correctly in each city could have an even more powerful effect, the power would intensify as more people grow closer to nature, from our self-imposed incarceration in a world of illusory materialism.

Never doubt that a small group of thoughtful people can change the world. Indeed it is the only thing that ever has.

Margaret Mead, Anthropologist

So let us celebrate the GREAT BIG TRUST. Global Respiratory Educational Advancement Trust. (ONLY BREATH IS GLOBAL.) Correct Breath can save the world. Correct Breath can create solutions to apparently insolvable problems. Correct Breath can make you happy, it can make everyone happy. Breathe correctly and regenerate your spirit. Breathe correctly because the children of the Universe desperately need you to breathe in that way, because they still know how, (until we spoil their ability).

Breathe correctly for only *you* can save them.

In Gunnel Minnet's excellent book *Exhale - An Overview of Breathwork,* she presents the fact that shared breathing sessions between people of different nations and cultures have been observed to have a unifying effect.

(I believe that the germination of this proven fact on a larger scale presents a possibility not yet conceived that could ensure our global survival as a species.)

WATCH FOR FURTHER NEWS ABOUT
THE GREAT BIG TRUST.
BECOMING THE GREAT BIG TRUST.
IT IS NOW A REGISTERED CHARITY.

Chapter 53

KARMA

DO YOU EVER READ something in a book, or hear some-one make a statement which synchronises with knowledge or a conviction within you, which you had never until then spoken about, or even acknowledged to yourself? Nevertheless it represented a deeply held certainty. This truth is what I call a *gut-feeling*, and such truths must never be disregarded.

Deep within me coincidences such as this give me a deep feeling of relief, confidence, even joy, because, until that moment, no one else I had ever met had voiced such words. I feel such a strong bonding with the person who shared my most precious thoughts, even although I might never meet them, and we lived on separate continents. Thought must exist on millions of wavelengths which I suppose crowd this great apparently empty area around us which we call space.

I experience on such occasions a profound sense of relief, because when we have very strong positive thoughts and feelings, which we do not feel able to share with anyone else we have yet met, we must realise that such *certainties* are not to be scoffed at. It is always a temptation to ally ourselves with the opinions of anything we share in common with our friends. We have to ensure that we do not become carbon copies of others in order to maintain a relationship, even if others in our circle of acquaintances do not share an important aspect (to us) of our reality. It is probably unrealistic to accept they will. We must respect and treasure whatever any of our relatives and acquaintances mean to us, but despite these ties, we must not deny our own uniquely different reality.

The most important aspect of our personality which we must defend and protect is that unique individuality, otherwise we shall not hear the real wisdom and truths which we share with others. We may never meet, but that truth represent the life-blood of who we really are, the spiritual links which give us such joy.

Whenever we are tempted to think and act out of accordance with our most deeply held certainties of conscience, we sin against our morality, and that of the unseen code of the earth's morality set in stone but impossible to read in material terms. The earth does not use a pen or paper to record her unchanging laws. Nevertheless we all know these truths within our hearts.

This brings me to the subject of karma, the meaning of which I am looking up in my two kilogramme *Readers' Digest Dictionary*, and see that they have it in a nutshell from Hindu and Buddhist origin. *'The sum of a person's actions during the successive phases of their existence. Regarded as determining their destiny in future incarnations.'*

Well that's quite a good summing up. I've had this dictionary for about eighteen years, and referred to it no more than a dozen times. This is thanks to my father spending time to read with me during our lunchtime break when I was about six. We read a book called *The Land of Nod*, and from those days I taught myself to read, aided by the ten volumes of *The Children's Encyclopedia* which arrived soon after. I was allowed to look at Volume One. For these books I shall always be grateful to my parents.

Some time age I was watching a TV programme soon after the Tsunami disaster. A group of leading figures from different religions were contributing to the discussion. The person who impressed me most was a beautiful, calm middle-aged Indian lady who spoke of the karmic implications of the disaster from her perspective. I shall never forget the emanations of love which flowed from her presence.

Her words seemed to come from the soul rather than the mind. She spoke with great certainty about her absolute conviction that the people involved in this great tragedy had been drawn to that spot and event because of their karmic debt.

So what is this karmic debt? It springs from a total acceptance that if we sin in any way and do not attempt to atone for it in this lifetime, then it still remains as a debt to be paid when we return again to our next existence. I am sure that you, like myself, understand our cultural laws of the need to pay back financial debts. Karma accepts that moral debts also exist which have to be paid back. I do not suggest that you have to accept this philosophy, it may be unthinkable to you when looking at terrible tragedies and violence. This was at first difficult for me too. On the other hand the beautiful Hindu lady impressed me with her spirituality. I trusted her words. Before I understood the form of words she used, I had been increasingly aware that many people in Western culture also shared her conviction. I certainly believe that we have to pay for our moral wrongdoing at some stage. Since I do believe in reincarnation, it makes sense to consider that payback time may not be in this present existence.

Listening to the media, or reading the news, it is obvious that some moral sins are horrendous, some very small. If we do not acknowledge our own moral errors or try to atone, perhaps payback may be in the form of something negative happening in our lives which represents the energy power of the original sin. We have to find a loving solution, difficult as it may be. Especially when someone has badly hurt us in any way.

Of course I cannot prove this form of logic, but am sure

that I have experienced situations in my own life, which have convinced me of the sensible thinking behind the law of Karma. I do not know, but I have freedom to speculate.

From my own perspective, I seem to learn about other faiths by osmosis, rather than by learning the doctrine. We all have to trust our own intuition, and by trusting in that I have learned to respect some of the teachings of other faiths, especially that of Karma, while being unable to accept other aspects of those beliefs. I do not think that we can forever 'get away' with cold-blooded murder, or deliberate infliction of pain on another.

Just as some of the modern manifestations of Christianity seem to lack the clear message of the teachings of Jesus, I imagine all religions lose some of their original truths down the years. After all, religions are what man thinks God is about, and what man thinks always has to be a little suspect when viewed from the clarity of Higher Truths. Man usually creates what suits him at the time.

In considering some Eastern religious practices, how could one go along with the (until very recently) Indian practice of a widow being burnt alive on her husband's funeral pyre? How could one understand such macabre and negative thinking? By contrast I can empathise with some aspects of the Hindu faith as expressed by that beautiful spiritual Hindu lady I mentioned earlier. Particularly the possibility of the law of Karma.

For many years during my own journey of what I know to be spiritual growth, certainly as far as I have progressed to this present time, the word karma has assumed a growing significance, particularly as I came through the process called 'When the Universe Came to Call', experienced by many, a very potent phrase used by that special remarkable writer, lecturer and intuitive Caroline Myss. For her the Universal visitation left her jobless, homeless and with a broken relationship. From this withdrawal of total security her life then blossomed. Something of the same happened to me many years ago. Not quite the same set of circumstances, but certainly a visit by the Universe!

When we reach a certain level of spiritual consciousness, we may have our security mat withdrawn, as that is the next spiritual lesson we have to learn. We have to grow with no other security than our spiritual trust. Reflecting on this often apparently cataclysmic event from a personal perspective, I know that it was bound to happen.

Outwardly I had committed no sin, indeed to the onlooker my life probably represented a success story, but it did not represent the truth of who I really was. To that extent it was a lie, and deep within myself I knew it I had built a life which represented a false security, because I had never faced up to my *floating fears*. I suppose many of these were inherited from my parents, ancestors if you like. Nevertheless, a part of me I had to acknowledge knew I had not been given life in order to feel afraid.

I have now come to the conclusion that whatever we create in our lives based on fear will then lead us on to thoughts and actions based on that fear, which will affect our lives like a virus. We are false to ourselves and false in our dealings and relationships. Fear cannot see the helpline always available to us from Higher Power. Naturally there are many degrees of fear, each degree is an energy which has its own vibration, attracting back to itself equally negative events in a person's life. Eventually a life crisis will arise, which we have to deal with. If we do not face the fear, catastrophe will return. Some people prefer to die, because they do not believe they have the power to change their lives.

This is where cunning karma starts to operate. I believe that we have to keep returning to this life time and again, until we have discovered how to live from a love rather than a fear basis. Therefore when we are born again as a dear little baby, we still have imprinted on our souls the fact that we have the unfinished business of trusting *love* rather than *fear*. As we are all unique we all have special but never identical gifts to anyone else, and if we do not fulfil our life's purpose, a vacuum is created, which can only ever be filled by our own loving actions. We are as important as that.

If we do decide to face the fear, and start to climb out of the abyss, we are faced with a series of actions based on trusting courage, in which we deal with a situation or people with courage instead of fear. This constitutes another upward step up the karmic ladder, so that our future actions relating to this particular situation will be positive and life-enhancing. We have paid off some of our karmic debt, and the Universe will be spiritually richer. So it goes on.

I repeat, do not feel that you have to agree with me. My thoughts and feelings are the result of the events of my life, and how I healed myself of fear. As I did, I began to love myself a great deal more. I still think I could love myself even more!

As I healed my fear I became a great deal more qualified to start my life's work, *to do good instead* of *'do-gooding'*. When you realise the enormous difference between the two you may understand that do-gooders may have quite a lot of *karmic pay-back time*. Now here comes an important piece of information, which the do-gooders find difficult to swallow, and can be recognised precisely by that problem. How can you do good to others, unless you know how to good to yourself? Do-gooders will disagree with you, they think you should always consider yourself last. How can you put anyone else first if you do not know how to do this, starting with yourself? Another chance, another karmic lifetime?

I hope you can understand that there is a difference between putting yourself first and being intentionally selfish; this concept has been part of my maturation. Putting yourself first is acknowledging that you have a right to respect and prioritise your unique gifts and talents. Only then can you appreciate other people's gifts.

When you have learned how to climb out of your own particular abyss, you then possess the blueprint to be a support and assistance to others who may ask you to be of help. Not that you can do the climbing out for them, but you know the route and the false detours. The fact that you have made it, without assuming superiority in any way, makes you a trustworthy friend in need. As a therapist you really have to have *walked the walk* whatever your discipline. The ability to *empathise*, not the patronage of sympathy.

In climbing from the abyss by yourself, which can only be done by love, you are really paying off your karmic debt; it is something that clarifies itself in retrospect. What happens eventually is that the wonderful joy and humour of your loving child finds security again within you, and you realise how vital it is to love and care for that child. Otherwise I do not think that we can truly understand and be sensitive to a child.

Here are some of the *nasty* negativities we have to conquer in order to climb out of the abyss. Self and other's hatred, accumulated anger, greed, jealousy, envy, malice, lust, feeling sorry for myself. In past lives when we have been under the influence of any of the foregoing, and others you can think of for yourself, we will have sinned in some way, and hurt others. Such debts have to be paid off.

You may agree with me that all of us have some degree of the above disharmony within us, they can become permanent mind-sets, and from time to time we act in a way which reflects the vibration of that harmful frequency. Unless we realise this and take action to make good that wrong, it will be incorporated into our psyche in the same way as a virus pumps its poison through our system. The longer it resides within us, the harder it will be to dislodge.

I cannot see how we can escape this law, whether as an individual or a nation.

The comforting fact is that those who consciously develop the process of corrective breathing, start to intuitively understand these truths that I have discovered, and begin to put their lives in order often without a great deal of counselling or therapy. Paying back karma cheerfully and willingly renders it much less painful, although I personally know that there is no growth without pain, usually mental and emotional pain. Physical symptoms also usually need to be cleansed from the system.

A client may of course volunteer information about their problems, and we may discuss them, but my opinion cannot be given nor sought. Each time we have to return the question by another question, 'what do you think is right for your deepest self?'

This return to the knowledge contained within the deepest self has to be sought time and time again, until it becomes the first point of referral. In other words a revitalisation and regeneration of the intuitive instinct which is a vital part of our make-up as a baby. Few people acknowledge that a baby knows what is right for itself. It is so difficult to remember this as we immerse ourselves in the baby books and articles on child rearing. It is essential to regain our trust in our own inner intuitive friend, our true inner guide. In order to retrieve its power we have to throw off the shackles of any other influence in our lives which we have allowed to dominate us. Another name for this domination is *subjugation*.

The pruning process of correct breathing and intuitive health are our guides in the essential self-changing process which is an automatic accompaniment to finding the courage to recognise and eliminate karmic habits and actions which we unknowingly still harbour.

Each karmic trait released must be replaced by spiritual

wisdom and right action, the communication of self with self, or we will re-absorb the karma. The greatest skill that I can bring to this client growth process, is to learn how to be present, and yet keep out of the way.

We can put our lives back in order which involves acting on these intuitive insights, which come to us in the deeply relaxed state which accompanies correct breathing These insights play back to us the original causes of our problems together with intuitive information on how to reverse them. Such information is the fruit of a brain rhythm which is restoring itself to the Alpha dominant frequency, the rhythm of nature.

The moral code of right living encoded within the Alpha vibration can change the actions of the hardened criminal. I wonder how long it will be before we use the treatment of correct breathing within the prison service. The prison officers would have to learn the process first of all, in fact all within the penal service, including the police, lawyers and magistrates! I am talking of *my* ideal world of course.

This process of healing our karma is paralleled by the release of the toxins of old harmful negative energy. For a time while this energy is being *excreted,* it seems to attract events and negative people into our lives which appear as apparent dangers which we have to deal with by creating good energy. Learning how to do this represents another phase of karmic pay-back. This negativity has had a good and safe *bed and breakfast* lodging within us for many years, and will not go without a struggle.

What I find intriguing, is that people going through this karmic process almost invariably realise that the apparent trauma of this temporary struggle is recognised as a *release* by the client rather than a new life-crisis. It is an illusion and yet a solid process. Difficult to convey its reality, you really have to go through it to understand how it works.

I recall reading an article, I believe by Catherine Ponder who wrote some wonderful books about prosperity, where she describes this process of change as *chemicalization*. In my own terminology *all hell seems to be let loose* for a period when we face the challenge and responsibility of healing our karma, even if we may not call it by that name. We feel like a container filled with a variety of conflicting elements all shaken up, fizzing and fighting for dominance. Our karma is coming to the surface to be confronted and dealt with.

Breath correction separates the contents of the container, causing the unwanted negative toxins and dross to be dispersed and eliminated, while the precious spiritual gold elements of our physical, mental and emotional essence is retained for its higher use in our life's purpose.

I am sure that our Higher Purpose in life is what really excites Higher Power, and we receive unexpected help in quite subtle ways as we begin to make spiritual progress.

It seems to help us to pay off our karma, that accumulated load of bad action inherited from past lives.

This time round, the strength of the inner true self will no longer tolerate the impurity within us, which perhaps only we ourselves can see. Other people may want us to stay the same, perhaps for their own need to dominate or be dominated, but the changes happening within us cannot be halted just to please others.

We discover life-enhancing ways to deal with the erupting poisonous foam of the toxins as they emerge. Unforgiveness, greed, dishonesty, love of power for power's sake, violence, malice, lust, you name it, it has to be excreted. They are all part of the negative fruits of our spirit. Gradually we begin to wonder why certain unsavoury people and events have been part of our lives, we discover how to face up to them with love, reinforced with a positive 'No.' As we fail to respond to their negative energy it is amazing how they fade from our lives. It may at times feel like facing a vampire, our only armour a spiritual or material crucifix, even occasionally by banshee-like shrieks. Just stay firm!

Increasingly permeating from our deepest awareness an inner voice appears to speak to us, whose advice we learn to trust, respect and act upon. Even when this advice seems difficult and we would do anything rather than act on its promptings. However we *do* listen, we *do* follow its promptings, and guided by correct breathing, our circumstances change favourably, and problems are resolved.

Once again we have dealt with another layer of our karma.

We recognise that in the past we would probably have succumbed to the artificial temptations represented by the karmic layer we have just released, and we know that we have been taught another valuable lesson in learning to trust the moral truths of life. Such laws *have* to be obeyed in order to progressively deal more easily and effortlessly with karmic clearance, and the ways in which we have in the past abused these laws.

The next work in all this spiritual growth is reparation for such past abuses. In this *re-learning* period we are given the opportunity to deliberately acknowledge, maybe only to ourselves, the harm we have done to ourselves and others, to consciously feel grief and regret, and then to let go of these negative thought forms. Our work is to forgive ourselves and others, never to wallow in the grief and regret. That was then, but this is now.

We are now required to choose a new way of being, in order to contribute consciously the gift of our talents to the world's bank of loving creative action.

This is what is meant by overcoming, cancelling or paying back karma. It is not punishment, but an opportunity, always available once we decide to listen and obey our heart's promptings and intuition. From now onwards when we encounter events and people who seem too difficult to cope with, who maybe represent negativity and spiritual danger, we refuse to take the '*I can't*', or '*everyone is better than me*' attitude. We speak to Higher Power within ourselves as to a friend, asking why these circumstances have appeared in our lives and how we can crack the code of solution in a good and loving way. Otherwise we could return to our past habits of attempting the apparently easier path of a shallower and third-rate life-style choice.

So now in this present lifetime we continue pruning our old ways, cutting out diseased branches of old behaviour. However difficult this new path, we begin to experience a keen sense of relief and enjoyment of simple pleasures. Furthermore as people walk this new walk they begin to understand the meaning of reincarnation, without anyone mentioning it They take it for granted as I began to myself. To try to persuade them of such issues as a therapist would not be ethical.

The fact that so many people come to these conclusions with no prompting, seems to me to be more than coincidence. I have begun to share with an increasing body of *ordinary* people in the community, a certainty that when we leave this present existence, we take with us the spiritual luggage of what we have accomplished in this lifetime.

It appears logical to me that that we go to some other level of existence which parallels our spiritual attainment. I believe we get a spiritual wash and brush up, revue our past lifetime, and agree a return trip.

There are probably loving supporters in this other level of existence, who help us to revue our next lifetime, which I believe will match the karmic debt we still have to pay back. We then agree to go back for another life-experience. It is said by some that we choose our parents, and they choose us.

I am sure that we come back into a new life with no memory of this spiritual pit-stop.

We return to life again as a beautiful loving child but carrying the seed of any unfinished karma within us, to be worked through during this present lifetime, which many now recognise and naturally verbalise as such.

Within all this I believe we always have free will. After observing my own life and that of thousands of other fellow travellers, I believe we make our own heaven and hell.

Some say that groups of people incarnate together, being involved in group karma. I have not explored this in depth in my mind, but again can understand the possibility. Eventually when we encounter problems, we start to talk to life as if to a loving teacher. 'So what is it I have to learn now, what are you telling me?' Life then starts to become the Game of Life, fascinating, often hilarious, always surprising, loving, deeply rewarding.

When we re-correct our breathing, and then make a karmic error, feedback happens very quickly in some form of apparent misfortune, to be solved by right action which I have learned has a direct karmic value to our error. *It is not punishment*, but to me a practical demonstration of the verse in *The Aquarian Gospel* which states so clearly 'a little sin in him who walks in Holy Breath, is greater far than sin in him who never knew the way.'

Be warned when you take on correct breath, you may take on the responsibility of healing your remaining Karma in one lifetime. I think the Earth desperately needs the help of people who have healed their Breath, and healed their Karma.

Think about that.

To lighten what may seem to be a heavy task, remember the saying, 'don't sweat the small stuff, it's all small stuff.' Once you apply that formula, it becomes magically true!

★ ★ ★

ALL IT TAKES IS A CHANGE
OF THOUGHT, AND YOU ARE IN
CHARGE OF YOUR THOUGHTS.

MY LAW

Tieme Ranapiri

The sun may be clouded, yet ever the sun
Will sweep on its course till the Cycle is run.
And when into chaos the systems are hurled,
Again shall the Builder reshape a new world.

Your path may be clouded, uncertain your goal,
Move on, for your orbit is fixed to your soul,
And though it may lead into darkness of light,
The torch of the Builder shall give it new light.

You were, you will be, know this while you are,
Your spirit has travelled both long and afar.
It came from the Source, to the Source it returns,
The spark that was lighted, eternally burns.

It slept in a jewel. It leapt in a wave,
It roamed in the forest. It rose from the grave.
It took on strange garbs for long aeons of years,
And now in the soul of yourself it appears.

From body to body your spirit speeds on,
It seeks a new form when the old one has gone
And the form that it finds is the fabric you wrought,
On the loom of the mind from the fibre of thought,

As dew is dawn upward as rain to descend,
Your thoughts drift away and in destiny blend.
You cannot escape them for petty or great,
Or evil or noble, they fashion your fate.

Somewhere on some planet, sometime and somehow,
Your life will reflect the thoughts of your Now,
My Law is unerring, no blood can atone -
The structure you built you will live in - alone,

From cycle to cycle, through time and through space,
Your lives with your longings will ever keep pace.
And all that you ask for and all you desire,
Must come at your bidding, as flame out of fire.

Once list to that Voice and all tumult is done -
Your life is the Life of the Infinite One.
In the hurrying race you are conscious of pause,
With love for the purpose, and love for the Cause.

Your are your own Devil, you are your own God,
You fashioned the paths your footsteps have trod.
And no one can save you from Error or Sin,
Until you have hark'd to the Spirit within.

Attributed to a Maori

Chapter 54

REINCARNATION

THIS IS MY SECOND ATTEMPT to write about reincarnation. I got up to page seven and by some action not yet understood wiped the whole lot off my computer. Some of you will understand my feelings. Perhaps this second attempt will make better reading, I hope I can remember the original gems!

For the first sixty years of my life the word reincarnation would have caused me to roll my eyes *as you do*, to indicate that the believers must be a little off-centre. Still, to be truthful, I probably had a sneaking suspicion that those who courageously pronounced their conviction in the process were not totally mad. Nowadays in this later era of my life, I have the courage to say that I do believe that we lived before, and will do so again, unless we have reached such a state of spiritual perfection that we have learned all the lessons required, and then can go on to undertake other work in another dimension.

Nowadays I realise that you have to be true to your deepest spiritual convictions, and not suppress them in order to please other people. Of course we must never try to force those convictions on others, it's a question of being as 'wise as the serpent and gentle as the dove.'

Do you believe that you have lived before, and will probably return again? Perhaps you will say 'rubbish' as I once did. I wouldn't want to change your opinion. Read on!

If I seem to digress a little, bear with me, you will soon understand the reason.

Anyone who has become interested in Alternative or Complementary therapies will these days encounter a fantastic selection of books, articles and people who have had some life experience which has caused them to question deeper issues. Quite often it has been a life crisis of fear for which our *polite* society has provided no tools to cope, except for drugs or alcohol, and many people have had to delve deeper into hitherto untapped mental and spiritual resources in order to survive without addictive props.

Such experiences cannot be disregarded when there are so many people who could be helped by the knowledge gained by the sufferers. The once-sufferers know that they have to use their new knowledge of self-healing to help others, for it does not seem to be known or available within the orthodox establishment.

Well, that is not exactly true, for a few brave colleges and universities are beginning to embrace the more easily accepted alternative therapies, such as massage, aromatherapy, reflexology, Reiki, although I don't know how they teach the spiritual aspect of the latter.

I often wonder if they have been allowed to trickle in because female relatives of principals or lecturers at such establishments have discovered these other therapies, and their influence has opened the creaking door of orthodoxy. Maybe that's just my imagination, but you can never give a university degree for spirituality, (who would be so audacious?) Perhaps they will give a certificate for knowledge of the Spiritual Masters, but that is not spirituality.

I have found in my professional life, that a considerable number of college-taught alternative therapists have asked me for assistance, and I am convinced that this is because it is not possible to teach such a subject intellectually. If the student has not experienced depth of life experiences, or has not healed their breathing pattern, they will be extremely

626

vulnerable when working with highly stressful clients, who may appear quite aggressive.

Aggression, particularly overt aggression in a client, can have a powerfully draining effect on the energy of a therapist unless they are spiritually strong, otherwise any immaturity in the therapist will not be able to cope. They will lose confidence and become as stressed as the client!

This is a very discouraging set-back for a newly intellectually trained therapist, optimistically established in their new therapy room with certificates on the wall, and incense sticks smoking away! The problem clients are often not intentionally aggressive, or mentally ill, but their emotional armoury prevents creative communication which becomes interpreted as hostility, and atmospheric negative energy starts to permeate the therapeutic session.

Infected and affected by this negative energy the therapist can suffer from burnout and depleted confidence, which becomes a spiral of apparent failure. A very real sense of career stress often results in the therapist giving up. Their stress causes exhaustion. If they had received instruction in correct breathing they would have received the missing vital link in their training. They would have walked the really confident walk, rather then talked the talk. Able to cope with clients with difficult intense stress problems, and not be negatively affected by them.

My apparent digression in referring to one of the biggest problems in the growing army of alternative practitioners is because we are moving very quickly from one era into another, where we shall have to make a quantum leap in having to understand many issues that have been swept under the formal educational discussion carpet. These issues are perhaps more important than spending untold billions in space travel.

I am positive that we need to come nearer home and fully

realise that 'the proper study of man is man.' In that respect the study of childhood assumes, I believe, enormous importance. 'Except ye become as little children', 'a little child shall lead them' come from the Bible. Wordsworth's wise comment that 'the child is father to the man' picks up the same reminder. 'Man know thyself' is a clarion call from another wise mind.

Living in the present, I think we can exist more intuitively and enjoyably in this present by having a healthy understanding that the spirit can never die. Our present body is the living house of our *now*, but we have come from another existence and will move on to others. That is unless our present perfection removes our need to return to this world, which I believe to be a spiritual training-school.

'Trailing clouds of glory do we come,' says the poet Wordsworth. I believe that to be so, we have to learn how to hold on to, or re-find that glory in order to be joyful in the present. From my experience the correction of the spirit breath is the surest way. I believe we *can* have heaven on Earth.

So, what about reincarnation? My present convictions have come about in unexpected and unsought ways, but always when a specific but unusual *happening* has occurred in my life, *after* which a person, book or event has confirmed that my interpretation of the happening is a valid one, in so far as anyone can *prove* the world invisible. This corroboration has underlined information which has come to me from within. Therefore what I write about reincarnation has come about by such unusual coincidences.

In this way, layer upon layer of information has been added to my growing certainty of the existence of things which must to my mind exist beyond our everyday consciousness.

Many years ago I met a very gifted and spiritual lady who remarked that if I understood her work, she would have made it! She obviously was well aware of my suspicious and at that time virtual cynicism about the validity of Higher Power. Conversely she must have been aware that I had potential!

It was some time after I started my teaching work on correct breathing that I was in a therapeutic session sitting very quietly in silence, providing a supportive environment. My client was lying comfortably, replicating a steady corrective breathing movement which she had been maintaining for some minutes. In such calm periods a client might speak from time to time without feeling the need to open their eyes, through the deep pleasurable relaxed state which they themselves had brought about because of their correct breathing. This seems to re-connect them to Nature's blissful Alpha energy.

Eventually a client is able to maintain a constant awareness of calm confidence in the waking state, or in any social or work situation, without massage, manipulation, or touch of any kind. The only help required in corrective breath training is not touch, but a temporary support provided by the quiet presence of the therapist.

It was in just such a situation that I was sitting beside a client aged about thirty-five. I was not maintaining a continuous visionary assessment, because I believe that it constitutes an invasion of the sense of privacy needed. Obviously my *detached* observance was regular, and at one point I became aware that over the face of the lady of whom I write appeared a kaleidoscope of other faces, which came and went in quick succession. The faces could be either male or female, from any historical era, geographical area, social class, primitive or aristocratic, beautiful, ugly, old or young.

The phenomena were extremely interesting, and more so because Jean, as I shall call her, seemed in no discomfort.

The images faded quite naturally, and when she decided to finish the breathing session, I noticed that she seemed much stronger, as if she had integrated important information from an unknown source which had strengthened her personality.

Situations similar to this happened on several occasions with other clients, as if I needed to learn something, although there was no conscious effort on my part. Later client appointments using the same process did not reveal the phenomena to me nor did I feel the need to bring them about, although I am sure I could have done so, through eye and brain focus. But you do not need to test Higher Power, which I eventually realised was revealing the actuality of reincarnation to me, a vision of previous existences of my clients, which I had not discussed with them at the time.

I must mention here that during my seventeen years as a local authority councillor, I attended a number of conferences on various issues, mostly very informative, some rather boring. Of course it is the quality of the speaker which often greatly helps to make the subject come alive. It was at some point towards the end of my career as a regional councillor, when changes were beginning to happen in my life which persuaded me that my skills needed to be used in another direction (which direction I did not then know), that I was watching a speaker who was standing in front of a plain white wall.

I had discovered by that time the ability to become relaxed in order to recharge my batteries, so was sitting in a peaceful frame of mind. Now when one relaxes, the brain relaxes, and so do the eyes which are part of the brain. Indeed the muscles at the back of the eyes control a third of brain activity, so as the brain relaxes while still being alert, the eyes feel relaxed as well. You can consciously relax the muscles at the back of the eyes.

In looking at the speaker, I realised that there was a band of colour, varying in intensity between yellow, green and blue, around his head, which moved as the speaker moved.

In fact I began to see this colour around the whole body. The colour watch continued during several lectures by various speakers; it created a harmless diversity while still being able to hear what was being said. I discovered that the more dynamic the speaker, especially if they seemed to be of attractive personality and integrity, the clearer were the colours, with blue predominating. In my room at night, I began to remember snippets I had read somewhere about the human aura, and realised that this was what I was being shown. Again I had not actively sought these manifestations.

I was later to learn more about the probable meaning of the colours of this energy band which exists around all of us. On one occasion I saw a dull brown colour around another speaker (an MP). Intuitively I felt that he was not well, indeed he did not look very healthy. Several months later I read that he had died. There was nothing that I could have done, but I was aware that such knowledge could not be taken lightly.

Illuminating information leads to a great deal of subsequent deep thinking. The perception of what I had interpreted as past lives had come about while the client was quietly breathing correctly and under no pressure. Although I subsequently shut down my ability to see these energy waves, I am sure that they still manifest during a relaxed session of correct breathing.

I am positive that such balanced respiratory action helps to stimulate quite naturally the auto-immune area between the pelvic bone and the navel. It is from this area that the power of our spiritual blueprint flows through our cells. When we breathe inadequately this spiritual awareness becomes suppressed and its availability to us is limited.

It seems obvious that the first cell at our conception contains this blueprint of who we were meant to be, and our ability to project into appropriate activity the meaning of that blueprint is dependent upon being able to access the information, the creative meaning of our life's purpose. If in any lifetime we do not fulfil that purpose, it is unfinished, and because we are all unique, the work will never be done, unless *we* do it.

I remember reading an article by the writer Catherine Ponder, who suggested that at the end of our lives 'most of us are sick with guilt at having lived below our authentic potential.' A well-known actor said, during his last days, that his only regret was not realising that he 'could have had everything.' By that he was not meaning material possessions, but in the clear sightedness available to him at the end of his life he recognised his true potential, and that he had not fulfilled that potential.

The real reason we do not fulfil our potential is, I am sure, *fear*, and in fear we restrict our breathing. You may say *laziness* but laziness, I believe, comes from a fear of *doing*.

Having free will we are the only ones who can *de-restrict ourselves from fear*, and I believe that this planet could well be our spiritual University of Learning. We cannot go on to higher levels of existence until we have completed a fearless or ultimately fearless existence with love predominating. I understand our fear represents a magnetic force field, which then attracts negative situations into our lives, unless correct breathing changes our magnetic force field positively.

You may disagree with me, but if we have not overcome our fears which represent our immature child, (a mature adult has overcome fear), we then depart this lifetime's existence without having carried out the work demanded by our spiritual potential for a fulfilled life.

Perhaps in one former lifetime we were a male of an Eastern nationality, it may be that in order to progress on our spiritual path in the next we need to become a female in a Western culture. So on and so on. It is possible that the kaleidoscope of images I saw appear on my client's faces were little bits leftover from previous lifetimes. Through the miraculous power of correct breathing they were being reintegrated into the present personality, through a vibrationary process, which acts like a combined code breaker to magnetise into our spirit in this life, left-over bits of past lives. The increased mental and emotional strength I have observed in those who have got their lives together in this way is heart warming, and the whole process comes over as a wholesome experience.

Naturally some people have told me that while they were quietly breathing correctly, they felt that they had slipped into a perfectly safe place, not awake, but certainly not asleep, and have reported scenes and images, definitely not dreams, which they felt certain without any prompting from me represented flashbacks to past lifetimes. It would never occur to me to question their conclusions, why should I? Sometimes these flashbacks are triggered off by quite mundane events in daily life, which produce amazing coincidences relating to the dream content.

There is, from time to time, media interest in the subject of reincarnation, but it is unfortunately usually presented in a way which highlights a sensational flippancy, rather than the spiritual dimension.

If each lifetime gives us an opportunity for that spiritual improvement, the only self-improvement path available to us is to use ourselves with love, the highest energy. Whatever we did not do from a love impulse in a past life provides the lesson material for the present. Whether we are of royal blood or a road-sweeper, the same rule applies.

It is understandable that we return to life again and again in order to have the chance to go on learning the amazing miracle and mystery of the power of love, until we completely trust it.

When we have completed this beautiful non-intellectual education, we probably do not need to materialise again on this earth, but I do believe that there will be work for us on another plane of existence. Feel free to disagree!

Without actively searching for information on my own past lives, as I seem to have been too busy to do consciously in this, I am positive that information has percolated down to me about two of my possible past existences. Although very interesting, they represent unfinished business which has certainly taken all my time and effort since the age of fifty-nine, and at eighty there is so much that I still wish to accomplish. My main concern is to be given the time to do that work.

Certainly possible past-life information which has been given to me has felt rather like a pat on the head from *them up there* and made life more fascinating, but without this bonus I think I would still have chosen my present path. That is after 'The Universe came to call', as Caroline Myss says in one of her lectures, meaning one's artificial *security rug* is pulled from under us. The space under the rug represents all our untruths, ego-created life-styles and unresolved fears, requiring our immediate attention. It leaves us with no option but no learn to swim in a loving environment, and create it around us or to drown in negativity, for we have been thrown into the deep end, with no apparent lifebelt. For me the lifebelt was the discovery of correct breath, the lifebelt which rescued me, but I had to almost drown to reach out for its rescue.

The discussion about past lives (I will not begin to discuss future lives, as I do not think we are meant to explore that dimension) appears in the media from time to time as a subject for entertainment, which when presented from that aspect raises viewer figures, or sells more papers/magazines.

On the subject of reincarnation I believe it would be a great help to many people if the main religions were to invite public discussion on the subject, in the healthy wholesome way it deserves, but that might prove too challenging, and risk relinquishing some of the loss of power implied by having to say 'I don't know', or even acknowledging its possibility.

Some of our religions imply that it is a sin even to contemplate reincarnation, many religious attitudes haven't changed since the Middle Ages, and are no longer tenable in an intelligent society, unable to accept rigid doctrines based on fear and superstition. Too many people are longing for open discussion, acknowledgement that reincarnation *may* be a possibility even if not provable. So many are earnestly searching for the deeper truths of their own spiritual path and identity.

The subject of remarkable coincidences has come up time and time again in my own life, and the lives of many others I have met. These coincidences may seem haphazard, but link up in a deeply fascinating way, like a treasure trail requiring constant awareness. The search which can transform our lives, reminds me of the words of Leonard Orr, 'am I ready to let go of who I am, in order to be what I have not yet become?' As we move forward guided by clues many of which appear to come from past lifetimes, we learn how to take the right intuitive path to our destiny. We certainly know when we are travelling on it.

As I corrected my own breathing pattern and passed on the information to others who requested it, I noticed that with all of us the choice of the right path to choose, was always the most loving. Using that yardstick, what was really right spiritually for us. It takes a while to understand that what is right for us on a spiritual level cannot be wrong for anyone else. This is one of the most important lessons of life, and helps us to be released from leaning on others too much, or them from leaning on us. It may have been all too easy to have been a prop for others all our lives, or allow others to be too dependent on us. That is no one's higher destiny.

Had we taken the dependency path, our actions would have replicated past problems, our lives would seem to be going round and round like a treadmill, with disaster after disaster, difficulties with relationships, work, money, home, chaos. So many reach the end of their lives stuck in this muddle without feeling that they have used their gift of life in any satisfactory way. What a shame.

The question then arises naturally. If we leave this present lifetime with so much wonderful potential undeveloped at the end of our lives I believe we have to realise how important we are, how necessary it is to be true to ourselves and that only *we* have stopped ourselves. It makes sense to come back and have another shot at life. Of course that depends on whether you can believe that your spirit cannot die. I am sure that it goes to some dimension out of time, probably needing a good rest, but carrying an urgent need eventually to go on with the journey of life here on earth until we have learned the lesson of love. I think we re-enter this life at the same spiritual level we left the last one, our learning has to be done on this earthly plane; we just get a fresh lifetime to start again.

It was after I had begun to have very definite thoughts and feelings about the probability of reincarnation, based upon the experiences I have mentioned in this chapter, that I came upon the book called *The Aquarian Gospel of Jesus the Christ*, by Levi. Those who have an understanding, accept this wonderful book's historical concept that man progresses through ages of two thousand years, each era represented by one of the signs of the Zodiac. We have just left the Piscean age, which started after the birth of Christ, and have now moved into the Aquarian Age. At least that is what I have read and can comprehend. I am no astrologer. The Aquarian Age is supposed to be an age of high development for mankind, and we are now in its very early years.

I had first noticed the *Aquarian Gospel* in the houses of two friends, picked it up, and turned the pages. I was no Bible-thumper nor intended to be one, and yet the few sentences I read made an impact, if there had been time I would have read more.

After going home I thought that I would like to read more, but in telephoning my friends, the book could not be found. It had been loaned out or returned to the actual owner.

From time to time I wished I could find a copy, but made no attempt to do so. However it turned up by chance (?) in a tea-chest of books given to a charity with which I was involved. You may have read about this in a previous chapter.

Not being one to read such a book from cover to cover, I would pick it up from time to time and read the verse or chapter which I opened at random.

When I read the following verses, the implication of its meaning did not come to me immediately, but then suddenly I realised what the words were talking about. Reincarnation. Chapter 105. In this chapter Jesus is talking about hypocrisy, and advising people not to pretend to be a friend or foe in order to please another person, saying that the thoughts of our hearts cannot be hidden and are always known on another level. I suppose He was really talking about honest communication and advised people to recognise and discuss our anger with others involved, 'for if you hold and *swallow down* that anger or curse it never will digest, lo it will poison every corner of your soul.' He advises us. 'And if you sin against another man, you may be pardoned and your guilt be cleansed by acts of kindness and of love.

But if you sin against the Holy Breath (Spirit) by disregarding her when she would open up the doors of life for you, your guilt shall not be blotted out in this nor in the life to come. An opportunity has gone to come no more (in this lifetime) and you must wait *until the Ages roll again.* Then will the Holy Breath again breathe on your fires of life and fan them to a living flame. (Reincarnation?)

Then she will open up the door of life again for you, (next lifetime) and shine the light of love into your hearts and you may let her in to sup with you for evermore, or you may disregard her again and yet again.' We always have free will. No one *forces* us to be loving or breathe correctly, each of us has to do that for ourselves, and discover the resulting changes in our lives. Both require an active use of will. Since we are all unique, the results will have unique yet similar benefits for each individual yet all on separate paths.

We soon realise that something special and *wholesome* is happening in our lives, as we start to recognise the amazing coincidences which then start to happen.

In another chapter Jesus talks of master-minds, great souls or prophets. 'And backwards down the Ages Master minds can recognise themselves, and so they know.'

Perhaps we are all Master minds in training!

To me Reincarnation simply means another opportunity to decide how we are going to use our loving Spirit within our new present life-form. It just makes sense. I cannot believe in the death of the Spirit, and so I suggest to you that each of our lives on earth is just another learning stage in the everlasting,

UNIVERSITY
OF THE SPIRIT